PATERNOSTER THEOLOGICAL MONOGRAPHS

The Trinity, Creation and Pastoral Ministry

Imaging the Perichoretic God

PATERNOSTER THEOLOGICAL MONOGRAPHS

A full listing of all titles in this series and Paternoster Biblical Monographs will be found at the close of this book.

PATERNOSTER THEOLOGICAL MONOGRAPHS

The Trinity, Creation and Pastoral Ministry

Imaging the Perichoretic God

Graham Buxton

Foreword by Jürgen Moltmann

Wipf & Stock
PUBLISHERS
Eugene, Oregon

Wipf and Stock Publishers
199 W 8th Ave, Suite 3
Eugene, OR 97401

The Trinity, Creation and Pastoral Ministry
Imaging the Perichoretic God
By Buxton, Graham
Copyright©2005 Paternoster
ISBN: 1-59752-760-2
Publication date 6/8/2006
Previously published by Paternoster, 2005

This Edition Published by Wipf and Stock Publishers
by arrangement with Paternoster

Paternoster
9 Holdom Avenue
Bletchley
Milton Keyes, MK1 1QR
Great Britain

PATERNOSTER THEOLOGICAL MONOGRAPHS

Series Preface

In the West the churches may be declining, but theology—serious, academic (mostly doctoral level) and mainstream orthodox in evaluative commitment—shows no sign of withering on the vine. This series of *Paternoster Theological Monographs* extends the expertise of the Press especially to first-time authors whose work stands broadly within the parameters created by fidelity to Scripture and has satisfied the critical scrutiny of respected assessors in the academy. Such theology may come in several distinct intellectual disciplines—historical, dogmatic, pastoral, apologetic, missional, aesthetic and no doubt others also. The series will be particularly hospitable to promising constructive theology within an evangelical frame, for it is of this that the church's need seems to be greatest. Quality writing will be published across the confessions—Anabaptist, Episcopalian, Reformed, Arminian and Orthodox—across the ages—patristic, medieval, reformation, modern and counter-modern—and across the continents. The aim of the series is theology written in the twofold conviction that the church needs theology and theology needs the church—which in reality means theology done for the glory of God.

Series Editors

David F. Wright, Emeritus Professor of Patristic and Reformed Christianity, University of Edinburgh, Scotland, UK

Trevor A. Hart, Head of School and Principal of St Mary's College School of Divinity, University of St Andrews, Scotland, UK

Anthony N.S. Lane, Professor of Historical Theology and Director of Research, London School of Theology, UK

Anthony C. Thiselton, Emeritus Professor of Christian Theology, University of Nottingham, Research Professor in Christian Theology, University College Chester, and Canon Theologian of Leicester Cathedral and Southwell Minster, UK

Kevin J. Vanhoozer, Research Professor of Systematic Theology, Trinity Evangelical Divinity School, Deerfield, Illinois, USA

This monograph is dedicated to my wife, Gill

"The good does not begin in the consciousness of man. It is being realized in the natural cooperation of all beings, in what they are for each other. Neither stars nor stones, neither atoms nor waves, but their belonging together, their interaction, the relation of all things to one another constitutes the universe. No cell could exist alone, all bodies are interdependent, affect and serve one another. Figuratively speaking, even rocks bear fruit, are full of unappreciated kindness, when their strength holds up a wall."

Rabbi Abraham Joshua Heschel (1907-1972), theologian, educator, philosopher and author

"At moments of wonder, it is easy to avoid small thinking, to entertain thoughts that span the universe, that capture both thunder and tinkle, thick and thin, the near and the far."

Yann Martel, *Life of Pi*, Edinburgh, Canongate Books: 2002: 223

Contents

Foreword by Jürgen Moltmann   xiii

Preface   xv

Acknowledgements   xvii

Chapter 1
The Road Less Travelled – **Science and the Christian Faith**   1
The Shape of 'Scientific Theology'   2
Clarifying Terms   7
Connecting Science and Theology   10
The Science-Religion Relationship: Conflict   16
The Science-Religion Relationship: Independence   20
The Science-Religion Relationship: Dialogue   23
Alternative Theological Approaches to Dialogue   31
Dialogue, Truth and the Postmodern Culture   41

Chapter 2
In Solidarity with Beasts, Plants and Stones – **Theology, Science and Pastoral Ministry**   53
Ministry as *Praxis*   54
Theological Reflection and *Theologia Viatorum*   61
Theological Method in Pastoral Ministry   64
Defining Pastoral/Practical Theology – A Historical Perspective   71
Pastoral Ministry as Contextual Activity   79
The Contemporary Scientific Context for Ministry   84
Imago Dei and the Natural World   92

Chapter 3
***The Coping-stone of Christian Doctrine* – The Resurgence of Trinitarian Thinking**   97

Beginning with Barth   97
Being and Becoming   103
'Rahner's Rule'   105
The Cappadocian Connection   107
The Trinity and the 'History of God'   112
God for Us: The Trinity as Soteriology   119
The Trinity and Creation   124
The Doctrine of *Perichoresis*   129
Perichoresis and the Nature of Reality   136

Chapter 4
***Redressing the 'Failure of Nerve'* – *Perichoresis* as a Dialogical Construct at the Level of Pastoral Practice**   143

Particularity – Contexts and Persons   144
Perichoretic Themes in Pastoral Life   149
Community Formation – Difference and Diversity   153
Community Realisation – Love   167
Community Operation – Worship   176
Community Operation – Mission   183
Community Operation – Compassion   188

Chapter 5
***Probing the 'Web of Life'* – *Perichoresis* as a Principle of Cosmological Unity**   195

Quantum Theory and Holistic Non-Locality   197
Quantum Mechanics, Entanglement and the Doctrine of *Perichoresis*   205
Fractals and Holograms   211
Chaos, Complexity and Self-Organisation   221
Evolutionary Emergence   225
The Ubiquity of Pain, Suffering and Death   235
God's Perichoretic Presence in Creation   238

Chapter 6
Imaging the Perichoretic God – Towards a Model of Scientific and Pastoral Coherence — 247

Exploring Metaphors of Ecological Promise — 250
Moltmann's 'Ecological Concept of Space' – Pastoral Implications — 253
Nature as an Enchanted and Interconnected Reality — 261
The Spirit as *Anima Mundi*, or Cosmic *Élan Vital* — 266
The Integrating Concept of *Imago Dei* — 272
Nature as *Imago Dei*? — 276
Imaging the Perichoretic God in the Community of Creation — 282

Bibliography — 289

Author Index — 305

Foreword

It is with pleasure that I take this opportunity to recommend this excellent book by Graham Buxton, who has managed to achieve a praiseworthy integration of contemporary thinking ranging from theology to modern physics. The author handles with great aptitude issues including recent trinitarian theology, quantum mechanics, and David Bohm's holistic thought. Such wide ranging competence is not often encountered today and is therefore particularly to be commended. The author is concerned in this work neither with a simplistic religious worldview that explains everything, nor with a Christian metaphysics. Rather he is much more concerned to put forward a model that has emerged out of such diverse fields as theology, sociology and the natural sciences that allows us to understand the interrelationship between these fields and that will lead to a fruitful exchange between them.

I am particularly impressed that the trinitarian concept of *perichoresis* has been employed as leitmotif to facilitate this exchange. It seems to me, in fact, that the subtitle of the book, 'Imaging the Perichoretic God,' is really the main title because it explains why the author has entered into such diverse areas as the doctrines of the Trinity, creation, pastoral care and the church. In this way Graham Buxton is able to uncover the perichoretic interconnectedness within the perichoretic nature of the universe. Although I myself have been concerned very much with developing both a perichoretic understanding of the Trinity and an ecological doctrine of creation, I have found new insights and stimulus for further reflection in every chapter of this book. For this reason I am personally grateful for the appearance of this present work.

A foreword, of course, is not a review, but an invitation to read. I shall therefore restrict myself to points that should be kept in mind while reading this book. *Perichoresis* means mutual interpenetration, movement into one another, and mutual indwelling. This perspective allows us to see unity within diversity and diversity within unity. Individuality and community, movement and rest, life and living space, person and relationship, relationship and the group, the parts and the whole – all complement one another in perichoretic thought, analogous to Niels Bohr's Copenhagen interpretation of quantum mechanics. They complete one another and that which they hold in common appears either in one connection and perspective or the other. Precisely because this perichoretic dialectic can be applied at so many levels, it is important that one be aware of these levels.

Within trinitarian theology the first level is the inner life of the triune God. The Father, Son and Holy Spirit express their unique trinitarian unity through their mutual *perichoresis*. They are persons and movements for one another as well as sharing at the same time a common 'living space.' The second level is the exterior life of the triune God in relation to the world in its creation, redemption, sanctification and completion. With regard to kenosis, incarnation, salvation and eschatological completion we have to do with the indwelling of the created world in God, as well as God's indwelling in God's created dwelling place. To bring this concept to life I would point the reader to the simple words of 1 John 4:16 – "those who abide in love abide in God, and God abides in them." In this second level of *perichoresis* God and humanity come together and live within one another: Trinity and creation. It is the *perichoresis* of unequals. At a third level we once more encounter something corresponding to the *perichoresis* of equals in the inner trinitarian life. We find this in the human community, which is "a heart and soul", and in the perichoretic nature of the interconnectedness of the universe. Here again we find a *perichoresis* of equals. Graham Buxton introduces us to these different levels and clarifies their relationship to one another. In reading this work, however, one must be mindful of which level of *perichoresis* the author is treating at any given point.

Before me lie two other books on the same theme that I would like to mention. The first is by the Slovenian theologian Ciril Sorč: *Entwürfe einer perichoretischen Theologie* (Münster: 2004); and the other by the recently deceased Canadian theologian Stanley Grenz: *Rediscovering the Triune God: The Trinity in Contemporary Theology* (Fortress Press: 2004).

The new trinitarian thinking takes a great step forward in this book by Graham Buxton. It may well be the future of Christian theology.

Jürgen Moltmann
Tübingen
June 2005

Preface

Throughout this book a 'trialogue', or three-way conversation, between theology, science and pastoral ministry is proposed. The goal of this conversation is apologetic, and is predicated on a number of observations. Firstly, there is a growing awareness within the Christian community of the impact of science and technology on contemporary life. Secondly, pastoral theologians need to focus their sights on a more sympathetic engagement with those in the scientific community in order to combat the (sometimes substantial) residual prejudice in the minds of many Christians against the contribution of the natural sciences to an understanding of what it means to live as human beings in God's world. Conversely, the natural sciences have much to gain from the insights of theology. Thirdly, those who are engaged in Christian ministry of all types need to be more adequately informed about the culture in which they seek to serve, a culture in which the scientific worldview is a dominant feature. These three reasons for a 'trialogue' between systematic theology, scientific theology and pastoral theology – the ethical/pastoral implications of scientific advances, the corrective to historical misunderstandings for the mutual benefit of both science and theology, and the potential apologetic opportunities in pastoral ministry – point to the value of a project which seeks to integrate insights from all three disciplines.

The approach developed in this study is based on a trinitarian understanding of God as a relational being of love who invites human beings into the dynamic life of his perichoretic being-in-community, a life that 'spills over' into all created reality, human and non-human. The trinitarian concept of *perichoresis* is therefore helpful at a number of levels of reality, as well as *between* those levels. As a *theological* doctrine, it is helpful as a way into understanding the communion of being and action that is at the heart of the life of the Trinity. *Pastorally*, *perichoresis* is significant in expressing not only the relationship between God and human beings, who are invited to participate in the divine life, but also the nature of ecclesial life (so the church may be viewed as an image of the Trinity). *Scientifically*, the concept correlates with an understanding of the interconnectedness of all creation in a coherent, open-ended and complex system (a freedom made possible because of the humility of a kenotic God).

The purpose of the book is to demonstrate the relevance of the *perichoresis* motif for the realms of both pastoral and scientific theology, thus helping to bridge the gap between the two disciplines. Additionally, it is argued that a pastoral theology that has no place for a sacramental understanding of the world of nature is a deficient theology: the doctrine of *imago Dei* requires a healthy and positive interaction between human beings and their environment. Not only does *imago Dei* encapsulate in all its richness human participation in God's perichoretic life; it also explains why people throughout the ages have sought to understand the physical universe in which they are privileged to participate. To be made in God's image expresses both the *desire* and the *capacity* to investigate God's world, as well as the act of *living* human life within the created order. The scientific endeavour is one expression of this ancient quest to locate human meaning and purpose within the perichoretic community of creation. For those who are critically involved in the pastoral ministry of the Christian faith-community, it is a quest that is enticingly situated at the nexus of science and faith. And, as demonstrated throughout this book, one of the pivotal theological concepts that nourishes the dialogue between science and faith is the trinitarian idea of *perichoresis*.

Acknowledgements

Many people have made this book 'come alive' for me. My interest in the theology-science interface began only recently. In the first two months of 2001, at the instigation and encouragement of my friend and colleague at Tabor College, Dr. Mark Worthing, I prepared a submission to the Center for Theology and the Natural Sciences (CTNS) in Berkeley, California, for a teaching course in the developing 'science-and-religion' discipline. The course was selected for an award in the CTNS 2001 Science & Religion Course Competition, sponsored by the Templeton Foundation. I wish to express a debt of gratitude to both CTNS and the Templeton Foundation for opening up the way for me to explore this exciting and challenging field. Little did I know then the implications of my early foray into this growing field of academic study and research. I have been passionately committed to fostering dialogue between science and religion ever since.

As one of my doctoral supervisors, Mark Worthing has been a continuous source of encouragement to me. Not only has he persisted in believing in my capacity to engage at a scholarly level in a new field of enquiry, but he has also motivated me to stretch my vision, to see beyond the detail and to capture something of the 'big picture' that lies at the heart of the science-religion debate. I am grateful to both Mark and Dr. Stephen Downs for keeping me focused throughout my reading and writing, and for their advice when I was tempted to stray beyond appropriate limits for a study of this nature. I am also grateful to Dr. Denis Edwards and Professor Celia Deane-Drummond, both of whom read drafts of portions of the material, and whose comments both encouraged me and added depth to the final work. Many others, committed to working in the growing field of science and religion, have inspired and motivated me, but they are too many to be named. I would also like to thank Professor Jürgen Moltmann, whose theological insights have enriched my own thinking for many years, for his gracious foreword.

My thanks also go to Tabor Adelaide, for allowing me release from my immediate college responsibilities for a day each week over a period of two years so that I could complete this study. I have also benefited from exposure of my ideas in the classroom over the past three years: students often ask searching questions, and many times I have been forced to think through more clearly some of my proposals. I would also like to express my gratitude to my publishers at Paternoster, especially Robin Parry, whose belief in the central propositions developed in this book has been unswerving. I am grateful for the opportunity to make my research available to a wider audience through the Paternoster Theological Monograph series.

Finally, I would like to express my gratitude to my wife, Gill, who has been wonderfully caring throughout, bringing me much-appreciated sandwiches and coffee to keep me going, and patiently enduring many long silences as I grappled with some of the complexities of trinitarian theology and quantum mechanics! My immediate family has also been enthusiastic in their support, and together they have given me new insights into what it means to belong to a perichoretic community of life.

Needless to say, I am solely responsible for the final outcome. My hope – and prayer – is that those who are involved in the demanding and rewarding task of Christian pastoral ministry may find inspiration in these pages to explore sympathetically and openly the contributions of those who work in the natural sciences. And I sincerely trust that the traffic will be two-way.

Graham Buxton
Adelaide, South Australia
June 2005

CHAPTER 1

The Road Less Travelled – Science and the Christian Faith

If, as McGrath suggests, the natural sciences represent the contemporary handmaid of Christian theology – following a similar role for philosophy in the ancient world and the social sciences in the modern world[1] – then it may not be inappropriate to propose one particular doctrine of Christian theology as a handmaid to a more sympathetic engagement between scientific theology and pastoral theology. It is the purpose of this book to critically examine one such doctrine, that of the Trinity, with a particular focus on the theological construct of *perichoresis*, which (as we shall see in Chapter 3) conveys the richness of mutuality, reciprocity and interconnectedness discernible not only in the divine life of the triune God of grace, but also in all created reality, both human and non-human.

As an expression of inner-trinitarian life, *perichoresis* is a term that shifts us away from the static language of persons to the dynamic language of relationships. Defined thus in terms of relational interconnectedness and movement, the concept may be helpful at a number of levels of reality, as well as *between* those levels. As a *theological* doctrine, it is helpful as a way into understanding the communion of being and action which is at the heart of the life of the Trinity. *Pastorally*, *perichoresis* is significant in expressing the relationship between God and human beings, who are invited to participate in the divine life: this expression of dynamic participation in a trinitarian life of relations opens up the way for interpreting the life of the church as well as the nature of pastoral practice in perichoretic language. But we can go further by considering the concept scientifically, or, more specifically, *cosmologically*: increasingly scientists perceive the cosmos as a coherent whole, in which the notion of *perichoresis* may be viewed as a principle of cosmological unity and interconnectedness. So we recognise three significant – and interrelated – perspectives for examining the doctrine of *perichoresis*: theological/trinitarian, pastoral/ecclesial and scientific/cosmological.

---

[1] McGrath, Alister E., *A Scientific Theology,* Vol I - *Nature*, Edinburgh: T. & T. Clark, 2001: 7-20; McGrath's technical term for 'handmaid' is *ancilla theologiae*.

The Shape of 'Scientific Theology'

The aim of this chapter is to examine the strides that have taken place in the emerging field of science and religion over the past four decades, ever since Ian Barbour, the *doyen* of contemporary writers in the field,[2] published his landmark book, *Issues in Science and Religion*.[3] In the first volume, *Nature*, of *A Scientific Theology*, in which Alister McGrath "aims to examine, critically yet appreciatively, the way in which the working assumptions and methods of Christian theology and the natural sciences interact with and illuminate each other"[4], the author raises the critical problem of transient theological trends. He identifies two writers who have made significant contributions to the current dialogue between theology and the natural sciences – Ian Barbour and Arthur Peacocke – and argues that both are guilty of succumbing to "significantly weakened variants of the classic statements of Christian orthodoxy."[5]

A similar point is made with regard to the provisionality of scientific conclusions. Thomas Torrance, arguably the greatest twentieth-century British theologian, reprimands those scientists whose Promethean attitudes lead them to "extend their knowledge of contingent processes beyond the boundaries of what is creaturely, contingent and relative."[6] Later in this chapter we will refer to the philosophical concept of critical realism, which acknowledges that scientific – and theological – observations or understandings are predicated on a 'real world', whether physical or spiritual, but that our knowledge is necessarily finite and theory-laden and therefore only partial (though quite possibly very close approximations to) representations of reality.[7] In other words, neither theology nor science can claim to be infallible conveyors of all that there is to see and know.

---

[2] As acclaimed by John Polkinghorne in his endorsement of Barbour, Ian G., *When Science Meets Religion: Enemies, Strangers or Partners?*, San Francisco: Harper Collins, 2000.

[3] Barbour, Ian G., *Issues in Science and Religion*, New York: Harper & Row, 1966.

[4] McGrath, *A Scientific Theology,* Vol I - *Nature*: 3.

[5] *Ibid*: 37. McGrath singles out Ian Barbour for special criticism (contra Polkinghorne!) in this regard, taking exception to "the disproportionate extent to which he relies upon process theology in the course of his analysis" (*ibid*: 38). Hence the particular attention paid by McGrath in his text to the classic themes of Christian theology explored by such theologians as Athanasius, Augustine, Aquinas and Barth, as well as to the central philosophical themes of Plato and Aristotle.

[6] Torrance, Thomas F., *Theological Science*, London: Oxford University Press, 1969: 283.

[7] In his assessment of the postmodern view of science and the contemporary undermining of the epistemological foundations of the scientific enterprise, Denis Alexander concludes that "the stance of 'critical realism' provides an appropriate middle way between the Scylla of naïve realism and the Charybdis of systematic relativism": see Alexander, Denis, *Rebuilding the Matrix: Science and Faith in the 21st Century*, Oxford: Lion Publishing, 2001: 461.

This insight is of critical importance for McGrath because it exposes the fallacy of relying upon either transient revisionist theologies or allegedly secure scientific conclusions in exploring the relationship between theology and the natural sciences. This is not to imply that McGrath eschews *any* theological position: he is adamant that "the classic Christian formulations of faith are perfectly adequate to function as the basis of a scientific theology."[8] So the term 'scientific theology' is offered as an expression of the *methodological* parallels between theology and the natural sciences. In this way, McGrath avoids the temptation to ground his work in the sort of naïve realism that has characterised some approaches to the scientific enterprise, whilst in the same vein acknowledging what Peacocke describes as "our incapacity ever to express in human language the nature of that ultimate Being who is called 'God'."[9]

Following McGrath, scientific theology may therefore be defined as that project which seeks to identify and examine the common epistemological ground between Christian theology and the natural sciences as they seek to interpret the nature of reality. However, this procedural definition, which eschews reliance upon both contemporary theological trends and the agreed consensus of the scientific community, should not blind us to the plausibility that valuable insights may be gained by serious reflection upon the *substance* of contemporary thinking and outcomes in both disciplines. A major proposition sustained throughout this book is that whilst both theology and science are 'works in progress', *theologia viatorum* and *scientia viatorum*, such that their relationship at any one time reflects the unique and particular demands of social or historical circumstance,[10] each may generate data or insights which enrich the other, even pointing us towards a rational and orderly coherence present in all reality. It is helpful therefore to widen the scope of scientific theology to allow for this possibility, without in any way diminishing McGrath's *caveat* regarding the provisional nature of both theology and the natural sciences.

McGrath's suggestion that the natural sciences represent a convincing *ancilla theologiae*, following the earlier contributions of philosophy and the social sciences as 'profitable dialogue partners',[11] epitomises the sort of cultural

---

[8] McGrath, *A Scientific Theology,* Vol I – *Nature*: 42.

[9] Peacocke, Arthur R, *Theology for a Scientific Age: Being and Becoming – Natural, Divine and Human*, Minneapolis: Fortress Press, 1993: 16.

[10] As demonstrated in Brooke's magisterial volume on the historical relationship between science and religion, in which the author exposes the often subtle and complex interactions in the shifting relationship between the two: see Brooke, John Hedley, *Science and Religion: Some Historical Perspectives*, Cambridge: Cambridge University Press, 1991.

[11] McGrath is critical of the value of the social sciences as a valid *ancilla theologiae*: "Precisely on account of their radical and often aggressive commitment to a naturalistic world-view, the social sciences offer a skewed perspective on religion which, in the first place, refuses to acknowledge an ancillary role to theology, and, in the second place, denies the entire legitimacy of the theological project, as this is traditionally conceived."(McGrath, *A Scientific Theology,* Vol I – *Nature*: 15).

and interdisciplinary engagement that Christian theology needs if it is to survive as more than just an academic discipline. If the modern era "has suffered a culture split where understanding (*Verstehen*) has been separated from explanation (*Erklären*) with the result that questions of meaning have been isolated from questions of nature and behaviour"[12], it is even more urgent that theology does not retreat into its own corner, but identify appropriate 'dialogue partners' in its quest for relevance in today's world. The discipline of the natural sciences is one such partner, for a number of important reasons, which will be outlined shortly. In a fascinating review of three recent books exploring the relationship between science and religion, Margaret Wertheim titles her article "The Odd Couple", subtitled: "Can science and religion live together without driving each other crazy?"[13] In this chapter we will offer some responses to this question. But the title of the article betrays a narrower perspective than that envisaged in this book, which is that a contextually-aware practical theology cannot ignore explicit engagement with the natural sciences if it is to have contemporary relevance in the practice of ministry.

This proposition widens the dialogue into a 'trialogue', a three-way conversation between theology, science and pastoral ministry. The goal of this conversation is apologetic, and is predicated on a number of observations. Firstly, there is a growing awareness within the Christian community of the impact of science and technology on contemporary life, particularly in terms of the ethics of new scientific capabilities, such as genetic engineering. Human beings, for example, have engaged in intentional genetic modification at the agricultural level for many years, often resulting in such damaging environmental consequences as deforestation, pesticide pollution and the narrowing of plant and animal gene pools. Haught comments that "religion and theology have the reputation of not caring very much about the welfare of the natural world."[14] In the next chapter we shall note that a pastoral theology that has no place for a sacramental understanding of the world of nature is a deficient theology; moreover, a comprehensive theology of *imago Dei* requires a healthy and positive interaction between human beings and their environment.

Ronald Cole-Turner observes that with the technology of genetic engineering now available to meet human objectives, something new has taken

---

[12] Anderson, Ray S., "Isomorphic Indicators in Theological and Psychological Science" in *Journal of Psychology and Theology*, Vol. 17 No.4 (1989), 373-381, in which Anderson credits his mentor Thomas Torrance with this suggestion, as articulated in Torrance, Thomas F., *Theology in Reconstruction*, London: SCM Press, 1965.

[13] Wertheim, Margaret, "The Odd Couple" in *The Sciences*, March/April 1999, 38-43, in which the author reviews Polkinghorne, John, *Belief in God in an Age of Science*, New Haven CT: Yale University Press, 1998; Ward, Keith, *God, Faith and the New Millennium: Christian Belief in an Age of Science*, Oxford: One World, 1998; and van Huyssteen, J. Wentzel, *Duet or Duel?: Theology and Science in a Postmodern World*, Harrisburg PA: Trinity Press International, 1998.

[14] Haught, John, *Science and Religion: From Conflict to Conversation*, New York: Paulist, 1995: 183.

place: "While the chemical processes of natural recombination are billions of years old, and while they occur naturally and all around us and even inside us, as *technology* – conscious, intentional, and purposive – genetic engineering or artificial recombination is new."[15] This means that "our choices have skewed the value-neutrality of the microbiological in the direction of our values and desires."[16] The speed with which this has happened, with the consequent lack of time to adequately discuss the issues involved, has created tensions and difficulties between scientists and the general public (and within the scientific community as well) both in terms of ethics and in the context of public policy and legislation.[17] Recent developments in the contentious area of human cloning have generated the most vocal opposition, and the pastoral responsibilities of the Christian community obligate it to engage with scientists more urgently than ever before.

A second reason why those engaged in pastoral ministry need to dialogue with the scientific community is grounded in the historical relationship between science and religion. In their respective typologies of the science-religion relationship, both Barbour and Haught adopt the word 'conflict' to describe the assumed (and, in some cases, actual) position of irreconcilable difference, even to the point of 'warfare'.[18] The general impression gained by many people today is that science and religion are diametrically opposed: science deals with facts and religion deals with – to put it as charitably as possible – untestable dogma. Some would want to subvert the religious perspective as so much 'supernatural mumbo-jumbo',[19] hardly consistent with the scientific age in which we now live. We noted earlier the presence of social and historical factors which shaped the particular contexts within which the relationship between science and religion was played out over time. Citing the example of

---

[15] Cole-Turner, R. *The New Genesis: Theology and the Genetic Revolution*, Louisville: WJKP, 1993: 42, author's italics. By 'natural recombination', Cole-Turner means the continuous activity of a range of chemical processes, involving such natural agents as restriction enzymes, ligases, plasmids and viruses, which cut and splice the DNA of all organisms, creating the genetic variety implicit in biological evolution.

[16] Cole-Turner, *The New Genesis*: 43.

[17] On the bioethical issues associated with genetic technology, see Dixon, P. *The Genetic Revolution*, Eastbourne: Kingsway, 1993; Peters, T. (ed) *Genetics: Issues of Social Justice*, New York: Pilgrim, 1988; Peters, T. *Playing God?: Genetic Determinism and Human Freedom*, New York: Routledge, 1996; Dutney, Andrew, *Playing God: Ethics and Faith*, East Melbourne: HarperCollins*Religious*, 2001; and Cole-Turner, *The New Genesis*.

[18] See Barbour, *When Science Meets Religion*: 10-17; and Haught, *Science and Religion*: 9-12.

[19] Typical of this view would be the writings of the neo-Darwinist reductionist Richard Dawkins, the Charles Simonyi Professor in the Public Understanding of Science at Oxford University, in such books as *The Blind Watchmaker,* New York: W.W. Norton & Co., 1986; *River Out of Eden*, New York: Basic Books, 1995; and *Climbing Mount Improbable*, New York: W.W. Norton & Co., 1996.

Galileo in his relations with the Roman Catholic Church, Brooke reminds us that because both science and religion "are rooted in human concerns and human endeavour, it would be a profound mistake to treat them as if they were entities in themselves – as if they could be completely abstracted from the social contexts in which those concerns and endeavours took their distinctive forms."[20] The two have not been pitched against each other over the centuries, as some would like us to believe. It has often been claimed that were it not for the stimulus provided by early Christian thinkers in the sixteenth and seventeenth centuries, then scientific endeavour would not have been so rapid.

The warfare motif has its origin in two books among many spawned by the Darwinian controversy. The first is Draper's *History of the Conflict between Religion and Science*, published in 1875, followed twenty years later by White's *A History of the Warfare of Science with Theology in Christendom*.[21] Both were avowedly anti-Christian, heavily influenced by humanistic reasoning, and intent on demolishing any support for what they regarded as a bigoted ecclesiastical establishment. However, despite

> the sometimes poor documentation and obvious prejudice of the Draper-White thesis, as well as its eventual rejection by most respected historians of religion and science, it contained (unfortunately) a sufficient measure of truth to sustain its influence and to color the views of many in both the scientific and the religious communities. Its influence continues to this day.[22]

For this reason, if for no other, pastoral theologians need to focus their sights on a more sympathetic engagement with those in the scientific community in order to combat the (sometimes substantial) residual prejudice in the minds of many Christians against the contribution of the natural sciences to an understanding of what it means to live as human beings in God's world. In the process, as we shall discover later, the natural sciences have much to gain from the insights of theology.

A third reason in favour of a three-way conversation between theology, science and pastoral ministry is essentially apologetic, relating to the nature of pastoral ministry as an incarnational imperative: those who are engaged in Christian ministry of all types need to be more adequately informed about the culture in which they seek to serve, a culture in which the scientific worldview is a dominant feature. Authentic Christian ministry, as we shall develop in Chapter 2, is expressed most helpfully in terms of participation in the Spirit-empowered ministry of Christ in the world. So the Lord of creation graciously

---

[20] Brooke, *Science and Religion*: 8.
[21] Draper, John W., *History of the Conflict Between Science and Religion*, New York: Appleton, 1875; and White, Andrew Dickson, *A History of the Warfare of Science with Theology in Christendom*, New York: Appleton, 1895.
[22] Worthing, Mark W., *God, Creation and Contemporary Physics*, Minneapolis: Fortress, 1998: 23.

invites us to participate in his glorious creative energies, which are manifestations of his creative and reconciling ministry in the world. To be uninformed about the scientific understandings of the nature of reality, both human and non-human, may therefore result in forfeiting useful apologetic insights. This is a perspective which is grounded in the Christian doctrine of creation: "If God made the world, which therefore has the status of being 'creation' as well as 'nature', it is to be expected that something of the character of God might be disclosed through that creation."[23] In Chapter 3 we shall see how this might be explored within a trinitarian understanding of God as a relational being of love who invites human beings into the dynamic life of his perichoretic being-in-community, a life that 'spills over' into all created reality: the pastoral and apologetic implications of such a perspective are evident.

The three reasons elaborated above for a three-way dialogue between systematic theology, scientific theology and pastoral theology – the ethical/pastoral implications of scientific advances, the corrective to historical misunderstandings for the mutual benefit of both science and theology, and the potential apologetic opportunities in pastoral ministry – point to the value of a project which seeks to integrate insights from all three disciplines. This present work is predicated on the hypothesis that there is a significant 'gap' between the practice of ministry within the Christian faith community and the insights of the scientific community. The hypothesised neglect of scientific insights within pastoral ministry will be examined in Chapter 2, drawing on a thorough review of pastoral theology literature published during the second half of the twentieth century. In Chapter 3 trinitarian theology, and its associated *perichoresis* construct, will be presented as a fruitful avenue for encouraging a more constructive engagement between those who are involved in pastoral ministry and those whose energies are devoted to the science-theology interface. The remainder of this chapter traces the key elements in that interface.

Clarifying Terms

Science is typically defined as the attempt to understand the world of physical reality (as distinct from ideas) through what has been called *the scientific method*, an empirical process that involves such things as observation, data-gathering, experimentation and theory formulation. But it is far too simplistic to propose the existence of a single unique scientific method – scientists use a cluster of procedures and practices in their work, and their approaches are almost always coloured by personal presuppositions and motivations. In his historical survey of the science-religion debate, Brooke points to "the diversity, the subtlety, and ingenuity of the methods employed, both by apologists for science and for religion, as they have wrestled with fundamental questions

---

[23] McGrath, *A Scientific Theology,* Vol I – *Nature*: 21.

concerning their relationship with nature and with God."[24] Alongside differentiation in methodology, therefore, we need to understand the scientist as a person before we can fully understand the science he or she may be doing. It is also important to avoid the oversimplified notion that the conversation between science and theology is concerned about the relationship between 'science' and 'religion' in a singular sense. We usually find ourselves talking of 'the sciences' in the *plural*: so biology, cosmology, physics, neurology and psychology. Moreover, as a discipline, science cannot be viewed in isolation from other disciplines, such as philosophy or anthropology. It is often held that science is distinct from the subjectivity of other disciplines like philosophy or theology because it is concerned with physical, measurable data only – that which you can observe, touch, taste, feel – in other words, it is concerned with *empirical* analysis. But science has an interest in other fields of enquiry that do not easily lend themselves to measurement or quantification, such as the spread of bacteria in the environment, or psychological enquiries into human behaviour.

One further example may suffice, drawn from the recent science of 'sociobiology', which explores the relationship between culture and evolution. E. O. Wilson – the principal architect of sociobiology – argues that such cultural features as altruism and religious belief are present in human society because they are effective in ensuring the survival of the human gene pool.[25] Many have disputed Wilson's strong reductionist line, insisting that human beings are not rigidly determined 'from below': "It is in those regions left unspecified by chemistry that the emergent freedom of life, mind, and soul are given a very real place in our evolving universe."[26] Accordingly, it is better to define science in terms of its intent to *explain*, rather than just measure: and that means that science necessarily has to integrate with other disciplines. The example quoted above indicates that some scientists recognise that there are

---

[24] Brooke, *Science and Religion*: 5. "Such is the richness of the subject," Brooke goes on to write, "that it is well to set aside one's preconceptions." Recognising the diversity within the natural sciences, McGrath considers three areas of scientific research – cosmology, biology and psychology – noting that each "has a quite distinct way of understanding its goals, evaluating evidence and formulating research strategy": see McGrath, Alister E., *Science and Religion: An Introduction*, Oxford: Blackwell, 1999: 178.

[25] See Wilson, Edward O., *Sociobiology: The New Synthesis*, Cambridge MA: Harvard University Press, 1976. Wilson asserts that if "religion, including the dogmatic secular ideologies, can be systematically analyzed and explained as a product of the brain's evolution, its power as an external source of morality will be gone forever." (Wilson, Edward O., *On Human Nature*, Cambridge MA: Harvard University Press, 1978: 201). For a critical response to Wilson, see Rolston, Holmes, III, *Genes, Genesis, and God: Values and Their Origins in Natural and Human History*, Cambridge: Cambridge University Press, 1999.

[26] Haught, *Science and Religion*: 90.

important connections between what we observe physically around us and what is unobservable, such as the concept of the human soul ... or even the 'soul' of the universe, a theme which we will explore more fully later in this book.

As for science, we cannot talk of religion as if we were describing one single uniformly-accepted set of beliefs. Some would argue that all of life is religious, in the sense that we are all concerned about finding some way of organising and directing our lives. There is some validity in that perspective – philosophers are basically addressing the age-old human question: "How can I obtain a worthwhile life?"(which is what the Greek philosopher Aristotle described as *summum bonum*, the 'highest good'). The renowned theologian, Albert Schweitzer, brought philosophy and religion together, writing that "the religious world-view which seeks to comprehend itself in thought becomes philosophical ... On the other hand a philosophical world-view, if it is really profound, assumes a religious character."[27] We recognise a very broad definition of religion here. Albert Einstein, a self-confessed atheist, admitted that he was a 'religious man', in the sense that he acknowledged and revered the 'mystery' of the universe. So an atheist can be a religious person. Perhaps, then, it is more helpful to think of religion as a set of beliefs, or faith, in a personal "God", the sort of God we associate with the universal faiths of Judaism, Christianity and Islam. Reflection on such religious faith we may call 'theology'.

McGrath notes the problems associated with defining the term 'religion', concluding that "there appears to be at least some measure of genuine agreement that religion, however conceived, in some way involves belief and behaviour linked with a supernatural realm of divine or spiritual beings."[28] This substantive view of religion contrasts with the functional view, which emphasises personal experience and the role of ritual within a sociocultural context. Barbour identifies six types of religious experience which recur in a variety of traditions around the world: numinous experience of the holy, mystical experience of unity, transformative experience of reorientation, courage in facing suffering and death, moral experience of obligation, and awe in response to order and creativity in the world. All occur in the context of a community, the members of whom are strengthened in their beliefs through stories and rituals.[29] Religious beliefs, therefore, are closely related to the cultural life of a community. Hoebel defines culture as "the integrated system of learned behaviour patterns which are characteristic of the members of a society and which are not the result of biological inheritance."[30] So culture is a

---

[27] Schweitzer, Albert, *Civilization and Ethics,* Adam & Charles Black, 1949: 30.
[28] McGrath, *Science and Religion*: 30.
[29] Barbour, Ian G., *Religion and Science: Historical and Contemporary Issues*, London: SCM, 1998: 110-115.
[30] Hoebel, E. Adamson, *Anthropology: The Study of Man*, New York: McGraw Hill, 1972: 6.

social concept, reflecting patterns and rules that arrive through consensus over a period of time. All religions, whether they are the great monotheistic faiths of Judaism, Islam and Christianity, or indigenous, localised belief systems, are culturally-determined within a historical framework. This suggests that when we talk about religion, we are talking about a dynamic and contextual experience amongst particular groups of people. The question of the relationship between science and religion is therefore even more problematic, especially in the light of Cobb's assertion that there is no such thing as 'religion': "[t]here are only traditions, movements, communities, people, beliefs, and practices that have features that are associated by many people with what they mean by religion."[31] Even within the Christian tradition, there is enough diversity to confound any attempt to propose a consensus view of the relationship between science and Christianity.[32]

Our thoughts about science and religion lead us to the conclusion that neither are fixed, complete disciplines – in fact, they are evolving, open to change and revision. This suggests that both scientists and theologians should adopt an attitude of humility, willing to learn and change.

Connecting Science and Theology

One perspective from which to view alternative approaches to the science-religion debate is to ask the question: What sort of thinkers are we? In other words, is our instinct to start with a particular phenomenon or experience and seek to build our understanding of reality from that[33] (the 'bottom-up'

---

[31] Cobb, John B. Jr., "Beyond Pluralism" in D'Costa, G. D. (ed), *Christian Uniqueness Reconsidered: The Myth of a Pluralistic Theology of Religions*, Maryknoll NY: Orbis, 1990: 83.

[32] For an excellent assessment of four major schools of thought in the modern period – Liberal Protestantism, Modernism, Neo-Orthodoxy and Evangelicalism – and their respective interaction with the natural sciences, see McGrath, *Science and Religion*: 31-44; the variety of positions held within these school of Christian thought are epitomised in McGrath's statement that "Liberal protestantism has tended to have a very positive attitude towards the natural sciences, whereas Neo-Orthodoxy has tended to insist that religion and science belong to totally different spheres of activity." (*Ibid*: 31).

[33] For example, a 'bottom-up' thinker observes the changing weather patterns in a particular location, and then probes to see what they might say to us about the world in which we live. Another example would be the investigation of strands of DNA in order to contribute to an understanding of what it means to be a human being. 'Top-down' thinking works in the opposite direction. Christians believe in a God of love who has made all things well. They might also want to assert that God acts in certain ways in the world (though there will be disagreement among Christians as to how exactly he acts). These fundamental beliefs then influence how events or experiences such as earthquakes, shooting stars and human suffering are interpreted.

approach)? Or do we prefer to start with broad, general principles, and then work downward from there (the 'top-down')? The two approaches need not imply conflict, because they are both, in different ways, tackling the same sort of questions. Both are attempting to get to grips with the nature of reality. The "bottom-up" approach relates closely to the scientific way of looking at things. "Bottom-up thinkers "feel it is safest to start in the basement of particularity and then generalize a little."[34] The ''top-down' approach presupposes some form of metaphysical framework – such as a Christian theistic framework – within which to interpret the nature of reality. The theoretical physicist-cum-Anglican priest John Polkinghorne is a 'bottom-up' thinker, who instinctively builds up from observable phenomena in the "one world of human experience and human understanding that we are trying to come to grips with."[35]

Science and religion are both motivated by our experience of the world, and seek to answer questions like: What sort of world do we live in? How does it work? However, religious belief and scientific belief are not the same. Polkinghorne suggests the following difference between them:

> In science, we are in contact with the physical world treated as an object, treated as an "it", open to us to manipulate through the marvellous resource of the experimental method ... But religion is part of a broad spectrum of personal encounter with reality. In that domain of our experience, testing has to give way to trusting.[36]

In common with other Christian scientists, Polkinghorne argues that we cannot simply reduce the amazing complexity of creation to purposeless physical matter. There has to be more behind it all, he claims. How do you explain the amazing power we have to understand the physical world? The Adelaide physicist Paul Davies acknowledges that there must be a Mind behind everything scientists see, although his perception inclines towards the demiurge

---

[34] Polkinghorne, John, *Science and Christian Belief: Theological Reflections of a Bottom-Up Thinker*, London: SPCK, 1994: 11.

[35] Polkinghorne, John, *Serious Talk: Science and Religion in Dialogue*, Harrisburg PA: Trinity Press International, 1995: 1.

[36] *Ibid*: 2; this statement needs to be modified in the light of our earlier comment that scientists are beginning to grapple more seriously with metaphysical concepts like the human soul. Later on in this chapter we will recognise important points of correspondence between science and religion: Fuller makes reference to a continuous scale with knowledge at one end and belief at the other, suggesting that "[s]cience tends to yield us information that is nearer to the 'knowledge' end of the scale, and theology tends to yield us information that is nearer to the 'belief' end of the scale, but in fact there are elements of knowledge in theological statements and elements of belief in scientific statements ... Scientists are to a certain extent necessarily 'believers', and believers are to some extent necessarily 'scientists'." (Fuller, Michael, *Atoms and Icons: A Discussion of the Relationships Between Science and Theology*, London: Mowbray, 1995: 29).

of classical Platonic thought rather than the God of classical Christian theism.[37] And human beings somehow have a mind to grasp this amazing reality, reminiscent of Einstein's famous remark that 'the only incomprehensible thing about the universe is that it is comprehensible.'

Polkinghorne's second argument for the existence of a creative and purposive Mind behind creation has to do with the remarkable characteristics of the laws of nature, summed up in the well-known 'anthropic principle', which proposes that the whole cosmos, right from the very beginning, was 'fine-tuned' in such a way that life as we know it today would not have been possible if conditions had been ever so slightly different.[38] Further arguments are presented, such as the presence of beauty in the world, the source of moral choice, and the reality of spiritual encounter, or worship. For Polkinghorne, as for others, science has little to offer in these areas. These intimations of *beauty*, *ethics* and *worship* in our human experience of reality mean that not only must we make connections between science and theology, but we also need to draw art and spirituality into the wider picture.[39] They suggest to us that behind the extraordinary physical reality, of which we are a part, there is a God who wills

---

[37] See, for example, Davies, Paul, *The Mind of God: Science and the Search for Ultimate Meaning*, London: Penguin, 1993, in which the author states that he belongs to "the group of scientists who do not subscribe to a conventional religion but nevertheless deny that the universe is a purposeless accident. Through my scientific work I have come to believe more and more strongly that the physical universe is put together with an ingenuity so astonishing that I cannot accept it merely as brute fact. There must, it seems to me, be a deeper level of explanation. Whether one wishes to call that deeper level 'God' is a matter of taste and definition. Furthermore, I have come to the point of view that mind – i.e. conscious awareness of the world – is not a meaningless and incidental quirk of nature, but an absolutely fundamental facet of reality. That is not to say that *we* are the purpose for which the universe exists. Far from it. I do, however, believe that we human beings are built into the scheme of things in a very basic way." (*Ibid*: 16, author's italics).

[38] Specifically, the anthropic principle proposes that astrophysical conditions such as the force of gravity, the density of the cosmos, the rate of expansion of the universe, and values attributed to particles in the cosmos all cohere in such a way as to provide an unexpectedly welcoming place for human habitation. The *strong anthropic principle* insists that into the picture we have to introduce the *mind*. Human beings with their conscious and complex minds are the result of the universe being as it is: if the universe had been any different – younger or older – life as we know it would not have come into being. Haught puts it this way: "If there was ever to be anything like mind, therefore, an incredibly delicate balancing of the numerical values of gravity and cosmic expansion was required *at the very beginning* of the universe." (Haught, *Science and Religion*: 127, author's italics). For a helpful discussion of the anthropic principle in its weak and strong variants, see Alexander, *Rebuilding the Matrix*: 407-425.

[39] With regard to moral choice – and, we might want to add, in the light of the events surrounding September 11th 2001 – Polkinghorne speaks about the "irreducible ethical element" present in our understanding of reality.

it all into existence. The universe has purpose.

Polkinghorne highlights the necessity for dialogue between science and theology by articulating eight assertions that reflect the essential interdependence between science and theology.[40] His first assertion is that both science and theology are concerned with the rational exploration of what is the case: all scientists are interpreters in their search for an understanding of the nature and pattern of the physical world. This means that they must necessarily be open to correction. Likewise, the theological enterprise also involves wearing "spectacles behind the eyes": as Christians we also need to be willing to allow our theology to be shaped as we go along.[41] Secondly, the physical world testifies to marvellous and transparent rationality: there is beauty and elegance in the mathematical equations and patterns that describe the universe. The Christian parallel to this rational mathematical harmony is found in the concept of the *Logos*, a Greek word that refers to 'divine rational order', conveying coherence and order, and embracing reason or Mind. The Creator God is a *rational* God. Science and theology converge here in presenting an understanding of ultimate reality that "is shot through with signs of mind."[42]

Polkinghorne's third assertion is that the universe is rich in fruitfulness because it is both historically fine-tuned (the 'anthropic principle' noted above) and theologically 'free'. Scientists have demonstrated that a universe as large as ours needs a very long history – perhaps 15 billion years – to bring into being the nuclear furnaces of stars that produce the carbon and oxygen necessary for human life. Theologically, we might interpret the process of evolution as the history that is necessary for the Big Bang to become God's fruitful universe that we know today.[43] Through a divine mix of regular and reliable (but not rigid) laws of nature, and irregular and unpredictable happenings (what we might call the 'chance' that is implicit in natural selection), God in self-limiting love allows his creation to evolve with the freedom with which he endows it. So 'chance' is God's gift to his creation: it is the gift of independence and freedom. Fourthly, suggests Polkinghorne, the physical world is endowed with

---

[40] See Polkinghorne, *Serious Talk*: 34-59.

[41] The essential difference between science and theology here is that science deals with *repeatable* phenomena, whereas theology usually deals with unique experiences; this is because science is concerned with impersonal material, whereas theology has to do with personal divine Reality. This echoes the insights of the Jewish mystical philosopher Martin Buber, who once distinguished between two different types of knowledge, "It" and "Thou": see Buber, Martin, *I and Thou*, translated by Ronald Gregor-Smith, New York, Charles Scribner's Sons, 1958.

[42] Polkinghorne, *Serious Talk*: 50.

[43] For helpful discussions of the relationship between Big Bang cosmology and the theology of original creation, see Worthing, *God, Creation and Contemporary Physics*: 85-93; Barbour, *When Science Meets Religion*: 39-64; Davis, John Jefferson, *The Frontiers of Science and Faith: Examining Questions from the Big Bang to the End of the Universe*, Downers Grove: IVP, 2002: 11-36; and Davies, *The Mind of God*: 39-72.

an open future that allows for God's providential action. In 1961 Edward Lorenz, Professor of Meteorology at Massachusetts Institute of Technology, accidentally discovered the so-called 'butterfly effect' in his computer simulations of weather patterns.[44] The phenomenon, technically known as 'sensitive dependence on initial conditions,' gave rise to the sciences of chaos and complexity, competitors to the predictable ordered linearity assumed in scientific activities.[45]

Alexander points out that 'chaos' is somewhat of a misnomer, "since chaos theory demonstrates how different *ordered* systems can arise from such different starting conditions."[46] Likewise, Gleick describes the 'butterfly effect' as "order *masquerading* as randomness."[47] The lesson to be learned from this is that physics – particularly at the quantum level – is not as predictable, as rigidly Newtonian or mechanistic as once thought. Theologically, this insight suggests a God who is not some divine clockmaker, a deistic God who set the whole universe in motion, and then withdrew to allow it to function according to some predetermined and unchanging principles of operation. Rather, God's involvement is hidden and at times (but not always) unpredictable – his activity is discernible through faith and not experiment. Both science and theology offer us here a God who acts not only according to predictable natural laws – such as the rhythms of the seasons that reflect his faithful character – but also in an open, indeterminate way.

Polkinghorne's fifth assertion is that both the physical world and theology are characterised by surprise. The emergence of quantum theory offers a logic that is at odds with the either/or logic that characterised earlier (Newtonian) physics.[48] Scientists are now open to exploring the universe in a more *imaginative* and less linear way than previously available or thought possible. We might want to say the same about theology. Is theology a purely systematic enterprise, based on propositional statements about what is and what is not? Are we not faced with paradox in our Christian experience? How do love and suffering cohere in God? How can we explain the mystery of the incarnation – Jesus as both fully God and fully man? In both science and theology, our finite

---

[44] For a compelling account of Lorenz's discovery, see Gleick, James, *Chaos: Making a New Science*, New York: Penguin Books, 1987: 11-31.

[45] Although, as Haught points out, we should not "trivialize or dismiss linear science, for without it we would have little control over our technological projects." (Haught, *Science and Religion*: 144-145). Without the predictability and exactness implicit in linear science, major engineering and technological schemes would be impossible.

[46] Alexander, *Rebuilding the Matrix*: 335, author's italics.

[47] Gleick, *Chaos*: 22, author's italics.

[48] See Wilkinson, David, *God, the Big Bang and Stephen Hawking*, Tunbridge Wells: Monarch, 1993, for an introduction to the basic principles of quantum mechanics; see also Barbour, *When Science Meets Religion*: 65-89, in which the author discusses the implications of quantum theory for an understanding of God as the "determiner of indeterminacies."

minds are confronted with infinite mystery. So we should not be surprised if both disciplines give rise to new, previously unimagined expressions of reality that may express paradox rather than conformity.[49]

Polkinghorne then suggests that the insights of both science, in its investigation of the pattern and structure of the physical world, and theology are exciting. 'Serendipity' is a word which scientists sometimes use to describe the rewards of scientific research. After all the hard work of investigation and experimentation, of theories dashed and ideas discarded, there comes that moment when it is all worth while – like Crick and Watson's discovery of DNA. Theoretical physicists are excited today about the possibility of drawing together the theories of general relativity and quantum mechanics into a Grand Unified Theory (GUT). Theologians are similarly imbued with a sense of expectation and wonder as they contemplate the grandeur of God. This happens not only as Christians meditate on the glorious truths of the gospel, the God who has come to us, and the eschatological hope of resurrection life. There is excitement too as believers open themselves to the divine mystery that somehow integrates all the many diverse aspects of human experience.

> The religious believer can perceive the divine unity that underlies and unites this polyvalent diversity: science is exploring the rational order of creation; our aesthetic pleasures are a sharing in God's joy in that creation; our moral intuitions are intimations of God's will; our religious experience is the true meeting with him.[50]

Yet – and this is Polkinghorne's seventh assertion – both science and theology are problematic. The problem with the latest developments in science is that they are decidedly non-rational! Traditionally science has dealt with the 'how?' questions relating to reality, with the 'why?' questions left to theology. But now scientists acknowledge that they cannot explain how quantum theory works – except to agree that it does work. Theology has its intractable questions too. There are some obvious ones – like the problem of God and suffering. The response that human beings are given free will, and that creation has a freedom given to it by its creator, go some way to answering the problem … but not fully. Polkinghorne also addresses the problem of the diversity of religious belief: one of the greatest challenges facing Christians today is how to respond to the many different belief systems around. The presence of difficulties reminds us that neither science nor theology has all the answers – both are imperfect, evolving enterprises seeking in their unique ways to discover what each is capable of with regard to ultimate reality.

---

[49] The idea of mystery is given explicit treatment by Haught in his examination of the relationship between religion and the environment, in which he espouses the twin themes of sacramentalism and silence: "Without being identified with nature, the divine mystery is nevertheless deeply interior to it – at least according to the sacramental vision." See Haught, *Science and Religion*: 198-201.

[50] Polkinghorne, *Serious Talk*: 56.

The consequences of all that Polkinghorne has been asserting are then summed up in his final point: science and theology have things to say to each other. It is precisely because both science and theology are incomplete that they can each learn from the other. Science reminds Christians that God's creation is characterised by an evolving history: God is a patient God, whose actions in the universe are subtle and deep. And in ways that we cannot easily fathom, this world is shaped by both predictable natural laws and unpredictable randomness, both of which are expressions of God's love. Theology reminds science that science does not – and ultimately cannot – have all the answers to life's mysteries. The great questions of meaning and purpose are ultimately *theological*, not scientific, questions.

The Science-Religion Relationship: Conflict

If, as Polkinghorne suggests, science and theology have things to say to each other, how might we represent the nature of that conversation? In recent years, a number of writers in the science-religion field have offered a range of alternative schematic outlines, or typologies, for consideration. Perhaps the most famous is that developed by Ian Barbour, whose scheme allows for four categories of relationship, which he first presented in abstract form in the 1990 Gifford Lectures, and first written up in his book, *Religion in an Age of Science*.[51] Barbour's typology is summarised in the four words 'Conflict', 'Independence', 'Dialogue' and 'Integration'. They represent the variety of ways in which people have related science and religion. They range from the openly hostile – signified by the 'warfare' metaphor – to the desire for some form of synthesis between the two. John Haught proposes a slightly different typology, which is more easily remembered because each category begins with the letter 'c' – 'Conflict', 'Contrast', 'Contact' and 'Confirmation'.

The Lutheran theologian Ted Peters, of the Centre for Theology and the Natural Sciences in Berkeley, California, has offered a rather more extensive eight-fold classification scheme, and his categories range (in popular language) from what he calls 'pitched battle to an uneasy truce'. He also introduces the category of 'Ethical Overlap', which not only is significant in contemporary concerns regarding the ethics of applied technology but also reflects Peters'

---

[51] Barbour, Ian G., *Religion in an Age of Science*, San Francisco: HarperSanFrancisco, 1990. Southgate critiques Barbour for being too abstract in his Gifford Lectures, and Barbour may have taken that on board, because his latest book, *When Science Meets Religion*, presents the same classification scheme, and unpacks it in the context of four key areas of concern: astronomy and creation, quantum physics, evolution and continuing creation, and neuroscience and human nature. He concludes with a broad look at the topic of 'God and nature' within his fourfold schema. See Southgate, Christopher *et al., God, Humanity and the Cosmos: A Textbook in Science and Religion*, Edinburgh: T & T Clark, 1999.

specific interest in genetic technology.⁵² A very simple demarcation is made by Alister McGrath, who distinguishes between what he calls 'confrontational models' and 'non-confrontational models', though he does differentiate in the latter category between science and religion that are *convergent*⁵³ and science and religion that are *distinct*.

The fundamental question is that of 'enmity or alliance?' Notwithstanding the problem of the plurality of sciences and the plurality of religious – and Christian – beliefs, the historical relationship has been characterised by both mutual hostility and mutual friendship ... or, if not warm friendship, at least, a willingness to talk together! Both Barbour and Haught offer the term 'conflict' to describe the position of irreconcilable difference, even to the point of 'warfare', in the science-religion relationship. However, it wasn't until well towards the end of the nineteenth century that open warfare was declared. Until then, science and religion enjoyed a reasonably good, if unstable, relationship, punctuated by tensions that existed as the result of the dispute between Galileo and the Catholic Church at the beginning of the seventeenth century, the rise of natural theology in the eighteenth century, and the Darwinian controversy in the middle of the nineteenth century.

For example, Cardinal Bellarmine, who was the Vatican's key protagonist in dealing with Galileo and his support of Copernicus' heliocentric model of the universe, had a far more open attitude to Copernican theories than is often supposed. He wrote on one occasion in a letter:

> I say that if there were a true demonstration that the sun is at the centre of the world and the earth in the third heaven, and that the sun does not circle the earth but the earth circles the sun, then one would have to proceed with great caution in explaining the Scriptures that appear contrary, and say rather that we do not understand them than that what is demonstrated is false.⁵⁴

Early on there were those within religious circles who were very much aware that the issues raised by the science-religion debate critically related to biblical interpretation, and it did no one any good – least of all within the Christian community – to insist upon one single, dogmatic interpretation of the biblical record. Furthermore, Galileo himself sought to relate his growing scientific understanding to his Christian faith. So, the Galileo affair is not a good representative of the 'pitched battle' scenario suggested by some.

---

⁵² See, for example, Peters, T. (ed) *Genetics*; Peters, T. *Playing God?*
⁵³ In a recent interview in the CTNS publication *Research News and Opportunities* (January 2001: 21,25) McGrath eschews the use of the term 'convergence' in favour of 'resonance'.
⁵⁴ Quoted in Finocchiaro, M. P. (ed), *The Galileo Affair*, Berkeley and San Francisco: University of California Press, 1989: 68. For a discussion of the relationship between Galileo Galilei and Robert Bellarmine in the context of intellectual freedom, see Brooke, *Science and Religion*: 99-105.

A similar statement applies to the rise of Newtonian mechanics in the late seventeenth and eighteenth centuries. On the basis of his observations regarding mass, space and time, Isaac Newton was able to demonstrate that the world functioned according to certain mathematical principles. These laws of motion and gravity gave rise to the mechanistic worldview, lending weight to Christian beliefs about a provident designer, and accelerating the subsequent rise of natural theology – from data and empirical observations 'down below' we can intuit the nature and character of the divine author, or Creator, 'up above'. However, secular interpretations encouraged the view that perhaps the world was in fact a self-sustaining deterministic mechanism, in need neither of a divine author nor of a divine sustainer.[55] Newtonian ideas were originally seen as consistent with Christian notions of divine creation – they helped us to understand how God was at work in his world – Newton himself regarded God as the mediator of gravitational forces. But later in the eighteenth century, other forces began to erode theistic interpretations of Newtonian mechanics: the industrial revolution and the major social and economic changes of the time were strong secularising influences, along with increasing scientific endeavours.

In 1859 Charles Darwin published *The Origin of Species*, an evolutionary proposal that was not without its Christian apologists: there were those who supported what he had to say, and those who vigorously attacked him. Brooke notes that at the famous Huxley-Wilberforce encounter in Oxford in 1860, Frederick Temple, later to become Archbishop of Canterbury, "made room for Darwin's science and was even said by one observer to have espoused Darwin's ideas fully."[56] In a letter to Darwin, Charles Kingsley remarked that the theory of natural selection provided "just as noble a conception of deity, to believe that he created primal forms capable of self-development ... as to believe that he required a fresh act of intervention to supply the *lacunas* which

---

[55] "The problem for Christian apologists was this: In seeking to capitalize on the most accessible proof of God's existence, and one having the authority of the sciences behind it, they came close to saying that what they meant by God was the craftsman, the mechanic, the architect, the supreme contriver behind nature's contrivances. From this to atheism *could* be one short step. It only required an alternative metaphysics in which the appearance of design could be dismissed as illusory ... If the *only* proof came from design, one was left with nothing on its collapse. The point is not that science undermined the design argument – certainly not in the eighteenth century. Quite the contrary. It was rather that religious apologists were asking too much of it." (Brooke, *Science and Religion*: 195, author's italics).

[56] *Ibid*: 41. Brooke notes, along with others, that the debate between Huxley and Wilberforce was not as one-sided as legend has it. Indeed, Wilberforce was not as obscurantist as Huxley sought to convey: Darwin acknowledged some weaknesses in his argument pointed out by the bishop in a review in the *Quarterly Review* of *The Origin of Species*: "it picks out with skill all the most conjectural parts, and brings forward well all the difficulties."

He Himself had made."[57] However, the assault on the ecclesiastical establishment of the day by Draper and White fuelled the flames of conflict; the result was that the 'warfare' metaphor had particular relevance towards the end of the nineteenth century. Those who attacked Darwinism argued on the basis that belief in Darwinian evolution and belief in a Creator God were incompatible and therefore irreconcilable. So the debate was simplified down to creation *or* evolution. Huxley was perhaps more subtle than the aggressive, polemical stance of people like Draper and White. He saw in Darwinianism a powerful antidote to what he saw as the poison of Roman Catholicism. Rather than attacking the church, Huxley developed a strategy of imitation – he spoke of the "new Reformation" heralded by science. He preached "lay sermons" on scientific subjects, spoke of his colleagues as "the church scientific" and of himself as its "bishop" ... at some lectures a hymn to creation, or 'Mother Nature', was sung by the attendant audience.

In the twentieth century, the conflict thesis is clearly discernible in the psychoanalytic theories of Sigmund Freud, especially in his notion of the irrationality of religious beliefs. Freudian theories about human nature contained a deterministic fatalism, suggesting that human beings were victims of unresolved inner conflicts, so challenging the possibility of a free and open relationship with God. During Freud's lifetime, a philosophical movement called 'logical positivism' was developed by a group of philosophers called the Vienna Circle. They believed that science gave 'certain' or 'positive' knowledge through the senses, a theory they believed followed as a matter of logic from the positivism of science. Taking an epistemological stance, logical positivism declared that only science had meaningful answers regarding knowledge, thus dismissing the metaphysical contributions of religion. Since science is 'provable' and religion is not, then religion can be discarded.

However, what logical positivism failed to appreciate was that science focused on questions of mechanism, whereas religion tended to focus less on mechanism than meaning. Recent thinking has posited some convergence between science and religion with regard to meaning.[58] Haught, for example,

---

[57] Quoted in Alexander, *Rebuilding the Matrix*: 199, original author's italics. Here Kingsley, with others like the nineteenth-century Oxford Anglo-Catholic Aubrey Moore, was concerned to resist suggestions of a 'God-of-the-gaps' who was introduced only at those points where science was unable to offer an explanation for the operation of the natural world; so Alexander quotes Moore: "There are not, and cannot be, any Divine interpositions in nature, for God cannot interfere with Himself. His creative activity is present everywhere. There is no division of labour between God and nature, or God and law ... *For the Christian theologian the facts of nature are the acts of God*" (*Ibid*: 199, original author's italics).

[58] For example, the 'naïve realist' view of science, which claims that scientific discoveries correspond to truth – the logical positivist position – was attacked by the philosopher Karl Popper, whose proposal of a 'reverse methodology' in scientific rationality was influential in twentieth-century philosophy of science. He argued that *falsification* rather than verification was the appropriate criterion for distinguishing

argues that developments in physics and astrophysics "challenge the dualistic assumption that mind is fundamentally alien to the cosmos,"[59] and bring us face to face with the reality of mystery. A further criticism of logical positivism is that science demands that assumptions be made – such as the uniformity of nature – which cannot be proved by our senses.[60] Philosophically, logical positivism is unsustainable, for science itself is an evolving discipline – or, rather, the sciences are evolving disciplines. Science cannot give the final answer because science itself is changing, as twentieth-century developments in physics clearly show: "Far from demystifying the world, as the reductionist agenda proposed to do, science is now opening up the horizon of an inexhaustibly indeterminate universe."[61]

The Science-Religion Relationship: Independence

Questions of meaning point us away from the confrontational approach to non-confrontational models. Whereas McGrath distinguished between convergent and distinct in his discussion, the term employed by Barbour is 'independent', whilst Haught prefers to think of 'contrast': in both, science and religion are regarded as two distinct ways of approaching reality. Perhaps the most famous expression of this independence of two valid approaches is what has come to be known as the 'Baconian compromise', after Francis Bacon (1561-1626). One of Bacon's statements is called the "two-books" statement – "Let no man upon a weak conceit of sobriety or an ill-applied moderation think or maintain that a man can search too far, or be too well studied in the book of God's word, or in the book of God's works."[62] In effect, Bacon sharply separated the two,[63] and

---

science and non-science: see Popper, Karl, *The Logic of Scientific Discovery*, London: Hutchinson, 1959. For a fine discussion of logical positivism and Popperian falsificationism in the context of truth and reason in science and theology, see Southgate *et al., God, Humanity and the Cosmos*: 49-92; see also Alexander, *Rebuilding the Matrix*: 230-239.

[59] Haught, *Science and Religion*: 193; Haught maintains that "[w]e are now becoming convinced that mind is much more deeply embedded in the universe than we had for centuries suspected" – so quantum physics and the principle of indeterminacy imply that "the observed world cannot be sharply segregated from the human observer or instruments of observation". This link between mind and matter is, for Haught, integral to his understanding of meaning attributable to the physical universe, a theme which he expounds within an ecological – and eschatological – frame of reference (*Ibid*: 183-201)

[60] Freud – himself a Viennese – captured the spirit of logical positivism by insisting that his interpretation of human nature was no illusion!

[61] Haught, *Science and Religion*: 153.

[62] Bacon, Francis, *The Advancement of Learning*, London: Dent, 1965: 8.

[63] However, as Brooke points out, "Bacon remained convinced that scientific conclusions had still to be limited by religion ... he gave science a religious sanction, in

subsequent advocates of this approach have suggested that science and religion, though equally valid, are basically tackling different questions.

One of the greatest advocates of separation between the two is Karl Barth, whose emphasis on revelation allows no place for what is known as 'natural theology', which argues that it is possible to know something about God through empirically-derived knowledge and the data of the sciences. At the heart of natural theology lies the premise that the world is God's world, and it must therefore tell us something about its Creator. The claims and counter-claims of natural theology will be examined later in this chapter, but the point to appreciate here is that conflict, or 'warfare', between science and religion is avoided by keeping them as far apart as possible. Each maintains its own integrity, and cannot be threatened by the advances of the other. In the seventeenth century, the French philosopher René Descartes (1596-1650) reinforced the 'independence' between science and religion, regarding revelation as a separate form of knowledge,[64] and laying important foundations, along with Bacon, for the Newtonian mechanistic worldview.

One mid-twentieth-century writer who has clearly articulated the 'independence' thesis is the North American neo-orthodox author Langdon Gilkey. Ian Barbour summarises his argument in terms of four clear distinctions:

> (1) Science seeks to explain objective, public, repeatable data. Religion asks about the existence of order and beauty in the world and the experiences of our inner life (such as guilt, anxiety, and meaninglessness, on the one hand, and forgiveness, trust, and wholeness, on the other). (2) Science asks objective 'how' questions. Religion asks personal 'why' questions about meaning and purpose and about our ultimate origin and destiny. (3) The basis of authority in science is logical coherence and experimental adequacy. The final authority in religion is God and revelation, understood through persons to whom enlightenment and insight were given, and validated in our own experience. (4) Science makes quantitative predictions that can be

---

that it promised a restoration of a dominion over nature that had been God's intention for humanity' in Brooke, *Science and Religion*: 57.

[64] Descartes' distinction between reason and revelation corresponds to the sharp dualism between body and soul in his understanding of human nature, both of which reflect his rationalist epistemology. Whereas Bacon's methodology was essentially inductive, Descartes' scientific approach was deductive, starting from his well-known statement, *cogito ergo sum*, and then moving downward from that primary certainty to the physical world. For a study of Descartes' philosophy and scientific method, and an acknowledgement of the inconsistencies in his methodology, see Smith, Norman Kemp, *New Studies in the Philosophy of Descartes*, London: Lowe and Brydone, 1966; and Westfall, Richard S., *Science and Religion in Seventeenth Century England*, New Haven CT: Yale University Press, 1958.

tested experimentally. Religion must use symbolic and analogical language because God is transcendent.[65]

Haught's way of expressing this distinction between science and religion – his 'contrast' category – is to suggest that advocates of this approach want to "avoid conflating science and belief into an undifferentiated smudge."[66] For example, in recent decades there have been significant attempts made by 'creation scientists' to demonstrate that science is fully in support of a literal interpretation of the Genesis account of the creation of the world, especially through what is known as 'flood geology'.[67] Advocates of the independence thesis want to avoid such examples of what they see as unfounded and unsubstantiated rejection of scientific accounts of biological and cosmological evolution. They argue that 'creation science' is turning belief into a pseudo-scientific form, offering an alternative scientific theory. What supporters of the independence approach to the science-religion debate would say is that religion must not use science as its ally in such a fraudulent, and essentially unscientific, way.

In his recent book, *Rock of Ages*, the evolutionist Stephen Jay Gould presents science and religion as occupying different domains.[68] His basic principle is known as NOMA, or 'non-overlapping magisteria', and he echoes the perspective offered by Langdon Gilkey when he argues that: "The magisterium of science covers the empirical realm: what is the universe made of (fact) and why does it work this way (theory). The magisterium of religion extends over questions of ultimate meaning and moral value."[69] Gould is equally trenchant in his criticism of scientists in any attempt they might make to derive theological insight from their scientific endeavours. His rejection of purpose in creation[70] strikes at the very heart of religious convictions. For Gould, biological (or cosmological) evolution is totally incompatible with

---

[65] Barbour, *When Science Meets Religion*: 18, with reference to Gilkey, Langdon, *Maker of Heaven and Earth*, Garden City NY: Doubleday, 1959, and *Creationism on Trial*, Minneapolis: Winston Press, 1985: 108-16.

[66] Haught, *Science and Religion*: 13.

[67] See, for example, Morris, Henry (ed), *Scientific Creationism*, El Cajun CA: Master Books, 1985; Whitcomb, J.C. and Morris, H.M., *Genesis Flood*, Philadelphia: Presbyterian & Reformed Publishing Company, 1961; Numbers, Ronald L., *The Creationists: The Evolution of Scientific Creationism*, Berkeley: University of California Press, 1992.

[68] Gould, Stephen Jay, *Rock of Ages: Science and Religion and the Fullness of Life*, New York: Ballantine, 1999.

[69] *Ibid*: 6.

[70] Human beings, argues Gould, are "a wildly improbable evolutionary event, and not the nub of universal purpose" (*Ibid*: 206), a contrast to the closing words in Davies' *The Mind of God* (p.232): "I cannot believe that our existence in this universe is a mere quirk of fate, an accident of history, an incidental blip in the great cosmic drama ... We are truly meant to be here."

purposeful creation.

Such a view can be found in the work of the Nobel Prize-winning theoretical physicist Steven Weinberg, who famously wrote in his book *The First Three Minutes* that "the more the universe seems comprehensible, the more it also seems pointless."[71] Later in his book he wrote that it is very hard to realise that the world is just a tiny part of an overwhelmingly hostile universe. Such purposelessness and hostility suggest a bleak, even chilling, evaluation of creation, contradicting the Christian claim that the universe is inherently intentional and teleological. However, Weinberg does redeem himself by insisting that human beings can give the universe a purpose through the way we live our lives: although we may not be the stars in any great cosmic drama, we can nonetheless create for ourselves what he calls 'a little island of warmth and love and science and art' in an unloving and impersonal universe.

The Science-Religion Relationship: Dialogue

We now need to consider the idea that science and religion – and specifically Christianity – need be neither in conflict with nor independent of each other. For Haught, words like contact and confirmation are employed, whilst Barbour speaks of dialogue and integration. McGrath collapses all these typological categories under the heading convergence, but here we will use the word 'dialogue'. There are many theologians and scientists who have spoken wisely about the need for dialogue, and to this group we might add churchmen too: Pope John Paul II once declared: "Science can purify religion from error and superstition; religion can purify science from idolatry and false absolutes. Each can draw the other into a wider world, a world in which both can flourish."[72]

The dialogue approach suggests that we are wise to be cautious about the two extremes of biblical literalism and fundamentalist scientism identified in the pages above. In a critique of fundamentalist scientism, which claims that all meaningful reality can be reduced to materialistic statements, the Christian astrophysicist, Dr Bernard Haisch, castigates those who claim that "investigation of the physical world rules out anything spiritual", criticising such a position as both irrational and dogmatic. He goes on to say, "Rejection of evidence that cannot yet be measured with instruments in a laboratory is contrary to the scientific spirit of enquiry. It is time to move beyond dogmatic fundamentalism in both religion and science."[73] The dialogue approach

---

[71] Weinberg, Steven, *The First Three Minutes: A Modern View of the Origin of the Universe*, New York: Basic Books, 1977: 144.

[72] These words are taken from a message by John Paul II in Russell, Robert John, Stoeger, William R., and Coyne, George V., S.J. (eds), *John Paul II on Science and Religion Reflections on the New View from Rome*, Vatican: Vatican Observatory, 1990: M13.

[73] Haisch, Bernard, "Freeing the Scientific Imagination from Fundamentalist Scientism" in *Research News and Opportunities* (January 2001), 22.

maintains that the sciences have much to learn from religious insights about the real world in which we live. Conversely, Christians need to listen to the voice (or, rather, the many voices) of the sciences, as they offer insights about how God's world works.

When Haught uses the term 'contact' between science and religion, he means that the two inevitably interact – though they are distinct, they have implications for each other. So 'contact' "insists on preserving differences, but it also cherishes relationship."[74] In his quest for ultimate answers, Paul Davies, the well-known physicist, comes to the conclusion that "it is hard not to be drawn, in one way or another, to the infinite."[75] He continues: "I have never had a mystical experience myself, but I keep an open mind about the value of such experiences. Maybe they provide the only route beyond the limits to which science and philosophy can take us, the only possible path to the Ultimate."[76] Similarly, whether they are willing to acknowledge it or not, theologians bring to their thoughts about God certain pre-understandings about the nature of the physical world.

Dialogue means that there must be some thoughtful and intelligent contact between the sciences and Christian faith. Haught's 'contact' approach proposes that "scientific knowledge can broaden the horizon of religious faith and the perspectives of religious faith can deepen our understanding of the universe."[77] Both theologians and scientists are therefore in the business of 'doing theology' or 'doing science', an imperative that highlights the philosophical notion of critical realism.[78] Critical realism acknowledges that there is a real world 'out there', the operation of which we can begin to understand through our 'models' and theories. The knowledge human beings have of the real world is both provisional and fallible: the real world, whether the universe or God, is too vast for the human mind to encompass. It follows, then, that our knowledge – whether scientific or theological – can never be independent of the 'knower'.

Critical realism has been helpfully defined as

> a way of describing the process of 'knowing' that acknowledges the *reality of the thing known, as something other than the knower* (hence 'realism'), whilst also fully acknowledging that the only access we have to this reality lies along the spiralling path of *appropriate*

---

[74] Haught, *Science and Religion*: 18.
[75] Davies, *The Mind of God*: 229.
[76] *Ibid*: 232.
[77] Haught, *Science and Religion*: 18.
[78] See Chapter 2 for a discussion of the notion of 'doing theology' (or *theologia viatorum*): it should be noted in the discussion that follows above that the philosophical approach of critical realism may be applied to *scientia viatorum* as much as to *theologia viatorum*.

dialogue or conversation between the knower and the thing known (hence 'critical'). This path leads to critical reflection on the products of our enquiry into 'reality', so that our assertions about 'reality' acknowledge their own provisionality. Knowledge, in other words, although in principle concerning realities independent of the knower, is never itself independent of the knower.[79]

The provisionality implicit in the critical-realist position means that we cannot close the door on new, future understandings: the universe in which we live and the God who is worshipped are both far greater than ourselves – so both science and religion (as human endeavours to understand reality) need to be open to correction.

Peacocke is one of many contemporary writers who espouse a critical-realist perspective towards both science and theology.

> Critical realism recognizes that it is still only the *aim* of science to depict reality and that this allows gradations in acceptance of the 'truth' of scientific discoveries ... It must never be forgotten that the realism is always qualified as 'critical' since the language of science is ... fundamentally metaphorical and revisable ...[80]

With regard to theology, Peacocke distinguishes between referring to and describing God, a distinction that is crucial to a critical-realist stance in theology. Alongside the approach to theology known as *via negativa*, which recognizes that all we have to say about God is ultimately fallible, and therefore a potential "slippery slope to atheism",[81] we need to more positively affirm the reality of God in metaphors and models (*via positiva*). "The metaphors of theological models that explicate religious experience can refer to and can depict reality without at the same time being naively and unrevisably descriptive, and they share this character with scientific models of the natural world."[82]

---

[79] Wright, N. T., *The New Testament and the People of God*, London: SPCK, 1992: 35, author's italics.

[80] Peacocke, *Theology for a Scientific Age*: 12, 13, author's italics.

[81] *Ibid*: 15.

[82] *Ibid*: 15. For a fuller discussion of metaphors and models in theology, see Barbour, Ian G., *Myths, Models and Paradigms*, New York: Harper & Row, 1974; Soskice, Janet, *Metaphor and Religious Language*, Oxford: Clarendon Press, 1985; and McFague, Sallie, *Metaphorical Theology: Models of God in Religious Language*, Philadelphia: Fortress Press, 1982. Barbour comments on the methodological and conceptual parallels between science and theology in response to those who contrast the 'objectivity' of science with the 'subjectivity' of religion: "Scientific data are theory-laden, not theory-free. Theoretical assumptions enter the selection, reporting and interpretation of what are taken to be data. Moreover, theories do not arise from logical analysis of data but from acts of creative imagination in which *analogies* and *models* often play a role ... In religious language, too, *metaphors* and *models* are prominent ... Clearly, religious

In the second volume of *A Scientific Theology*, McGrath presents a thorough defence of theological realism, arguing that theology, like any other responsible discipline, "is accountable for its rendering of reality, and must be called upon to reform and revise its ideas if these can be shown to be out of line with what they purport to represent."[83] The philosophical concept of 'realism' – of which critical realism is one option – represents a specific aspect of epistemology and ontology which maintains that there exists a real world which is external to the human mind, a reality which can be accessed through a range of disciplines, such as the social sciences, the natural sciences and theology. McGrath notes approvingly that realism is now 'back in fashion', pointing out that it is clearly presupposed and applied by the classic theological tradition in its affirmation that "responsible theological statements *about* God can be taken to refer *to* God."[84]

McGrath observes that realism actually represents a family of philosophical positions, noting three general approaches: the world is mind-independent; (only) non-mental entities exist; and mental and non-mental entities exist. All these variations challenge the idealist, or anti-realist, position that argues that what human beings perceive derives from mental construction and does not lie outside the human mind. Realists, however, agree that "the human mind generates ideas – yet it generates those theories *in response to what it encounters outside itself.*"[85] This is the case not only within the natural sciences, which lend themselves particularly to a realist epistemology, but also within theology. For example, the fundamental Christian doctrine of creation presents us with an ontological imperative since "the nature of reality is such that the question of how it is to be known is imposed upon us."[86]

However, as McGrath points out, citing the work of the philosopher Roy Bhaskar, reality may be viewed as multi-layered, an ontological insight which has important epistemological implications, as each layer – or stratum – of reality demands a methodology appropriate to its ontology. Bhaskar's argument challenges "both reductionist approaches which collapse reality into a single observable stratum, and pluralist theories which affirm the existence of

---

beliefs are not amenable to strict empirical testing, but they can be approached with the same spirit of inquiry found in science." (Barbour, *When Science Meets Religion*: 25).

[83] McGrath, Alister E., *A Scientific Theology,* Vol II - *Reality*, Edinburgh: T. & T. Clark, 2002: 4.

[84] *Ibid*: 199, author's italics.

[85] *Ibid*: 134, author's italics.

[86] *Ibid*: 248; for a full discussion of the foundations of realism in the natural sciences, setting the scene for an investigation of the term 'critical realism', see *ibid*: 121-193; on critical realism, and its preference as an alternative to naïve realism (which eschews reflection on the part of the human knower so that reality impacts directly upon the human mind) and postmodern anti-realism (in which the human mind freely constructs its ideas without any reference to an alleged external world), see *ibid*: 195-244.

different strata, but decline to see them as dependent upon each other."[87] It follows from this argument that reality cannot be determined by whether or not it is known, a particularly significant observation in the light of the reductionist claims of those scientists with an anti-religious agenda. The significance of the concept of a stratified understanding of reality for the developing dialogue between science and theology is that it

> allows us to argue that the natural sciences investigate the stratified structures of contingent existence *at every level open to human inquiry*, while a theological science addresses itself to God their creator *who is revealed through them* ... It is not the position of *theology* within the stratification of reality which is of critical importance, but the position of *God*.[88]

McGrath's affirmation of natural theology here[89] should not be interpreted as "constituting 'proof' of God's existence or the intellectual credibility of the Christian faith."[90] Throughout his many writings as an evangelical theologian, as in this volume, he insists upon the validity of revelation as the *primary* source of knowledge about God within the Christian faith; so natural theology derives its intellectual foundations from *within* the Christian tradition. McGrath helpfully points out that the Enlightenment critique of revelation's 'scandal of particularity' – with the moral problem of its universal inaccessibility – is paralleled by "the fictitious notion of universal reason", as disclosed by the insights of the sociology of knowledge.

As an alternative to the evident limitations of a universal rationality, the writings of the philosopher Alisdair McIntyre are put forward in support of the importance of the community and its traditions in rational discourse, legitimising the validity of the Christian tradition of God as creator of humanity and the world. McGrath concludes that because the Christian concept of natural

---

[87] *Ibid*: 226, and developed in Baskhar, Roy, *The Possibility of Naturalism: A Philosophical Critique of the Contemporary Human Sciences*, 3rd edition, London: Routledge, 1998: 97-107.

[88] McGrath, *A Scientific Theology*, Vol II- *Reality*: 227, 228-229; McGrath develops the notion of stratified reality in *theology* with reference to Karl Barth's theology of the Word of God and Thomas Torrances's theology of the Trinity, arguing that both in fact deal with stratification within *theory* – i.e. at the level of explanation – rather than within *reality*: so Barth distinguishes between the Word of God as revelation, Scripture and preaching, and Torrance distinguishes between Christian trinitarian experience, the economic Trinity and the ontological Trinity (*ibid*: 232-238). McGrath agrees with Bhaskar's critical-realist proposal that we live in a world characterised by a multi-layered reality that requires investigation and explanation within a multi-disciplinary framework – theology, amongst other disciplines, therefore faces the task of addressing the stratified world of nature within the construal of critical realism.

[89] See, especially, his chapter "Natural Theology and the Trans-Traditional Rationality" (*ibid*: 55-120).

[90] *Ibid*: 74.

theology maintains that something of God may be known outside the Christian tradition, it "offers us an interpretative grid by which other traditions may be addressed on the common issues of existence, enabling the coherence and attractiveness of the Christian vision to be affirmed."[91] In a plea to take seriously the processes of human cognition and rationality, Peacocke puts forward a case for a critical realist epistemology known as 'inference to the best explanation' (abbreviated to IBE), according to which we infer what would appear to be the best possible explanation from all available data: "In IBE, the process of argument is to present those features of a case which severally cooperate in favour of a conclusion."[92]

For Peacocke, theology is a particularly apt discipline for the application of IBE, on the specific grounds that "strict falsifiability is not emphasised nor any absolute requirement for novel predictions" and in theology "overt falsifying of theological affirmations is notoriously unavailable."[93] Peacocke proposes five criteria for the 'best' explanation amongst a range of possible candidates, namely comprehensiveness, fruitfulness, general cogency and plausibility, internal coherence and consistency, and simplicity or elegance. These criteria, which need to be held in tension with each other within a web of beliefs and knowledge,[94] suggest for Peacocke a 'theology at the crossroads':

> it is now essential that the theological pier of the bridge to science be subject to the same demands for epistemological warrant and intellectual integrity as other disciplines, especially science – and to relinquish any unestablished confidence that the content of traditional theological affirmations is divinely warranted.[95]

In the development of his argument, Peacocke is anxious to avoid any over-simplistic parallels between traditional natural theology – to be addressed

---

[91] *Ibid*: 75.

[92] Peacocke, Arthur, *Paths from Science Towards God: The End of all our Exploring*, Oxford: Oneworld Publications, 2001: 27.

[93] *Ibid*: 27; Peacocke's advocacy of IBE within a critical realist framework is expressed forcefully in a number of places in his book, for example: "I urge that IBE is the procedure that best leads to public truth about the relation of nature, humanity and God which is both communicable and convincing by its reasonableness through reflection on our most reliable and generally available knowledge of nature and humanity. To most in Western culture such knowledge is pre-eminently forthcoming from the sciences. Such an approach might even open a path towards God for the many wistful agnostics and the 'cultured despisers' of any form of theism." (*Ibid*: 30).

[94] On the nature of the reconstructive development of webs of knowledge as new data are introduced, see Gregersen, Niels H., "A Contextual Coherence Theory for the Science-Theology Dialogue" in Gregersen, Niels H. and van Huyssten, J. Wentzel (eds), *Rethinking Theology and Science: Six Models for the Current Dialogue*, Grand Rapids: Eerdmans, 1998: 181-231.

[95] Peacocke, *Paths from Science Towards God*: 30.

shortly – and his own proposal, insisting that the IBE process is rather more subtly nuanced than the weak links characteristic of those who seek to deduce the nature and attributes of God from empirically derived data about the physical world. However, in his methodology – which gives central place to IBE within the science-theology dialogue – Peacocke warns against too sharp a discrimination between various modes of revelation in God's self-communication with humanity, preferring to speak of 'gradations' between different categories of revelation.[96] The result is an 'open theology' characterised by a hesitancy about the *primacy* of the doctrine of special revelation in Christian theology (without, however, dismissing its importance), an openness to "the Word/*Logos* as it is manifested in other religions as not at all derogating from the Christian revelation"[97], and a web of beliefs[98] which favours describing God in the language of Ultimate Reality rather than the orthodox trinitarianism of Christian revelation.[99] McGrath's concern about Peacocke's Christian orthodoxy, cited earlier, would seem to be well grounded.

Nonetheless, what does emerge from Peacocke's recent writing is the recognition that, whether we are scientists or theologians, we are necessarily pilgrims, and that demands an attitude of humility, and a willingness to learn

---

[96] We noted earlier that the term 'gradation' is used by Peacocke in his critical-realist approach to the sciences.

[97] *Ibid*: 170.

[98] The concept of a 'web of beliefs' should not be regarded as epistemologically inferior to revelation, but rather as a different way of *ordering* knowledge. In her response to a paper presented by Owen Gingerich at a conference in New Zealand, Nancey Murphy advocates such a holistic model as a replacement for the traditional linear geometric model of reasoning; so "the epistemological task is to seek coherence and consistency within the web without losing touch with experience" (see Gingerich, Owen, "Is There a Role for Natural Theology Today?" and Murphy, Nancey, "Response" in Rae, M., Regan, H. and Stenhouse, J. (eds), *Science and Theology: Questions at the Interface*, Edinburgh: T. & T. Clark, 1994: 29-48, 65-71). Murphy argues in her paper that coherence and consistency within a web may strengthen Christian claims to truth, although she confesses that "some of the proponents of an atheistic worldview have been much more effective rhetorically than Christians have been" in sustaining their position (*Ibid*: 68).

[99] Peacocke is cautious with respect to differentiation in his trinitarian understanding of God: "I prefer to be non-assertive about the nature of any differentiation within the divine Being and Becoming, willing to accept that it is threefold but not to speculate about the relationship of the three to each other. The triple nature of Christian experience certainly points to a threefoldness in the modes of Being and Becoming of God, but I prefer to remain reticent about any more positive, ontological affirmations concerning the, by definition, ineffable and inaccessible Godhead." (*Ibid*: 168). Accordingly, he proposes a modalistic trinitarian schema in which transcendence belongs properly to the Father, incarnation to the Son and immanence to the Spirit, but in his affirmation of the unity of the Godhead he is unwilling to speculate about the relationship between the three and the one (see Chapter 3 for a more complete discussion of trinitarian theology).

from others. Karl Popper, perhaps the greatest twentieth-century philosopher of science, has argued that the scientific quest is not in fact a quest for absolute truth: rather, it is a quest for greater *verisimilitude* – a more accurate 'model' – in our understanding of reality.[100] The same is true with regard to theology. No theologian can claim to have the last word about the God who is greater than finite minds.[101] It is with this provisionality in mind that we might usefully approach the idea of dialogue in the relationship between science and religion. McGrath, as we noted, expresses this friendship between science and religion in terms of resonance: theologians and scientists must at least listen sympathetically to each other, with a willingness to adjust where it may seem appropriate, in order to avoid the charge of arrogance.

Barbour suggests that science and religion are similar, or converge (to use McGrath's phrase), in a number of important respects. Philosophically and methodologically, dialogue "emphasizes similarities in presuppositions, methods and concepts."[102] We noted a number of significant methodological parallels between science and religion in our discussion of critical realism, with particular reference to metaphors and models. In addition, Barbour observes that science raises a number of questions that it is unable to answer – these are called *limit-questions*, or *boundary questions*. For example, at the cosmological level, theories about the origin of the universe raise questions related to temporal, spatial and conceptual boundaries: Why is there a universe at all?[103]

---

[100] On Popper's understanding of verisimilitude, see Popper, Karl, *Conjectures and Refutations*, London: Routledge and Kegan Paul, 1963.

[101] One Christian writer put in the index at the back of his book a number of references to 'Truth, ultimate': the pages indicated are all completely blank! See Sanders, E.P., *Paul and Palestinian Judaism*, London: SCM, 1977.

[102] Barbour, *When Science Meets Religion*: 23. Barbour (*ibid*: 24-27*)* refers to the insights of Kuhn (Kuhn, Thomas, *The Structure of Scientific Revolutions*, Chicago: Chicago University Press, 1962), who argued that shifts from one scientific paradigm to another usually occur as crisis shifts, rather than through gradual change (examples might include the heliocentrism of the Copernican revolution, and, more recently, the insights from quantum physics which have led to the acceptance of indeterminacy in the operation of the real world, contradicting the deterministic character of Newtonian physics). Kuhn's revolutionary theory challenged Popper's dependence upon falsification within the framework of steady progress through the piecemeal testing of discrete hypotheses and theories (see Southgate *et al., God, Humanity and the Cosmos*: 72-76). In the light of Kuhn's proposal, Barbour proposes a particular methodological parallel between science and religion, suggesting that both are paradigm-dependent in their interpretation of data: "Ad hoc assumptions are often introduced to reconcile apparent anomalies, so religious paradigms are even more resistant to falsification, but they are not totally immune to challenge." (Barbour: *When Science Meets Religion*: 26).

[103] In his book *The Mind of God*, Paul Davies raises a number of issues which relate to the boundaries and limits of science; for example, in a philosophical excursion entitled "Why Is the World the Way It Is?", he addresses such questions as: Is the universe necessary? Is a Theory of Everything feasible? Why is the universe as ordered and

At the microbiological level, and in the light of recent neuroscientific research into the link between the mind and the brain, is it really conceivable that such human characteristics as love, compassion, altruism and honesty are nothing but the result of survival-oriented neurobiological regulation? Are not human beings more than a bundle of chemicals? The boundaries of science are evident whenever scientific reductionism "shouts out too profanely and prematurely that it has finally plumbed the depths of all reality and brought the long human quest for coherence to its final stage."[104]

Alternative Theological Approaches to Dialogue

Barbour then discusses three theological ideas – *natural theology*, *theology of nature* and *process theology* – under the rubric of 'integration'.[105] Each of these theological dimensions of constructive relationship will be considered in turn. Natural theology first emerged in seventeenth-century England as a means of reinforcing the validity of Christian revelation, known in its original context at that time as 'physico-theology', and given rich expression in, amongst other texts, John Ray's 1691 work *The Wisdom of God Manifested in the Works of Creation*.[106] McGrath notes a number of interconnected developments during this period that fostered interest in "the revelatory capacities of the natural world": the rise of biblical criticism, with a consequent openness to other means of knowing the divine; the rejection of ecclesiastical authority, leading to a desire for emancipation from the church; the quest for a primordial 'religion of nature' as an alternative to the pomposity and conservatism of organised religion; and the rise of the mechanical world-view, which encouraged a purely naturalistic understanding of the universe.[107] The polemical social context within which natural theology developed at this time – in contrast to the earlier less abrasive 'natural theologies' of Aquinas and Calvin – corresponds to the polemical *religious* context which contributed to Barth's furious critique of natural theology three centuries later.[108]

In natural theology, dialogue between science and religion is predicated on the assumption that it is possible to know about God through what he has

---

stable as it is? Is God necessary and does God have to exist? (Davies, *The Mind of God*: 161-193).

[104] Haught, *Science and Religion*: 98.

[105] Barbour, *When Science Meets Religion*: 28-36.

[106] For a study of Ray, see Raven, Charles E., *John Ray, Naturalist: His Life and Works*, Cambridge: Cambridge University Press, 1986. Brooke comments that in Ray's work there is "a sense of exultation in the wonders of nature. So marvellous was the migrating instinct of birds that he could only ascribe it to the superior intelligence of their Creator." (Brooke, *Science and Religion*: 24).

[107] McGrath, *A Scientific Theology,* Vol I - *Nature*: 244-248.

[108] *Ibid*: 268.

created, and specifically that the existence of God can be discerned from the evidence of design in nature. It is a well-known axiom of revelation-based Barthian neo-orthodoxy that all attempts to understand God through the natural senses or through human reason should be eliminated. Barth was dismayed by the impotence of liberal theology in the face of the horrors of World War I, and appalled by the capitulation of German theology to Nazi propaganda in the 1930s. He also wanted to dispense with any suggestion that natural theology could prove the existence of God: hence his resistance to the construction of a Christian theology from secular – that is, *human* – data: "One of Barth's central concerns is to expose the myth of human autonomy, and identify its consequences for theology and ethics."[109] Contra Barth, Brunner argued that there was 'a point of contact' for divine revelation within human nature: since human beings are created *imago Dei*, then we are analogous to the being of God.[110] In his *Church Dogmatics* Barth acknowledges "the existence of other events and powers, forms and truths alongside the one Word of God",[111] but this "possibility of a natural theology as such" can never represent an alternative, independent source of Church proclamation. It is legitimate only if it is predicated on the prior recognition that God has made himself known in Jesus Christ: in other words, natural theology is valid if, and only if, it is located within the structure of divine revelation.[112]

One particular representation of natural theology is the 'design argument', otherwise known as the teleological argument, which states that the beauty, order and elegance discernible in creation imply a 'cosmic architect' behind it all.[113] The 'design argument' can be traced to early Greek thought. For

---

[109] McGrath, *A Scientific Theology,* Vol I - *Nature*: 269; McGrath adds that "Barth's attitude to natural theology rests partly on his concern that the assertion of the human autonomy to find God in whom or where it pleases inevitably leads to the enslavement of theology to prevailing cultural and ideological currents." (*Ibid*: 271).

[110] Brunner used the example of sin and repentance – human beings have an intrinsic understanding of these two concepts, and fuller understanding is provided through revelation. For a full account of the arguments on either side of the Barth-Brunner debate see Barth, Karl and Brunner, Emil, *Natural Theology*, London: SCM Press, 1947.

[111] Barth, Karl, *Church Dogmatics* 2/1, Edinburgh: T. & T. Clark, 1957: 178.

[112] This interpretation of natural theology *within* revealed theology in Barth's thinking is explored most fully in Torrance, Thomas F., "The Problem of Natural Theology in the Thought of Karl Barth" in *Religious Studies* 6 (1970), 121-135.

[113] The parallel with William Paley's well-known argument from design in his 1802 publication *Natural Theology* is apparent – Paley, a nineteenth-century Anglican priest, suggested that the discovery of a watch with its meticulous design pointed to a transcendent Designer; likewise, the complexity of human beings argues in favour of a God with a mind and a personality. See Paley, William, *Natural Theology*, Boston: Gould, Kelly & Lincoln, 1850, and especially Brooke's discussion of Paley in his chapter on "The Fortunes and Functions of Natural Theology" in Brooke, *Science and Religion*: 192-225.

example, Cicero, in his book *On the Nature of the Gods,* refers to the order and beauty of the heavens, the design of the human body and earthly provision for people's needs: all these things pointed towards design in the world. The Stoics in the Roman world believed the universe to be unified and intelligible, a single, well-ordered system. Further philosophical underpinnings can be found in Aristotle's notion of the 'unmoved mover', and theological origins can be traced to the thought of Augustine and Aquinas. The scientific discoveries of the sixteenth and seventeenth centuries actually bolstered the idea of intelligent design, implicit in the equal validity of Bacon's "two books", and scientists and theologians alike were united in championing the design argument as the anticipated 'nail in the coffin' of atheism. More recently, the 'design argument' spawned the concept of the anthropic principle, discussed earlier, which supports the idea of a transcendent and purposeful Creator, a providential God who had planned everything from the very beginning.

Earlier in this chapter, we noted Polkinghorne's observation that the physical world testifies to marvellous and transparent rationality: there is beauty and elegance in the mathematical equations and patterns that describe the universe. Many scientists and theologians during the centuries leading up to the Enlightenment held to the rationality of the universe, interpreting this within a solid theistic framework: for them, God was the common ground of rationality. The great physicist, Albert Einstein, once confessed to what he described as a deep faith in the rationality of the world. He did not ascribe this rational orderliness to a God who acts in some way upon his creation; rather, he subscribed to a pantheistic sort of God who was identified with the creation itself. He also rejected the idea of an open universe – for Einstein, the universe operated as a deterministic mechanism: hence his frequently quoted remark that "God does not play dice." Einstein's opposition to the idea of chance as a player in the cosmic drama was shared by many others, including the eighteenth-century French mathematician Pierre Laplace, who claimed that if we knew the position of every particle in the universe we could calculate all future events.

Linked to the idea of order is the notion of beauty. Cicero once remarked that a person who cannot feel the power of God when gazing at the stars is probably incapable of any feeling at all! Throughout the ages, scientists and theologians alike have enthused about the beauties of earth and sky, seeing them as clear pointers to the beauty and majesty of the Creator God. The Bible too bears witness to the glory and majesty of God's creation, as expressed in Psalm 8 and Psalm 19:1-6. Haught argues that the universe is influenced by an 'aesthetic' cosmological principle that causes it to expand and intensify its inherent beauty: the Christian God is therefore best understood as "One who wills the maximization of cosmic beauty."[114] Similarly, Polkinghorne refers to the world as a 'carrier of beauty': "Beauty is not just a sort of froth on the surface of things. It is something very deep about the world."[115] The theologian

---

[114] Haught, *Science and Religion*: 140.

[115] Polkinghorne, *Serious Talk*: 8.

Jeffrey Sobosan writes of "the commonness of the beauty always available, one that does not hide itself in secret nor show itself only to the elect".[116]

But the 'design argument' is not without its limitations, nor its detractors. Problems in relation to the 'design argument' arose in the nineteenth century as a result of the impact of Enlightenment thinking, and the subsequent arrival of Darwin's *The Origin of Species* in 1859: both contributed to a growing disaffection with the idea of intelligent design. How, for example, was it possible to reconcile evolutionary theories about natural selection and survival of the fittest with any form of *benevolent* design? Furthermore, the idea of randomness in Darwinian natural selection begs the question: how can an intelligent cause – who may or may not be expressed in theistic language – be reconciled with the 'accidental' mutations of evolutionary processes? Similar questions apply to disorder in the cosmos, such as earthquakes and other natural catastrophes.

One inherent problem associated with the 'design argument' as a category of natural theology is that, *by itself*, it could just as easily posit a God of the deists, outside his creation, remote and uninvolved, a God who 'wound up the clock' and has since long departed. Throughout the eighteenth and nineteenth centuries, the orthodox idea of God as Creator supplanted the biblical view of a God who is immanent as well as transcendent. God was seen increasingly as a distant God as natural theology's 'design argument' began to squeeze out the idea of a God who is immanent in his creation. Contemporary exposés of the weakness of the design argument are represented in Davies' suggestion of a 'space age astro-engineer': "it is perfectly possible for much, if not all of what we encounter in the universe to be the product of intelligent manipulation of a purely natural kind: within the laws of physics."[117]

The debate is still very much alive today, fuelled by the antagonism between evolutionary scientists such as Richard Dawkins[118] and the Intelligent Design Movement (IDM). The IDM began in the 1980s and is, in fact, theologically minimalist, presupposing neither a Creator nor miracles: it tracks intelligence without speculating on the nature of that intelligence. As a result, the movement embraces a wide range of philosophical, theological and scientific

---

[116] Sobosan, Jeffrey G., *Romancing the Universe*, Grand Rapids: Eerdmans, 1999: 39. Sobosan rebukes four great theologians of the twentieth century – Barth, Brunner, Bultmann and Bonhoeffer – for their failure to acknowledge the way science can inform our understanding of God's beautiful creation: commenting on Barth's presentation of the doctrine of creation in his *Church Dogmatics*, he writes that "he relied on a dazzling display of exegesis that attended to Genesis but refused the insights of science, ignoring almost all the currently pertinent data of geology, evolutionary biology and astrophysics." (*ibid*: 11). For a contrasting perspective on Barth – and the place of Mozart in theology! – see Sherry, Patrick, *Spirit and Beauty: An Introduction to Theological Aesthetics*, Oxford: Clarendon Press, 1992.

[117] Davies, Paul, *God and the New Physics*, New York: Simon & Schuster, 1983: 208.

[118] Dawkins' book *The Blind Watchmaker* has the explicit subtitle: *Why the Evidence of Evolution Reveals a Universe without a Design.*

perspectives, united in their opposition to all forms of naturalism: intelligent design is therefore predicated on the observation that intelligent causes can do things which undirected natural causes cannot.[119] But what exactly do we mean by 'intelligent design'? In order to address the difficulties raised by those who are hostile to the very notion of purposeful design, it may be helpful to think less in terms of fixed, totally fore-ordained and detailed plans for the unfolding of the universe and human life, and more in terms of a universe which has been given freedom by God to develop within God-given built-in self-organising capacities.

Those scientists who insist that the universe is a meaningless and purposeless zigzag path of evolutionary development, without any intelligence or reason behind it, embrace a view which is called metaphysical reductionism: there is no need to posit an author behind nature, because ultimately all things are reducible to scientific explanation. For Richard Dawkins, Stephen Jay Gould, and other scientific reductionists, there is no ultimate teleology, or purposeful goal in creation, let alone a divine plan. Their position is avowedly atheistic, and their perspective has been well stated by the Harvard astrophysicist Owen Gingerich in his critique of Dawkins, who

> seems to feel that by defending the view that a mechanistic process could have brought about humankind, his case against design had been made. But we can look at the same data and come to opposite conclusions. He is no more able to *prove* the non-existence of a Creator than I, by arguments from design, can prove the existence of a super-intelligent Designer and Creator.[120]

In an attempt to facilitate genuine dialogue with regard to God's relationship to the world, a number of scientists and theologians have recently begun to take seriously the idea of God as the intelligent designer of an amazingly complex self-organising system. Barbour therefore directs us to what he calls a *theology of nature* as another expression of the positive relationship between science and religion. Here, doctrines of creation and human nature are influenced by scientific findings. For Barbour, the starting point for a theology of nature is not science but religion, expressing a 'top-down' approach as distinct from the 'bottom-up' approach of natural theology. The theme of 'downward causation' is evident in the work of Peacocke, whose starting point is a God who is an

---

[119] Examples of this minimalist philosophy – which *allows* for theistic creation, but does not require it – are William Dembski's *complex specified information*, Michael Behe's *irreducible complexity*, David Bohm's *active information* and Marcel Schützenberger's *functional complexity*. See, for example, Behe, Michael J., *Darwin's Black Box*, New York: Free Press, 1996; Dembski, William A., *The Design Inference*, Cambridge: Cambridge University Press, 1998; Dembski, William A. and Behe, Michael J., *Intelligent Design: The Bridge between Science and Theology*, Downers Grove: IVP, 1999.

[120] Gingerich, "Is There a Role for Natural Theology Today?": 44, author's italics.

improvising choreographer or composer, ever at work continuously creating in and through 'the stuff of the world' which has always had inherent within it the potentialities for higher forms of life.[121] So Peacocke defends the idea of God as 'top-down cause', beyond whom there is no further causation, but below whom lower-level laws and interactions take place: "these new perceptions of the way in which causality actually operates in our hierarchically complex world provides a new resource for thinking about how God could interact with that world."[122]

The model advocated here is essentially panentheistic.[123] Peacocke quotes

---

[121] More recently, Peacocke has shifted away from the language of causation, preferring the phrase 'whole-part influence' in order to accommodate a more holistic systems-based understanding of the relationship between God and the world: see Peacocke, *Paths from Science Towards God*: 116-125; also Peacocke, Arthur, "The Sound of Sheer Silence: How Does God Communicate with Humanity?" in Russell, Robert John *et al.* (eds), *Neuroscience and the Person: Scientific Perspectives on Divine Action*, Vatican City State: Vatican Observatory Publications, California: CTNS, 1999; for a discussion of this revised direction in Peacocke's thought, see Wiseman, James A., *Theology and Modern Science: Quest for Coherence*, New York: Continuum, 2002: 116-117.

[122] Peacocke, *Theology for a Scientific Age*: 158.

[123] Panentheism has been defined as "the belief that the Being of God includes and penetrates the whole universe, so that every part of it exists in Him but (as against pantheism) that His Being is more than, and is not exhausted by, the universe" in Cross, F. L. and Livingstone, E. A., (eds) *Oxford Dictionary of the Christian Church*, 2nd edition, revised, Oxford: Oxford University Press, 1983: 1027. Whilst panentheism maintains that God and the world are *not* identical (unlike pantheism, in which deity is *wholly* immanent), the term is, in fact, difficult to define with exactness, because the distinction between God as a *transcendent* Being and the reality included in God is notoriously imprecise. Citing Hans Frei's famous phrase about hermeneutics, panen-theism is thus a word that is "forever chasing a meaning" (Frei, Hans, *Types of Christian Theology*, New Haven: Yale University Press, 1992: 16). The German philosopher Karl Krause (1781-1832) introduced the term as a means of reconciling pantheism and theism, maintaining that "God includes in His being, *while transcending them*, both nature and humanity." (See http://www.geocities.com/SoHo/Lofts/2938/poly2.html#panentheism, accessed 25.03.04, my italics). Krause goes on to say that "the world is a finite creation within the infinite being of God." Matthew Fox, however, interprets panentheism as 'all things in God and God in all things', thus melting "the dualism of inside and outside – like fish in water and the water in the fish, creation is in God and God is in creation" (Fox, Matthew, *The Coming of the Cosmic Christ: The Healing of Mother Earth and the Birth of a Global Renaissance*, San Francisco: Harper & Row, 1980: 57). Just as there are different varieties of pantheism (see, for example, the list of basic schools of pantheistic thought, which can be divided further, in Reese, William L., *Dictionary of Philosophy and Religion: Eastern and Western Thought*, New York: Humanity Books, 1996 – hylozoistic, acosmic, immanentistic, stoic, emanationist, identity of opposites, monistic, relativistic monistic, and absolutistic monistic) so there appear to be different understandings of panentheism. Moltmann, for example, seems to give panentheism his own meaning, tying his interpretation to a strongly trinitarian

approvingly Augustine's vivid description of the whole creation as a 'huge sponge' penetrated by a boundless sea: "that sponge must needs, in all its parts, be filled with that unmeasurable sea: so conceived I Thy creation, itself finite, full of Thee, the Infinite; and I said, Behold God, and behold what God hath created; and God is good, yea, most mightily and incomparably better than all these ..."[124] A panentheistic interpretation of God's interactions with his creation differs from pantheism in holding together God's transcendence with his immanence *without confusing the two*. In other words, God's otherness is not compromised since he is continually interacting with the whole world system in a top down causative influence, culminating in events observed in the regularities and laws operative within the universe and explained by the natural sciences. This enables us to hold scientific theories about the universe in creative tension with fundamental Christian beliefs about the transcendent sovereignty of God.

But we need to go further, and introduce into the picture the notion of chance, a "slippery word" because, as Alexander demonstrates, it can be used in three different ways.[125] The first meaning relates to events that are unpredictable because we cannot, for *practical* reasons, possess the necessary information needed to predict the outcome – such as in the tossing of a coin.[126] Secondly, chance may refer to "events that are physically indeterminate, as in the conventional interpretation of quantum mechanics"[127] – these quantum

---

theology of the cross: "in the hidden mode of humiliation to the point of the cross, all being and all that annihilates has already been taken up in God and God begins to become 'all in all'"(Moltmann, Jürgen, *The Crucified God: The Cross of Christ as the Foundation and Criticism of Christian Theology*, London: SCM Press, 1974: 277).

[124] Edward Bouverie Pusey's translation of Augustine, *The Confessions* VII, 7, in Hutchins, Robert Maynard (ed), *Great Books of the Western World*, Vol 18 *Augustine*, Chicago: Encyclopaedia Britannica Inc., 1952: 45. God's ontological interaction with the world, or 'world-System' (a phrase used by Peacocke) is given spatial representation in a diagram in Peacocke, *Paths from Science Towards God*: 112-113, a model which, as the author himself points out, suffers from the limitations not only of the two-dimensional plane of a text-book page, but also of impersonality: "if God is going to effect events and patterns of event in the world, then we cannot avoid attributing the personal predicates of intentions and purposes to God – inadequate and easily misunderstood as they are." (*ibid*: 114).

[125] See Alexander, *Rebuilding the Matrix*: 330-359, for a comprehensive discussion of chance and necessity.

[126] Alexander illustrates this type of chance – what he calls Chance A – as follows: "Out in the forest a deer is frightened by the sound of a hunter's gun and runs into the path of an express train that happens to be passing at that moment. Both sets of events have separate causal antecedents and it is their intersection by chance that results in the death of the deer." (*ibid*: 334).

[127] *Ibid*: 334. Alexander discusses whether or not 'chaos theory' (which deals with situations in which outcomes are highly dependent on small variations in the starting conditions – the well-known 'butterfly effect') belongs to Chance A or this second category of Chance B, deciding to locate it – "for the sake of tidiness" – under Chance A

events could be described in terms of 'pure chance' because they are indeterminate in *principle*, and not just in practice. The third type of chance Alexander calls 'metaphysical chance', a descriptive metaphor – unrelated to the first two technical categories of chance – which corresponds to the principle or power that rules the universe.[128] Dismissing this third type of chance – not only because it rests on a number of false assumptions but also because it is purely descriptive and *does* nothing[129] – Alexander argues that the first two types of chance are both very real in the world in which we live.

Tracing the relationship between chance and order in the origin and evolution of life at both the microbiological and the cosmological level, he suggests that if we rerun the tape of life, "given time plus chance plus natural selection plus the occasional catastrophe … it is not impossible that the rerun might not turn out so very different."[130] For Alexander, as for Peacocke and others, chance is not inconsistent with theistic top-down causation, as further supported by Ilya Prigogine, whose work demonstrates the creative interplay between chance and law within the evolutionary process.[131] For Peacocke, chance is

> the eliciting of the potentialities that the physical cosmos possessed *ab initio*. Such potentialities a theist must regard as written into creation by the Creator's intention and purpose and must conceive as gradually

---

"in recognition of the fact that it refers to classes of events that are unpredictable in practice, not unpredictable in principle."

[128] This understanding of chance – Chance C – is explicitly stated by Monod, who insists that "chance *alone* is at the source of every innovation, of all creation in the biosphere. Pure chance, absolutely free but blind, at the very root of the stupendous edifice of evolution. This central concept of modern biology is no longer one among other possible or even conceivable hypotheses. It is today the *sole* conceivable hypothesis" in Monod, Jacques, *Chance and Necessity*, London: Collins, 1972: 110, author's italics, and quoted in Alexander, *Rebuilding the Matrix*: 339.

[129] *Ibid*: 340. It is evident that Chance C is diametrically opposite to Peacocke's theistic 'top-down causation'.

[130] *Ibid*: 349, a conclusion resisted by reductionists like Richard Dawkins and Stephen Jay Gould, whose interpretation of sheer chance in the evolutionary process means that any number of reruns would result in any number of quite different outcomes.

[131] Prigogine, Ilya, *From Being to Becoming*, San Francisco: W.H. Freeman, 1980. See also Prigogine, Ilya and Stengers, Isabelle, *Order Out of Chaos: Man's New Dialogue with Nature*, New York: Bantam Books, 1984; Prigogine, Ilya and Nicolis, G., *Exploring Complexity*, New York: W.H. Freeman, 1989. Stuart Kauffman draws from Prigogine in his proposal that organisms evolve the property of 'evolvability', so that even before nature has a chance to select some few species for survival and reproduction, living systems have already organised themselves spontaneously. To propose self-organisation prior to selection is, at the very least, to point us in the direction of order prevailing over disorder – theologically, this is extremely suggestive, for it begs the question: who designed creation with this self-organising capability? See Kauffman, Stuart, *At Home in the Universe*, Harmondsworth: Penguin, 1995.

The Road Less Travelled 39

being actualized by the operation of 'chance' stimulating their coming into existence ... Hence we infer *God is the ultimate ground and source of both law ('necessity') and 'chance'*.[132]

In this view, chance is God's 'radar beam' sweeping through the diverse potentialities that are invisibly present in every configuration in the world.[133] So God might be expressed as the 'determiner of indeterminacies',[134] operating in his universe with what Peacocke calls 'self-limited omnipotence and omniscience'.[135] We see here a God whose love for his creation is expressed in terms of the gift of *autonomy* not only at the human level (free will) but also at the level of natural processes (contingency).

In an article in the CTNS publication *Research News*, the theologian Keith Ward quotes from Tennyson's well-known poem *In Memoriam*:

> Who trusted God was love indeed
> And love Creation's final law –
> Tho' Nature, red in tooth and claw
> With ravine, shriek'd against his creed

Ward echoes the thoughts of many when he writes: "There can hardly be a theology of nature, if nature is such an amoral, purposeless, irresistible power."[136] However, challenging the simplistic arguments of those who, like Paley two centuries ago, exalt the 'Designer God' who has designed every detail of nature for the best, he argues that chance, accident and competition are all parts of the evolutionary process, though – crucially – they are not the products of sheer chance. There is no reason to suppose, he maintains, that a purposive Creator might not have set up the unfolding process of evolution so that it would eventually result in intelligent life. Denis Edwards observes that "although evolution is entirely dependent on random mutation, *evolution itself is not random*."[137] So a coherent 'theology of nature' may reasonably reflect the

---

[132] Peacocke, *Theology for a Scientific Age*: 119, author's italics.

[133] The metaphor of chance as the search radar of God was explored by Peacocke in an earlier work, and suggests a creative and imaginative dimension to God which is highly suggestive: see Peacocke, Arthur R., *Creation and the World of Science*, Oxford: Clarendon Press, 1979: 95.

[134] See, on this, Barbour, *When Science Meets Religion*: 170-172.

[135] The idea of a God who voluntarily limits himself in terms of both power and knowledge in order to allow his creation to exist in open-ended freedom is dealt with more fully in later stages of this book.

[136] Ward, Keith, "'Nature, Red in Tooth and Claw': Keith Ward asks, "Can There be a Theology of Nature'?" in *Research News and Opportunities*, March 2002 (Vol.2 No.7), 20-21; see also Ward, Keith, *God, Chance and Necessity*, Oxford: One World, 1996; Ward, Keith, *Divine Action*, London: Collins, 1990.

[137] Edwards, Denis, *The God of Evolution: A Trinitarian Theology*, Mahwah, NJ: Paulist, 1999: 45, my italics.

wisdom of a God who has set in motion a process with a general direction and goal, but the realisation of that goal is left not only to the operation of the laws of nature but also to free choices, random events and other unpredictable interactions.[138]

The possibility of integrating the insights of science and religion are further discussed by Barbour in the form of a Thomist-type synthesis, but without the dualistic categories discernible in Aquinas' thinking. The vehicle he adopts for this 'systematic synthesis' is process philosophy. In the theological realm, process thought tackles the tension between divine transcendence and immanence by eliminating the transcendent God of classical theism. The emphasis is on God as one entity among others – God is therefore not ontologically different from the cosmos. In its rejection of the fixed, or unchanging, nature of reality, common in Western philosophy, process theologians focus on the dynamic process of becoming.[139] They emphasise God as one who understands as a fellow-sufferer with all humanity, sympathetically interacting with human beings. Process theology is therefore attractive in presenting God as one who is responsive to the world. It is sympathetic to evolutionary models of a God involved in his creation, with all its attendant notions of chance and novelty.

One particular feature of process theology, as articulated by Barbour, is the identification of the Spirit with divine action and energy in creation, not only in a general sense but also in the particularity of divine initiatives.[140] But its failure to account for the distinctively Christian idea of a God who is transcendent, and whose purpose is to offer hope to a suffering world, causes concern as to how much of a God is actually left. Ultimately, process theology has no eschatological promise: it offers no absolute victory over evil, as even Barbour

---

[138] Other dimensions to Barbour's 'theology of nature' include the insights of feminist theologians who emphasise the pervasive dualisms that have characterised Western thought: they argue that dualisms like mind/body, reason/emotion, objectivity/subjectivity, domination/submission and power/love have male/female implications inherent in Western culture, in which the first term of each pair is often associated with science and its attempt to control nature. So patriarchal models of historical Christianity need to be re-evaluated in the light of insights from feminist theology. Barbour also points out that science offers the raw data to enable Christianity to articulate an environmental ethic based upon responsible stewardship of the earth, which can have sacramental significance. See Barbour, *When Science Meets Religion*: 32-34.

[139] See, on process theology, Cobb, John B. and Griffin, David Ray, *Process Theology: An Introduction*, Philadelphia: Westminster Press, 1976; Hartshorne, Charles, *Creative Synthesis and Scientific Method*, London: SCM Press, 1970; and Cobb, John B., *A Christian Natural Theology: Based on the Thought of Alfred North Whitehead*, London: Lutterworth, 1966.

[140] The activity of the Spirit within world religions – and not just within the Christian faith – is offered by Barbour as a helpful encouragement to interreligious dialogue: see Barbour, *When Science Meets Religion*: 179.

has to admit. Accordingly, at the scientific level, it is not immediately clear "how such a scheme would be reconciled with contemporary cosmological predictions about the end of the present universe, which are that either a 'Big Crunch' or an infinite expansion will eventually lead to a state quite incompatible with life."[141]

Both theologically and scientifically process thought is problematic, but a number of contemporary thinkers at the science-religion interface are sympathetic to its insights, though with reservations. Ian Barbour acknowledges his debt to the concepts of process philosophy, but he is aware that "a single coherent set of philosophical categories may not do justice to the rich diversity of human experience."[142] In his desire to affirm that God both is causally independent of the world and interacts continuously with it, Peacocke rejects the two extremes of pantheism and classical theism. He recognises the value of process thought's affirmation of divine responsiveness to events in the world, but criticises its over-emphasis on God's *total* receptivity to all events in the world in a way that seems to allow God little discrimination[143]: hence his preference for a panentheistic perspective. Another theologian who displays process sympathies is the Roman Catholic John Haught; although he makes a clear distinction between God and his world, he is keen to affirm the idea of a God who interacts compassionately and sensitively with human beings in their suffering. However, his description of God's influence upon the world as persuasive love rather than domineering force steers him away from the distinctive redemptive work of Christ, and echoes process themes: "God struggles along with all beings, participating in both their pain and their enjoyment, ultimately redeeming the world by an infinite compassion – so that in the end nothing is ever forgotten or lost."[144]

Dialogue, Truth and the Postmodern Culture

In attempting to summarise the dimensions of dialogue discussed above, we should note Haught's proposal that religion essentially fortifies the humble desire to know. This reflects his conviction – which he labels 'confirmation' –

---

[141] Southgate *et al., God, Humanity and the Cosmos*: 214.
[142] Barbour, *When Science Meets Religion*: 180.
[143] Peacocke, *Theology for a Scientific Age*: 371-372, fn.75.
[144] Haught, *Science and Religion*: 69; although Haught is writing here within the framework of one who sympathises with the 'Contact' approach in the author's typology, it is evident not only in other comments but also in the overall tenor of his writing that Haught is amenable to the insights of process theology. It is noticeable too that he prefers to write within a theistic framework which embraces the three great monotheistic faiths – Christianity, Judaism and Islam – rather than confining himself to the Christian faith, as both Barbour and Peacocke do.

that religion actually supports the entire scientific enterprise. For Haught this is an epistemological issue: both enterprises – science and religion – seek to discover that which is true about reality. Haught reasons that science has religious – or theological – dimensions because scientists start from an *a priori* 'faith' that the universe is a rationally ordered totality of things; they believe that this real world hangs together intelligibly; they operate on the basis that the human mind has the capacity to comprehend at least some of the world's intelligibility; and they accept that no matter how far we probe there will still be further intelligibility to uncover.[145]

Paul Davies claims that

> even the most atheistic scientist accepts as an act of faith that the universe is not absurd, that there is a rational basis to physical existence manifested as a lawlike order in nature that is at least in part comprehensible to us. So science can proceed only if the scientist adopts an essentially theological worldview.[146]

But if we insist with Davies that scientists must be 'theologians', then it is equally valid to demand that theologians must be 'scientists', at least in outlook if not in practice. We have argued that, methodologically, both disciplines take place within a framework of values, assumptions and interpretations. Both are involved in truth-seeking. If it is true that our world is an evolving world, in which God is involved in continuous creation, then science is constantly engaged in the enterprise of formulating models of a universe that is moving towards the new creation of Christian eschatology. Christians should be stimulated about the sort of future that science might propose, without losing sight of the biblical hope of the *eschaton*. It follows, therefore, that orthodox Christian faith must critique evolutionary models that postulate the gradual creation of perfected persons into a final state that is ultimately 'this-worldly'. Christian eschatology anticipates a new creation that *transcends* the possibilities of this world, demanding that we think in terms of radical newness. Openness to the scientific endeavour must not destroy Christian hope in God's radical intervention to bring about the new creation.[147]

---

[145] *Ibid*: 23.

[146] Davies, Paul, "Physics and the Mind of God" in *First Things* 55 (August-September 1995), 32.

[147] For a helpful discussion of the issues involved in creation and eschatology from the perspective of the science-theology interface, see Worthing, *God, Creation and Contemporary Physics*: 159-198. See also Dyson, Freeman J., *Infinite in All Directions*, New York: Harper & Row, 1988; Polkinghorne, *Science and Christian Belief*: 162-175; Wiseman, *Theology and Modern Science*: 96-111. For two theologically rigorous explorations of eschatology by theologians who are sympathetic to the science-theology dialogue, see Moltmann, Jürgen, *Theology of Hope: On the Ground and the Implications of a Christian Eschatology*, Minneapolis: Fortress Press, 1993; and Pannenberg, Wolfhart, *Theology and the Kingdom of God*, Philadelphia: The Westminster Press,

We noted earlier in this chapter that the issues raised by the science-religion debate around the time of Galileo in the seventeenth century related in large measure to the problem of biblical interpretation. No one doubted the authority of the Bible: rather, they were wrestling with how that authority should be understood. This was important in Galileo's time, because if the Catholic Church allowed alternative interpretations of biblical passages, such as those Galileo was presenting, then they might have to give ground to central Protestant teachings, thus undermining their own claim to be the guardians of biblical truth. We are reminded again of Brooke's thesis that the science-religion relationship at any one time reflects the unique and particular demands of social or historical circumstance. All interpretation is an epistemological discipline within a particular historical framework, concerned with seeking truth, and in both science and theology 'truth-telling' "plays a critical role because the task is no less than trying to describe accurately, though incompletely, what God has done in the created order."[148] During the period of the Reformation, for example, Calvin argued that study of the created order through the natural sciences was of great value in discerning the existence of God, and his wisdom in creation. Brooke points out that it "has been well said of the Reformers themselves that the Bible was the sole norm and guide in matters of faith and conduct, not in everything under the sun."[149] Calvin also taught that God's self-revelation *accommodates* to the conditions of human beings, who are limited both in their understanding and by their cultural contexts. So God 'adjusts' to human capacities and minds: he 'stoops down' to our level, revelation expressed in terms of divine condescension. For example, in the biblical accounts of creation, the author of Genesis is communicating divine truth within a primitive worldview, accommodating to the understanding of the people of those days.[150]

1969: some of their ideas are considered briefly within a trinitarian framework in Chapter 3 of this book.

[148] Alexander, *Rebuilding the Matrix*: 245.

[149] Brooke, *Science and Religion*: 97; earlier, Brooke records Galileo's quip that "the Bible teaches how to go to heaven, not how the heavens go" (*ibid*: 54).

[150] In the development of his trinitarian theology of God and creation, Denis Edwards similarly resists a historical interpretation of the Genesis accounts of creation, preferring to view them as theologically rather than cosmologically authoritative for today. Edwards identifies a number of 'salvific truths' communicated in these creation narratives, truths that he takes with absolute seriousness. These truths are: the pre-existence and transcendence of God over all creatures; the ongoing relationship of all things to God as creatures to their Creator; God's delight in creatures; the divine proclamation of the goodness of creation; the blessing that makes creation fecund; the creation of human beings in the image of God; the call of the human being to work with creation but also to take care of it as God cares for it; the social nature of the human person; the insight that male and female represent the divine image; the goodness of human sexuality and marriage; the reality of human sinful rebellion against God, bringing alienation from God, from other human beings, and from creation itself; and

Throughout this chapter we have addressed a number of aspects of this search for truth in our discussion of the historical development of the science-religion debate, the rise of natural theology in the eighteenth century, the inherent rationality in both science and theology, and the more recent philosophical concept of critical realism. Whilst both biblical literalism and fundamental scientism have had their advocates and are still strongly championed in some quarters, contemporary developments in both science and theology suggest the growth of a more constructive interchange between the two disciplines. Southgate alludes to the contemporary renaissance in Barthian studies, reminding us, as we pointed out earlier in this chapter, that "Barth himself acknowledged that his Christocentric focus and starting point in Christian theology was by no means in tension with a recognition as to there being truth (what he referred to as 'other lights') outside the sphere of Christian faith."[151]

The point here is not that Barth's position is being re-interpreted in any novel way, but that the current climate is encouraging a re-evaluation of Barth's theological statements with regard to how God speaks today. If the constructive aspects of Barth's 'other lights' were obscured by the prevailing context of liberal theology in the early years of the twentieth century, as well as by Barth's own resolute stand against natural theology, the new millennium offers a radically new context for hearing Barth – without diminishing what Bonhoeffer calls his 'positivism of revelation'[152] – as scientific insights open up new opportunities for understanding God's world.

The contemporary postmodern culture – what Lundin has described as 'the culture of interpretation'[153] – invites some final comments in this chapter on the structure of the science-religion dialogue within the framework of postmodern thought. The French social theorist, Jean-Francois Lyotard, argues that the essence of postmodernism is the "incredulity toward metanarratives": that is, there are no overarching explanations of the human condition, such as those

---

the enduring divine promise of salvation. These truths represent for Edwards truth as a trinitarian reality; his text holds together the Christian view of God and the insights of evolutionary science by rethinking our theology of the trinitarian God at work in creation (Edwards, *The God of Evolution*: 12-13).

[151] Southgate *et al.*, *God, Humanity and the Cosmos*: 63.

[152] Bonhoeffer, Dietrich, *Letters and Papers from Prison*, London, SCM Press, 1953: 148.

[153] Lundin, Roger, *The Culture of Interpretation: Christian Faith and the Postmodern World*, Grand Rapids: Eerdmans, 1993. For a helpful introduction to the philosophy and culture of postmodernism, see Harvey, David, *The Condition of Postmodernity: An Enquiry into the Origins of Cultural Change*, Oxford: Blackwell, 1990; Middleton, Richard J. and Walsh, Brian J., *Truth Is Stranger Than It Used To Be: Biblical Faith in a Postmodern Age*, Downers Grove: IVP, 1995; Grenz, Stanley J., *A Primer on Postmodernism*, Grand Rapids: Eerdmans, 1996; Erickson, Millard J., *The Postmodern World: Discerning the Times and the Spirit of Our Age*, Wheaton: Crossway Books, 2002.

claimed by either Christianity or any other political or social 'order'.[154] However, postmodernism is, as hermeneutics was once described in the memorable phrase of Hans Frei, "a word that is forever chasing a meaning."[155] Inbody has referred to postmodernism as "intellectual velcro dragged across culture"[156] – an adhesive label picking up anything random that floats across our culture. Whatever else one may think about such a label, at least it has the merit of alerting us to an important signifying motif in postmodernism: its rejection of transcendent absolutes of any kind. Taking a philosophical perspective, McGrath suggests that the heterogeneity of postmodernism argues against any generalised postmodern attitude to the natural sciences: what is more useful, in his view, is to explore "how anti-realism has become accepted – without any real engagement with the issues – as the working philosophy of postmodernism."[157] Anti-realism refers to the philosophical claim that the human mind freely constructs its ideas without any reference to an alleged external world. Just as the philosophical structure of postmodernism resists the *grand récit* of the Christian worldview, it also dethrones the privileged status of scientific knowledge, treating it "as one option in the worldview shelf displayed by multicultural societies in which occult or mystical worldviews may be looked on as equally valid."[158]

However – as discussed earlier – since both science and religion are involved in truth-seeking, both are attempting to chart objective reality and therefore cannot dispense with the notion of Lyotard's *grands récits*. The problem with anti-realism for both science and religion, as ably demonstrated by McGrath, is that it espouses a social construction of reality that serves the interests and purposes of specific social groupings rather than responding to reality.[159] Of importance here is the distinction he makes between weak and strong approaches to the relationship between social factors and the scientific method in the natural sciences. At the weak level, social factors evidently play a part in scientific discovery and theory, since historicity and social location inevitably determine access to the external world. A similar observation may be made with regard to the way communities of faith are shaped in their religious belief. In other words, social and historical factors *condition* the acquisition and representation of knowledge, whether, scientific, religious or social; but they do not *determine* it. The deterministic position characterises the strong approach,

---

[154] Lyotard, Jean-Francois, *The Postmodern Condition: A Report on Knowledge*, Minneapolis, University of Minneapolis Press, 1984.
[155] Frei, *Types of Christian Theology*: 16.
[156] Inbody, Tyron, "Postmodernism: Intellectual Velcro Dragged Across Culture?" in *Theology Today*, Vol 51 No 4, January 1995: 524-538.
[157] McGrath, *A Scientific Theology,* Vol II- *Reality*: 178.
[158] Alexander, *Rebuilding the Matrix*: 239.
[159] See, especially, Berger, Peter L. and Luckmann, Thomas, *The Social Construction of Reality: A Treatise in the Sociology of Knowledge*, Harmondsworth: Penguin, 1971.

which allows no input from the external world of reality. [160]

McGrath acknowledges the anti-realist attack on such despised 'soft' targets as religion,[161] but he examines more critically the anti-realism of the strong social constructivists with regard to the natural sciences. Ultimately,

> the critiques directed by postmodernity against the alleged claims to objectivity of the natural sciences proved embarrassingly self-referential. Most damning of all, postmodernity has signally failed to explain why it is the case that the natural sciences continue to produce useful knowledge.[162]

McGrath's anti-realist critique leads him to state that all is not well with postmodern thinking and to advocate a critical realist agenda. However, whilst postmodernism may resist the specific claims of the Christian faith at the level of dogma, it may have some important contributions within the context of Christian *ministry*. In my book *Dancing in the Dark*, I argue that we must look beyond the initially negative interpretations of postmodernism, which question how Christians can ally themselves with a life-philosophy that rejects any notion of absolute truth and advocates not just an epistemological shift but an epistemological *vacuum* into which people are invited to construct their own versions of reality, with the inevitable consequences of ethical pluralism.

In an evangelical response to postmodernism, Erickson distinguishes between two varieties of postmodernism, which he labels 'hard' and 'soft', echoing the strong and weak distinction advocated by McGrath with regard to social constructivism. Hard postmodernism reflects the radical deconstructive elements of the movement, which deny objectivity and rationality, and takes up an extreme pluralistic position with regard to truth. Soft postmodernism, on the other hand, rejects dogmatic naturalism and antisupernaturalism and "the type of naïve objectivity that denies the effect of historical and cultural situations. In

---

[160] The contribution of communities of faith in the shaping of religious belief has been consistently articulated in the writings of Stanley Grenz, who argues that "theological construction needs no elaborate, foundation-setting, certainty-gaining prolegomenon. Instead, it arises out of the life of the discipleship community, persons who are joined together by the Spirit and who join together in living out the mandate they share. Therefore, presence within the Christian community itself leads to the theological task." (Grenz, Stanley J., *Renewing the Center: Evangelical Theology in a Post-Evangelical Era*, Grand Rapids: Baker Academic, 2000: 214).

[161] In his analysis, McGrath draws helpfully from the insights of Latour, who exposes the implausibility of social constructivism in the 'hard' targets, such as the natural sciences: see Latour, Bruno, *We Have Never Been Modern*, Cambridge MA: Harvard University Press, 1993.

[162] McGrath, *A Scientific Theology,* Vol II- *Reality*: 191. Postmodernism's lack of intellectual rigour is exposed in Sokal's celebrated 1996 academic hoax, where the author mimicked postmodernism's shallow, even ignorant, critiques of the natural sciences; for a summary of Sokal's hoax and its implications for postmodernism, see *ibid*: 188-191.

other words, it rejects logical positivism, behaviourism, and all other artificially scientistic approaches to reality."[163] This distinction leads Erickson to view hard postmodernism as a threat to Christianity, but to support the presence of soft postmodernism as an encouragement to believers "to contend for the truth of the Christian faith, in contrast to a secular world that formerly excluded any faith of this type."[164]

The redeeming feature of soft postmodernism for Christian ministry within the contemporary cultural context may be its opening of the door to new and optimistic expressions of freedom, imagination and creativity, epitomised in the challenge to Le Corbusier's architectural straight lines. Right-brain creativity, with all its ambiguities, flamboyance, irreverence and stylised pastiche, offers hope and encouragement (if at times only transitory) to a generation tired of structure, order and left-brain sterility. It is too easy for those who mourn the loss of stable values and the abandonment of unequivocal truth-statements, particularly in the realm of theology, to dismiss this more positive evaluation of postmodernism for the practice of Christian ministry.[165]

If the soft variety of postmodernism has something to say to us by virtue of its challenge to a hierarchically-structured and propositional way of ordering and presenting reality, then it may have a contribution to make to the conversation between the natural sciences and the Christian faith, without our having to endorse its intrinsically fatal philosophical weakness.[166] The idea of

---

[163] Erickson, Millard J., *Postmodernizing the Faith: Evangelical Responses to the Challenge of Postmodernism*, Grand Rapids: Baker Books, 1998: 19.

[164] *Ibid*: 20.

[165] See Buxton, Graham, *Dancing in the Dark: The Privilege of Participating in the Ministry of Christ*, Carlisle: Paternoster, 2001: 173-186; it will be noted here that the *philosophical* underpinnings of postmodernism are not being advocated: rather, the *experiential* consequences are acknowledged as relevant within the context of a more sympathetic engagement with the contemporary postmodern culture. McGrath comments on the philosophical appeal of anti-realism for certain postmodern writers "not on account of its intellectual *credentials*, but on account of its intellectual *consequences*. It thus serves the agenda of postmodernity well, in that all can be accounted for as a human construction which may immediately be deconstructed by those with the necessary skills to yield a more pleasing intellectual artifice in due course." (McGrath, *A Scientific Theology,* Vol II- *Reality*: 178, author's italics).

[166] This fatal weakness has been summarised by Alexander: "The claim that there is no 'grand narrative' that can validate particular forms of human knowledge is of course itself a 'grand narrative' on a majestic scale which itself lacks validation, and indeed there seems no particularly good reason for believing it. The beliefs of postmodernism therefore find themselves hoist by their own petard in rather the same way the Logical Positivism came aground on the realization that its own claims could not be validated by empirical data. In some ways postmodernism is in a worse position than this, because its new 'grand-narrative' – that no branch of human knowledge can be legitimated – must, if believed, lead to the conclusion that the claims of 'postmodernism' themselves comprise a language-game that need not detain us for very long. Indeed, it is difficult to avoid the slide from such conclusions into futility and cynicism. If various branches of

dialogue coheres well with a number of insights implicit in postmodern thinking, one of which is a holistic interpretation of reality. It has frequently been observed that Western thought has been characterised by dualistic interpretations of reality,[167] such as mind *versus* body, objective *versus* subjective, reason *versus* emotion, and – by implication – science *versus* religion, even evolution *versus* creation. Postmodernism prefers to think in *holistic* terms, in which we conceive of a fluid *web* of knowledge, rather than hierarchical and reductionist constructions built upon fixed foundations of right

---

human knowledge are ultimately mere sets of language games, why bother to play them? We may as well stick to trivial pursuits." (Alexander, *Rebuilding the Matrix*: 241).

[167] See, for example, Barbour, *When Science Meets Religion*: 32-33, 129-132. For a helpful introduction to the dualistic separation between the sacred and the secular, see Brown, Robert McAfee, *Spirituality and Liberation: Overcoming the Great Fallacy*, London: Spire, 1988; and Walsh, B. J. and Middleton, J. R., *The Transforming Vision: Shaping a Christian World View*, Downers Grove: IVP, 1984: 93-105. In an extensive series of volumes on dualism, Fontaine argues that dualism exists where "there are two systems or concepts or principles or groups of people or even worlds that are utterly opposed and cannot be reduced to each other ... One of the two is always thought to be of a much higher quality than the other, so much so that one pole is always seen as distinctly inferior, fit to be neglected, repudiated, or even destroyed." (Fontaine, Petrus Maria, *The Light and the Dark: A Cultural History of Dualism*, Amsterdam: J. C. Gieben and Gopher Publishers, 1986-2002). The term 'dualism' was actually coined at the beginning of the eighteenth century in the writings of Thomas Hyde, a Professor of Hebrew at Oxford University. He, like many others, referred to the ancient Persians, especially their notion of two principles, one *eternal* and one *created*. Fontaine disputes this, insisting that dualism as such cannot be traced to a historical origin. For him, it has always existed: it is not so much a historical phenomenon as an *anthropological* one: "It occurs in every conceivable field of life, in religion and philosophy, in history and politics, in literature and art, in social relationships and in personal life. Wherever we are looking, we see people grappling with or suffering from or trying to accommodate themselves to unbridgeable oppositions. We are in presence of a general human phenomenon; since it fundamentally forms part of our human make-up, we are entitled to call it anthropological. The origin of dualism is not to be found in history or mythology, in philosophy or religion (not even in the dualistic Iranian religion), but in the human condition." But the term can be most easily understood with reference to the metaphysical ideas of Plato, who postulated two worlds, "a world of sense, always in flux, and a unified world of Ideas, not available to our senses but only to thought, which alone are fully knowable" (Hare, R. M., *Plato*, Oxford: Oxford University Press, 1983: 13). In *The Republic* these two worlds are defined in terms of the higher world of knowledge, on the one hand, and the lower world of opinion on the other. In Plato's thinking, the dimension of knowledge is subdivided into pure thought or intelligence and mathematical reasoning, which alone are capable of apprehending the intelligible world of Forms; and the dimension of opinion is subdivided into belief and illusion, which reflect the nature of the physical world in which we live (see Plato, *The Republic*, translated by H. D. P. Lee, London: Penguin Books, 1955: 231-286).

versus wrong. The notion of dialogue therefore sits well – at a conceptual level – with this idea of web-like connections of belief and insight.[168]

We have elucidated hard postmodernism as a highly subjective enterprise, challenging the concept of objective reality. Not only does Erickson's hard version seek to pull the carpet away from under the feet of many scientific claims, but Christianity also finds itself under attack as objective 'truth-claims' about the 'God who is' are repudiated. However, both science and Christianity may find common ground within the contemporary postmodern climate with the acknowledgment that both stand on the threshold of ultimate mystery. In an editorial in the CTNS *Research News and Opportunities*, Karl Giberson argues that there is

> no abstract, universal scheme into which 'timeless truths' of both science and religion can be placed once and for all, snugly juxtaposed and eternally secure. Human beings know a tiny bit about the world and an even smaller bit about God. But the bit that we don't know – the *Cloud of Unknowing* – is so much larger. And in that larger cloud lies the possibility that what may seem to be contradictory truths are not what they seem. [This may be] the beginning of wisdom.[169]

The danger, of course, is that 'wisdom' may be interpreted in an epistemologically suspect way, serving as a disguise for a pragmatic pseudo-reconciliation of incompatible beliefs. This seems to be where Giberson is heading when he invites us to "suppose that we do not define compatible beliefs as 'those that can be philosophically reconciled' but rather 'those that can be simultaneously believed.'"[170]

Whilst the idea of a 'cloud of unknowing' resonates more sympathetically with a critical-realist understanding of a reality which is not limited to what can

---

[168] Gregersen likens the concept of a web of beliefs to a raft with planks, in his outline of a 'contextual coherence theory' for the science-theology dialogue: so human knowledge is viewed as an intersubjective enterprise, "like *a raft with planks* of different size and color. The raft as a whole (the web of beliefs) is corroborated by the planks (the truth-candidates) that constitute that raft, and knowledge is enlarged when new planks are added which fit into the raft and strengthen its structure. No plank forms a raft in itself but is only a distinctive part of the raft, and belongs as such to the family of planks constituting the raft as a whole." (Gregersen, Niels H., "A Contextual Coherence Theory for the Science-Theology Dialogue": 189). The 'coherence model' directs us from the foundational notion of a 'chain of knowledge' to the web-like 'raft of knowledge'. For Gregersen, though the model "always prefers stronger ties of interconnection, it also allows for looser connections between different epistemic approaches to reality. In this respect *the coherence model can be seen as steering a middle course between critical realist and nonintegrative approaches to the interface of science and theology*, though coherence is closer to the former than the latter." (*Ibid*: 227, my italics).

[169] Giberson, Karl, "Where It All Comes Together: *The Beginning of Wisdom*" in *Research News and Opportunities*, July/August 2001: 4.

[170] *Ibid*: 4.

be observed,[171] rather than with the anti-realist presuppositions underlying the more radical philosophical underpinnings of postmodernism, the themes of mystery, wisdom and wonder have a suitably postmodern ring about them. They resist clear definition and boundary. The Princeton theologian J. Wentzel van Huyssteen suggests that, as a result of the contemporary postmodern challenge,

> many of the stereotyped ways of relating theology and science through models of conflict, independence, consonance, harmony, or dialogue are revealed as simplistic generalisations about the relationship between these two dominant forces in our culture. The challenge so typical of postmodernist pluralism not only implies a heightened awareness, and a historical sensitivity, to the shifting boundaries between theology and science, but in fact makes it impossible even to speak so generally about 'rationality', 'religion', 'theology', 'God', or 'Divine action'.[172]

Ultimately van Huyssteen's approach favours the primacy of what he calls 'experiential accountability', which "reveals that in both theology and the sciences we relate to our world epistemically through the mediation of interpreted experience"[173] within the context of living, developing and changing traditions.

Whilst contemporary scientist-theologians like Ian Barbour, John Haught and Arthur Peacocke gravitate towards a process-type of integration between science and religion, the philosopher Holmes Rolston III insists that science needs religion in order to make sense of its discoveries and theories – it needs the *wisdom of God* to keep science humane, to give it a conscience:

> too much emphasis on the pragmatic utility of science is increasingly likely to obscure the most genuine reason for doing it, which lies in the joy of, and human need for, inquiry into the nature of things ... Among the humanities, religion pushes science toward questions of ultimacy, as well as of value, and it can keep science from being blinkered, or, more elegantly put, religion can keep science down.[174]

---

[171] This statement underscores Bhaskar's distinction between epistemology and ontology – the epistemic fallacy "that statements about being can be reduced to or analysed in terms of statements about knowledge": see Bhaskar, *The Possibility of Naturalism*: 38, and McGrath, *A Scientific Theology,* Vol II- *Reality*: 218-219.

[172] van Huyssteen, J. Wentzel, "Postfoundationalism in Theology and Science: Beyond Conflict and Consonance" in Gregersen and van Huyssteen, (eds), *Rethinking Theology and Science*: 13-49

[173] *Ibid*: 45.

[174] Rolston, Holmes, III, "Science, Religion and the Future" in Richardson, W.M. and Wildman W.J. (eds). *Religion and Science: History, Method, Dialogue*, New York: Routledge, 1996: 61-82.

The Road Less Travelled

This notion of wisdom is characteristic of postmodern thought, particularly in its resonance with ethical issues of justice and ecological concern for the physical world in which we live.

In his concluding comments in an edited book on the relationship between science and the quest for spiritual truth, the philosopher Philip Clayton notes appreciatively the stress placed by contributing scientists on the spiritual life at a personal level, a recognition that empirical knowledge is not all there is, that there are questions that lie beyond the domain of the natural sciences. These questions often lead to a sense of wonder:

> when you raise questions of ultimate meaning, when you ask about the beauty of a mountain lake or a Mozart symphony, when you experience wonder at the sheer size of the universe or the complexity of its structures, you concentrate on experiences that are not, at least not directly, part of the subject matter of the natural sciences.[175]

At the scientific level, that wonder may translate into a sense of mystery implicit in such notions as the curvature of space and the phenomenon of quantum mechanics, reminiscent of Niels Bohr's famous comment that "whoever says they understand quantum mechanics does not understand quantum mechanics."

Commenting on Rahner's understanding of God as unfathomable mystery, Denis Edwards notes "the ever-amazing mystery of our own profound interconnection" with the incomprehensible processes in the cosmos, leading to a more 'theological' interpretation of the cosmos itself: "The experience of the profound mystery of our existence in relation to a wondrously mysterious universe can open out into self-acceptance before Holy Mystery."[176] For Edwards, this may be viewed as an authentic experience of the Spirit of God at the heart of creation. An appreciation of wonder and mystery – whether it is triggered by a profound awareness of humanity's place in the cosmos, the affective experience of a Mozart symphony or the intellectual bafflement at quantum mechanics – resonates with the 'soft postmodern wisdom' that challenges the purely dispassionate analysis associated with rationalistic scientific endeavour.

The Quaker scientist Jocelyn Bell Burnell expresses this well at a personal level:

> Whilst attributes like academic argument, careful experimentation, clear thinking, physical insight and logic are important, I also honor

---

[175] Clayton, Philip, "Some concluding reflections" in Richardson, W. Mark, Russell, Robert John, Clayton, Philip and Wegter-McNelly, Kirk (eds), *Science and the Spiritual Quest: New Essays by Leading Scientists*, London and New York: Routledge, 2002.

[176] Edwards, Denis, "Ecology and the Holy Spirit" in Pickard, Stephen and Preece, Gordon (eds), *Starting With the Spirit*, Adelaide: Australian Theological Forum, 2001: 238-260.

and value qualities such as beauty, compassion, connectedness, empathy, genius, glory, insight, inspiration, the numinous, wisdom, and wonder.[177]

Human beings do well to take stock of their own lives, and to ask, with Eliot, "Where is the Life we have lost in living?" Immediately preceding this searching question, Eliot remonstrates against the incessant, and ultimately fruitless, pursuit of idea and action that drives us further from God, rather than towards him:

> The endless cycle of idea and action,
> Endless invention, endless experiment,
> Brings knowledge of motion, but not of stillness;
> Knowledge of speech, but not of silence;
> Knowledge of words, and ignorance of the Word.
> All our knowledge brings us nearer to our ignorance,
> All our ignorance brings us nearer to death,
> But nearness to death no nearer to God.
> Where is the Life we have lost in living?
> Where is the wisdom we have lost in knowledge?
> Where is the knowledge we have lost in information?
> The cycles of Heaven in twenty centuries
> Bring us further from God and nearer to the Dust.[178]

For those who are engaged in Christian ministry, seeking to articulate the gospel of Jesus Christ in a way that resonates with the culture of pluralism and tolerance, a culture which responds sympathetically and often unquestioningly to the claims of the scientific community, the invitation is to listen with openness to what the natural sciences are saying without peddling a trite and unthinking Christianity. That same invitation is open to scientists: it is the invitation to lift their eyes higher, to look beyond the academy, the observatory and the laboratory, because both science and religion "ultimately flow out of the same 'radical' eros for truth that lies at the heart of our existence. And so, it is because of their shared origin in this fundamental concern for truth that we may never allow them simply to go their separate ways."[179]

---

[177] Burnell, Jocelyn Bell, "Science, spirituality and religion: An exploration of bridges and gaps" in Richardson *et al* (eds), *Science and the Spiritual Quest*: 21-27.

[178] Eliot, T. S., 'Choruses from "The Rock"' (Chorus I) in *Selected Poems*, London: Faber and Faber, 1961: 107.

[179] Haught, *Science and Religion*: 203.

CHAPTER 2

In Solidarity with Beasts, Plants and Stones – Theology, Science and Pastoral Ministry

In his discussion of the nature of pastoral care in the church, Brister identifies a range of images that have represented guiding visions for ministry through the years, such as preacher, discipler, servant leader and wounded healer, amongst others. None of these images, however, as Brister acknowledges, adequately reflects the core purpose of the Christian faith-community, a task compounded by what he identifies as cultural fragmentation, loss of prophetic vision and increasing secularisation.[1] In this chapter we address the nature of the church's ministry – its core purpose – in the world, in which the concept of *praxis* is introduced as an inner dynamic that informs the ongoing practice of ministry. A number of interrelated motifs are presented which converge to offer a well-rounded understanding of pastoral ministry within the overarching rubric of participation[2], namely trinitarianism, incarnation, contextualisation and Christopraxis. These themes articulate the fundamental truth that all ministry is God's ministry and Christians are privileged to cooperate with him in his work of grace as they engage in the *praxis* of ministry. The gospel – if it is to be faithfully heard as the gospel of *God* – therefore straddles the twin themes of transcendence and immanence.[3]

In Chapter 1 we noted the significant developments that occurred during the final quarter of the twentieth century at the interface between science and theology, particularly with reference to the natural sciences. During the same period – following the insights of the Dutch theologian Jacob Firet in the late

---

[1] Brister, C.W., *Pastoral Care in the Church*, (3rd edition, revised and expanded) San Francisco: HarperCollins*Publishers*: 1992: 4.

[2] Sections of this chapter first appeared in Buxton, Graham, *Dancing in the Dark: The Privilege of Participating in the Ministry of Christ*, Carlisle: Paternoster, 2001, especially Part One: 'A Theological Paradigm for Ministry': 13-114; and also in Buxton, Graham, 'The Failure of Functional Theologies of Ministry and the Promise of a Relational Alternative' in *Ecclesiology* 1.3 (May 2005): 27-43 (© Sage Publications Ltd., London).

[3] These two themes are given important emphasis in Chapter 3, where the tension between the transcendent absoluteness and the dynamic reciprocity of God are examined within the framework of trinitarian theology.

1960s[4] – a new paradigm of "practical theology as a theory of action" emerged in America and Europe[5]. Though the literature on pastoral and practical theology over the past fifty years regularly refers to the contribution of the *human* and *social* sciences and scientific *methodologies* to pastoral ministry, specific mention of the *natural* sciences is conspicuously lacking. The thesis proposed here is therefore an apologetic one: a contextually-aware practical theology cannot ignore explicit engagement with the natural sciences if it is to have contemporary relevance in the practice of ministry.

In developing this thesis, we will need to clarify the meaning of *imago Dei* within the specific context of a theology of creation: Luther's warning of our tendency to define humanity self-referentially – *incurvatus in se*[6] – needs to be addressed not only christologically, but also within the context of humanity's relationship with the physical creation. Commenting on the Judæo-Christian ontology of communion that interprets the doctrine of *imago Dei* in relational terms, Douglas John Hall observes that

> the natural sciences, which official religion has consistently feared (because, one suspects, they threatened to transfer to the world some of the wonder religion wanted to reserve for its own special preserve) – even the natural sciences learned from this same Judæo-Christian ontology that human spirituality is cheapened when it fastens on the divine in such a way as to exclude nature and even history from the realm of transcendent wonder.[7]

Ministry as *Praxis*

It is not uncommon to hear of pastoral ministry expressed in terms of the familiar pastoral triad of *kerygma*, *koinonia* and *diakonia*, which speak of the outward, observable expression of the life of the church in proclamation, fellowship and service. These characteristic features of Christian ministry are all vital components of the active life of the church: however, they fail to do

---

[4] Firet, Jacob, *Het agogisch moment in het pastoral optreden*, Kampen: 1968 (translated by Vriend, J. as *Dynamics in Pastoring*, Grand Rapids: Eerdmans, 1986), and cited by Heitink, Gerban, *Practical Theology: History, Theory, Action Domains: Manual for Practical Theology*, Grand Rapids: Eerdmans, 1999: 3; under Firet's leadership the Institute of Practical Theology was founded in Holland in the late 1960s.

[5] Heitink, *Practical Theology*: 2. It is significant to note that the emergence of the discipline of practical theology as *praxis* also parallels the 'rediscovery' of trinitarian theology, which, as expounded in the next chapter, is similarly concerned with the transcendent-immanent tension.

[6] See Luther, Martin, *Lectures on Romans* (translated and edited by Wilhelm Pauck), Philadelphia: Westminster, 1961: 23-27.

[7] Hall, Douglas John, *Imaging God: Dominion as Stewardship*, Grand Rapids: Eerdmans, 1986: 138.

justice to ministry as that which finds its source and purpose in the will of God. Thomas Oden points us to the centre of ministry by reminding us that this centre is "Christ's own ministry for and through us, embodied in distortable ways through our language, through the work of our hands and quietly through our bodily presence."[8] The major limitation of the typical functional terminology proposed is that it focuses primarily on practical actions without offering us any insight into the essentially revelatory and christological basis of Christian ministry.[9] It is not the task of the church to decide how and when to make God known: it is the privilege and responsibility of those who confess Christ to discern the will of the Father, and in obedience to respond to the Spirit who ever seeks to glorify Christ in the world. So ministry is not what *we* do, but is "determined and set forth by God's own ministry of revelation and reconciliation in the world, beginning with Israel and culminating in Jesus Christ and the Church."[10]

The implications of this are profound, for to view ministry in this light is to emphasise the crucial relationship between the ministry of Christ and the ministry of the church. Furthermore, the present ministry of Christ in the world may be described as revelatory, for human attempts to disclose Christ fail to reveal God in his saving grace. Truly we may say with Barth that "it is not [Christ] that needs proclamation, but proclamation that needs him ... He makes himself its origin and object."[11] Only Christ in the power of the Spirit is able to make God known to us, to reveal God as he truly is. And when we are confronted with God as he truly is, that revelation in itself effects reconciliation. So we are invited to be participants in God's self-revelation: that is the privilege of those who are called to be co-workers with Christ in his ongoing ministry in the world.

However, we may go further and articulate Christian ministry within a trinitarian framework. In systematic theology, we are accustomed to identifying

---

[8] Oden, Thomas C., *Pastoral Theology: Essentials of Ministry*, San Francisco, Harper & Row, 1983: 3.

[9] Bromiley articulates the christological basis for ministry well: "Christians may press others with cogent arguments, move them by eloquent addresses, manipulate them by clever techniques, influence them by efficient organization, capture them by attractive personality, but they cannot alone do the one thing that finally counts: i.e. give the inner enlightenment and bring about the inner conversion that mean eternal salvation. God uses their ministry as a means to this end, but the power of Christian evangelism and edification is the power of the Word's own ministry by the Spirit and in high-priestly intercession." (Bromiley, Geoffrey W. "The Ministry of the Word of God" in Kettler, Christian D. and Speidell, Todd H. (eds), *Incarnational Ministry: The Presence of Christ in Church, Society and Family*, Colorado Springs: Helmers & Howard, 1990: 84).

[10] Anderson, Ray S., "A Theology for Ministry" in Anderson, Ray S. (ed), *Theological Foundations for Ministry: Selected Readings for a Theology of the Church in Ministry*, Edinburgh: T. & T. Clark Ltd, 1979: 7.

[11] Barth, Karl, *Church Dogmatics*, 4/1, Edinburgh: T. & T. Clark Ltd, 1956: 227.

the elements of God's action in Christ in history as distinct, even separate, events. So we develop a doctrine of the incarnation, a doctrine of the atonement, a doctrine of the ascension, and so on. However, it is far more appropriate to view the various dimensions of the christological event as the interconnected aspects of one multi-faceted jewel, from the incarnation through to the *parousia* (the return of Christ), in which all three members of the Trinity are intimately and necessarily involved. This overarching framework for understanding God's redemptive work, in which the community of the Trinity takes an active part in the economy of salvation, is helpful in thinking about the nature of the church's ministry. Not only are we alerted to the importance of sourcing all ministry in God himself, but we are encouraged to interpret ministry as that which flows out of the corporate life of the church. It follows from this that outmoded concepts of ministry, which ascribe responsibility for the various dimensions of church life to only a few people (the 'ministers'), are therefore replaced by an understanding of the ministry of the community of God's people that reflects the communal life of the Trinity.[12]

Before elaborating further on these insights, which posit a *relational* – as distinct from a functional – understanding of ministry, it is instructive to note how ministry has been interpreted by pastoral/practical theologians[13] in the second half of the twentieth century. Writing in 1956, H. Richard Niebuhr cites Mark May's 1934 study of the profession of the ministry, in which the author pointed out evidence of confusion about the role and function of pastoral ministry. Niebuhr suggests that "in large areas the indefiniteness, vagueness and conflict characteristic of thought about the ministry in the 1930s continues to prevail."[14] So ministry training (and Neibuhr was addressing the American context) focused on ministry as 'a series of loosely connected acts' without any evident thread tying them together. Ministry was thus reduced to a manual of 'hints and helps', a form of applied theology, or 'theological technology'.[15] It is

---

[12] See Chapter 4 for a more detailed examination of the relationship between persons and community within the life of the church as an expression of the life of the Trinity. Note there, especially, the insights of Miroslav Volf in *After Our Likeness: The Church as the Image of the Trinity*, Grand Rapids: Eerdmans, 1998, and John Zizioulas in *Being as Communion*, London: Darton, Longman & Todd, 1985.

[13] The distinction between 'pastoral theology' and 'practical theology' will be considered in a later section of this chapter. As Elaine Graham has pointed out, the two terms are often used interchangeably, but because they have specific historical and normative values, it is important to recognise the differences of tradition and emphasis behind them. See Graham, Elaine, *Transforming Practice: Pastoral Theology in an Age of Uncertainty*, London: Mowbray, 1996: 11-12 (fn.1).

[14] Niebuhr, H. Richard (in collaboration with Williams, D. D. and Gustafson, James M.), *The Purpose of the Church and Its Ministry: Reflections on the Aims of Theological Education*, New York: Harper & Bros., 1956: 52.

[15] The term 'theological technology' is used disparagingly by Edward Farley in his essay "Theology and Practice Outside the Clerical Paradigm" in Browning, Don S., (ed) *Practical Theology,* San Francisco: Harper & Row, 1983. Similarly, Forrester, who like

not uncommon today to hear pastors and other Christian leaders speaking about ministry using comparable pragmatic language.

Seward Hiltner, one of the most influential pastoral theologians of the mid-twentieth century, had a strong empirical bent, with a concern for experience and function. In his groundbreaking *Ferment in the Ministry* he declares that "my implicit argument all the way through is that a lot of the modern arguments about the ministry can be solved if they are approached through the analysis of functions of ministry."[16] In this regard, Hiltner is an avowed 'functionalist' – he disavows being called a 'pragmatist' "only because that term connotes a certain opportunism that I deny."[17] Similarly, Urban Holmes argues, on the questionable basis that we are what we do, not the other way round, that any "doctrine of the ministry must therefore ultimately fall back on function."[18] Whilst both were troubled about the significance attributed to status and "ontological theories of ministerial order"[19], neither looked beyond function to the christological source of ministry.

In his 1956 text, *The Church's Ministry*, Manson insists that the doctrine of the church is a branch of Christology:

> There is one 'essential' ministry, the only ministry that is unchallengeably essential. That is the ministry which the Lord Jesus Christ opened in Galilee after John the Baptist had been put in prison, the ministry which he carried on in Galilee and Judæa, the ministry which he continues to this day in and through the Church, which is His body.[20]

Over the years, however, this christological perspective to ministry has been either undervalued or neglected as different emphases have been given to the discipline of pastoral ministry. Amongst the many themes that have been suggested are ministry as interconnection with God and the world,[21] ministry as community formation,[22] ministry as functional competence,[23] ministry as

---

others is concerned to see ministry and theology more closely integrated as *praxis*, notes Schleiermacher's apparent elevation of practical theology as the 'crown of theological study', but ultimately dismisses the early nineteenth-century German theologian's schema, in which "it seems that practical theology is really nothing more than *applied* theology ... a kind of technology." (Forrester, Duncan B., *Truthful Action: Explorations in Practical Theology*, Edinburgh: T. & T. Clark, 2000: 36-37, author's italics).

[16] Hiltner, Seward, *Ferment in the Ministry*, Nashville: Abingdon Press, 1969: 48.
[17] *Ibid*: 31.
[18] Holmes, Urban T. III, *The Future Shape of Ministry: A Theological Projection*, New York: Seabury, 1971: 96.
[19] *Ibid*: 95.
[20] Manson, T., *The Church's Ministry*, London: Hodder & Stoughton, 1956: 21.
[21] Brister, *Pastoral Care in the Church*.
[22] Poling, James N. and Miller, Donald E., *Foundations for a Practical Theology of Ministry*, Nashville: Abingdon, 1985.
[23] Hiltner, *Ferment in the Ministry*.

compassion,[24] ministry as presence,[25] and ministry as reconciliation.[26] More recently, Thomas O'Meara maintains that ministry "begins with the Christian community, flows out of the community and expands the community."[27]

Whilst these perspectives are helpful and revealing, with the emphasis on action – doing something – as an imperative which cannot be avoided, many recent pastoral/practical theologians are deeply critical: the ministry area "is not simply the marketing subdivision for an enterprise that sees 'real' theology as biblical, historical, or systematic."[28] In order to investigate this insight concerning the intrinsic theological nature of ministry, we need to introduce the idea of ministry as *praxis*, a term which Ray Anderson has expanded into 'Christopraxis', referring to the reality that "truths of God are discovered through the encounter with Christ in the world by means of ministry."[29] In this paradigm, theology and ministry are integrated powerfully within a christological, trinitarian and ecclesial framework: so we may define ministry as participation by the people of God in the relational life of God who is continuously working in his creation through his Spirit to reconcile all things under Christ (as Paul articulates in Ephesians 1:10). In this process we are necessarily engaged in 'doing theology', what Anderson calls 'theological innovation'.[30]

In his dialectical theology made explicit – and famous – in the preface to the second edition of *Der Römerbrief*,[31] Karl Barth expresses his debt to the Danish

---

[24] Stone, Bryan P., *Compassionate Ministry: Theological Foundations*, New York: Orbis, 1996.

[25] Augsburger, David, *Pastoral Counseling Across Cultures*, Philadelphia: Westminster, 1986: especially pp. 37-38.

[26] Neuhaus, Richard J., *Freedom for Ministry*, San Francisco: Harper & Row, 1979.

[27] O'Meara, Thomas F., *Theology of Ministry* (rev ed), New York: Paulist Press, 1999: 146. In one place, O'Meara acknowledges that ministry's "sublime, encompassing, and intimate source is the personal inviting presence of the Spirit of the risen Christ" (*Ibid*: 148), but he does not make explicit the insight that the ministry of the church is a participation in the ministry of *Christ*. Rather, his emphasis is on what he calls a 'developmental theology of charisms'; accordingly, his interpretation of ministry is essentially functionalist.

[28] Mudge, Lewis S. and Poling, James N., "Editors' Epilogue" in Mudge, Lewis S. and Poling, James N. (eds), *Formation and Reflection: The Promise of Practical Theology*, Minneapolis: Fortress Press, 1987: 157.

[29] Anderson, Ray S., *The Soul of Ministry: Forming Leaders for God's People*, Louisville: John Knox Press, 1997: 29; in a later book Anderson critiques Don Browning's model of practical theology on the grounds that it is christologically deficient, a claim which we will consider later in this chapter: see Anderson, Ray S., *The Shape of Practical Theology: Empowering Ministry with Theological Praxis*, Downers Grove: IVP, 2001: 26-31.

[30] Anderson, *The Shape of Practical Theology*: 17-24.

[31] See, in particular, Barth, Karl, *The Epistle to the Romans* (translated by Edward C. Hoskyns from the Sixth Edition), London: Oxford University Press, 1933: 2-15.

philosopher Kierkegaard. Mueller observes that "Barth's frequent references to 'paradox', 'decision' and 'crisis' in the attempt to describe the divine-human encounter are all reminiscent of Kierkegaard."[32] For Barth, the dialectical method, which he advocated in his earlier theological writing, enabled him to propose a theological 'system' which was, in essence, a form of dialogue between God and man, recognising Kierkegaard's 'infinite qualitative distinction' between the divine and the human. This theological paradigm represented for Barth a 'pilgrim theology', or *theologia viatorum*, a continuous dialogue involving "speech and response, 'yes' and 'no', question and answer."[33] Whilst Barth's later theology became more explicitly Christocentric, motivated by his aversion to any form of natural theology, he never deserted his dialectical approach, which was, as Mueller suggests, "the medium he adopted to point to the message of the Word of God to man as he stands in the situation of crisis between time and eternity."[34] So, for Barth, the dialectical approach was the methodology *within which* faith seeks understanding: ultimately dialectical theology begins with the Word of God – *Deus dixit* – and points towards true knowledge of God, summed up in the person of the one who is both God and man, Jesus Christ, who is the beginning and end of faith. All theology is therefore predicated on the divine initiative, and it is this conviction that circumscribes Barth's interpretation of the task of pastoral ministry.

This brief summary of Barth's dialectical methodology is central to an understanding of the concept of *praxis* in pastoral ministry. Dialectical theology as developed by Barth affirms that human beings are drawn by the Spirit into *theologia viatorum* as they journey towards knowledge of God: God is both the beginning and the end of the process, which itself is totally dependent upon revelation. Likewise, Christian ministry starts and ends with God, who is ever at work throughout his creation and in whose activity Christians are invited – or summoned! – to participate. *Praxis* may be defined as 'truth in action', which is radically distinct from 'practice'. This phrase brings ministry and theology, or

---

[32] Mueller, David L., *Karl Barth*, Waco: Word Books, 1972: 24.

[33] *Ibid*: 25.

[34] *Ibid*: 26. It is important to recognise Barth's later theological movement towards a theology based on analogy, in order to combat any drift towards anthropocentrism in theological method. As fully developed in his *Church Dogmatics*, Barth's theology is a theology of the Word of God – *Deus dixit* – such that all pastoral activity (and Barth was acutely concerned by the problem of preaching) finds its source in the revealed truth of God's speech to humanity. So Webster: "What is most important here is to grasp how radically Barth revised the whole shape of the theological enterprise: no longer concerned with universal reason, morals or experience, the theologian is set firmly within the church, alongside the preacher who has been disturbed by the imperious summons to pass on in human words the *Deus dixit* of revelation." (Webster, John, *Barth*, London: Continuum, 2000: 41). For a full discussion of Barth's shift in theological thinking, see von Balthasar, Hans Urs, *The Theology of Karl Barth* (translated by John Drury), New York: Holt, Rinehart & Winston, 1971.

behaviour and belief, into close proximity: "Theology is properly conceived as a performative discipline, in which the criterion of authenticity is deemed to be *orthopraxis*, or authentic transformatory action, rather than *orthodoxy* (right belief)."[35]

So, as Anderson rightly points out, *"actions are themselves theological"*[36], an insight which has transformed recent approaches to the discipline of practical theology. The significance of the relationship between theory and practice should not be underestimated:

> If theory precedes and determines practice, then practice tends to be concerned primarily with methods, techniques and strategies for ministry, lacking theological substance. If practice takes priority over theory, ministry tends to be based on pragmatic results rather than prophetic revelation.[37]

In his discussion of ministry as theological *praxis*, Anderson distinguishes between two different ways of viewing an action, after Aristotle.[38] The first is *poiesis*, which is an act of making something or producing a result where the final meaning, purpose or character of that which is produced – its *telos* – lies outside the act of making. A carpenter who creates a table is engaged in *poiesis* when the future use of that table is not intrinsic to its manufacture. However, *praxis* includes the *telos* within the action itself: the end purpose informs the nature of the action itself. Anderson illustrates the distinction with reference to homiletics: once a sermon has been constructed and presented, we have *poiesis*; but the sermon has not realised its *telos* until it has had its effect upon its hearers. *Praxis*, therefore, is "an action in which the truth is discovered through action, not merely applied or 'practiced'."[39]

Implicit in the idea of *praxis* is the discipline of theological reflection: *praxis* critically has to do with *reflective* action. Forrester speaks of "a deeper reciprocity between theory and practice, whereby theological understanding not only leads to action but also arises out of practice and involvement in the life of the world."[40] This renewed understanding, the wisdom that represents the fruit of theological reflection, is what Aristotle called *phronesis*. More recently, Farley has helpfully distinguished between theology as "an *episteme*, a *scientia*, an act or cognitive disposition in which the self-disclosing God is grasped as disclosed …[and] theology [as] *habitus*, a disposition, power, act of the soul

---

[35] Graham, *Transforming Practice*: 7, author's italics.
[36] Anderson, *The Shape of Practical Theology*: 48, author's italics.
[37] *Ibid:* 14.
[38] *Ibid*: 48-51.
[39] *Ibid*: 49.
[40] Forrester, *Truthful Action*: 22-23.

itself."[41] Forrester defines *habitus* as "a disposition of the mind and heart from which action flows naturally, in an unselfconscious way."[42] This particular sense of 'practice' is quite different from the regular, routine and non-reflective pattern of activity that characterises the mere application of theological principles. Forrester borrows from modern philosophy the concept of the 'hermeneutical spiral' as a helpful corrective to the simple linear relationship which has often been presumed to exist between theory and practice: so, "engagement, action and understanding interact with one another to seek a strengthening of commitment, a more just and caring social order, which all reflect the coming reign of God."[43]

Theological Reflection and *Theologia Viatorum*

In order to set the scene more thoroughly for an understanding of the contextual nature of pastoral ministry, we need to underscore the importance of theological reflection. The Catholic theologian Neil Darragh argues that ministry engagement demands that we seek a balance between implicit and explicit theology.[44] He advocates the necessity for all who are involved in Christian mission of 'doing theology' in context[45]: we are all theologians, on a journey of discovery. This is not to argue for an abandonment of inherited, implicit truth, but to be willing to expose our 'received theology' to critical analysis, to wrestle with it such that the Eternal-in-Time is not displaced by a preoccupation with the Eternal[46]: thus Hall affirms the necessity for contextual

---

[41] See Farley, Edward, "Theology and Practice Outside the Clerical Paradigm" in Browning (ed), *Practical Theology*: 1983: 21-41, in which the author presents a theology of 'ecclesial redemptive presence' as the necessary paradigm required in order to deliver practical theology from its captivity to the skills, techniques and strategies adopted by professional ministers; so Farley points away from a functionalist interpretation of ministry which alienates theology from practice, and re-establishes the roots of practical theology away from the 'faculty' back to where it belongs, within the redemptive life of the community of the church. For a similar understanding of the church as the context within which practical theology may be reintegrated in terms of practical wisdom, see Fowler, James, *Faith Development and Pastoral Care*, Philadelphia: Fortress Press, 1986.
[42] Forrester, *Truthful Action*: 5.
[43] *Ibid*: 30.
[44] Darragh, Neil, "Theology from Elsewhere" in *South Pacific Journal of Mission Studies* 2, 1/1991: 2-8. 'Implicit theology' is the dogma, the theological understanding we inherit, perhaps unconsciously, as we journey through life and ministry; much of this may not be very carefully thought through – hence the importance of making explicit the beliefs to which we adhere, so opening them to correction, revision or affirmation.
[45] See, in particular, Darragh, Neil, *Doing Theology Ourselves*, Auckland: Accent, 1995.
[46] Hall, Douglas John, *Thinking the Faith*, Minneapolis: Fortress Press, 1991: 99.

theology, which, for him, is a tautology. All theology, all ministry, is an enterprise that involves flesh-and-blood people in given contexts; it is a creative activity, mirroring the creative activity of the Holy Spirit, who is the Spirit of life and movement in a world in which God is continuously and intimately involved. So, as people of the Spirit, as the disciple-community, we are necessarily driven to engagement, taking us beyond a "fundamentalist treatment of *the Bible* as the locus of once-for-all Truth."[47]

'Doing theology' involves us in the ongoing process of theological reflection, and the motif of journey is consistent with the notion of *theologia viatorum*. In his exploration of the limitations of the Socratic approach to thinking, which seeks to arrive at 'truth' through an inductive process of questions and statements, Edward de Bono, the popular 'guru' of thinking, argues that the Western mind has been hi-jacked into a straitjacket, locked into a logical 'left-brain' paradigm of thinking.[48] He illustrates his point with a simple exercise involving a sequence of pieces of card that are presented one or two at a time. The person receiving these pieces has to arrange them according to what he or she thinks is 'best' at that time. The other pieces are offered, to be added to the original arrangement, and the final piece is given with the invitation to 'complete the square'. Unless the final objective is declared at the outset, the person attempting the exercise is initially unlikely to arrange the pieces satisfactorily. The implications for the evolution of ideas are spelled out by de Bono in the form of a fundamental principle:

> In any system in which information comes in over time and there is a need to make the best use of it at every moment, there is an absolute need to be able to go back and to rearrange the components in order to make the best use of the available information.[49]

Change, therefore, is not just about being willing to move forward, embracing new ideas: it may be necessary to *move back* to change something which seemed perfectly right in the light of the available information at the time. This is a threatening and risky enterprise, but an essential aspect of all theological reflection as it is of all personal growth. De Bono suggests that any new ideas that involve a rearrangement of components should ideally be held 'in parallel' alongside the old idea, so that over time that which is preferable becomes the chosen approach. His methodology invites a spirit of creativity as we are encouraged not just to move forward logically in our thinking, but to be willing to move backwards and to switch between options in order to arrive at

---

[47] *Ibid*: 104, author's italics.
[48] de Bono, Edward, *Parallel Thinking: From Socratic Thinking to de Bono Thinking*, London: Penguin Books, 1995.
[49] *Ibid*: 51.

the best paradigm to fit the prevailing conditions.

Stephen Pattison has developed an approach to theological reflection modelled on what he calls 'critical conversation', which has more to do with discovering the right questions than arriving at the right answers.[50] He suggests that success in theological reflection has less to do with academic ability (though this is not to be derided!) than with inventiveness and imagination - a sort of 'right-brain' creativity that seeks to discern what we may call 'patterns of truth' within the triad of student presuppositions, Christian tradition and the appropriate context. An alternative model has been put forward by David Lyall, whose approach is a classic model of doing theology within a strongly contextual framework, drawing from the work of Farley.[51] It demands that all theological reflection carries with it a necessary freedom to either respond or stay silent, depending on how one interprets the situation under review. In this respect, it involves a process that has its genesis not in our own 'inherited' theology but in the givenness of the particular issue under examination. Farley's emphasis on history and systems analysis is particularly helpful in the light of temptations to evaluate situations within a *too-localised* time and space framework: we are encouraged to think more widely than we are accustomed to as we interact with those around us.

The dialectic between gospel and culture is presented here as that which takes place within our own personal faith-journey as we engage in theological reflection. The integrating concept is that of context. God is a God-in-context, who lives and moves amongst his people, whose story is not a story in isolation, but one that interacts with every human story. We are all participants in God's story, engaging in *theologia viatorum* as we witness to Christ in the world. There are many advantages in starting with the context: we are required to listen in a way that helps us to truly understand what is going on in a person's life. Rather than taking the gospel and trying to work it into the context, it may be far more fruitful to start with the context and work backwards from that to the gospel: what has the gospel to say in this situation or that set of circumstances?

This is not to argue for a model of ministry that permits the context to set the agenda for the Christian church: the gospel is a proactive and transformative presence in the world. So the challenge is to engage with the world in such a way as to retain both cultural relevance and gospel-faithfulness, without falling into either cultural naivety or dogmatic fundamentalism. Faithfulness to the gospel involves both doctrinal and ethical fidelity, both of which are necessary expressions of Christian witness. Doctrinal faithfulness refers to adherence to historic biblical truth-statements, whereas ethical faithfulness has to do with personal integrity in living out these truth-statements ('practising what we

---

[50] Pattison, Stephen, "Some Straw for the Bricks: A Basic Introduction to Theological Reflection" in *Contact*, Vol 99 (1989): 2-9.

[51] Lyall, David, "Pastoral Action and Theological Reflection" in *Contact*, Vol 100 (1989): 3-7.

preach'). In the process, precisely because we are active participants in God's world, our own story and faith-development cannot be divorced from our engagement in ministry. We must change even as we seek change in others - this is *theologia viatorum*. The missionary theologian Vincent Donovan quotes some advice given to him by a young person in an American university:

> In working with young people in America, do not try to call them back to where they were, and do not try to call them to where you are, as beautiful as that place might seem to you. You must have the courage to go with them to a place that neither you nor they have ever been before.[52]

Theological Method in Pastoral Ministry

Approaches to pastoral ministry which are predicated on *praxis* – 'truth in action' – and *theologia viatorum* – 'doing theology' – highlight the importance of theological method, or how we approach Christian theology as a discipline in order to better interpret, communicate and apply it. In his assessment of the engagement between Christianity and North American culture, Douglas John Hall contrasts the methods of Barth and Tillich.[53] Barth emphasises the Word of God as that which addresses the human condition because it is final truth that comes to us as revelation: so *Deus dixit*. Any condescension towards a world that is fallen creates the possibility of a message distorted by contact with sinful humanity. This 'positivism of revelation', a phrase coined by Dietrich Bonhoeffer,[54] emerged out of a deep concern to reaffirm the gospel in a world that was confused and in crisis between two world wars. Barthian methodology understandably – perhaps necessarily, given the historical context – insisted upon "the dissociation of the Christian message from the aspirations, mores, wisdom and (especially!) religion of its culture."[55]

Tillich's methodology has its source in the human predicament – what he calls the conflicts of our existential situation – and proceeds to "the positive or constructive exposition of the meaning of the Christian message pertinent to that aspect of reality."[56] Tillich refers to this as 'the method of correlation' because it connects the theological tradition with the issues and concerns within the unique context or situation encountered. The starting point for Tillich in his theological method is therefore the world rather than (for Barth) the Word. The issue, as Hall rightly points out, is one of continuity versus discontinuity. For Tillich, theology reflects the existential nature of our beingness in continuity

---

[52] Donovan, Vincent J., *Christianity Rediscovered*, London: SCM Press, 1978: vii.
[53] Hall, *Thinking the Faith*: 349-367.
[54] Bonhoeffer, Dietrich, *Letters and Papers from Prison*, London, SCM Press, 1953: 148.
[55] Hall, *Thinking the Faith*: 349.
[56] *Ibid*: 352.

with the beingness of God, with the result that his theology lacks the prophetic cutting edge typical of Barth.

Barth's approach acknowledges the reality of the discontinuity between God and human beings: "For I am God, and not man, the Holy One among you" (Hosea 11:9). In his insistence upon the sovereignty of the Spirit, who alone interprets the will of God in the world, Barth stands against any theological position that has its origin in corrupt human nature. We must be careful, however, not to minimise his recognition of the need to keep in close touch with the realities of the human condition – so we hold a Bible in one hand and a newspaper in the other! The Catholic pastoral theologian Richard McBrien argues that indifference to contemporary context is a denial of the incarnational principle implicit in John 1:14: "[T]hose who sometimes pride themselves on never watching television or never following news events actually convict themselves of a lack of readiness for important ministries in the Church."[57] Ironically, Barth's theological method was shaped and conditioned by the exigencies of his day. In particular, his confessional approach challenged the subjectivism of the nineteenth-century German theologian Friedrich Schleiermacher. Furthermore, his rejection of the theology of his liberal teachers was provoked by their endorsement of German imperialist policy at the onset of the First World War. Faced with these two situational realities, Barth espoused a kerygmatic theology of Word and Spirit that was 'from above' rather than 'from below'.

Poling and Miller propose a range of six models of practical theology derived from the two axes of critical methodology and church-society relationship.[58] Whilst their methodology begins and ends with experiences and their analysis leads them to favour an open dialogue between all the types, maintaining that they all enrich each other, their preference is for a confessional model of ministry with its locus of interest in the church: "truth moves through concrete praxis, and therefore we favor the community of faith reaching out in mission."[59] Community formation therefore becomes for Poling and Miller the primary task of ministry, though it is important to recognise that intrinsic to their understanding of the life of the community of faith are its relationships with other communities within a historical and socio-political framework in order to avoid "an idolatry of community that focuses only on the internal dynamics and makes of consensus a god which does not take into account the

---

[57] McBrien, Richard P., *Ministry: A Theological, Pastoral Handbook*, San Francisco: Harper & Row, 1987: 70.

[58] Poling and Miller, *Foundations for a Practical Theology of Ministry*: 29-61, where three types of method are elaborated: critical science, critical correlation and critical confession, and two expressions of the church-society relationship are presented (one tending towards society-formation, the other towards church-formation); the relationship between church and society is described as "the social horizon and context of the locus of praxis."

[59] *Ibid*: 61. Poling and Miller acknowledge that their position as seminary teachers may "unduly influence" them in favour of a "dialogical confessional community stance."

historical identity of the community and its movement toward universal values."⁶⁰ Neuhaus is similarly concerned that pastoral ministry does not perpetuate a false choice between an "otherworldly" and a "worldly" Christianity: "if we are truly converted to God in Christ, then we participate in *his* conversion to the world. We cannot love him if we do not share his love for his creation."⁶¹ However, whilst espousing a synthesis of immanence and transcendence, he is clear in his affirmation that the religious commitment to the immanent is finally *for the sake of the transcendent,* for the unlovable

> are not loved for their own sake, because we do not encounter them on their own but within the sacramental bonding of a double and doubling conversion; conversion to the transcendent God who in Christ has made himself vulnerable to our loving and our hurting in the immanent.⁶²

This Christocentric perspective is reinforced by Lesslie Newbigin, who offers two sharply contrasted models of the Christian life that correspond to the transcendent-immanent tension implicit in the relationship between the church and the world.⁶³ The first is what he calls the 'Pilgrim's Progress Model', which emphasises a decisive break from the world: in this model the world is perceived as a contaminating influence upon the community of faith, which must adopt a separatist stance if it is to remain 'holy'. The second model is the 'Jonah Model', after the prophet who is summoned by God to enter Nineveh and engage in his prophetic ministry amongst the people. Newbigin insists that Christian life – and ministry – is characterised by both radical separation and total engagement: "If we are not to be pulled aimlessly back and forth between these two models, we have to go down to the very heart of our faith, which is the Cross."⁶⁴ It is precisely this radical Christocentrism which is lacking in the proposals of key pastoral theologians such as Hiltner, Browning and Patton, whose method of theological reflection finds its starting place in human situations.

Hiltner, for example, speaks of "a creative theologizing that even a Barth should envy" when a minister, driving back to church after a hospital call or returning home after a frustrating committee meeting or a freedom march, reflects about what he or she has been involved in, even though such reflections may be rudimentary and uncritical. For Hiltner, such reflection is governed by a functionalist agenda, for "it cannot be done except in the context of preparing

---

⁶⁰ *Ibid*: 137.
⁶¹ Neuhaus, *Freedom for Ministry*: 94, author's italics.
⁶² *Ibid*: 95.
⁶³ Newbigin, Lesslie, *The Good Shepherd: Meditations on Christian Ministry in Today's World*, Grand Rapids: Eerdmans, 1977: 96-99, where the writer cites the example of Dietrich Bonhoeffer, whose life was a powerful expression of both radical inner consecration and active political engagement.
⁶⁴ *Ibid*: 97.

for future occasions of function and service."⁶⁵ Referring to the danger of the church ignoring the world, his critique is based upon the minister's preoccupation with such practical, functional items as "pulpit robe equipment, the shape of the baptistry, the architecture of the sanctuary, and perhaps the related facilities such as the educational rooms and the kitchens"!⁶⁶ The overriding impression is that for Hiltner ministry is less about participation in Christ's ministry and more about what *we* do in the concrete pastoral situations encountered from day to day. His pastoral theology is essentially an empirically-based, operation-centred discipline: Graeme Griffin observes that, in distinction to Eduard Thurneysen⁶⁷ – a close friend and colleague of Barth – "Hiltner sought to derive theological insights from the participation in and examination of particular human situations ... illuminated by whatever disciplines may contribute to their understanding."⁶⁸

With similar intent, Don Browning – a student of Hiltner – proposes a theological model that is "practical through and through and at its very heart."⁶⁹ He challenges what he refers to as Barth's *theory-to-practice* model of theology and proposes a view that goes from practice to theory and back to practice. He criticises Barth's interpretation of theology for not providing any "role for human understanding, action, or practice in the construal of God's self-disclosure."⁷⁰ His theological model begins with an 'inner core' of practical concerns based upon human experiences that prompt the questions 'What should we do?' and 'How should we live?' Each community of interpreters brings these questions to an 'outer envelope' of normative texts and events, engaging in critical reexamination of its religious meanings and practices in the light of these questions.⁷¹ This 'outer envelope' corresponds to what we

---

⁶⁵ Hiltner, *Ferment in the Ministry*: 170.

⁶⁶ *Ibid*: 26.

⁶⁷ See Thurneysen, Eduard, *A Theology of Pastoral Care*, Atlanta: John Knox Press, 1962, whose approach, based on the primary role of the Word of God and proclamation, was *deductive*, rather than *inductive* (so Hiltner): so the two approached practical theology from two different starting points, Thurneysen from Scripture and tradition, Hiltner from practical ministry functions.

⁶⁸ Griffin, Graeme, "Pastoral Theology and Pastoral Care Overseas" in Oglesby, William B. (ed), *The New Shape of Pastoral Theology: Essays in Honour of Seward Hiltner*, Nashville: Abingdon, 1969: 54.

⁶⁹ Browning, Don S., *A Fundamental Practical Theology: Descriptive and Strategic Proposals*, Minneapolis: Fortress Press, 1991: 7.

⁷⁰ *Ibid*: 5. Browning acknowledges that Barth's model of practical theology is "partially right", but criticises his epistemological realism: "He believed that the interpreting community should empty itself of its usual attempts to verify things morally, experientially, or cognitively. The believing community should conform itself totally to the Word of God revealed in Scripture." (*Ibid*: 7).

⁷¹ The approach suggested here is similar to Stephen Pattison's 'critical conversation' approach to theological reflection, discussed earlier in this section, in which questions

identified earlier as the Aristotelian concept of *phronesis*, or practical wisdom, which Browning prefers to call 'practical reason': "The outer envelope of practical reason is its fund of inherited narratives and practices that tradition has delivered to us and that always surrounds our practical thinking."[72] The 'overall dynamic' implicit in Browning's model is the reconstruction of experience as an interpretive and reinterpretive process, a 'hermeneutical spiral' in which "these new, reconstructed religious meanings and practices continue until this religious community meets a new crisis."[73]

In adopting the term 'contextuality', the contemporary American pastoral theologian John Patton means that "the social situation in all its uniqueness informs the thought and action of the reflection of the Christian community."[74] Arguing that the classical paradigm for pastoral care is too universalistic in its understanding of human problems, and that the clinical model is overly focused on psychological interpretation, he proposes a *communal contextual* paradigm which "emphasizes the caring community and the various contexts for care rather than focusing on pastoral care as the work of the ordained pastor."[75] Patton cites the work of Douglas John Hall[76] and Peter Hodgson [77], who identify a number of contexts that theology needs to acknowledge today: the end of the political establishment of Christianity; a multi-religious society; the radical nature of human evil (eg. Auschwitz); a growing awareness of the oppressed peoples in our world; the ecological crisis; fear of nuclear accident; religious simplism and apocalyptic consciousness; growth of the African American church; Latin American sacramental communities; and the feminist vision. Rather than explore these in turn, Patton identifies five specific contexts for discussion: race, gender, power, problem (recognising that human problems are the contextual background for the more important task of care) and morality.[78] As Brister notes, Patton's method of theological reflection does not begin with God: "Rather, he advocates imaginative focusing on 'a specific character and need of the world' through a three-storied process of caring event, symbolic construction and theological reflection."[79]

---

arising out of specific pastoral contexts represent the catalyst for a 'conversation' between student presuppositions, Christian tradition and the appropriate context.

[72] Browning, *A Fundamental Practical Theology*: 11.

[73] *Ibid*: 6.

[74] Patton, John, *Pastoral Care in Context: An Introduction to Pastoral Care*, Louisville: Westminster/John Knox Press, 1993: 39.

[75] *Ibid*: 5.

[76] Hall, *Thinking the Faith*.

[77] Hodgson, Peter, *Revisioning the Church: A Theology of the Church in the New Paradigm*, Philadelphia: Fortress Press, 1988.

[78] Patton, *Pastoral Care in Context*: 39-61.

[79] Brister, *Pastoral Care in the Church*: 24, citing Patton, John, *From Ministry to Theology: Pastoral Action and Reflection*, Nashville: Abingdon Press, 1990: 97, 18. In an earlier footnote, Brister notes Patton's dependence upon theological methods associated with Edward Farley and John Macmurray.

Anderson affirms Browning's model but adjusts it at a critical point, at its centre. Consistent with the christological and trinitarian orientation of his theology, he replaces Browning's focus on experience at the 'inner core' with Christopraxis, which he defines as the continuing ministry of Christ through the power and presence of the Holy Spirit. He acknowledges Browning's inclusion of Christology, though only as a component of systematic theology in the 'outer envelope' of the community's memory, expressed in creed and dogma. Anderson's critique of Browning is fundamentally theological rather than methodological: along with Hiltner and Patton, Browning lacks a "christological core of praxis within a trinitarian structure of God's ministry as the basis for all ministry."[80] So, for Anderson, theological reflection has its starting point in what *Christ* is doing in the power of the Holy Spirit in specific situations of crisis and consolation.[81]

Expressed more formally in trinitarian language, "practical theology is grounded in the intratrinitarian ministry of the Father toward the world, the Son's ministry to the Father on behalf of the world and the Spirit's empowering of the disciples for ministry."[82] The Spirit of God is ever at work in the world, touching lives, revealing the life of God in situations of distress and hopelessness, *in whose ministry we are invited to participate.* Caught up in the love of the Trinity, we are privileged to dance with God in the darkness of his

---

[80] Anderson, *The Shape of Practical Theology*: 34. Elsewhere, Anderson argues that this "christological, and actually trinitarian, basis for ministry rules out both utilitarianism, which tends to create ministry out of needs, and pragmatism, which transforms ministry into marketing strategy." (*Ibid*: 63).

[81] "Theological reflection does not ask the question 'What would Jesus do in this situation?' because this question would imply his absence. Rather, it asks the question 'Where is Jesus in this situation and what am I to do as a minister?" (*Ibid*: 56). In recent years a movement has gathered pace in America called WWJD? – *What Would Jesus Do*? It started with bracelets with the letters WWJD inscribed for young people to wear, reminding them to continually ask the question "What would Jesus do?" as they journey through life. Now all kinds of merchandise are offered, from mugs to notebooks to tee-shirts; whilst there is something very commendable about encouraging Christians to live a Christ-centred life, there is a subtle trap in the message because taken by itself it could be interpreted as a moral aphorism – "Look at Jesus: he's done it, now it's over to you!" This is what the American theologian Daniel Thimell calls "bootstraps theology". It's up to us to go out and imitate Christ – reminiscent of the moral influence theory of the atonement. A better slogan would be WIJD? – *What Is Jesus Doing?*

[82] *Ibid*: 40. The paradigm presented by Anderson is fundamentally a theology of Pentecost: he quotes John Taylor, for whom the practical theologian is the theologian of the Holy Spirit, who points to and participates in the creative invisibility of the God who holds all things together (see Ballard, Paul and Pritchard, John, *Practical Theology in Action: Christian Thinking in the Service of Christ and Society*, London: SPCK, 1996: 41, fn.2, referring to Taylor, John V., *The Go-Between God: The Holy Spirit and the Christian Mission*, London: SCM Press, 1972). The Holy Spirit also makes known to human beings the truth concerning the inner life of God as dynamic trinitarian being.

world.[83] Christian ministry has, as its starting point, God himself. In fact, we are unable to develop sound theological foundations for ministry until we have critically examined God's ministry in the world. What God has done incarnationally in Christ is the starting point for our theology: ministry thus precedes theology.

> The ministry of Jesus to the Father on behalf of the world is the inner logic of all ministry ... On behalf of the world, Jesus offers up to the Father a ministry of prayer, worship, obedience and service. His ministry is first of all directed to God and not to the world. The needs of the world are recognized and brought into this ministry but do not set the agenda.[84]

The issue of contextualisation in both theology and ministry has much to do with the tension that exists between Barthian and Tillichian theological method. The poet Alexander Pope once penned these words: "Know then thyself, presume not God to scan; the proper study of Mankind is Man."[85] Although we are no longer living in the Enlightenment period in which Pope wrote, liberal theology's emphasis on human experience at the expense of supernatural revelation as the basis for truth and knowledge – and therefore ethics as well – is conspicuous in contemporary Western society and threatens to undermine the efforts of those who seek to direct people back to the reality of a God who is outside time and space and yet intimately involved in the lives of those whom he has created in love. The Christian God is both transcendent and immanent: he is the supreme, absolute Other, who is beyond the world, and yet also the God who is ever present in the world. With Barth, we declare that the Christian message has its source in the unchanging nature of God, who is final truth, and which has no need of any human instrument to be effective in the world. Through the prophet Isaiah, God declares that his word "will not return to me empty, but will accomplish what I desire and achieve the purpose for which I sent it" (Isaiah 55:10). But it is also a message that needs to be *heard* by those to whom it is sent, heard in a language that they can understand, and presented in a way that acknowledges the uniqueness of each specific and concrete time-and-place context.

Hiltner's concern for the particularity of the human predicament, Browning's emphasis on God's self-disclosure in creation and Patton's communal contextual paradigm are important Tillichian voices that need to be acknowledged. Consequently all three point to the need to reconcile the contrasting theological approaches of Barth and Tillich. Barth's insistence that

---

[83] An insight which gave rise to the title of the author's recent text on the theology of Christian ministry; see Buxton, *Dancing in the Dark*, esp pp 1-42.

[84] Anderson, *The Shape of Practical Theology*: 42.

[85] Pope, Alexander, *An Essay on Man*, Epistle II in Butt, John (ed), *The Poems of Alexander Pope*, London: Methuen, 1963: 501-547.

natural theology has no "legitimate function in the sphere of the Church"[86] and his priority of the theological task over any form of philosophical inquiry self-evidently conflict with Tillich's reliance on existential philosophy to formulate the questions that theology answers.

Barth is uncompromising in his theology of the mystery of creation: "in the Christian sense it cannot be that *first of all* we presuppose the reality of the world and then ask whether there is also a God"[87] (which is his chief complaint against natural theology). His exposition of the Apostles' Creed affirms the primacy and self-sufficiency of the *Creator*; it is only incidentally, that the Confession speaks of the created world, or the work of creation. For Barth, creation is grace, invested by God with its own freedom and reality.[88] But if the goal of creation is to declare the glory of God – "its goodness incontestably consists in the fact that it may be the theatre of His glory, and man the witness to this glory"[89] – then the door is clearly open to the possibility that God may speak to a person through the glory of his creation. Tillich is also constrained by his adherence to the classical Christian tradition, especially in his acknowledgment of the place of revelation in Christian theology. But whilst Barth's emphasis on revelation as that which stands outside experience is absolutely central, the hinge on which his whole theological endeavour turns, Tillich believed that "revelation is the answer to reason's questions and that reason does not resist revelation."[90] For Tillich, revelation is "*first of all* the experience in which an ultimate concern grasps the human mind and creates a community in which this concern expresses itself in symbols of action, imagination, and thought."[91] So the door is kept firmly open to human social and cultural experience as the medium through which God may be known. Although both theologians accord revelation different places in their theological schemas, they concur in preserving Christian revelation as final in humanity's knowledge of God.

Defining Pastoral/Practical Theology – A Historical Perspective

It is helpful to adopt a historical perspective in order to clarify terminology with regard to the theology of pastoral ministry. In the process we will discern some important themes and distinctions with respect to the language of 'pastoral

---

[86] Barth, Karl, *Church Dogmatics* 2/1, Edinburgh: T. & T. Clark, 1957: 178.
[87] Barth, Karl, *Dogmatics in Outline*, London: SCM Press Ltd., 1949: 53, my italics.
[88] For Barth, creation is neither an emanation from God "something divine which wells out of God like a stream out of a spring" (*ibid*: 55), nor is it a manifestation of God, in the philosophical sense that "God would to some extent be the Idea" (*ibid*: 55).
[89] *Ibid*: 58.
[90] See article on Paul Tillich on http://www.faithnet.org.uk/Theology/tillich.htm, © Pelusa 2003, accessed on 14.01.04.
[91] Tillich, Paul, *Dynamics of Faith*, New York: Harper & Row Publishers, 1957: 78, my italics.

theology' and 'practical theology'. Our discussion so far has introduced a number of these themes, which we now draw together within a coherent historical survey of the discipline. The contemporary focus on *praxis* is not, in fact, new: in the pre-modern era, Anselm's well-known dictum, *fides quaerens intellectum* – faith seeking understanding – implied a practical dimension to theology:

> Inasmuch as faith involved discipleship and was an orientation of the whole person rather than a simple act of intellectual assent, theology was understood as a practical matter. Contemplation could not be separated from action, any more than faith could be separated from the Church, the community of faith.[92]

This was evident during the earliest years in the life of the Christian church, as witnessed in the New Testament. Heitink suggests that the locus of action is "the church as it meets together",[93] and in the Acts of the Apostles and the Pauline and pastoral epistles there is evidence of patterns of ecclesial activity which reflect a number of distinct yet complementary modes of pastoral ministry, which Firet has summarised as *kerygma*, *didache* and *paraklesis* (proclamation, catechesis and pastoral care).[94] Heitink uses the term 'pastoral theology' to refer to the *ecclesiological* context of pastoral ministry, as the emerging church wrestled with its identity as a community of faith, particularly towards the end of the first century as the expected return of Christ did not materialise: pastoral structure was needed to ensure the continuity of the community of believers.

In the early centuries of the church, the practice of Christian ministry was given pastoral-theological shape in the writings of such leaders as Cyprian, Gregory of Nazianzus and Augustine.[95] At the end of the sixth century, Gregory the Great produced *The Book of Pastoral Rule*, a systematic account of the scope and practice of pastoral ministry within the church. However, as the universities assumed greater responsibility for the study of theology in the Middle Ages in Europe, theology forfeited its practical orientation and became an academic discipline *par excellence*, given pre-eminence during that period

---

[92] Forrester, *Truthful Action*: 33-34.

[93] Heitink, *Practical Theology*: 92.

[94] Firet, *Dynamics in Pastoring*: 43ff. For a brief discussion of the *praxis* of the New Testament see Heitink, *Practical Theology*: 91-92.

[95] For a comprehensive introduction to the historical development of pastoral care as *cura animarum* within the Christian church see Clebsch, W. and Jaekle, C., *Pastoral Care in Historical Perspective* (2nd edition), New York: Aronson: 1983, where the four frequently-cited primary functions of pastoral care are enumerated: healing, sustaining, guiding and reconciling. To these, Clinebell adds a fifth – nurturing – in Clinebell, Howard J., *Basic Types of Pastoral Care and Counselling* (revised edition), Nashville: Abingdon, 1984.

as the 'Queen of the Sciences'.[96] In the pre-Reformation era, Aquinas's thirteenth-century vision of theology as a theoretical discipline (*sophia*) vied with the more practical interpretations of Duns Scotus, William of Ockham and other medieval theologians, who emphasised the concept of *phronesis* as practical wisdom.[97] Whilst the theologians of the Protestant Reformation followed in the tradition of *phronesis*, with particular emphasis on the theology of the Word,[98] the Catholic Church focused on the work of the priest and the pastoral role of the liturgy and the sacraments.

In their recent encyclopedic volume on pastoral/practical theology, Woodward and Pattison acknowledge that there is a good deal of overlap between the terms 'practical theology' and 'pastoral theology', with the difference between them more one of emphasis than substance.[99] As an amusing aside, they comment that for "the pragmatic British, either name will do as a broad designation of the subject area that deals with the relationship between the faith and theological traditions, and practical issues and actions that are concerned with human wellbeing."[100] Such blurring between the two, however, is not appropriate with regard to the American scene, nor in some parts of Europe. In order to clarify how others perceive the difference between the two, we need to go back to the middle of the eighteenth century in Europe to trace the beginning of what came to be known as 'practical theology' (*praktische Theologie*) as a distinct academic discipline within the curriculum of German Protestant ministry training. Shifts took place in theological education throughout that century, following Buddaeus in 1711, who suggested that "one part of theology should deal with the *agenda* (things that must be done), while another should deal with the *credenda* (things that must be believed)."[101] So the way was paved for a separation between that part of theology which was dogmatic in content and that part which was essentially

---

[96] For an impassioned plea "to rediscover and remine the classical models of Christian pastoral care and to make available once again the key texts of that classical tradition" see Oden, Thomas C., "Recovering Pastoral Care's Lost Identity" in Aden, Leroy and Ellens, J. Harold (eds), *The Church and Pastoral Care*, Grand Rapids: Baker, 1988: 17-32.

[97] As Forrester points out, both terms, *sophia* and *phronesis*, can be traced to Aristotle, for whom *sophia* was an end in itself, whereas *phronesis* represented practical knowledge directed towards other ends and other goods: see Forrester, *Truthful Action*: 34. The distinction between *sophia* and *phronesis* is not unlike that between *poiesis* and *praxis* discussed earlier.

[98] Heitink cites in particular the contribution of Martin Bucer, whose outline of a pastoral theology "emphasized the church as the body of Christ, where the community of the Word, the sacraments, and discipline must receive their rightful places": see Heitink, *Practical Theology*: 93-94.

[99] Woodward, James and Pattison, Stephen (eds), *The Blackwell Reader in Pastoral and Practical Theology*, Oxford: Blackwell, 2000: 1-3.

[100] *Ibid*: 3.

[101] Heitink, *Practical Theology*: 108.

practical, with little real integration between the two: so practical ministry was regarded as an appendix to systematic theological study, in effect a junior partner within the academic community.

Schleiermacher's *A Brief Outline on the Study of Theology*, published in Germany in 1811,[102] challenged the inferior role[103] attributed to the practical branch of theology by integrating it into a coherent proposal for theology as a whole. His radical proposition was based on the conviction that theology should be located not just within the university but also, critically, within the province of the community of faith: the real 'princes of the Church' are those who most effectively integrate 'scientific spirit' and 'ecclesial interest': "Even the especially scientific work of the theologian must aim at promoting the Church's welfare and is thereby clerical; and even those technical prescriptions for essentially clerical activities belong within the circle of the theological sciences."[104] Schleiermacher identified philosophical theology as the pure 'root' (*Wurzel*) of theological study within a hierarchy of three sub-disciplines. The second was historical theology – the 'body' (*Körper*) – embracing exegesis, dogmatics and church history (a consolidation of theoretical disciplines which had already been established by the middle of the eighteenth century). The final sub-discipline is what Schleiermacher called 'the crown' (*Krone*) of theological study on the grounds that "the practical should be given preferential status in assessing the authenticity and validity of the truth-claims of theological discourse."[105]

His schema is, in *principle*, a model of theological *praxis* in its recommendation to integrate theory and practice within a paradigm of Christian faith and action, but, as Burkhart observes, Schleiermacher never fully thought through the implications of his outline. Whilst his schema derived from his concern for the intellectual formation of clerical leadership in the church, he failed to present a truly *interdependent* relationship between philosophical, historical and practical theology. The traffic was still, in effect, one way – from theory to practice – with the result that *praktische Theologie* consisted of "the

---

[102] See Schleiermacher, Freidrich, *A Brief Outline of the Study of Theology* (translated by Terrence N. Tice), Richmond VA: John Knox, 1966).

[103] So the "relationship between practical theology and historical and dogmatic theology was seen largely as a deductive one, practical theology being understood as *applied* theology, just as, say, civil engineering is applied physics." (Campbell, Alistair, "The Nature of Practical Theology" in Woodward and Pattison, *The Blackwell Reader in Pastoral and Practical Theology*: 79, authors' italics).

[104] Schleiermacher (trans by Tice), *A Brief Outline of the Study of Theology*: 8; note that Schleiermacher's reference to a 'scientific spirit' relates to the domain of scientific *methodology* only, and should not be interpreted as an allusion to specific academic disciplines within the human and natural sciences, such as sociology or physics.

[105] Graham, *Transforming Practice*: 60.

consequences and applications derived from thought done elsewhere."[106] For Schleiermacher, *praxis* was more of a vision than a reality, and ironically the consequent inevitable tendency of practical theology towards *Technik* reinforced the 'hints and helps' interpretation of the discipline: *praxis* as a hermeneutical spiral of action-theory-action failed to assume the significance that Schleiermacher's structural paradigm promised. Nevertheless, his determination to lift practical theology out of the 'poor relation' status into which it had fallen, and his emphasis on the discipline as essential for 'maintaining and perfecting the Church' may be seen as prophetic for the future status and development of practical theology.[107]

Post-Schleiermacher, two distinct approaches to theology may be discerned which are significant with regard to the development of practical theology. The first is what Farley has labelled the 'encyclopaedic' approach, in which four specific areas may be identified: exegetical, historical, systematic and practical.[108] This line of development was particularly evident in Europe, and intensified the dichotomy between practical faith and theological education. The second approach is what we have defined earlier as *habitus*, which demands a closer correlation between the two. Heitink comments that

> European theologians think primarily in encyclopaedic terms, while American theologians think primarily in hermeneutical terms ... The Europeans first of all search for the proper distinctions by clarifying differences, while the Americans focus on good correlations and possible connections.[109]

A further differentiation may be offered, that between the inductive method favoured by American pastoral theologians like Hiltner and Browning, and the deductive approach, which draws its strength from an emphasis on the Word of God as the controlling dynamic for practical theology, reflected in the theological systems of Thurneysen and Barth. Urban Holmes is particularly critical of the inductive model's emphasis on psychology and sociology and the empirical methodology that is central to its structure.[110] He traces the Hiltnerian school of pastoral theology to the influence of Anton Boisen, the 'father' of Clinical Pastoral Education (CPE), which came into being in the 1930s. Boisen, who had experienced mental illness, developed what was in effect a 'crisis' model of therapy: his starting place for theological study was the 'living human

---

[106] Burkhart, John, E., "Schleiermacher's Vision for Theology" in Browning (ed), *Practical Theology*: 1983: 53; as Burkhart expresses it in other terms, "there is *lex credendi, lex orandi*, but no *lex orandi, lex credendi*".

[107] For an excellent summary and evaluation of Schleiermacher's schema, see *ibid*: 42-57.

[108] See Farley, Edward, *Theologia: Fragmentation and Unity in Theological Education*, Philadelphia: Fortress Press, 1983.

[109] Heitink, *Practical Theology*: 110.

[110] Holmes, *The Future Shape of Ministry*: 167-194.

documents' of human beings in crisis.[111] The impetus for a pastoral theology grounded in the human sciences was solidly established through Boisen and CPE, and this, together with Tillich's theological correlation methodology and Carl Rogers' 'client-centred therapy',[112] laid firm foundations for the inductive psychologically-oriented approach typical of American pastoral theology for much of the twentieth century.

Holmes critiques the inductive psychological model of pastoral theology on the grounds of its inadequate anthropology, persistent anti-intellectualism, theological poverty and loss of transcendence.[113] It is the latter omission that represents the central platform in the deductive approach. Thomas Oden remonstrates against the 'liberal pietism'[114] and task-oriented empiricism[115] of the Hiltnerian school, appealing for a return to the more robust theologically-informed approach characteristic of the neo-orthodoxy of Thurneysen and Barth. Oden's criticism of Hiltner and his tradition is incisive, condemning it for dispensing with the 'excess baggage' of Nicaea and Chalcedon:

> It has been content to derive its 'theological' bearings essentially from psychological case studies and clinical pastoral relationships, the result of which is a *derivative* or functional theology, in which theology *functions* now and then to help out in the solution of some practical problem.[116]

For both Thurneysen[117] and Barth[118] – contemporaries and close companions

---

[111] "This program is frequently criticized in that it trains men to minister to abnormal people or people in abnormal situations, and consequently does not prepare them to counsel people who are not psychotic in a normal setting." (*Ibid*: 173).

[112] During the middle decades of the twentieth century, the parallel influence of Carl Rogers should not be underestimated. Rogers espoused a humanistic approach to counselling involving a 'self-actualising' potential in human nature which many regarded as preferable to the concept of human sinfulness: many Christian pastors adopted the Rogerian themes of 'unconditional positive regard' and 'empathy' as constructive approaches to solving human problems. See Rogers, Carl, *Client-Centred Therapy: Its Current Practice, Implications, and Theory*, London: Constable, 1951.

[113] Holmes, *The Future Shape of Ministry*: 175-177. The author, whilst not dismissing the importance of a dialogic relationship between theology and the human sciences, follows his trenchant critique of the psychological model implicit in Clinical Pastoral Education with an outline and evaluation of the sociological model of sensitivity training, based on the theories of Kurt Lewin (*ibid*: 178-193).

[114] See Oden, Thomas, C., *Contemporary Theology and Psychotherapy*, Philadelphia: Westminster Press, 1967: 81-91.

[115] See, on this, Graham, *Transforming Practice*: 73.

[116] Oden, *Contemporary Theology and Psychotherapy*: 57.

[117] See Thurneysen, *A Theology of Pastoral Care*.

[118] See Barth, Karl, *Evangelical Theology: An Introduction*, London: Collins Fontana, 1965. In his discussion of theological work as service, Barth observes that theology " is an enterprise in whose performance one question can all too easily be forgotten: For what purpose?" – to which his response is "that the service of God and the service of

– theology was a supremely practical discipline operating within the walls of the faith-community: "the theologian cannot present or conduct himself as the expert or superior authority in contrast to the fools *intra et extra muros ecclesiae*."[119] All theological work therefore takes place within the context of the church and 'attendance on the divine Word': so theology cannot be divorced from the proclamation of the gospel. In fact, theology derives its meaning and purpose from the event of proclamation. Barth is sympathetic to the insights and contributions of the human sciences as they operate within the social context of the day, but neither he nor Thurneysen give any ground to a theological method that denies the primacy of revelation and *Deus dixit*.

Barth is therefore close to Schleiermacher's heart in his desire to locate practical theology, in which preaching and prayer are for him central acts, as an ecclesial discipline. As his Romans commentaries demonstrate, he is also passionate about theology being relevant, though Heitink argues that he allows little room in his writings for an inductive approach to practical theology, citing Bastian's complaint that Barth's theology is "a theology that immediately knows all the answers and loses sight of the questions faith evokes, and that fails to do justice to humans as questioning beings."[120] However, in the preface to the second edition of *Der Römerbrief*, Barth emphasises the vital hermeneutical task involved in biblical interpretation:

> how energetically Calvin, having first established what stands in the text, sets himself to re-think the whole material and to wrestle with it, till the walls which separate the sixteenth century from the first become transparent! Paul speaks and the man of the sixteenth century hears.[121]

For Barth, proclamation – the goal of theology – is both ecclesial, and evangelical in its summons to the world, and there is, as Forrester observes, a circular, dialectical movement in his theology "whereby theological discoveries and rediscoveries are stimulated by discerning the work and Word of God in the struggles and problems of the day."[122]

In the 1980s a recognisable linguistic shift took place from 'pastoral theology' to 'practical theology' with the publication of Browning's edited volume of essays,[123] designed to respond to "the growing hunger to make

---

man are the meaning, horizon, and goal of theological work ... If theological work is not to become sterile in all its disciplines, regardless of how splendidly it may develop at one point or another, it must always keep sight of the fact that its object, the Word of God, demands more than simply being perceived, contemplated, and meditated in this or that particular aspect." (*Ibid*: 174-175).

[119] *Ibid*: 176.
[120] Heitink, *Practical Theology*: 12.
[121] Barth, *The Epistle to the Romans*: 7.
[122] Forrester, *Truthful Action*: 39.
[123] Browning (ed), *Practical Theology*, 1983.

theology in general more relevant to the guidance of action and to bridge the gap between theory and practice, thought and life, the classical theological disciplines and practical theology."[124] Elaine Graham helpfully observes that

> The usage of 'practical theology' is problematic given its associations with a division between practical and systematic theology since Schleiermacher, and an implicit separation of theoretical and applied knowledge. However, 'pastoral' carries implications of individually based pastoral care and counselling, with a similar neglect of the theological dimensions of Christian action. It also represents an unfortunate narrowing of focus into ameliorative ministry at the expense of wider functions of education and formation amongst the community of faith and the Church's mission (in its widest sense) in the world at large.[125]

Whatever terminology is preferred, it is clear that the notion of *praxis* is useful in articulating the nature and scope of practical theology today.

The tension between inductive and deductive approaches to pastoral theology – epitomised in the Hiltner-Thurneysen/Barth polarity – and the growing awareness of the need to integrate theory and practice within a coherent framework of *praxis* have become more critical as the Christian community faces up to the challenges of postmodernism and pluralism. Pannenberg locates the issue in the realm of epistemology, specifically in the search for truth: "the question of the truth of Christianity cannot be enquired into without also enquiring into the question of the truth of all areas of human experience."[126] In her critique of Browning's model of 'practical moral reasoning', in which congregational life is "the expression of ethical principles and pastoral actions the outworking of moral reasoning"[127], Elaine Graham proposes a contrary perspective by locating pastoral activity in the pastoral practice of intentional faith-communities. By asserting that the "*practical wisdom* of the faithful and practising community is the medium by which truth-claims and value-commitments come into existence"[128], Graham's vision is essentially inductive in orientation and is biased towards a *phronesis* which embraces the distinctive postmodern themes of alterity, diversity and inclusivity. The transcendent dimension, though acknowledged, plays no essential part in her proposal: "although God is understood as transcendent reality, the theological values of practice are only manifested in the concrete *praxis* of the community in a given context."[129]

---

[124] *Ibid*: 3.
[125] Graham, *Transforming Practice*: 11-12.
[126] Pannenberg, Wolfhart, *Theology and the Philosophy of Science*, London: Darton, Longman & Todd, 1986: 264.
[127] Graham, *Transforming Practice*: 140.
[128] *Ibid*: 140.
[129] *Ibid*: 140.

Pastoral Ministry as Contextual Activity

This brief survey of the historical development of pastoral and practical theology has identified two significant polarities that correspond to the transcendent-immanent tension implicit in a contextual understanding of Christian pastoral ministry. The word 'polarity' is used here to express the possibility of two extreme positions within a spectrum of possibilities, but is not meant to imply that there cannot be a meeting somewhere between those extremes: for example, as noted in Chapter 3 of this book, the trinitarian debate throughout the twentieth century has been characterised by a creative tension between the transcendence and immanence of God. The first polarity is the distinction between an encyclopaedic and a hermeneutical approach to pastoral theology, evidenced in the contrasting theological perspectives in Europe and America, as observed by Heitink. Secondly, we noted the tension between deductive and inductive approaches to pastoral theology, again associated with the characteristic orientations of European and American pastoral theologians, epitomised in the theologies of Thurneysen and Barth on the one hand and Hiltner and Browning on the other. The tension may also be expressed as a contrast between theocentrism (given a specific christological interpretation by Anderson in terms of Christopraxis) and anthropocentrism[130] as the primary orientation in the *praxis* of pastoral ministry. The concept of *praxis* bridges the gap between theory and practice in a way that permits theological truth to be discerned as the church – participating in the ministry of Christ – engages in contextually-relevant ministry in the world. The result is a hermeneutically coherent model of *orthopraxis* in which theory and practice interact in a way that both deepens faith and transforms lives.

The polarities identified in the preceding paragraph have a lot to do with the concept of contextualisation and may be usefully incorporated into a more comprehensive typology of analogous polarities, drawing further from insights considered in earlier sections of this chapter, where a number of prevailing tensions characteristic of the contextual nature of Christian pastoral ministry were presented. Firstly, we noted that all who are engaged in the authentic *praxis* of ministry are inevitably drawn into the tension between gospel-faithfulness and cultural – or contextual – relevance, seeking to enrich their faith and their understanding of the gospel at the same time as they participate in Christ's transformative actions in the world. Secondly, in his approach to theological reflection, Stephen Pattison points to the role of Christian tradition and the appropriate context as two partners in a three-way 'critical conversation' model, in which personal presuppositions also play a vital role.

---

[130] For example, Anderson refers to Balsinger, who faults Browning for "an overly anthropological bias in his approach, lacking sufficient focus on faith contents" in Anderson, *The Shape of Practical Theology*: 29, citing Balsinger, Todd, "The Transforming Communion: A Trinitarian Spiritual Theology" (Ph.D. diss., Fuller Theological Seminary, 2000).

Thirdly, the postmodern context reminds us of the tension between the universal truth-claims of the Christian metanarrative and the locally-mediated – and inherited – truth-claims of particular communities of faith.

Finally, practical theology has been shaped over the years by a healthy and constructive tension between ecclesial and missional perspectives.[131] The New Testament witnesses to the role of the Spirit in incorporating believers into the one body of Christ, whose primary purpose in the world is essentially evangelical. Heitink outlines the *praxis* of the Acts of the Apostles (*Praxeis Apostolōn*) by which men and women "receive spiritual gifts (*charismata*), enabling them to proclaim the gospel (*kerygma*), to support each other in the establishment of a community (*koinōnia*), and to be servants in the kingdom of God that is being established in this world (*diakonia*)."[132] This reflects Farley's understanding of the world-transforming nature of 'ecclesial redemptive presence', which "is in part something that is constitutive, that perdures through changing historical epochs, and at the same time is perpetually incarnated in the specific historical situation."[133] For James Fowler, the relationship between church and world is encapsulated in the phrase *ecclesial praxis*, which embraces "the specific ways in which the church attempts to work in partnership with God and to remain faithful to God and God's mission."[134] Pannenberg gives the ecclesial and missional orientation of practical theology a firm eschatological twist, observing that mission

> is not simply the practice which originally created the church, but also the ultimate horizon on which the whole life of the church must be understood. By its origin in mission the individual community is drawn into a history of divine election which looks towards a future in the kingdom of God.[135]

Drawing these insights together, we may therefore propose a comprehensive typology for contextual pastoral ministry represented by the following

---

[131] The incarnational thrust of the church in the world may be articulated in terms of a tension between the radical separation implicit in Newbigin's 'Pilgrim's Progress Model' and the total engagement of the 'Jonah Model', two polarities (cited earlier in Newbigin, *The Good Shepherd: Meditations on Christian Ministry in Today's World*) which should be interpreted not as necessary opposites but as two dimensions of authentic Christian ministry.

[132] Heitink, *Practical Theology*: 91.

[133] Farley, "Theology and Practice Outside the Clerical Paradigm": 39.

[134] Anderson, *The Shape of Practical Theology*: 33; see Fowler, James, "Practical Theology and the Shaping of Christian Lives" in Browning (ed), *Practical Theology*: 148-166. Anderson develops the concept of mission theology as a form of practical theology in Anderson, Ray S., *Ministry on the Fireline: A Practical Theology for an Empowered Church*, Downers Grove: IVP, 1993: 114-118.

[135] Pannenberg, *Theology and the Philosophy of Science*: 438-439.

overlapping polarities, which combine to constitute a coherent framework for a contextually-relevant *orthopraxis*: *transcendent-immanent*; *encyclopaedic-hermeneutical*; *deductive-inductive*; *theocentric-anthropocentric*; *faithful-relevant*; *traditional-contextual/communal*; *universal-particular*; and *ecclesial-missional*. It is the task of practical theology to reflect upon the *praxis* of ministry as shaped by these critical dimensions, and "to ensure that the church's public proclamations and praxis in the world faithfully reflect the nature and purpose of God's continuing mission to the world."[136] This involves authentic engagement with the contemporary context, and earlier we noted the challenge to engage with the world in such a way as to retain both cultural relevance and gospel-faithfulness, without falling into either cultural naivety or dogmatic fundamentalism.

In their discussion of 'contextuality' Mudge and Poling express the dilemma as follows: "If one can no longer take for granted that the formative interaction between tradition and one's own context is simply normative, one must ask *how* such interactions take place and how 'other' interactions are to be regarded."[137] Ultimately, 'contextuality' for them is not so much a question of adaptation, but essentially about "fundamental differences of perspective, divergent ways of conceiving what the gospel is about."[138] Augsburger illustrates this with reference to a group made up of Africans and Western missionaries who were asked to identify the main point of the story of Joseph in the Old Testament: the Africans interpreted the narrative as a model of tribal identity, of a young man who never forgot his family; the Westerners saw the Joseph as an individual whose example of faithfulness to God represents a model of personal strength.[139] Augsburger comments that whilst both meanings are legitimate, we need to acknowledge both in order to establish a responsibly inclusive theology, rather than a neutral theology (which is actually a 'homeless theology'):

> The beginning point for pastoral theology must be both local – with a particular case, person, instance – and universal – with all humankind, human culture, and human history. Awareness of both the universal and the particular offers a constant corrective and directive to creative theologizing.[140]

The sort of creativity to which Augsburger alludes is precisely the task of a practical theology that is grounded in the church's participation in the incarnational and contextual ministry of Christ in the power of the Spirit. James Torrance points out that the prime purpose of the incarnation is to "lift us up

---

[136] Anderson, *The Shape of Practical Theology*: 22.
[137] Mudge and Poling, "Editors' Epilogue" in Mudge and Poling (eds), *Formation and Reflection*: xx-xxi, authors' italics.
[138] *Ibid*: xxi.
[139] Augsburger, *Pastoral Counseling Across Cultures*: 81-82.
[140] *Ibid*: 73.

into a life of communion, of participation in the very triune life of God."[141] So incarnational theology firstly has to do with God's deepest desire in relation to humanity, which is to renew his image in us. In his treatise *De Incarnatione Verbi Dei* the early church father Athanasius taught that no one could do this save God alone: "Therefore he assumed a human body, in order that in it death might once for all be destroyed, and that men might be renewed according to the Image."[142] This is what Athanasius describes as 'the good pleasure of God', so enabling us to participate in the gift of life in the Spirit, redeemed and made new by the grace of God, and free to share in the fullness of life and ministry within the community of the triune God. The implications are that we must now interpret all ministry from a new vantage point: ministry does not depends upon human effort but originates in the heart of God, finding its source in our relationship with the triune God. It is within this interpretation of the theology of the incarnation that we understand the ministry of the church in its mission orientation towards the world.

This leads us to a view of ministry which focuses on the church as a servant people ready to listen to and identify with the world in its diversity and pluralism. It is a mission of justice, salvation and restoration for the peoples of *all* nations - an inclusiveness picked up in Simeon's hymn of praise in Luke 2:29-32 as he held the Christ-child in his arms. In other words, God became involved with the whole world in Christ. He became involved at the most personal level possible, and he became involved with us all. The God who has come to us, who has entered our lives and simultaneously drawn us into his life (John 14:20) is our model for ministry. Marion Ganey, a Christian who made the villagers of Fiji amongst whom he worked feel that he believed in them because of his empathetic respect for them, once wrote: "You will never do very much for people until you realise in your whole heart and soul that you are not doing them a favour by being with them. They do us a favour by permitting us to enter their lives; we are their servants, not their bosses."[143] Here was a man who understood the nature of incarnational, servant ministry. Ganey immersed himself in the Fijian culture, determined to understand the villagers from whom he was so different.

In a study of local church ministry, the Australian theologian Denham Grierson examines the characteristic features of local congregations, arguing that each faith-community is unique in its history and identity. 'Naming' those characteristics (signs of meaning in the local context) will help to determine purpose and direction in the church's ministry in the community, and, to aid the process, Grierson proposes a simple sequential model: *understanding* → *accepting* → *loving*. Grierson's framework is incarnational, earthing pastoral

---

[141] Torrance, James B., Worship, *Community and the Triune God of Grace*, Downers Grove: IVP, 1996: 32.

[142] See *St. Athanasius on the Incarnation*, translated and edited by a religious of C.S.M.V. (Crestwood: St Vladimir's Orthodox Seminary, 1993: 41.

[143] Quoted in Arbuckle, Gerald, *Earthing the Gospel*, Homebush NSW: St Paul Publications, 1990: 218.

ministry in the actualities of congregational life. This focus on understanding others is central to his model of ministry, which is presented as a framework within which a faith community can discern openings for ministry. Only in understanding a given local context is it possible to avoid "the dogmatism that teaches us nothing and the scepticism that does not promise us anything."[144] Such understanding enables us to accept and love others more readily, thus creating ministry opportunities as we share more significantly in their lives. To Grierson's framework we should add 'listening' as a necessary first stage: we will never understand others until we are willing first to listen to them.

The American missiologist Charles Kraft confesses to fears of slipping out of theological conservatism into liberalism in his early missionary endeavours, fears fuelled by opening the door to new contextual interpretations of the gospel. Later, he realised that to be contextual was a methodological rather than a theological modification, requiring him to seek new truths even at the expense of previously held understandings. He saw himself increasingly as an 'open' conservative, "open to learning things from people of a different culture concerning what biblical Christianity should look like in their culture."[145] This methodological transformation is central to an understanding of ministry as *praxis* in its shift away from a propositional, dogmatic approach to one that has its roots in a willingness to learn from others. Instead of telling others, we listen to them. Christian ministry demands a willingness to engage in 'paradigm shifts'[146] in order to creatively interact with people whose perceptions of reality may be very different from our own.

As noted earlier in this chapter in our discussion of *theologia viatorum*, this creative approach can create considerable tension amongst those Christians who are motivated by a desire to see God as the source and author of all ministry. To focus initially on the recipients of ministry rather than on the one in whom all ministry originates may be regarded by some as a retrograde step, an approach which runs the risk of responding to the needs of people rather than to the initiative of God. However, we need to avoid putting a wedge between an approach to ministry that starts with God's agenda and an approach that starts with people's needs. Perhaps in the actual practice of ministry it does not really matter too much where we start: what is more important is where we end up, and the journey we are willing to travel along the way. So, with Barth, we might wish to affirm a dialectical approach to pastoral ministry based on the primacy of *Deus dixit*, an approach *within which* faith seeks understanding, and in which God is both the beginning and the end, Alpha and Omega, the end point of the hermeneutical spiral of practical theology, irrespective of the point of insertion.

---

[144] Grierson, Denham, *Transforming a People of God*, Melbourne: JBCE, 1984: 11.
[145] Kraft, Charles H., *Christianity in Culture*, Maryknoll NY: Orbis, 1979: 8.
[146] See Kuhn, Thomas, *The Structure of Scientific Revolutions*, Chicago: Chicago University Press, 1962, for an introduction to the concept of 'paradigm shift'.

The Contemporary Scientific Context for Ministry

In Chapter 1 we identified a number of reasons why those who are engaged in pastoral ministry need to be open to developments in science and technology as a contextual imperative. Firstly, there is a growing awareness within the Christian community of the impact of science and technology on contemporary life, particularly with regard to the ethical implications of new scientific capabilities, such as genetic engineering. The second reason relates to the historical mutual suspicion between theology and science, and the contemporary openness to the need for some sort of dialogue between the two. Finally, we argued that those who are engaged in Christian ministry need to be more adequately informed about the culture in which they seek to serve, a culture in which the scientific worldview is a dominant feature. In order to examine these more fully within the context of a contextually dynamic pastoral practice, it is helpful to establish a clear theological framework within which to articulate the relationship between God and his creation. This can be most usefully accomplished through the Christian doctrine of *kenosis*.[147]

In a discussion on the phenomenology of love, W. H. Vanstone, an English parish priest, argues that Christ's self-emptying (*kenosis*) in his incarnation, far from impairing the fullness of his revelation of God, contains the very heart and substance of that revelation, which is of a kenotic God who is ever self-giving in authentic love.[148] This love is at once limitless, precarious (in that it does not force itself on another) and vulnerable. The servant heart of God is immediately evident in this understanding of kenotic Christology, which speaks of a God who stoops down from on high to take his place amongst sinful human beings. Vanstone has touched upon something that is at the heart of incarnational theology, namely the way of love as the motive for *kenosis*. God is not separated from his creation, uninterested and uninvolved. It is a mark of his great love, and of his freedom too, that he has chosen a relationship with human beings that is given its fullest expression in the incarnation (and ultimate suffering) of his Son. We might also understand God as one who freely limits himself out of love so that his *physical* creation might experience freedom in all its fullness. So the doctrine of *kenosis* speaks to us of a God who has freely

---

[147] A careful exegesis of Philippians 2:7 suggests that servanthood and suffering are closely connected with the concept of *kenosis*. We could say that Christ's glory, the glory of his pre-existent oneness with the Father, was concealed in 'the form of a servant' which he took when he assumed our nature, a *kenosis* which led ultimately to the obedience of the cross. The linguistic connections between the Greek word meaning 'to empty' and the Semitic original can be traced to Isaiah 53:12: "He poured out his soul to death" (see Martin, R.P., "Kenosis" in Douglas, J.D. (ed), *The Illustrated Bible Dictionary*, Part 2, Leicester: IVP, 1980: 848). This insight has important implications for the ministry of the church, reflected in Paul's words in Philippians 2:5 that self-sacrificing humility should mark the lives of Christ's followers.

[148] Vanstone, W.H., *Love's Endeavour, Love's Expense: The Response of Being to the Love of God*, London: Darton, Longman & Todd, 1977: 39-54.

chosen and accepted self-limitation for the sake of the freedom of *all* that he has created, human and non-human.

In a brief treatment of the relationship between the Trinity and creation in Chapter 3, reference is made to Colin Gunton, who transmutes the concept of freedom into one of contingence when moving from the personal to the non-personal sphere, and to Thomas Torrance's understanding of the unlimited freedom which characterises the being of the triune God, and the limited yet authentic freedom given to the whole universe. The American philosopher Diogenes Allen writes:

> When God creates, it means that he allows something to exist which is not himself. This requires an act of profound renunciation. He chooses out of love to permit something else to exist, something created *to be itself* and to exist by virtue of its own interest and value. God renounces his status as the only existent – he pulls himself back, so to speak, in order to give his creation room to *exist for its own sake*.[149]

John Polkinghorne suggests that when God created *ex nihilo* he brought into being "a universe which is free to exist 'on its own', in the ontological space made available to it by the divine kenotic act of allowing the existence of something wholly other."[150] God respects *free natural processes* as well as human *free will*. He respects the unfolding of his universe with its own inbuilt laws, initial conditions and potentialities, as well as respecting human beings as free agents created *imago Dei*. This is a different view of *divine omnipotence* from that which is associated with classical theology – rather than speaking about God as Almighty and all-powerful in a detached sort of way, God is understood here to exercise his power as a 'capacity to influence'.[151] So he releases human beings to freely participate in his ongoing creativity in the world. This creativity makes room for unpredictable novelty in the emerging of the potential of the natural world alongside the predictability of 'laws of nature'.

These propositions will be examined more thoroughly at a later stage in this book, but the point to note here is that it is precisely because God may be

---

[149] Allen, Diogenes, *The Traces of God in a Frequently Hostile World*, Cambridge MA: Cowley, 1981: 35, author's italics.

[150] Polkinghorne, John, *Science and Christian Belief*, London: SPCK, 1994: 167.

[151] This is not to suggest that God should be equated with the idea of 'process theology'. Process theology is strong on God's immanence in the world, but fails to give to transcendence the absolute status it has in traditional theism. For this reason, whilst it is attractive as presenting God as one who is responsive to the world, process theology's understanding of God is not convincing. See, on process theology, Whitehead, Alfred North, *Process and Reality: An Essay in Cosmology*, New York: Macmillan, 1929; Hartshorne, Charles, *Creative Synthesis and Scientific Method*, London: SCM Press, 1970; and Cobb, John B., *A Christian Natural Theology: Based on the Thought of Alfred North Whitehead*, London: Lutterworth, 1966.

viewed as a creator who is *still creating*, and who invites us into the unfolding newness of his glorious creative energies, that Christians should value the freedom to participate in his creative and reconciling ministry in the world. This is a privilege, but a costly one, as Anderson reminds us: "As Jesus exists in a community of relation with the Father characterized by self-emptying, so does the church exist as a community of self-emptying, or kenotic presence, in the world."[152] Responsibility with regard to the world is therefore measured by the faith-community's commitment to and solidarity with the world: "incarnational solidarity is the theological presupposition of all Christian mission in the world."[153]

A critical assumption in this book is that the world in which we live is a creation which is characterised by order, coherence, beauty and novelty: the universe can be described by elegant mathematical equations whilst also evoking a mystery and wonder which evade logic. Accordingly, it invites scientific enquiry into such diverse fields as cosmology, ecology, biology, neuroscience, genetic technology and psychology. In Chapter 1 we argued that both the natural sciences and theology are motivated by the same search for truth, or at least verisimilitude,[154] with the result that we cannot simply allow them to stand apart, let alone in opposition to one another. There is an absolute necessity for dialogue if, methodologically, both disciplines are involved in *truth-seeking* within a common framework of values, assumptions and interpretations: this was the conclusion reached at the end of Chapter 1.

However, there is little evidence, even in recent literature on pastoral and practical theology, that the relationship between theology and science – and our concern is specifically with the natural sciences – has attracted serious consideration. In the preparation of this book, a representative sample of over fifty texts on pastoral and practical theology published in the second half of the twentieth century was consulted in order to assess the attention given to the role of the natural sciences. In one recent text, a compendium of pastoral and practical theology illustrative of the material consulted, several chapters are devoted to particular disciplines and perspectives that influence the shaping of pastoral theological theory and the practice of pastoral care, and other chapters explore important contemporary issues and topics.[155] The editors also acknowledge that other topics could have been included, but in none of the chapters or the list of possible inclusions is there any reference to the

---

[152] Anderson, *The Shape of Practical Theology*: 116.

[153] *Ibid*: 118.

[154] The philosopher Karl Popper incorporates the notion of verisimilitude as a necessary building block in his philosophy of science. Whilst scientific realism insists that there is a final reality that may be summed up as 'truth', Popper argues that all theories of reality are necessarily false. Progress in science is therefore represented by advances towards truth as one theory replaces another. On Popper's understanding of verisimilitude, see Popper, Karl, *Conjectures and Refutations*, London: Routledge and Kegan Paul, 1963.

[155] Woodward and Pattison, *The Blackwell Reader in Pastoral and Practical Theology*: 149-150.

importance of the natural sciences.

The primary interest in science shown by pastoral theologians in the twentieth century has been in the realm of methodology, specifically the empirical methodology of the social or human sciences. Heitink suggests that practical theology, as a specific discipline, "now identifies itself as a theological *theory of action*, with a methodology that is closely linked to the social sciences."[156] Browning cites the close parallelism between pastoral care and psychotherapy as an example of the mutually critical correlation between practical theology and the human sciences,[157] but more generally the contribution of studies in such areas as developmental psychology, personality theory, sociobiology and social psychology were valued because they generated empirical data about human behaviour which are useful in providing not only skills needed for effective pastoral action, but also "a new angle of vision on our quest for the appropriate enactment of the Christian faith."[158] For example, within a clearly articulated social science framework, Hiltner was prominent in advocating the application of general systems theory to his shepherding perspective, which is central to his pastoral theology, on the grounds that shepherding deals with complex life processes, involving a holistic interdependence between the information governing living organisms and processes.[159]

In the mid-twentieth century in America the Harvard University Project on Religion and Mental Health was active in bringing together the religious understanding of humanity and findings in psychiatry and the social sciences, because of the prevailing conviction that everyone has "the innate and irrepressible urge to make sense of life and to have this sense expressed through the unique character of his own personality and in the precise context in which he lives and works."[160] This partly explains the burgeoning interest in the field of personality theory at the time. In the field of pastoral care and counselling, the twentieth century has witnessed the ascendancy of what Benner calls the 'therapeutic culture', dominated by Rogerian client-centred therapy, Freudian psychoanalysis, the growth and group therapies of the human potential movement, and a wide range of interpersonal therapies. Benner notes the inevitable compromise in the distinctiveness of pastoral counselling practice as a result of the "syncretistic incorporation of models and technologies that are

---

[156] Heitink, *Practical Theology*: 1, author's italics.
[157] Browning, Don S., "Introduction" in Browning (ed), *Practical Theology*: 14-16.
[158] Ogletree, Thomas W., "Dimensions of Practical Theology: Meaning, Action, Self" in Browning (ed), *Practical Theology*: 93.
[159] See MacDonald, Coval B., "Methods of Study in Pastoral Theology" in Oglesby, William B. (ed), *The New Shape of Pastoral Theology*: 164-176.
[160] Hofmann, Hans, "Introduction" in Hofmann, Hans (ed), *Making the Ministry Relevant*, New York: Charles Scribner's Sons, 1960: xvi; Hofmann was the Director of the Harvard University Project on Religion and Mental Health at the time.

more clinical and pastoral",[161] warning that the church must "be careful not to trade its soul for a mess of psychological pottage."[162]

However, in the midst of the profusion of interest shown in the human sciences by pastoral theologians (and practitioners), there are some hopeful, if infrequent, signs of interest in the relevance of the *natural* sciences for pastoral ministry. Parallelling the ferment in the study of human nature through the disciplines of psychology and sociology, Carr notes the struggle to discover the shape of theology in the closing years of the twentieth century in the light of "[m]acrocosmic speculation and microcosmic investigation [which] together yield phenomena and ideas which were until recently inconceivable," discoveries which perhaps are "too vast to be easily incorporated into the structures which have served the Church."[163] But the struggle is worth the effort, if the goal of pastoral ministry is to open the eyes of the blind so that each may become, in John Macquarrie's phrase about spirituality, "a person in the fullest sense."[164] The English Anglican pastor and theologian Frank Wright cites Ian Ramsey, who insists that the only starting place for spirituality is the created world around us. Spirituality is therefore " a matter not of striving after another world, but having a deepened awareness of this world."[165] Pierre Teilhard de Chardin writes in his foreword to *The Phenomenon of Man* that the whole of life lies in the verb 'to see': " ...the history of the living world can be summarized as the elaboration of ever more perfect eyes within a cosmos in which there is always something more to be seen."[166]

Wright's thesis is that a pastoral theology that has no place for a sacramental understanding of the world of nature is a deficient theology, echoing Hall's earlier-quoted observation that "human spirituality is cheapened when it fastens on the divine in such a way as to exclude nature and even history from the realm of transcendent wonder."[167] In an earlier discussion, we noted in Barth the possibility that God may speak to a person through the glory of his creation (Calvin's *theatrum gloriae Dei*), whilst Tillich kept the door firmly open to human social and cultural experience as the medium through which God may be known. Both theologians, therefore, recognise – though in different degrees – the sacramentalism of created reality, both human and non-human.[168] As an

---

[161] Benner, David G., *Care of Souls: Revisioning Christian Nurture and Counsel*, Grand Rapids: Baker Books, 1998: 39.
[162] *Ibid*: 40.
[163] Carr, Wesley, *The Pastor as Theologian*, London: SPCK, 1989: 4.
[164] Macquarrie, John, *Paths in Spirituality*, London: SCM Press, 1972: 40.
[165] See "Awareness and Self-Awareness" in Wright, Frank, *The Pastoral Nature of the Ministry*, London: SCM Press, 1980: 32-42.
[166] Teilhard de Chardin, Pierre, *The Phenomenon of Man*, London: Collins, 1959: 31.
[167] Hall, *Imaging God*: 138.
[168] "A striking Barthian parallel and contrast to Tillich's statement of the many sources of theology is that God may speak to man through 'Russian communism or a flute concerto, a blossoming shrub or a dead dog' (Barth, *CD* 1/1: 60), but these do not constitute the object of Christian theology in any sense. If one's faith is aroused by and

example, Wright commends the work of the American poet Theodore Roethke as a creative resource to feed the contemplative spirit of pastors. Roethke saw the world as a 'sacramental reality'[169] in which rocks and hills, water and light, flowers, trees and birds and all other created things represent 'holy forms of life' which have the capacity to make us more fully human.[170] Martin Thornton suggests that, in a comparative way, things are more *consistent* than human beings in giving glory to God: "Despite the possibility of original sin pervading creation, buttercups are nearer to fulfilling God's plan for them than are most men and women."[171]

A world that is 'charged with the grandeur of God', to quote the immortal words of Gerard Manley Hopkins, may not, however, be readily acknowledged as such, for "among those schooled in science and technology there has been an almost joyful discarding of religious faith; such boldness has gradually affected most of our society."[172] If, in Deeks' words, human beings are 'enmeshed' in a world that is coherent and meaningful, such a position is both myopic and

---

given in the self-communication of the God and Father of Jesus Christ in a way that, when all is considered, is without final analogy to one's response to the Eroica symphony, the spirituality of the Bhagavad Gita, or the mysteriousness of the universe, then the characterization of all these by the same title may be abstractly and formally possible, but materially irrelevant" (Dowey, Edward A., Jr., "Tillich, Barth, and the Criteria of Theology" – see http://theologytoday.ptsem.edu/apr1958/v15-1-article4.htm, accessed on 14.01.04).

[169] Here Wright cites a phrase in Scott, Nathan A. Jr., *The Wild Prayer of Longing*, New Haven CT: Yale University Press, 1971: 118.

[170] The relationship between human beings and the physical world around is expressed evocatively in a Latin text inscribed on the glass of the east window of the library at Montacute House in Somerset, England, the translation of which reads: "Happy is the man with the keen intellect and superhuman eagerness to reveal the innermost secrets of nature; happy is he who can grasp the causes and relationships of matter; who can walk in the footsteps of Newton as his companion. But happy too is the man who cares for his fields; who appreciates all the manifold riches of his garden; who has learnt the art of grafting trees that each may thrive in its favourite soil; and who knows which are the happiest in the rich mud and ooze of the pond; which rejoice on the rocky ridges; which shun the biting cold of the north wind; and which flower high up in the snowy wastes of Scythia. Do not scorn or grumble about this modest toil; it is shared by the greatest gardener of all. Do not look for Him only among the stars of heaven; for it is in the ordinary things of life that you may find God." (Translated by Jonathan H. Musgrave in the Preface to *Gardening Tips from the National Trust*, London: The National Trust (Enterprises) Ltd., 1994: 5).

[171] Thornton, Martin, *Pastoral Theology: A Reorientation*, London: SPCK, 1961: 171, author's italics; this echoes the words of Dostoevsky's Father Zossima: "Do not pride yourself on superiority to the animals, they are without sin, and you, with your greatness, defile the earth by your appearance on it ..." (in Dostoevsky, Fyodor, *The Brothers Karamazov*, London: Heinemann, 1912: 332, quoted in Hall, *Imaging God*: 201).

[172] Deeks, David, *Pastoral Theology: An Inquiry,* London: Epworth Press, 1987: 68.

irresponsible. Pastoral theology

> takes with complete seriousness every struggle we engage in to understand ourselves, our culture and the functioning of nature and society ... it encapsulates our imagination and feeling, and therefore our art, it digests our science, technology and history.[173]

Before exploring some of these ideas more fully within the context of the doctrine of *imago Dei*, we might note a few more allusions to the natural sciences within the pastoral theology literature of the past half-century. Some references are slight, as in David Switzer's text, *Pastor, Preacher, Person*, in which the author proposes an 'interdisciplinary correlation' as a necessary element in pastoral theology: all who minister in the church "hold membership in the larger world," and among the disciplines noted by Switzer are the physical sciences.[174] Whilst he does not elaborate on this in his book, it is an inclusion worth noting in the light of the dominant emphasis on the social sciences in pastoral texts. Another writer, David Tacey, addresses a perceived imbalance in the concerns of practical theology, arguing that, whilst recent attention given to political and liberation theologies in the context of religious pluralism is appropriate and understandable, issues of global injustice and suffering also need to be embraced within the fold of practical theology.[175] Accordingly he applies the method of critical correlation to two vital cosmic issues, the ecological crisis and the threat of a nuclear holocaust. Whilst Tacey's concern is primarily ethical, offering the opportunity for fruitful engagement between religious traditions on a global scale, his insights are suggestive in steering practical theology towards what we might call a more 'cosmocentric' orientation, a corrective to the predominant anthropocentric bias.

Thornton's understanding of the relationship between pastoral theology and the domain of the natural sciences is more explicit, but unfortunately his interpretation takes place within a narrow and exclusive 'Remnant' pastoral theology.[176] His opening statements are promising: it is because "Jesus Christ *is* the Son of the Father-creator ... [that] there is still an organic relation between the order of nature and the order of grace."[177] He suggests that if "the world of the spirit has common properties with the world of nature ... we must ask what are the properties of the natural world which faith carries over, creatively, into parochial theology."[178] In response, he articulates four significant scientific

---

[173] *Ibid*: 67.
[174] Switzer, David, K., *Pastor, Preacher, Person: Developing a Pastoral Ministry in Depth*, Nashville: Abingdon, 1979: 140-141.
[175] Tacey, David, "Practical Theology in the Situation of Global Pluralism" in Mudge and Poling (eds), *Formation and Reflection*: 139-154.
[176] Thornton, *Pastoral Theology*: 121-128.
[177] *Ibid*: 115, author's italics.
[178] *Ibid*: 121.

properties inherent in the natural world: an incomprehensible complex of interrelated cycles; a fundamental order and relative contingency; evolutionary processes which move to a teleological plan; and the hierarchical development from simple organisms to complex organic cycles. However, Thornton's advocacy of a spiritualised 'Remnant' theology, in which the vicarious worship of a few parishioners replaces what he calls the 'puerile evangelistic stunts' of a simplistic conversion theology, leads him to interpret these properties analogically rather than recognising their intrinsic scientific worth. Besides lacking "the theological relevance of the Reformation principle of the universal priesthood of believers,"[179] Thornton's creative and over-imaginative proposal within his pastoral 'reorientation' is hermeneutically suspect, pastorally exclusive and fails to treat scientific data with integrity. As an example of the latter, he infers from evolutionary theory "the spiritual importance of Remnant organism, growing, not only in progressive spirituality, but also in harmony with a specific parochial environment."[180]

In his exploration of the relationship between trinitarian theology and pastoral experience, Paul Fiddes raises a number of significant pastoral themes, some of which invite a specific scientific perspective.[181] For example, in a chapter on God's action in relation to intercessory prayer, he suggests that God works persuasively by his Spirit within creation, calling out response from it. That response may be expressed in three kinds of language: the capacity of all entities for feeling, the movement of all creation in praise, and a receptivity to the holistic forming of patterns.[182] This idea of 'grace finding new paths in nature' is highly suggestive and invites us to conceive of a 'family-likeness' within the cosmos which influences how we might pray with respect to the world of nature. In a further chapter on sacramental life, Fiddes draws from Sallie McFague's metaphor of the world as 'God's body', a cosmic unity characterised by the organic interconnectedness between all bodies in the universe.[183] Human participation in the life of the trinitarian God therefore implies sacramental participation in all that he has created, where sacrament is defined by Fiddes as a place of encounter with God.[184]

Fiddes' comments derive from his willingness as a theologian to engage constructively with the natural sciences. His book, *Participating in God*, is a

---

[179] See Brister, *Pastoral Care in the Church*, 105-106.
[180] Thornton, *Pastoral Theology*: 126.
[181] Fiddes, Paul S., *Participating in God: A Pastoral Doctrine of the Trinity*, London: Darton, Longman & Todd, 2000.
[182] *Ibid*: 144-148.
[183] Panentheistically, not pantheistically, since, in Wright's words, the natural elements are not to be "swallowed up in some nebulous unity in which all distinctions are annihilated" (Wright, *The Pastoral Nature of the Ministry*: 82).
[184] *Ibid*: 278-302, citing McFague, Sallie, *The Body of God: An Ecological Theology*, London: SCM Press, 1993.

rare creative blend of theological and pastoral insights, some of which will be examined more fully in Chapter 4. A number of contemporary trinitarian theologians have been active at the science-theology interface, including Wolfhart Pannenberg, Jürgen Moltmann, Colin Gunton and Thomas Torrance,[185] and although each contributes important pastoral insights which enable us to think about how we are to live in the world, it is inappropriate to describe them as practical theologians: their primary strength is in the area of dogmatic theology. For example, in a critical essay on Thomas Torrance, Anderson discerns several contours of practical theology in his writings, grounded in the concept of *praxis*, but notes that "he seldom ventures onto the turf where practical theologians ply their trade."[186] The result is that while Torrance's theological matrix "contains an inner logic that overcomes the older dualism between theory and practice"[187], commending him as a 'practical theologian' of sorts, it does not expound any clearly articulated relationship between pastoral theology and the natural sciences in a way that is immediately helpful to those who are engaged in the *praxis* of ministry 'at the coal face.'

Imago Dei and the Natural World

It is helpful at this stage to reintroduce the theological construct of *imago Dei* in order to demonstrate the critical link between human beings and the created world as a way into articulating more firmly the pastoral relevance of the physical sciences to the *praxis* of ministry. In his book *Imaging God* Douglas John Hall interprets the phrase 'the ontology of communion'[188] in the form of a theorem, or axiom: "the basic ontological category of the tradition of Jerusalem is not, as with Athens, that of 'being' as such, but *being with*. Or, as an equation: Being=Being-With."[189] What Hall, amongst others, advocates is an interpretation of *imago Dei* that is predicated on the theological statement that human beings are created for relationship. In developing this doctrine, Gunton argues that it is an unsatisfactory anthropology which requires a choice between an image of God grounded in the human stewardship of creation, and one

---

[185] See Chapter 3 for a survey of some of their representative works within the framework of trinitarian theology.

[186] Anderson, Ray S., "Reading T. F. Torrance as a Practical Theologian" in Colyer, Elmer M. (ed), *The Promise of Trinitarian Theology: Theologians in Dialogue with T. F. Torrance*, Lanham: Rowman & Littlefield Publishers, 2001: 176. The contours which Anderson discerns are predicated on praxis as a hermeneutical criterion: Christopraxis, Ecclesial Praxis, Missiological Praxis and Pastoral Praxis.

[187] *Ibid*: 178.

[188] The phrase 'ontology of communion' is drawn from Joseph Sittler, who proposes an ontological structure of reality that is relational, an ontology of 'community, communion, ecology': see Hall, *Imaging God*: 115.

[189] *Ibid*: 116.

In Solidarity with Beasts, Plants and Stones 93

located in the distinction between male and female, based on the Genesis creation account. His solution is to correlate the relatedness implicit in each of the two interpretations in the 'missing conceptual link', that of the person.[190] The notion of 'person' with respect to the divine nature of God as Trinity will be explored in the next chapter, but the central point here is that human personhood consists essentially in relatedness which, as Gunton shows, takes shape in a 'double orientation'. The first has to do with our relationship with God; the second – the 'horizontal' orientation – is predicated on the first and is expressed as relationship with others in human community, on the one hand, and relationship with the non-personal world, on the other.

This last dimension of relationality proposes a view of human beings as 'creatures of nature', "bound up closely with the fate of the rest of the material universe"[191], where responsible stewardship supersedes arrogant dominion. The corollary of this is that the world, created in the freedom of God's love, "is not impersonal process, a machine or a self-developing organism – a cosmic collective into which the particular simply disappears – but that which itself has a destiny along with the human."[192] This is a theological anthropology that contradicts a Platonic dualism which sets body apart from soul, the material apart from the spiritual[193]: the nature of human beings living in community within the love of God is bound up intimately and necessarily with human responsibility for the world. For Gunton, only a *trinitarian* theology grounded in dynamic relationship can unlock that reality. He warns against the opposite error of denying the 'otherness' of creation:

> of our relation to the non-human world, it must be said that we make a mistake if we do not take due account of our otherness from it. To personalize the world or to make it the object of worship, as may be the case in some forms of 'creation-centred spirituality', is to misconstrue its nature, and so our responsibility for its being truly itself.[194]

Similarly, Fiddes, in his discussion of McFague's 'body of God' theology, warns against a pantheistic way of thinking in which "everything gets

---

[190] Gunton, Colin E., *The Promise of Trinitarian Theology*, Edinburgh, T. & T. Clark, 1991: 104-121.
[191] *Ibid*: 120.
[192] *Ibid*: 13.
[193] Hare traces Plato's approach to the soul and its place in the material world to Pythagoras, although he concedes that both "may have been influenced by ideas from the East and by the 'mystery religions' such as Orphism which spread through Greece in this period. The early Pythagoreans seem (though this has been disputed) to have been mind-body dualists; that is to say, they thought, as Plato was to think, that the soul or mind (*psyche*) was an entity distinct and separable from the body. This was consonant with primitive Greek thinking about the soul, as found, for example, in the earliest Greek poet Homer." (Hare, R.M. *Plato*, Oxford: Oxford University Press, 1982).
[194] Gunton, *The Promise of Trinitarian Theology*: 171.

swallowed up into an indifferentiated oneness."[195]

Following Moltmann, Hall suggests that to be *imago Dei* means also to be *imago mundi*[196]:

> The peculiar form of receptivity that we bring to our contemplation of nature is not of a different kind from the attitudes of mind and spirit with which we consider our proximity to God and to our own kind ... whether we reflect on God, on our own species, or on trees, rocks, and whales, we are engaged in the same mode of contemplation, investigation, or reverie. For all three ... are present to us in such a way that the being of each mirrors the being of the others.[197]

Humanity's failure to grasp this insight is named by Hall in terms of three areas of negligence: the sacrificial element in the stewardship of nature; the preservational dimension in the stewardship of other forms of life; and the recognition of the spiritual element in matter.[198] All three invite us into the realm of the natural sciences. To live responsibly as human beings within the created order embodies such concerns as the treatment of animal species in genetic technology, the environmental management of forests and waterways, and the allocation of resources for effective global stewardship. Moreover, it is to move beyond a purely utilitarian ethic and to embrace a spirituality that acknowledges the wonder and mystery of creation as 'sacramental reality.' It is an underlying premise in this book that these are all issues of immense pastoral significance, touching as they do upon the central questions 'What should we do?' and 'How should we live?', which lie at the heart of practical theology.[199]

Peter Shaffer's controversial play *Equus* deals with a 17-year-old boy who is brought to a psychiatric hospital because he has deliberately blinded several horses with a metal spike, acts which force the characters to confront questions of responsibility and ultimate meaning.[200] The boy's passion for horses has the effect of revealing to the psychiatrist the barrenness of his own life. He envies the boy's secret, though terribly confused and abnormal, life (even calling his

---

[195] Fiddes, *Participating in God*: 291. In his exposition of 'Being-With-Nature', Hall suggests that "underneath the modern decision to master nature is a long history of human anxiety in the face of nature's otherness, its seeming indifference to human pursuits, its resistance to human ambition." (Hall, *Imaging God*: 164). So we may discern two human responses to nature that deny the fundamental core of *imago Dei* as a trinitarian construct: divinisation and domination.

[196] Hall, *Imaging God*: 179; Moltmann actually juxtaposes the two terms as alternatives, a rendering resisted by Hall (*Ibid*: 233, fn.37).

[197] *Ibid*: 178.

[198] *Ibid*: 195-204.

[199] Chapter 4 will develop further the concept of *imago Dei* as we look in more detail at the significance of the *perichoresis* construct in pastoral practice.

[200] Shaffer, Peter, *Equus*, London: André Deutsch, 1980.

In Solidarity with Beasts, Plants and Stones 95

secret passion 'worship') and feels that his own life in the service of science and rationality has diminished him: "It's not that I'm unworthy to fill the job," he says. "The job's unworthy to fill me." The confession evokes a sense of desperation about his failure to experience the fullness of his own humanness. Commenting on the play, Frank Wright asks: "How can you be whole and empty at the same time?"[201] In other words, how can we live authentic and fully human lives if we are denuded inside of all passion? *Equus* – in spite of its senseless violence and explicit religious and sexual themes – arouses in Wright a pastoral yearning to see human beings experience life in all its depth and intensity ... with *passion*. The passion that Wright calls us to enter into is a passion to engage intimately, sensually and adventurously in God's good and holy creation. It is to this reality that a truly Christian understanding of *imago Dei* witnesses. Our discussion of trinitarian thinking in Chapter 3 will rehearse these themes, with particular reference to the role of the Spirit, who holds the whole created order in the freedom of divine perichoretic love.

To summarise, authentic Christian ministry has been developed throughout this chapter in terms of participation in the Spirit-empowered ministry of Christ in the world. Rather than interpreting ministry as a form of pragmatic 'hints and tips' applied theology, we have emphasised the essentially theological nature of pastoral action, in which theory and practice interrelate within a hermeneutical spiral, a crucial methodological insight central to the developing discipline of practical theology throughout the latter half of the twentieth century. We have seen how the two concepts of *praxis* and *theologia viatorum* have been given Christocentric and trinitarian orientation in Anderson's development of Christopraxis, in which theological truth is predicated on Christ's ministry in the world, thus bridging the gap between the theological academy and the practice of ministry, a gap which has its historical source in the development of scholarly learning in the Middle Ages. Following Schleiermacher's groundbreaking – though ultimately inadequate – schema to locate theology as a whole within the community of faith, the emerging discipline of practical theology travelled down two paths that epitomise the tension between the transcendent and immanent approaches in theological method. In the twentieth century, these two perspectives were given representative expression in the neo-orthodox pastoral theology of Eduard Thurneysen, on the one hand, and the empirical functionalism of Seward Hiltner, on the other.

Two other theologically significant themes that we have explored with reference to the development of practical theology are contextualisation and incarnation. Practical engagement with the contemporary context cannot avoid the dialectic between transcendence and immanence, summed up in the motif of contextualisation. We have seen how this dialectic tension may be articulated in the form of a typology of overlapping polarities, which constitute a comprehensive framework for a contextually-relevant *orthopraxis*. Christian ministry, expressed as human participation in God's *continuing creation*, is predicated on the freedom of love implicit in the theology of the incarnation:

---

[201] Wright, *The Pastoral Nature of the Ministry*: 79.

God's voluntary self-limitation, represented by the kenotic Christology of the incarnation, speaks to us of a creation which is characterised not only by human free will but also, at the non-human level, by free natural processes. So ministry is the privilege of participation in Christ's reconciling work "in the company of beasts and plants and stones, accepting solidarity with them,"[202] as well as with our fellow human beings. This directs us to a practical theology which values contextual engagement with the natural sciences as much as with the social and human sciences.

However, our survey of representative texts in the discipline of pastoral/practical theology published in the second half of the twentieth century demonstrates a predominant interest in the social sciences, with only passing lip-service paid to the contribution of the natural sciences. There are positive signs that this trend is now being corrected, and within the field of theological anthropology the Christian doctrine of *imago Dei* may offer a helpful way forward in articulating the relationship between pastoral insights concerning human experiences of life and the nature of the physical world in which human beings are privileged to live ... if only their eyes were opened to the reality around them! The scientist Linus Pauling, enthusiastically exalting the physical properties of the universe at a conference in Vancouver in 1982, declared: "It is really wonderful, the world, and one wonderful part about it is that there are sentient beings here who are able to appreciate the wonders of the world, to understand them!"[203] The next chapter takes us further along this track by offering a perichoretic understanding of this 'wonderful world' to which Pauling testifies, drawing on the insights of a dynamic, relationally-oriented trinitarian theology. In the process, we will begin to outline the contours of a coherent theological framework in order to interpret more thoroughly what it means for human beings to 'appreciate the wonders of the world' and therefore to live more fully in the image of God. Such fulfilment may surely be regarded as the goal of all pastoral ministry.

---

[202] Barth, Karl, *Church Dogmatics*, 3/3, Edinburgh: T. & T. Clark Ltd, 1960: 242.
[203] Hall, *Imaging God*: 205 (quoting Barth).

CHAPTER 3

The Coping-stone of Christian Doctrine – The Resurgence of Trinitarian Thinking

In this chapter we trace the development of what the American theologian Ted Peters has called 'Trinity talk'[1], from its revival in the theological writing of Karl Barth in the 1930s to current insights which urge us to interpret the relationship between God and his creation – personal and non-personal – in terms of dynamic 'open' relationality. In the process we will examine the connection between the economic Trinity and the immanent Trinity, which some have collapsed into one, either to avoid the alleged irrelevance of metaphysical speculation regarding the ontology of the trinitarian being, or to give substantial weight to temporality within the life of God. In effect, the trinitarian debate throughout the twentieth century has been the story of the creative tension between the transcendence and immanence of God. The chapter closes with an evaluation of the concept of *perichoresis* as an expression of the dynamic relationality that characterises not only the inner life of Father, Son and Spirit, but also the life of the Trinity *ad extra* both in human society and within the natural world.

Beginning with Barth

Many contemporary theologians trace the resurgence in trinitarian thinking to Karl Barth, whose insights gave rise to a renewed emphasis on the doctrine of the Trinity during the second half of the twentieth century. Peters observes that during this period Barth's "method of *analysis* of scriptural revelation" as his basis for trinitarian theology has, in theological debate, triumphed over Schleiermacher's "method of *synthesis*" based upon human experiences of God.[2] For Barth, the Trinity was "decisive and controlling for the whole of dogmatics"[3]; it represented "the first word as that which gives us information

---

[1] See Peters, Ted, *God as Trinity: Relationality and Temporality in Divine Life*, Louisville: Westminster/John Knox Press, 1993.
[2] *Ibid*: 10.
[3] Barth, Karl, *Church Dogmatics* [hereinafter referred to as *CD* in these chapter footnotes] 1/1, Edinburgh: T. & T. Clark, 1936: 303.

on the concrete and decisive question: Who is God?"[4] Accordingly, the Trinity is not just one of many Christian doctrines: it is "the basic presupposition of the doctrine of God."[5]

Schleiermacher regarded the concept of the Trinity as "the coping-stone of Christian doctrine (*der Schlußstein der christlichen Lehre*)."[6] However, this metaphor greatly exaggerates his actual interpretation of trinitarianism: his overriding monotheistic emphasis on divine unity caused his advocacy of the Trinity to be located in his *epilegomena*. For Schleiermacher, Trinity language is secondary rather than primary: "It is not an immediate utterance concerning the Christian self-consciousness."[7] The American Lutheran theologian, Robert Jenson, dismisses Schleiermacher's doctrine of the Trinity as a "bungle", not only because of its summary relegation to the end of his systematics, but also because of its Arian characteristics.[8] Schleiermacher was unable to shake himself free from classical metaphysical conceptions of God, in which attributes of immutability and timelessness were central. As we shall see, it is precisely this rather flat Augustinian idea of "an abstractly simple divine essence"[9] which has dominated Western trinitarian reflection and explication, to the point where, until Barth, the doctrine tended to be articulated in philosophical rather than biblical language.

Barth was insistent that God's being and God's act were not to be isolated from each other: so "this subject, God, the Revealer, is identical with His act in revelation and also identical with its effect."[10] Barth does not follow through this insight as fully as he could have in terms of the relational dynamic intrinsic to the nature of the Trinity, although in his later theological writing, referring to theology as a 'bird in flight', in contrast to a 'caged bird'[11], he specifically

---

[4] *Ibid*: 301.
[5] Barth, *CD* 1/2, 1956: 312.
[6] Schleiermacher, Friedrich, *The Christian Faith*, Edinburgh: T. & T. Clark, 1928: 739.
[7] *Ibid*: 738.
[8] See Jenson, Robert, *The Triune Identity: God According to the Gospel*, Philadelphia: Fortress Press, 1982: 133-134. Invited to write an article entitled "What is the Point of Trinitarian Theology?", Jenson elaborates a disclaimer in his opening paragraphs: "Trinitarian theology does not have a point,' he asserts, " it *is* the point." (in Schwobel, Christoph (ed), *Trinitarian Theology Today: Essays on Divine Being and Act*, Edinburgh: T. & T. Clark, 1995: 31).
[9] Jenson, *Triune Identity*: 120.
[10] Barth, *CD* 1/1: 296.
[11] So, in his *Evangelical Theology*, Barth writes that "in its perception, meditation, and discussion, theology must have the character of a living *procession*. Evangelical theology would forfeit its object, it would belie and negate itself, if it wished to view, to understand, and to describe any one moment of the divine procession in 'splendid isolation' from others. Instead, theology must describe the dynamic
interrelationships which make this procession comparable to a bird in flight, in contrast to a caged bird." (Barth, Karl, *Evangelical Theology: An Introduction*, London: Collins Fontana, 1963: 15).

alludes to a more dynamic interpretation of the relationships between Father, Son and Holy Spirit. What is of major significance in Barth's thesis, however, is his explication of the doctrine of the Trinity in terms of his doctrine of revelation. In fact, we might say that, for Barth, revelation rather than relationality is the essential controlling paradigm for trinitarian discourse.

Barth expresses the sum of his revelational thought about the Trinity in the following words: "*God* reveals Himself. He reveals Himself *through Himself*. He reveals *Himself*."[12] So God is the 'Who', the 'How' and the 'What' of revelation – he is Revealer, Revealedness and Revelation, the self-revealing God and his own self-revelation. So for Barth the doctrine of the Trinity derives from a revelational basis, as distinct from philosophical, naturalistic or anthropological insights: "When we ask: Who is the self-revealing God? the Bible answers in such a way that we have to reflect on the triunity of God."[13] Accordingly, Barth's theological framework demands that the Christian concept of revelation already includes within it the concept of the doctrine of the Trinity, in which God reveals Himself as the Lord – Father, Son and Holy Spirit. So the Father is revealed in the Son, and this revelation is the distinctive work of the Spirit, who alone enables human beings to understand God's self-revelation *as revelation*. So Barth states his proposition that

> He whom the Christian church calls God and proclaims as God, the God who has revealed Himself according to the witness of Scripture, is the same in unimpaired unity and yet also the same thrice in different ways in unimpaired distinction.[14]

As dogma, trinitarianism is, in the first place, good interpretation of the Bible. Barth dismisses analogues of the trinitarian God of Christian revelation (he cites five categories of phenomena which might reflect *vestigia trinitatis*: nature, culture, history, religion and the human soul[15]) on the basis that *vestigia trinitatis in creatura* do not display the indissoluble unity and the indestructible distinction implicit in the biblical revelation of the divine Trinity. Ultimately, "revelation will submit only to interpretation and not to illustration."[16]

Barth has quite rightly been lauded for bringing the Trinity into the centre of the stage of theological discussion. With Augustine, he is content to affirm the *mystery* of the Trinity. The patristic scholar G. L. Prestige notes that "Augustine was neither alarmed nor surprised to find that the Greeks interpreted the Trinity differently from the Latins." He quotes Augustine:

> For the sake of describing things ineffable, that we may be able in some way to express what we are in no way able to express fully, our

---

[12] Barth, *CD* 1/1: 296, author's italics.
[13] *Ibid*: 303.
[14] *Ibid*: 307.
[15] *Ibid*: 336-338.
[16] *Ibid*: 345.

Greek friends have spoken of one essence and three substances, but the Latins of one essence or substance and three persons.[17]

For Augustine the notion of Trinity was mystery, challenging attempts to be precise with regard to terminology, and therefore surpassing human discourse. Likewise, Barth eschews speculation, maintaining that "all rational wrestling with this mystery, the more serious it is, can lead only to its fresh and authentic interpretation and manifestation as mystery."[18] Perhaps it is this espousal of mystery, as well as his inherent dislike of anything that might allude to tritheism or encourage comparison with modern concepts of human individual personality, that caused Barth to prefer the phrase "modes of being" (*Seinsweisen*) to "persons" in his trinitarian theology.[19] Barth has been criticised for his modalistic tendencies, though later on he explicitly rejected modalism in his affirmation of the distinctiveness of the three persons of the Trinity.[20]

Barth adopts the word "triunity" (*Dreieinigkeit*) as a linguistic conflation of "unity in trinity" and "trinity in unity", postulating the unity of Father, Son and Spirit among themselves. In this connection he introduces the concept of *perichoresis*, concurring with Pohle that it was legitimate to interpret the concept as the final sum of the doctrine of *unitas in trinitate* and *trinitas in unitate*.[21] It is noticeable, however, that Barth's discussion of *perichoresis*, defined as the participation of each mode of being in the other modes of being, does not convey any sense of dynamic movement or energy: rather, the language is one of co-existence *ad intra*. As Alan Torrance notes, Barth prefers the Latin translation *circuminsessio*, denoting a "dwelling in one another", to the alternative *circumincessio*, conveying the idea of "passing into one another", because the former notion of "spatial juxtaposition" is more appropriate than a "temporal sequence" implied in the latter translation.[22] For Torrance, Barth grounds his exposition of the Trinity dialectically rather than dynamically in terms of the category of communion.[23]

Why should this be so? Though Barth sees God's work and essence as not twofold but one, so making explicit the correspondence between *ad intra* and *ad extra*, he nonetheless maintains that we must also *distinguish* his essence from his work, since we are limited by creaturely comprehensibility with regard

---

[17] Prestige, G.L., *God in Patristic Thought*, London: SPCK 1959: 237.
[18] Barth, *CD* 1/1: 368.
[19] *Ibid*: 355-359.
[20] *Ibid*: 355-359.
[21] *Ibid*: 370-371.
[22] *Ibid*: 370. As we shall see later, it is just this notion of temporality that has exercised the minds of more recent trinitarian theologians, especially Jürgen Moltmann, Wolfhart Pannenberg and Thomas Torrance.
[23] Torrance, Alan J., *Persons in Communion: An Essay on Trinitarian Description and Human Participation*, Edinburgh: T. & T. Clark, 1996: 256.

to God's triunity.²⁴ Barth's emphasis in his *Church Dogmatics* is on the God who reveals himself, especially in the history of Jesus Christ, as *God*, and explicitly the triune God of grace (thus negating the claims of natural theology). Therefore, while he emphasises correspondence between essence and work, it is evident in his trinitarian theology that he wants to leave a space between them.

The result is that his discussion of the doctrines of *perichoresis* and appropriation in his theology of the Trinity speak to us more of the *being* of God than of the actions of God. Of course, for Barth, God's being *is* God's act, and the principle of correspondence means that we can work backwards from God's act to a statement about God's being. But at all times we have to keep in mind that the incarnation is God's *self*-interpretation, his *self*-communication: God does what he does because he is who he is. Our trinitarian statements are therefore predicated on God's self-revelation.

If, as Barth affirms, there is a correspondence between the Trinity *ad intra* and *ad extra*, one way of understanding God's self-communication in the history of the world through Jesus Christ is that in some way God's action in the world becomes constitutive of God's essential being *ad intra*. This takes us beyond the language of correspondence, and represents more closely the axiom proposed by the Catholic theologian, Karl Rahner, that the immanent Trinity *is* the economic Trinity and *vice versa*. Barth does not take us that far: in his concern to preserve the 'wholly otherness' of God, he falls short of *equating* immanent and economic Trinity, with the result that his theology of intratrinitarian divine life tends towards the historically static doctrine of relations, as developed by Augustine, Anselm and Aquinas, rather than the dynamic, interactive relationality characteristic of contemporary trinitarian reflection.

Alan Torrance rightly discerns some ambiguity in Barth's thought here, particularly in "his continual reminders of the need to interpret the *Seinsweisen* in relational terms."²⁵ For Barth, the idea of 'relations' appears to be rather elastic, taking on different nuances of meaning in his discussion, but in each case "radically different from that unique and specific redefinition of the term 'relation' denoted when reference is made to the dynamic mutuality of the inner communion between the Father and Son in the Spirit."²⁶ Besides noting the need in Barth's trinitarian theology for a "more unambiguous affirmation of the primordial nature of the intrapersonal communion of the Trinity"²⁷, Torrance

---

²⁴ Barth, *CD* 1/1: 371.
²⁵ Torrance, Alan J., *Persons in Communion*: 259. We might note here Torrance's observation that *Seinsweisen* encourages the feminist argument for a functionalist revision of trinitarian language from Father, Son and Holy Spirit to Creator, Redeemer and Sustainer/Giver of Life (a formula which Torrance regards not only as pseudo-trinitarian, but anti-trinitarian), because "*Seinsweisen* opens the door to functionalist interpretations in a way that the term *Personen* does not" (*ibid*: 237-238).
²⁶ *Ibid*: 259-260.
²⁷ *Ibid*: 258.

critiques Barth's overdependence on the biblical *concept* of revelation at the expense of the biblical *content* of revelation in his advocacy of the term *Seinsweisen*.[28]

Barth's preference for the language of 'I' at the centre of God rather than 'we' reflects his resolution to affirm the central thesis of the sovereignty of God, but the hazard here is that dynamic mutuality is diminished in the process. Barth is aware of this danger, but in Torrance's view fails to deal with the problem with adequate consistency. The underlying complaint in Torrance's critique is that Barth's trinitarian discussion is grounded in an abstract 'revelation model' that is too narrowly conceived: it fails to do justice to *human* participation in the intra-divine life. So Torrance proposes a 'doxological' or 'communion' model that offers "a closer integration of the *trinitas ad intra* and the divine economy"[29], in which the notion of *koinonia* as a dynamic reality takes its place as a "controlled reinterpretation" of Barth's triune structure of revelation.

Of course, Barth's understanding of the freedom of God expressed as love (particularly in terms of correspondence between essence and work) is suggestive of dynamic relationality *ad extra*. For example, he insists that an aspect of God's freedom is his right to be free with regard to his freedom. God is not a prisoner of his own freedom. Referring to God's activity as Creator, Reconciler and Redeemer, he argues that "God must not only be unconditioned but, in the absoluteness in which he sets up this fellowship, He can and also will be conditioned."[30] This is indicative of a free intercourse between God and humanity that cannot be reduced to static interpretation. Alongside this, however, Barth's conception of God's freedom is expressed supremely as *transcendence*: "The loftiness, the sovereign majesty, the holiness, the glory – even what is termed the transcendence of God – what is it but this self-determination, this freedom, of the divine living and loving, the divine person?"[31] God's freedom both preserves and is determined by his otherness, his absolute independence from all that he has created. Others following Barth have diluted transcendence to the point where the distinction between transcendence and immanence has been almost dissolved. But for Barth God's transcendence is the sum of his freedom, which incorporates his freedom to be immanent: it must not, indeed cannot, be weakened. For other theologians after him, God's freedom is expressed more impressively by his immanence. It is within the tension of these two positions that theologians have debated the relationship between God and the world.

---

[28] *Ibid*: 239ff.
[29] *Ibid*: 308.
[30] Barth, *CD* 2/1, 1957: 303.
[31] *Ibid*: 302.

Being and Becoming

Notwithstanding a number of limitations in Barth's trinitarian insights, it is clear that he opened the door, and opened it very widely, that others might enter into a rich exploration of the doctrine of the Trinity, particularly from the perspective of the *interaction* between God and the world. One of Barth's pupils, Eberhard Jungel, affirms his mentor's emphasis on revelation as the starting-point for all trinitarian reflection. He also reinforces Barth's christological assertion of God's self-communication as a reiteration of his innertrinitarian identity, made explicit in the historical person of Jesus Christ: "it is the event of Jesus Christ's death on the cross which calls the *being* of God into question and presses for a *trinitarian* statement."[32] Having asserted that the *Church Dogmatics* is "a brilliant and diligent attempt to reconstruct in thought the movement of the statement 'God corresponds to himself'"[33], Jungel then takes the theme of correspondence further.

But what exactly does Jungel understand by the term 'correspondence'? He argues that God's being *ad intra* is relationally structured: relationality, or *self-relatedness*, is ontologically characteristic of God himself: there is differentiation within the divine life. The question then arises: how does the "taking up of humanity into the event of God's being, which comes to us from God as salvation"[34], correspond with the divine life? Clearly incarnation implies relationality: Jesus, the word made flesh, is

> other from the perspective of the first person of the Trinity, the Father. This otherness permits us to think of him as God's Son while, at the same time, due to the unifying work of the Holy Spirit, he constitutes the presence of God in the finite world.[35]

For Jungel, there cannot be relationality in incarnation, that is in the economy of salvation, without there being antecedent relationality *ad intra*. There is therefore a correspondence which moves from *ad intra* to *ad extra*.

But can we posit a correspondence in the other direction? The problem here for Jungel is that we might find ourselves proposing some form of ontological dependence of the divine being on that which is other to himself. Put another way, can we say that God's being is *constituted* by his temporal relations with the world? Such a proposal would seem to contradict God's aseity, and Jungel is concerned to hold on to God's being as *pros ti* (in relation to something) and yet protected from being dependent on the *heteros* (other).[36]

---

[32] Jungel, Eberhard, *God's Being is in Becoming: the Trinitarian Being of God in the Theology of Karl Barth*, Grand Rapids: Eerdmans, 2001: 4.
[33] *Ibid*: 36.
[34] *Ibid*: 75-76.
[35] Peters, *God as Trinity*: 173-174.
[36] Jungel, *God's Being is in Becoming*: 114.

Jungel gets round this dilemma by introducing the eschatological notion of *becoming* on the basis that God has already in freedom taken up historicity into his divine life: God's becoming is therefore predicated on his relationship with creation. God could have been the same God had there been no creation, but God in his freedom *as God* chose to bring creation into being and to relate to humanity as an ontologically relational being. God does not become other than he always has been from eternity: rather, he "continues unceasingly to be what he always is and ever will be in the living movement of his eternal Being."[37] For Jungel, God's being is defined eschatologically as a becoming, a dynamic process in which the fullness of his being is expressed in his determination to fulfil his eternal purposes for humanity, the consummation of salvation.

Like Barth, Jungel's doctrine of the Spirit does not surface in his discussion of God's becoming, reflecting what Jenson regards as Barth's own "exemplary use of Western doctrine" which "displays what can only be called an 'I-Thou' trinitarianism."[38] Whilst acknowledging important trinitarian strands in Barth's doctrine of the Spirit, Tom Smail comments that "in his later theology there is a growing tendency to regard the Spirit as simply the way the risen Christ goes on acting in the church."[39] Other trinitarian theologians, including Jenson, interpret the dynamic relationship between the triune God and the world with a robust pneumatology, drawing their inspiration from Cappadocian theology. Before giving more detailed consideration to their contribution to contemporary trinitarian debate, it is worth noting Peters' criticism of what he interprets as Jungel's preoccupation with the internal relations within the Trinity that are independent of God's relations to the world:

> If Jungel is really serious when he says that the historical event of Jesus Christ means that 'God has defined himself as a human God', then why not make God's incarnate intercourse with the world part of that ongoing process of divine self-definition?[40]

John Webster's judgment that Peters' critique of Jungel is a "process-theological aversion to any notion of divine aseity"[41] highlights further the question of divine activity in the world, which Peters addresses in his discussion of the relationship between the temporal and the eternal Trinity.[42] However, the key to Peters' trinitarian theology is not the divine *limitation* of

---

[37] Torrance, Thomas F., *The Christian Doctrine of God: One Being Three Persons*, Edinburgh: T. & T. Clark, 1996: 242.
[38] See Jenson, Robert W., *Systematic Theology*, Vol I - *The Triune God*, New York: Oxford University Press, 1997: 153-159.
[39] Smail, Thomas A., *The Giving Gift: The Holy Spirit in Person*, London: Darton, Longman & Todd, 1988: 43.
[40] Peters, *God as Trinity*: 96.
[41] John Webster in "Translator's Introduction" in Jungel, *God's Being is in Becoming*: xii.
[42] Peters, *God as Trinity*: 146-187.

process thought but the divine *fulfilment* of eschatological convergence:

> the trail of salvation traversed by God implies that the divine life *ad intra* has been put at risk by the incarnation of the Son and the indwelling of the Holy Spirit so that it comes to incorporate the divine life *ad extra*. That which needs convergence, then, is temporal history and the otherness of the divine persons with the eschatological advent of the eternal perichoresis.[43]

This takes us beyond the ambiguity of correspondence to Rahner's axiom that the immanent and economic Trinity are in fact the same.

'Rahner's Rule'

Karl Rahner's theology was conceived, in part, as a major attempt to overcome the classical dualism between transcendence and immanence. Whilst Barth's starting point was the transcendence of God, Rahner's theological method employed the tools of philosophical anthropology in order to demonstrate that human beings are created with an in-built capacity for God. Rahner's starting point is that human beings are transcendental beings who, by virtue of their transcendence, are inevitably oriented towards the ineffable mystery of God. Writing of humanity's transcendental orientation towards mystery, he insists that "He who is essentially open to being cannot by his own capacities set limits to the possible object of a revelation."[44] Elsewhere, he writes that "In the fact that he experiences his finiteness radically, he reaches beyond this finiteness and experiences himself as a transcendent being, as spirit."[45]

It is precisely because this transcendent capacity is an experience of *grace* that Rahner sees no contradiction between the knowledge of God as that which is given *a priori* to human beings and knowledge that derives from God's self-revelation. These observations are significant, for mystery characterises his theology of the Trinity. For Rahner "the doctrine of the Trinity is not a subtle theological and speculative game" but represents "the simple statement which is at once so very incomprehensible and so very self-evident, namely, that God himself as the abiding and holy mystery, as the incomprehensible ground of man's transcendent existence is not only the God of infinite distance, but also

---

[43] *Ibid*: 178.
[44] Rahner, Karl, *Hearers of the Word*, translated by Michael Richards, New York: Herder & Herder, 1969: 112.
[45] Rahner, Karl, *Foundations of Christian Faith: An Introduction to the Idea of Christianity*, London: Darton, Longman & Todd, 1978: 32. For a discussion of Rahner's 'transcendental anthropological method' and his concept of revelation, see Worthing, Mark W., *Foundations and Functions of Theology as Universal Science: Theological Method and Apologetic Praxis in Wolfhart Pannenberg and Karl Rahner*, Frankfurt am Main: Peter Lang, 1996: 93-108.

wants to be the God of absolute closeness in a true self-communication."[46]

There are several strands in Rahner's theology that are relevant to our present discussion. Rahner insisted that in the economy of salvation history particular realities are not only appropriated to a certain divine person, but are 'proper' to him. His theology of the incarnation, as a prime example, demands that only the Son could have become incarnate; likewise, only the Spirit is able to sanctify. Writing of the 'sending' of the Logos, Rahner argues that "something takes place in the world itself, outside the immanent divine life, which is not simply the result of the efficient causality of the triune God working *as one nature* in the world."[47] This statement enables us to posit a clear correspondence between the economy of salvation and the immanent Trinity: for Rahner the Trinity is a mystery of *salvation*. We can have confidence that "the divine hypostasis we experience within history corresponds to the same hypostasis within the Godhead proper"[48]: what we know of God in his salvific acts in history reflect the reality of God's being-in-communion. Consistent with his desire to bridge the transcendent and the immanent, Rahner thus postulates an axiom (popularly known as 'Rahner's Rule') that has become a watershed in trinitarian theology: the immanent Trinity is the economic Trinity, and *vice versa*.

For Rahner, the doctrine of grace implies that God really gives *himself* to human beings: he really appears as he is in himself. This is God's self-communicated gift to creation through grace. This concept, when coupled with his doctrine of the transcendental openness of humanity, leads us to Rahner's integrated theology of divine communion and a participative anthropology[49] as formulated in his axiom. However, as in Barth, there is in Rahner's theology of the immanent Trinity a predisposition towards a static ontology, which does not sit well with the dynamic relationality implicit in the economy of salvation, causing Alan Torrance to raise the question as to "how seriously he is committed *in practice* to the two-way identification of the economic and immanent Trinities."[50] In particular, Torrance refers to Rahner's statement that "there is properly no mutual love between Father and Son, for this would presuppose two acts"[51], which suggests an abstract immanent Trinity very much at odds with the logic of the incarnation as dynamic event.

The problem here might lie with Rahner's interpretation of the word 'person', a concept which he recognises as both blurred and ambiguous: therefore "the statement that 'God is a person' can be asserted of God and is true of God only if, in asserting and understanding this statement, we open it to

---

[46] *Ibid*: 137.
[47] Rahner, Karl, *Theological Investigations, Vol IV*, translated by Kevin Smyth, London: Darton, Longman & Todd, 1966: 88, my italics.
[48] Peters, *God as Trinity*: 100.
[49] Torrance, Alan J., *Persons in Communion*: 265.
[50] *Ibid*: 276.
[51] Rahner, Karl, *The Trinity*, London: Burns & Oates, 1970: 106.

the ineffable darkness of the holy mystery."[52] Later in his *Foundations of Christian Faith*, he acknowledges the individualistic connotations of secular language about persons, asserting that "this is the very thing which is excluded by the dogmatic teaching on the single and unique essence of God."[53] Here we recognise Rahner's concern not to lose sight of classical and idealistic notions of God which focus on the primacy and perfection of the divine essence: "one single consciousness and one single freedom."[54]

Rahner's Barthian predisposition towards a classical ontology of the personhood of God should not, however, be interpreted in terms of detached aseity. His discussion of the incarnation makes this clear. God has become man: in some ineffable way there is change in God. "It will hardly be denied that here the traditional philosophy and theology of the schools begins to blink and stutter", Rahner wryly observes.[55] And so the *mystery* of the incarnation is invoked, in which "the change and transition takes place in the created reality which is assumed, *and not in the Logos*."[56] In this way, Rahner sustains the doctrine of the immutability of God, but only at the expense of making a questionable distinction between internal and external change.[57] For LaCugna, this is tantamount to positing two 'levels' to the Trinity, one *ad intra*, the other *ad extra*.[58] Alan Torrance is equally severe: alluding to Christopher Kaiser's comment about Augustine's "complete dissociation of [the] eternal intra-trinitarian relations from ordinary human relations"[59] he ascribes to Rahner the same Augustinian static concept of deity.

The Cappadocian Connection

The critical issue exposed in the above treatment of Barth and Rahner has been admirably expressed by Langdon Gilkey:

> the central problem for the doctrine of God is how to unite intelligibly the *absoluteness* of God as the unconditioned source of our total being with the dynamic *relatedness* and the *reciprocal activity* of God as the

---

[52] Rahner, *Foundations of Christian Faith*: 74.
[53] *Ibid*: 134-135.
[54] *Ibid*: 135.
[55] Rahner, *Theological Investigations, Vol IV*: 113.
[56] *Ibid*: 113, my italics.
[57] Peters, *God as Trinity*: 101.
[58] LaCugna, Catherine Mowry, *God For Us: The Trinity and Christian Life*, San Francisco: HarperCollins, 1991: 13.
[59] Torrance, Alan J., *Persons in Communion*: 28.

ground, guide, dialogical partner, and redeemer of our freedom.[60]

We turn therefore to a number of important theologians who have grappled with this dilemma and emerged with coherent trinitarian statements that give primacy to the Eastern (Cappadocian) emphasis on relatedness and reciprocity. The major contributors are Robert Jenson, Jürgen Moltmann, Wolfhart Pannenberg and Catherine LaCugna. The insights of Colin Gunton and Thomas Torrance will also be raised in the context of their contributions to the theology of creation and God's relationship with the natural world. This will set the scene for a more detailed examination of *perichoresis* as a dynamic relational concept within trinitarian thought.

The unique contribution of the Cappadocian Fathers to trinitarian theology in the second half of the fourth century lies in their determination to eliminate any notion of the Father, Son and Spirit as modalistic roles, an interpretation implicit in the Greek word *prosopon* with its theatrical associations. Rejecting the term *prosopon* to denote personhood, the Cappadocians revived the term *hypostasis*, stripped it of its earlier Athanasian associations with *ousia*, and attributed to it relational significance. In order to avoid the charge of tritheism, they made a clear distinction between substance in God (*ousia*) and the *hypostases* of the three persons: "each of the divine hypostases is the *ousia* or essence of Godhead determined by its appropriate particularizing characteristic"[61]; for Basil, bishop of Caesarea, for example, these identifying properties (*idiomata*) were paternity, sonship and sanctifying power. Other Cappadocian terms used to describe these properties were 'unbegottenness', 'begottenness' and 'spiration'. The important point here is that these particular identifying properties characterised not the substance or essence of God, but the *unique personhood* of Father, Son and Spirit.

It is clear that the properties identified by the Cappadocian Fathers are relational in their ontology, consistent with the relational properties implicit in the divine economy. The starting-point for Eastern trinitarian theology, therefore, was a redefined *hypostasis* with relational attributes, in contrast to the Western emphasis on the unity, or oneness, of God. However, the Cappadocians were clear in affirming the one nature of God, finding the ground of unity in the *person* of the Father, rather than in the indivisible nature of God. The result of the primacy of person over substance is to give not only ontological priority to the person, but also ontological freedom.

The Greek Orthodox theologian John Zizioulas elucidates this with reference to Neoplatonic thought, "which tended to give priority to the 'one' over the 'many'", identifying "the 'One' with God Himself, considering the multiplicity of beings, the 'many', to be emanations basically of a degrading

---

[60] Gilkey, Langdon, "God" in Hodgson, Peter C. and King, Robert H. (eds), *Christian Theology: An Introduction to Its Traditions and Tasks*, Philadelphia: Fortress Press, 1985: 108.

[61] Kelly, J. N. D., *Early Christian Doctrines*, London: Adam & Charles Black, 1965: 265.

nature, so that the return to the 'One' through the recollection of the soul was thought to be the purpose and aim of all existence."[62] The Cappadocian response gave ontological integrity to the 'many', which Zizioulas interprets as freedom not only for the three persons of the Trinity but also, via the concept of *imago Dei*, for human beings.[63]

> By distinguishing carefully and persistently between the nature of God and God as the Father [the Cappadocians] thought that *what causes God to be is the Person of the Father*, not the one divine substance. By so doing they gave to the person ontological priority, and thus freed existence from the logical necessity of substance, of the 'self-existent'.[64]

For the Cappadocian Fathers, therefore, the concept of person was not individualistic, but relational. God is actually God by virtue of the loving relationships that exist within the divine life: *it is the relations between the divine persons which constitute the unity of God*. Father, Son and Spirit are united in such perichoretic union that it is impossible to imagine any one person existing without the others. The being of each person of the Trinity lies in the fact that each exists for the other, which is the antithesis of individualism. Each person of the Trinity is thus free to relate to the other two, not by the necessity of the divine *nature* as exemplified in classical Greek thought, but out of self-giving love within the divine communion. "Generation (and spiration) are not necessary but free because although there is one will 'concurrent' (as St Cyril of Alexandria would say) with the divine substance, there is the 'willing one' (*ho thelon*) and that is the Father."[65] The priority of person over nature in Cappadocian trinitarian theology secures this revolutionary understanding of ontological freedom in God.

In his analysis of the *person* of the Spirit in trinitarian theology, Robert Jenson articulates the issue in the form of a question: "Is Pentecost a peer of Easter or does it merely display a meaning that Easter would in any case have?"[66] Thus he addresses what he calls "the pneumatological problem": "Do we truly think of the Spirit as person?" This is a critical question because, for Jenson, the Spirit is the key to his eschatological resolution of the immanent-economic debate within a Cappadocian framework. Throughout his writings, Jenson's depiction of the Spirit as the 'Power of the Future' or the 'Power of the Eschaton' is repeatedly sustained. Quoting Jesus' words in Matthew 12:28

---

[62] Zizioulas, John D., "The Doctrine of the Holy Trinity: The Significance of the Cappadocian Contribution" in Schwobel (ed), *Trinitarian Theology Today:* 52-53.

[63] This is developed most fully in Zizioulas, John D., *Being as Communion: Studies in Personhood and the Church*, London: Darton, Longman & Todd, 1985.

[64] Zizioulas, "The Doctrine of the Holy Trinity": 54-55.

[65] *Ibid*: 51.

[66] Jenson, *Systematic Theology, Vol I - The Triune God*: 146.

("But if I drive out demons by the Spirit of God, then the kingdom of God has come upon you") as indicative of the parity between the power of the Spirit and the immanence of the Kingdom, he defines the Spirit as "the Love into which all things will at the last be brought."[67] For Jenson, the Spirit's 'identity' (a term coined by Jenson to refer to the person of each of the three members of the Trinity[68]) is a *personal* one. He is more than a link between Father and Son, though Colin Gunton criticises Jenson for what he perceives to be an adherence to Augustinian binitarianism[69], a tendency which, admittedly, is not altogether absent in some of Jenson's writing.

Gunton's critique is related to his concern to maintain a clear distinction between immanence and otherness in trinitarian theology, so that freedom in God (and humans) is maintained. His interpretation of Jenson's pneumatology relates to what he discerns as a failure to attribute particularity and distinctness to the persons of the Godhead. Once that happens, then it is not too far a step towards the undifferentiated unity characteristic of Western trinitarianism. However, Jenson's debt to Cappadocian theology's emphasis on innertrinitarian relationality is explicit in his doctrine of the Trinity: he refers to Basil the Great, Gregory of Nyssa and Gregory of Nazianzus as powerful thinkers in "a brilliant new generation of bishops and teachers."[70] Approving the Eastern tradition in which 'God' denotes a lively complex of *energeia*, he brings the divine economy and immanence in close proximity by asserting that

> 'God' simply as such denotes the Father's sending and the Son's obedience, the Spirit's coming to the Son and the Son's thanksgiving therefore to the Father – and so on in a dialectic to which only failing insight or imagination sets limits.[71]

Jenson expounds Rahner's axiom by claiming that the temporality of salvation history is *intrinsic* to the life of Father, Son and Spirit. The biblical endorsement of the Cretan poet Epimenides' statement that "In him we live and move and have our being" (Acts 17:28) suggests that in some way God makes room for temporality in his eternity. Drawing from Gregory of Nyssa, Jenson argues that God is infinite "because time cannot exhaust or keep up with his activity"; so "Hellenic deity is eternal in that in it circling time has its motionless centre: Gregory's God is eternal in that he envelops time, is ahead

---

[67] *Ibid*: 157.

[68] See Jenson, *The Triune Identity*, 1982: 108-111, in which the author amusingly describes the language of *hypostasis* as "merely an item of linguistic debris knocked from Hellenic philosophy by collision with Yahweh."

[69] Gunton, Colin E., *The Promise of Trinitarian Theology*, Edinburgh, T. & T. Clark, 1991: 136-137.

[70] Jenson, *The Triune Identity*: 89.

[71] Jenson, "What is the Point of Trinitarian Theology?": 38.

of and so before it."⁷² Jenson's emphasis on the incorporation of time into eternity in God establishes the logic of his doctrine of the Spirit as both *personal* and *dynamic reality*: "The Spirit is the Liveliness of the divine life because he is the Power of the divine future."⁷³ What he does is to free the Spirit from narrow, static and impersonal conceptions and locate him at the very centre of a dynamic eschatologically-oriented Trinity, whose goal embraces all humanity. The promise of the gospel is God's faithfulness to his future, guaranteed by the Spirit of God who is the Power of his own and our future. Jenson agrees that the only theological reason why a distinction needs to be made between the economic and immanent Trinity is to preserve the freedom of both God and human beings. But, he says, "genuine freedom is the reality of possibility, is openness to the future; genuine freedom is Spirit"⁷⁴: acknowledging God's utter freedom as Spirit permits Jenson to collapse immanent and economic into each other eschatologically, such that the immanent Trinity is simply the eschatological reality of the economic.⁷⁵ At the *eschaton*, then, the economic Trinity will be fully realised in the immanent Trinity.

The concept of eschatology is an ambiguous one. In its original formulation it referred to the four *eschata*, or last things, in a chronological sense: death, judgment, heaven and hell. However, as Ingolf Dalferth, reminds us, these things are not just 'last': they are, by virtue of their ultimacy, the 'greatest'. So,

> eschatology is not simply an appendix to dogmatics which describes some future events that are in principle beyond our present life and knowledge. It discusses the fundamental normative orientation of our present life in terms of its final end and ultimate points of reference.⁷⁶

Thus it is more appropriate to define eschatology as that which expresses the *goal* of all creation, human and physical, rather than specific, identifiable *eschata*. The task of theology is therefore to elucidate "not a series of eschatological *topoi* but the one eschatological reality of the risen Christ." ⁷⁷

Jenson's approach is not without its critics. Wolfhart Pannenberg, for example, remarks that in his presentation the economic Trinity almost vanishes, arguing that there is

> a necessary distinction that maintains the priority of the eternal communion of the triune God over that communion's explication in the history of salvation. Without that distinction, the reality of the one

---

⁷² Jenson, *The Triune Identity*: 165.
⁷³ Jenson, *Systematic Theology, Vol I - The Triune God*: 157.
⁷⁴ *Ibid*: 141.
⁷⁵ *Ibid*: 141.
⁷⁶ Dalferth, Ingolf U., "The Eschatological Roots of the Doctrine of the Trinity" in Schwobel, (ed), *Trinitarian Theology Today:* 157.
⁷⁷ *Ibid*: 159.

God tends to be dissolved into the process of the world.[78]

Gunton has expressed the same concerns. However, these criticisms should not eclipse Jenson's major contribution to trinitarian theology, which lies in his dynamic interpretation of the Cappadocian emphasis on the relational character of the Trinity within a future-based concept of time. For Jenson, there is "a continuity over time that strains forward toward the future when Yahweh's identity will become fully revealed."[79] This narrative causality, or ordering, in God is mediated by the Spirit, who confronts Father and Son with novelty and surprise within the divine life. For Jenson, the Spirit connects past, present and future; he is "the future rushing upon us"; he is "the eschatological reality of God."[80]

The Trinity and the 'History of God'

The concept of futurity, or history, within the Trinity is one that has been further developed by Moltmann and Pannenberg, whom Grenz identifies as the two theologians who have been most influential in directing attention to the 'history of God': "They are convinced that the turn toward history facilitates what in their estimation is a necessary move away from the focus on the one divine subject that captivated the Trinitarian theology of Barth and Rahner."[81] Acknowledging that the primary role of the doctrine of the Trinity in the early church had more to do with the praise and vision of God than with the economy of salvation, Moltmann raises the question: "But does the doctrine of the Trinity in fact belong in the 'consideration of the divine majesty', quite separately from the revelation of God through Christ for us, in our history and in our flesh?"[82] In his book *The Crucified God*, Moltmann proceeds to refute such a disconnection, insisting that we cannot say of God "who he is of himself and in himself; we can only say who God is for us in the history of Christ which reaches us in our history."[83] In his trinitarian formulation, this history is encapsulated in the event of the cross, in which suffering is received into the triune life of God. But not only is suffering taken up into the life of God: history is too. For Moltmann the Trinity is an *open* Trinity, contradicting the immutability, impassibility and timelessness of classical theistic concepts of God. He critiques both Barth and Rahner, arguing that neither "does justice to

---

[78] Pannenberg, Wolfhart, "A Trinitarian Synthesis" in *First Things* 103 (May 2000): 49-53.
[79] Peters, *God as Trinity*: 129.
[80] Jenson, "What is the Point of Trinitarian Theology?": 41.
[81] Grenz, Stanley J., *The Social God and the Relational Self: A Trinitarian Theology of the Imago Dei*, Louisville: Westminster John Knox Press, 2001: 41.
[82] Moltmann, Jürgen, *The Crucified God: The Cross of Christ as the Foundation and Criticism of Christian Theology*, London: SCM Press, 1974: 237.
[83] *Ibid*: 238.

the history which is played out between Jesus the Son, 'Abba' his Father, and the Spirit."[84]

Moltmann's 'salvation-historical' approach to his doctrine of the Trinity is therefore a project that explores the collaboration between the three triune subjects in the history of the world, and it is ultimately eschatological in its orientation. Believers are, in the language of *theosis*, caught up into the inner life of God himself, and this is a process which takes place through history, culminating in the consummation of God's unconditional love which is full of hope: therefore, "the Trinity is no self-contained group in heaven, but an eschatological process open for men on earth, which stems from the cross of Christ."[85] In Moltmann's theology the source of trinitarian identity is the cross; indeed, the cross is the centre of *all* Christian theology. "The nucleus of everything that Christian theology says about 'God' is to be found in this Christ event."[86] To think otherwise is to "speculate in heavenly riddles"![87]

More specifically, Moltmann spells out a trinitarian interpretation of the cross within the framework of dynamic relationship. The cross is what transpires between Jesus and the Father in the realm of the Spirit: something of personal and cosmic significance happens between the triune persons which actually constitutes their unity as God. Moltmann's point of departure in his understanding of the Trinity is not the 'One God' of philosophical enquiry but the three persons of biblical history, made explicit in *Heilsgeschichte*.[88] At the cross, there is no death *of* God, but death takes place *in* God: Moltmann's language about the dying of the Son and the grief of the Father as a God-event in trinitarian terms is replete with the dynamic reality of abandonment, surrender and suffering. For example, the Son "suffers in his love being forsaken by the Father as he dies. The Father suffers in his love the grief of the death of the Son."[89]

Furthermore, Moltmann's trinitarian theology of the cross is given pneumatological shape - a *pneumatologia crucis* - in his discussion of the role of the Spirit as a 'companion in suffering' in the *kenosis* and dying of Jesus: "The path the Son takes in his passion is then at the same time the path taken by the Spirit, whose strength will be proved in Jesus' weakness."[90] Just as the suffering of the Father is different from the suffering of the Son, so too is the suffering of the Spirit a different form of suffering, for he is Jesus' strength in

---

[84] Moltmann, Jürgen, *History and the Triune God: Contributions to Trinitarian Theology*, London: SCM Press, 1991: 82.

[85] Moltmann, *The Crucified God*: 249.

[86] *Ibid*: 204.

[87] *Ibid*: 207.

[88] See Moltmann, Jürgen, *The Trinity and the Kingdom of God: The Doctrine of God*, London: SCM Press, 1981: 148-150.

[89] Moltmann, *The Crucified God*: 245; see pp. 235-249 for an exposition of Moltmann's trinitarian theology of the cross.

[90] Moltmann, Jürgen, *The Spirit of Life: A Universal Affirmation*, Minneapolis: Fortress Press, 1992: 62.

Gethsemane and at Golgotha. So Moltmann outlines his trinitarian *theologia crucis*, in which the three persons of the Trinity participate in the historic outworking of cross and resurrection in dynamic perichoretic interdependency.

This historic unfolding is given eschatological focus in Moltmann's 'twofold trinitarian order', in which the Spirit is vitally involved in the two historic movements of sending and gathering:

> In *the first order* the divine Trinity throws itself open in the sending of the Spirit. It is open for the world, open for time, open for the renewal and unification of the whole creation. In *the second order* the movement is reversed: in the transfiguration of the world through the Spirit all men turn to God and, moved by the Spirit, come to the Father through Christ the Son. In the glorification of the Spirit, world and time, people and things are gathered to the Father in order to become *his world*.[91]

For Moltmann, this is the 'eternal feast of heaven and earth', it is the 'dance of the redeemed', it is Dante's *riso dell'universo*.[92] This Spirit-mediated future is a feature of Moltmann's 'theology of hope'[93], in which he articulates the Spirit as 'the power of futurity'[94] acting in dynamic perichoretic power: "Just as the cross of the Son puts its impress on the inner life of the triune God, so the history of the Spirit moulds the inner life of the triune God through the joy of liberated creation when it is united with God."[95]

Moltmann's accent on the energetic perichoretic life within the Trinity is conspicuous in his theology of creation, in which he offers what he defines as a paradigm shift from a hierarchical to a relational theology of creation.[96] This shift towards dynamic perichoretic relationality as the fundamental hermeneutic of Moltmann's pneumatological doctrine of creation is made explicit in his movement away from the language of 'order of creation' to 'community of creation' in the "cosmic body and relationships of heaven and earth and the

---

[91] Moltmann, *The Trinity and the Kingdom of God*: 127, author's italics.
[92] *Ibid*: 128.
[93] See Moltmann, Jürgen, *Theology of Hope: On the Ground and the Implications of a Christian Eschatology*, Minneapolis: Fortress Press, 1993.
[94] See Shults, F. LeRon, "Sharing in the Divine Nature: Transformation, *Koinonia* and the Doctrine of God" in Speidell, Todd H. (ed), *On Being Christian ... and Human: Essays in Celebration of Ray S. Anderson*, Eugene OR: Wipf and Stock Publishers, 2002: 87-127.
[95] Moltmann, *The Trinity and the Kingdom of God*: 161.
[96] See Moltmann, *History and the Triune God*: 125-142, in which he critiques Barth's insistence upon superiority and subordination as normative for all the conditions in creation that correspond to God. For Moltmann, "the levels of relationship in *perichoresis* and mutuality within the Trinity, rather than the levels of constitution within the Trinity, are normative for the relationship of God to creation and all the corresponding relationships in creation" (p.132).

anthropological relationships of soul and man and woman."[97] Furthermore, and anticipating what we shall be discussing later on, he asks, "Why should not scientific descriptions also discover the complexes of life and thus also complexes of the Spirit?"[98] Moltmann's hint at a cosmic *perichoresis* is undeniable here.

In his desire to proclaim this narrative of the dynamic, shifting and essentially open relationships of fellowship and movement between Father, Son and Spirit, into which all humanity has been invited to participate, Moltmann has been criticised for emphasising the immanence of God at the expense of his transcendence. Where, for example, is the sense of *mystery*, implicit in the trinitarian theologies of Barth and Rahner? Moltmann's approach has laid him open to the charge of antimonotheism in his robust emphasis on mutual and dynamic relationality.[99] Though he acknowledges a distinction between the immanent and transcendent Trinity on doxological grounds[100] in order not to conflate the two, his critics are concerned that he gives too much ground to the notion of a social Trinity at the expense of divine unity. Whatever the final verdict, it is clear that Moltmann's major contribution to trinitarian theology is his exposition of a theology of 'openness'.[101] The result is that we should finally put to rest, in Peters' words, "some sort of second God, a trinitarian double, a ghostly immanence hovering behind while unaffected by the actual

---

[97] *Ibid*: 135-140.

[98] *Ibid*: 128.

[99] Interestingly, Pannenberg observes that Moltmann's polemic against monotheism in a number of his writings is addressed to the *abstract* monotheism typical of nineteenth-century thinking: Moltmann is thus, according to Pannenberg, guilty of a "wrong terminological decision", having "no wish to abandon the unity of God as such" (Pannenberg, Wolfhart, *Systematic Theology*, Vol. I, Grand Rapids: Eerdmans, 1991: 336, n.217).

[100] Moltmann maintains that the "assertions of the immanent Trinity about eternal life and the eternal relationships of the triune God in himself have their *Sitz im Leben*, their situation in life, in the praise and worship of the church." So, the "'economic Trinity' is the object of kerygmatic and practical theology; the 'immanent Trinity' is the object of doxological theology." (Moltmann, *The Trinity and the Kingdom of God*: 152).

[101] See, for example, Pinnock, Clark H. *et al*, *The Openness of God: A Biblical Challenge to the Traditional Understanding of God*, Downers Grove: IVP, 1994, for a review of the concept of 'openness theology': five authors propose an understanding of a God who desires 'responsive relationship' with his creatures, challenging Augustinian and Thomist notions of divine immutability, impassibility and foreknowledge. A more recent defence of 'openness theology' can be found in Pinnock, Clark H., *Most Moved Mover: A Theology of God's Openness*, Carlisle: Paternoster Press, 2001, where Pinnock reinforces the dynamic, interactive, risky give-and-take relationship between the trinitarian God and human creatures: "God's perfection is not to be all-controlling or to exist in majestic solitude or to be infinitely egocentric. On the contrary, God's fair beauty according to Scripture is his own relationality as a triune community. It is God's gracious interactivity, not his hyper-transcendence and/or immobility, which makes him glorious." (*ibid*: 5-6).

course of divine-historical events."[102]

Dalferth suggests that Moltmann's difficulties with the unity of God contributed to Wolfhart Pannenberg's search for another way forward. There are two ideas that are fundamental to Pannenberg's systematic theology, in which the doctrine of the Trinity is "an anticipatory sum of the whole content of Christian dogmatics."[103] These two central themes are 'reciprocal self-dedication' and 'the rule of God', which converge in his conclusion that "*God, through the creation of the world, made himself radically dependent on this creation and on its history.*"[104] Pannenberg draws from the Hegelian insight that the essence of a person is to renounce isolation and exist in self-dedication to another: so Hegel understood the Trinity as three divine persons united by virtue of their intense and lively reciprocal self-dedication. This, argues Pannenberg, is precisely the language implicit in the patristic doctrine of *perichoresis*, which he clarifies in his discussion of the doctrine of *unitas in trinitate*.[105] However, he does not eschew monotheism *per se*, which is where his appeal to the 'rule of God' is critical.

The key to Pannenberg's doctrine of God's rulership lies in the Son's obedience to the Father:

> lordship goes hand in hand with the deity of God. It has its place already in the intratrinitarian life of God, in the reciprocity of the relation between the Son, who freely subjects himself to the lordship of the Father, and the Father, who hands over his lordship to the Son.[106]

However, Pannenberg's argument goes further than a simple correspondence between God's rule *ad intra* and his rule *ad extra*. Having first established that the whole sending of Jesus, as Son of God, is for the glory of the Father and his lordship, and drawing from Athanasius' argument against the Arians that the Father would not be the Father without the Son, he poses the question as to whether in some way the Father's deity is in fact *dependent* upon the Son.[107] At no point does Pannenberg relinquish monotheism in his trinitarian thesis. On the contrary, he insists that Son and Spirit serve the monarchy of the Father, which is therefore "*not the presupposition but the result* of the common operation of the three persons. It is thus the seal of their unity."[108] As Grenz succinctly summarises, Pannenberg "understands the deity of each trinitarian

---

[102] Peters, *God as Trinity*: 110.
[103] Pannenberg, *Systematic Theology*, Vol. I: 335.
[104] Pannenberg, Wolfhart, "Problems of a Trinitarian Doctrine of God" in *Dialog*, Vol. 26 No. 4, 1987: 255, author's italics.
[105] Pannenberg, Wolfhart, *Jesus – God and Man*, London: SCM Press, 1968: 179-183.
[106] Pannenberg, *Systematic Theology*, Vol. I: 313.
[107] *Ibid*: 310-312.
[108] *Ibid*: 325, my italics.

person as a *received* divinity. Each receives divinity as a person-in-relationship with the other two."[109]

For Pannenberg, this 'received', or dependent, divinity is grounded in the economy of salvation: in other words, it is historically and not ontologically determined.

> At stake, then, in the creative work of the Father, as well as in the reconciliation imparted through the Son and in the work of the Spirit glorifying them both is the existence of God in the world, without which no existence of God before the foundation of the world could be affirmed either.[110]

Within this framework of the history of creation, Pannenberg's trinitarian construction assumes both pneumatological and eschatological importance. The Father has made himself dependent upon the course of history, in which the Son's obedience to death on the cross and the Spirit's work in consummating the kingdom reflect supremely the dependence of the trinitarian persons on one another in the history of the world.[111]

Peters suggests that the "picture one gets here is of a God who jeopardizes his own divinity in order to engage in historical intercourse with created reality."[112] But, for Pannenberg, this is precisely the exegesis of the phrase "God is love" for the reconciliation of the world. Love expressed in terms of trinitarian reciprocal self-dedication in the history of creation will find its eschatological completion through the activity of the Spirit in the world. So history determines God's divinity, such that the unity of God can only be finally established eschatologically, when the kingdom of God is fully realised.

Pannenberg's theology of the divine essence is thus historically-determined. He argues that we can no longer adopt "traditional ways of basing the trinity of persons on the unity of the Father or of the divine essence because they entail either subordinationism or Sabellianism."[113] God's unity cannot be derived

---

[109] Grenz, *The Social God and the Relational Self*: 49.

[110] Pannenberg, "Problems of a Trinitarian Doctrine of God": 255. Elsewhere, Pannenberg spells out "the contrast between the trinitarian concept of God and the idea of God as taught by philosophical monotheism in classical antiquity. The trinitarian concept describes the particular unity of the living God, while philosophical monotheism conceived of the dead or static unity of a supreme being as an existing entity indistinguishable within itself. The trinitarian idea of God is congruous with historical process, while the notion of a supreme entity speaks of a 'divine thing' outside man's history. The trinitarian doctrine describes the coming God as the God of love whose future has already arrived and who integrates the past and present world, accepting it to share in his own life forever." (Pannenberg, Wolfhart, *Theology and the Kingdom of God*, Philadelphia: The Westminster Press, 1969: 71).

[111] Pannenberg, *Systematic Theology*, Vol. I: 329.

[112] Peters, *God as Trinity*: 141.

[113] Pannenberg, *Systematic Theology*, Vol. I: 334.

"merely by considering the immanent Trinity before the foundation of the world and ignoring the economy of salvation."[114] The only resolution to this tension is to acknowledge that God's transcendent unity-in-divinity finds its fullest expression only when history has been finally and completely embraced within the divine life, that is when time has been assumed into eternity. At that time, God will show himself to be what he always has been. Only then will the existence of God be "conclusively decided"[115], because God has chosen from eternity to make himself dependent upon his creation for his identity. Peters explicates Pannenberg's rejection of traditional interpretations of the divine essence by observing that

> Son and Spirit share in the divine essence of the Father not just by being begotten or by proceeding from a divine origin, but also by contributing to the kingdom of the Father that is entrusted to the Son and returned to the Father through the Spirit.[116]

Dalferth argues that Pannenberg "does not succeed in offering a trinitarian solution to the problem of the unity of God which is more than an eschatological postponement."[117] In the light of the above, Dalferth's negative interpretation of Pannenberg's 'eschatological postponement' to the problem of God's unity appears to have some merit: the course of history actually 'hides' the reality of the divine unity. But Pannenberg's emphasis on the mutuality of relations within the economic Trinity does not lead him to surrender the notion of the transcendence of God. Rather, he gives it controversial expression in his pneumatology, in which he understands spirit as *field*, a concept drawn from nineteenth-century scientific field theory.[118] Pannenberg proposes that the divine essence can be likened to an 'incomprehensible field' of power, which also finds personal expression as the Holy Spirit within the Trinity. Whilst critics have questioned the appropriateness of such a metaphor in the light of God's personality, others have commended him for recovering the cosmic dimension of Spirit, offering us a more generous and universal perspective of God at work in creation, in which activity all humanity is offered

---

[114] *Ibid*: 327.
[115] Pannenberg, "Problems of a Trinitarian Doctrine of God": 255.
[116] Peters, *God as Trinity*: 142.
[117] Dalferth, "The Eschatological Roots of the Doctrine of the Trinity" in Schwobel, (ed), *Trinitarian Theology Today:* 157.
[118] The concept of field theory, which leads Pannenberg to reconceptualise God as an infinite field of power, and which enables him to make important connections between science and theology, will be examined in our discussion of *perichoresis* as a principle of cosmological unity. See Pannenberg, Wolfhart, *Systematic Theology*, Vol. II, Grand Rapids: Eerdmans, 1991: 79-102.

participation.[119] Pannenberg's conception of the transcendence of God, therefore, needs to be understood within a pneumatological frame of reference:

> As Spirit, God functions as the whole that provides meaning to the finite events of history. This meaning is profoundly future, for only at the end of history do we find the meaning of history and the connection of each event with that meaning.[120]

With Jenson and Moltmann, Pannenberg's vision of God is intimately related to the 'power of the future'. Whilst there are problems in reconciling his thesis of a future which defines and determines the present with a truly open view of the future,[121] the richness of Pannenberg's trinitarian theology lies in his insistence that the history of salvation is the concrete context on which God's identity actually depends, thus anchoring God's eternal constitution in the reciprocal self-dedicating love of Father, Son and Spirit. His debt to Cappadocian thinking is explicit in his recognition that "the differentiation of the trinitarian persons and the reciprocity of their relationships are foundational for the unity of the economic and immanent Trinity."[122]

However, most contemporary trinitarian theologians believe that the Cappadocians did not go far enough: they failed to develop an intimate connection between economic and immanent Trinity, initially posited by Rahner in his axiom, and subsequently explored most fruitfully by Moltmann, Jenson and Pannenberg. In fact, in the judgment of Catherine LaCugna,

> by accentuating the distinction between God's permanently unknowable divine essence, in contrast to what is knowable through God's self-manifestation in creation, the Cappadocians contributed to a further separation of economy and 'theology'.[123]

God for Us: The Trinity as Soteriology

LaCugna understands 'theology' as the 'mystery of God', expressed in classical theism in terms of the traditional metaphysical properties of immutability, omniscience, omnipotence and impassibility. In *God For Us*, she argues

---

[119] See, for example, Pinnock, Clark H., *Flame of Love: A Theology of the Holy Spirit*, Downers Grove: IVP, 1996: 49-77.

[120] Grenz, Stanley J. and Olson, Roger. E, *20th-Century Theology: God and the World in a Transitional Age*, Downers Grove: IVP, 1992: 194-195.

[121] For a discussion of the relationship between past, present and future within a trinitarian framework, see Pannenberg, Wolfhart, "Eternity, Time and the Trinitarian God", accessed on http://www.ctinquiry.org/publications/pannenberg.htm on 12.03.03.

[122] Pannenberg, "Problems of a Trinitarian Doctrine of God": 252.

[123] LaCugna, *God For Us*: 10; see also pp300-304, where LaCugna examines some of the classical attributes of God, arguing that they stand in need of reinterpretation.

passionately for a practical doctrine of the Trinity that eschews the refuge of metaphysical mystery, opting to ground it in God's life with us and our life with each other. In other words, she collapses the Trinity *ad intra* into the Trinity *ad extra*, giving priority in her proposal to soteriology. Using Rahner as her point of departure, LaCugna states her basic principle: "Theology is inseparable from soteriology, and *vice versa*."[124] God's mystery is the mystery of persons in communion, revealed in the economy of salvation:

> The possibility of a *deus absconditus* (hidden God) who lurks behind *deus revelatus* is banished once and for all. There is no God who might turn out to be different from the God of salvation history, even if God's mystery remains absolute.[125]

LaCugna's relocation of mystery away from classical ontological statements about God and into the realm of soteriology necessarily leads her to focus the doctrine of the Trinity on the communion between God and *ourselves*, rather than on the nature of the innertrinitarian life. She pursues the Cappadocian line of thought that the only way to interpret the concept of person is in terms of relationship. Preferring to set aside the metaphysical debate about the ontological constitution of the Trinity *ad intra*, Lacugna bases her thesis on the premise that "God's way of being in relationship *with us* – which is God's personhood – is a perfect expression of God's being as God ... God for us is who God is as God."[126]

LaCugna's debt to the insights of John Macmurray and John Zizioulas are evident in her discussion of persons in communion. The purpose of Macmurray's 1953-54 Gifford Lectures was not only to eradicate the philosophical notion of the solitariness of the 'thinking self' by emphasising the self as active agent in the world, but, perhaps more fundamentally, to "show how the personal relations of persons is constitutive of personal existence; that there can be no man until there are at least two men in communication."[127] In Macmurray's personalist philosophy the idea of an isolated self is self-contradictory: to argue otherwise is a self-deception from which we need deliverance. More specifically, he argues that the unity of the personal is found "in the community of the 'You and I', and since persons are agents, this community is not merely matter of fact, but also matter of intention."[128]

---

[124] *Ibid*: 211.

[125] *Ibid*: 211.

[126] *Ibid*: 305, author's italics.

[127] Macmurray, John, *Persons in Relation*, London: Faber, 1970: 12.

[128] *Ibid*: 27. LaCugna draws obvious parallels with the I-Thou philosophy of the Jewish scholar Martin Buber, for whom true personhood belongs to the realm of I-Thou in opposition to the subject-object duality of I-It: see Buber, Martin, *I and Thou*, New York: Charles Scribner's Sons, 1958. I-Thou "entails activity on both sides, in which both parties are free to either disclose themselves or withdraw. Characteristic of such a relationship is the involvement of the total person: at its highest level, *I-Thou* involves

Macmurray proposes three types of disposition which give rise to three modes of morality. The 'communal' mode is characteristically heterocentric, existing for the sake of friendship and grounded in love, whereas the 'contemplative' and 'pragmatic' modes are typically egocentric, existing for the sake of protection and based on fear.[129] Accordingly, Macmurray develops his philosophy of the person as a 'celebration of communion', which he succinctly identifies with religion.[130]

Introducing the idea of a universal personal Other, Macmurray acknowledges the idea of God as "a universal Person to whom all particular agents stand in an identical relation."[131] This emphasis on community and intentionality is central to LaCugna's trinitarian proposal, as she affirms the necessity for an ethical orientation to the Other (heterocentrism) as the basis for both human and divine action. She extrapolates from Macmurray's writings a definition of true personhood which emerges only within the context of community, and apart from which persons do not exist at all: "*A person is a heterocentric, inclusive, free, relational agent.*"[132] Though Macmurray was neither a theologian nor interested in the doctrine of the Trinity, his philosophical concept of the intentional action of a person-in-relation lies at the very heart of LaCugna's trinitarian theology. In order to develop her thesis further, LaCugna advances beyond the philosophical insights of Macmurray and draws from contemporary Orthodox theology, specifically the theology of personhood associated with John Zizioulas.[133]

The fourth-century Cappadocian theologians had earlier attributed relational significance to the term *hypostasis*; with Zizioulas, LaCugna combines this understanding with the notion of *ekstasis*, which refers to the process of going out from oneself in a continual move outward. These two ideas of *ekstasis* and

---

all of me and all of you, intellectually, emotionally, volitionally. Mutuality, liberty and totality are therefore the defining features of *I-Thou* knowledge." (Buxton, Graham, *Dancing in the Dark: The Privilege of Participating in the Ministry of Christ*, Carlisle: Paternoster, 2001: 63). Buber's philosophical treatise also affirmed the personhood of God as the one eternal, unalterable 'Thou'.

[129] Macmurray argues that "[F]or the contemplative mode, the *real* world is the spiritual world, and the *real* life is the spiritual life" (Macmurray, *Persons in Relation*: 123, author's italics), thus reducing a person to the role of spectator in the world. This interpretation corresponds with his insistence that self can only be properly understood as agent. The pragmatic mode is defined as a competitive mode of morality, in which the goal is "the appropriation of power: and the relation of agents becomes a competition for power" (*ibid*: 125).

[130] *Ibid*: 162.

[131] *Ibid*: 168-169.

[132] LaCugna, *God For Us*: 259.

[133] See, particularly, Zizioulas, *Being as Communion*. LaCugna appeals not only to philosophical and orthodox theological streams of thought, but also to feminist and liberation theologies, because of her concern that not every configuration of persons-in-relation images God: see LaCugna, *God For Us*: 266-270.

hypostasis integrate in a 'catholic' interpretation of personhood. 'Catholicity' as it relates to human personhood has to do with being intrinsically and constitutionally oriented towards another, whether spiritually, aesthetically, sexually, mystically or intellectually (so *ekstasis*), and, secondly, with being totally unique and unrepeatable yet also fully constitutive of what it means to be a human being (*hypostasis*).

> A person is thus not an individual but an open and ecstatic reality, referred to others for his or her existence. The actualization of personhood takes place in self-transcendence, the movement of freedom toward communion with other persons.[134]

For LaCugna, this interpretation of personhood correlates with God's own trinitarian being: favouring the term *perichoresis* as a model of all that it means to be ecstatic, relational, dynamic and vital, she is sympathetic to the metaphor of the 'divine dance' as an expression of the essence and unity of God, even if its philological warrant is scant.[135] Just as each human person uniquely exemplifies what it means to be ecstatically human, each divine person exemplifies what it means to be ecstatically divine. This is shown most completely in the economy of salvation, where the "God who *is* love (*Ipse Amore*) does not remain locked up in the 'splendid isolation' of self-love but spills over into what is other than God, giving birth to creation and history."[136] So God's life is 'distributed' in ecstatic love within a comprehensive plan reaching from creation through to eschatological consummation, one dynamic movement of God, *a Patre ad Patrem*. LaCugna represents this movement graphically in the form of a parabola, a 'chiastic model of emanation and return' that expresses the economy of salvation as *the sum total of Christian theology*.[137] Thus LaCugna disposes of the need for a static, ahistorical and transeconomic immanent Trinity: "there is only the *oikonomia* [Lacugna's term for the economy of salvation] that is the concrete realization of the mystery of *theologia* [God *in se*] in time, space, history, and personality."[138]

LaCugna's revision of the basic trinitarian framework precludes the need for two levels in the Trinity, one *ad intra* and the other *ad extra*. The doctrine of the Trinity is essentially the grammar of God's *being with us*, not God isolated from his creation. So history is internal to the divine life: our life *is* trinitarian life, and *vice versa*. God has graciously included us in his 'divine dance' of life, and to contemplate whether or not God would be trinitarian *apart* from the economy of salvation is pure speculation: revelation does not offer us that option. For LaCugna, the doctrine of the Trinity is supremely a practical, not a speculative, doctrine: to participate in the life of God through *theosis* is the

---

[134] LaCugna, *God For Us*: 260.
[135] *Ibid*: 270-278.
[136] *Ibid*: 353, author's italics.
[137] *Ibid*: 221-224.
[138] *Ibid*: 223.

ultimate outworking of Jesus' words in John 17:20-21, realised through the activity of the Holy Spirit, whom LaCugna identifies as the animating power of the economy, the personal principle of union and communion.[139]

Recognising the social implications of trinitarian theology, LaCugna argues that a theology of the Trinity which allows room for *any* form of metaphysical statement about the divine life *ad intra* – even a metaphysics of equality – runs the danger of promoting a political and social order which sanctions potentially oppressive hierarchies. She points out that the original insight of the Cappadocians of a *trinitarian* interpretation of the monarchy of God (*triadike arche* instead of *mone arche*) very soon gave way to the idea that, though the monarchy *within* God might be a shared one, *externally* God appears to us as one.[140] This 'theological defeat of the doctrine of the Trinity' opened the doors to a confusion between God's benevolent Fatherhood and all kinds of dominating hierarchies, religious, moral, political and sexual. This concern leads Moltmann, for example, to affirm the concept of *perichoresis* as the grammar of a kingdom without a monarch, the kingdom of God:

> It is only when the doctrine of the Trinity vanquishes the monotheistic notion of the great universal monarch in heaven, and his divine patriarchs in the world, that earthly rulers, dictators and tyrants cease to find any justifying religious archetypes any more.[141]

LaCugna, however, goes further, arguing that "*any theological justification for a hierarchy among persons also vitiates the truth of our salvation through Christ.*"[142] Her vision of trinitarianism repudiates every conceivable form of subordination among persons: to allow for subordinationism within the life of the Trinity undermines the very basis of the mutuality and ecstasy implicit in the economy of salvation. For LaCugna, the replacement of trinitarian monotheism by a hierarchical theism may be averted by collapsing the immanent Trinity into the economic Trinity, so avoiding the very dangers of injustice and oppression experienced throughout history. However, as Grenz observes, her critics fear that "by submerging *theologia* in *oikonomia*, she may in fact have lost the freedom of the divine grace, the concern for which motivated theologians such as Barth to retain the language of the immanent in distinction from the economic."[143]

---

[139] *Ibid*: 296-300.

[140] *Ibid*: 390-400.

[141] Moltmann, *The Trinity and the Kingdom of God*: 197. Another theologian who has explored the relationship between the notion of divine monarchy and the reality of oppression in human society is Leonardo Boff, who also adopts the idea of *perichoresis* as the necessary contour of innertrinitarian life: see Boff, Leonardo, *Trinity and Society*, Maryknoll NY: Orbis, 1988.

[142] LaCugna, *God For Us*: 400, author's italics.

[143] Grenz, *The Social God and the Relational Self*: 57. For a thorough critique of LaCugna's position, see the excursus in Weinandy, Thomas G., *The Father's Spirit of*

The Trinity and Creation

This central problem in trinitarian theology of the immanent-transcendent tension, expressed by Gilkey in terms of the connection between the absoluteness and the reciprocal activity of God,[144] is evident in the writings of the theologians cited above. Not only have they wrestled with the problem of 'one being, three persons', but they have sought to articulate an understanding of the relationship between the Trinity *ad intra* and the Trinity *ad extra*. This necessarily draws the dimensions of time and space into trinitarian theology, specifically God's relationship with his creation, in which history and eschatology play a central role. The development of trinitarian thinking has therefore taken us beyond what Gunton describes as the Augustinian position, which is preoccupied with the unity of the divine essence and intradivine relations, and which, therefore, "by losing the mediatorship of the Word, at once distances God from the creation and flattens out the distinctions between the persons of the Trinity",[145] into a strongly *relational* and *dynamic* interpretation, embracing not only the internal life of God, but also, critically, the relationship between God and the church, human society and all creation.

The first two concerns – the church and human society – remind us that the doctrine of the Trinity is not to be regarded as an abstract or speculative dogma to be believed, but, as LaCugna insists, *living trinitarian faith*. It has to do not with theory, but practice, the practice of life as God has it for us. Trinitarian theology is therefore doxological, because "right relationship in every sphere, according to that which God has ordained, everything that brings human persons closer to the communion for which we were made, glorifies God."[146]

Sonship: Reconceiving the Trinity, Edinburgh: T. & T. Clark, 1995: 123-136. Weinandy castigates LaCugna for her reductionist presentation of the Trinity, insisting that by collapsing the immanent into the economic Trinity we are left without a God 'in his wholly otherness'. In order for there to be a 'God-for-us' there needs to be '*a*' God, ontologically distinct from all else that exists. Commenting on her emphasis on relationality in the Trinity, Weinandy argues that "while LaCugna maintains the dynamism and even beauty of relational language, the notion of personhood, at least the personhood and subjectivity of the Father, Son and Holy Spirit, is abandoned. They are not divine subjects and therefore all that LaCugna says about our unity and communion with 'them' is vacuous." (*Ibid*: 133) Essentially, Weinandy is driven by an ontological integrity which demands that we retain a gulf between the God who is in himself and the God who is for us. See also Cunningham, David S., *These Three Are One: The Practice of Trinitarian Theology*, Oxford: Blackwell, 1998: 37-39.

[144] Gilkey, "God" in *Christian Theology:* 108.

[145] Gunton, Colin, "Augustine, the Trinity and the Theological Crisis of the West" in *The Scottish Journal of Theology* 43 (1990): 38.

[146] LaCugna, *God For Us*: 343. For an excellent trinitarian exposition of worship as the gift of participating through the Spirit in the incarnate Son's communion with the Father, linking the doctrine of the Trinity to the pastoral concerns of community life, see

Hence, the doctrine of the Trinity pertains to all of life, ecclesial, sacramental, sexual, ethical and spiritual – it is *the* theological criterion for both orthodoxy and orthopraxis.

God's relationship with the natural world is likewise the province of trinitarian theology, as Colin Gunton and Thomas Torrance, amongst others, have consistently argued. As the creation of the love of God "the world is not impersonal process, a machine or a self-developing organism – a cosmic collective into which the particular simply disappears – but that which itself has a destiny along with the human."[147] Gunton identifies three trinitarian concepts of which echoes are to be found in recent scientific thought – freedom, relation and divine energies.[148] As we have seen above, these concepts are fundamental to the dynamic relationality implicit in contemporary thinking about the Trinity. Dynamic loving relationships constitute the inner being of God: "God's being is a being in relation, without remainder relational."[149] Because these relations are relations of *love* they are not necessary in themselves and are therefore free. Freedom, or non-necessity, characterises not only the inner life of the Trinity, but also the created world because it is the product of the free creating act of God. For Gunton, this has to do with the action of the Spirit "who is the giver of freedom and the one who enables the created order to be itself: to become what it was created to be."[150] We see here the outline of a trinitarian theology grounded in a correspondence between relational freedom *ad extra* and *ad intra*. God freely relates to his world through what Irenaeus called his 'two hands', Son and Spirit: in other words, the God who is free and relational *in se* acts immanently in creative and redeeming love, investing the created order with the same relational freedom: so the world as a contingent creation "exists in its own way, but is nonetheless dependent for its existence on the activity of the creator."[151]

Gunton also postulates correspondence with respect to divine energies, which refer to God's activities in and towards his creation. The Orthodox theologian, Vladimir Lossky, states that these energies "signify an exterior manifestation of the Trinity which cannot be interiorized, introduced, as it were, within the divine being, as its natural determination."[152] Gunton views

---

Torrance, James B., *Worship, Community and the Triune God of Grace*, Downers Grove: IVP, 1996.

[147] Gunton, *The Promise of Trinitarian Theology*: 13.

[148] Gunton, Colin E., "Relation and Relativity: The Trinity and the Created World" in Schwobel (ed), *Trinitarian Theology Today*: 92-112. For a more complete study, see Gunton, Colin E., *The Triune Creator: A Historical and Systematic Study*, Grand Rapids: Eerdmans, 1998.

[149] Gunton, "Relation and Relativity: 92-112. For a more complete study, see Gunton, *The Triune Creator*: 1998.

[150] Gunton, *The Triune Creator*: 86.

[151] Gunton, "Relation and Relativity": 103.

[152] Lossky, Vladimir, *The Mystical Theology of the Eastern Church*, London: James Clarke: 1957: 80. Lossky understands the energies of God as a strictly *concrete* reality

Lossky's distinction between God's essence and his energies as problematic, rendering the being of God as static and "essentially unknowable in an epistemologically destructive sense."[153] Following Gunton, the whole sweep of salvation history from creation to redemption may therefore be understood in terms of *dynamic relational freedom* consistent with the inner dynamic of God's being, exemplified in LaCugna's chiastic model of emanation and return.

Gunton articulates the historical progression from classical models of a static universe derived from the Aristotelian conception of an 'unmoved mover' to contemporary scientific accounts of creation which are predicated on the active role of the Spirit at work in an evolving, indeterminate and 'open' universe.[154] Here we are reminded of the pneumatological contributions of Jenson, Moltmann and Pannenberg, whose vision of the Spirit as the eschatological power of God at work within creation is, as discussed above, central to their trinitarian theology. Ultimately, for Gunton, the Spirit

> is a way of speaking of the personal agency of God towards and in the world; anthropologically a way of speaking of human responsiveness to God and to others; cosmologically a way of speaking of human openness to the world and the world's openness to human knowledge, action and art.[155]

Whilst dynamic relationality is an appropriate term to apply to the operations of the natural world, the concept of freedom is problematic, as Gunton acknowledges. Divine and human life is *personal* and intrinsically free, but the natural world, though given existence by its creator as the *theatrum gloriae Dei* (to use Calvin's phrase), is not. Gunton therefore transmutes the concept of freedom into one of contingence when moving from the personal to the non-personal sphere. As a contingent creation, the universe is an open, incomplete system, exhibiting a freedom that is limited by virtue of its dependence upon the free grace of God as creator. It is contingent in the sense that "it is not self-sufficient or ultimately self-explaining but is given a

---

of the religious order, appropriate to creatures but not, in themselves, expressions of God in his essence (for a full discussion of his theology of 'uncreated energies', see *ibid*: 67-90).

[153] Gunton, "Relation and Relativity": 100. Eastern theologians, in contradistinction to their Western counterparts, prefer to understand energies as *subsequent* to essence, *external* to the nature of the Trinity (see Lossky, *The Mystical Theology of the Eastern Church*: 81).

[154] Gunton, "Relation and Relativity": 100-109. For a fuller discussion of the role of Spirit as the agent of relation in otherness, such that the other is established - and not subverted - in its true reality, see, Gunton, Colin E., *The One, the Three and the Many: God, Creation and the Culture of Modernity*, Cambridge: Cambridge UP, 1993: 180-209.

[155] *Ibid*: 187.

rationality and reliability in its orderliness which depend on and reflect God's own eternal rationality and reliability."[156] Thomas Torrance expresses the contingent nature of God's creation in terms of correspondence, an *analogia relationis* in which the elusiveness and unpredictability of the natural world is "marvelously coordinated with the transcendent rationality and infinite freedom of its Triune Creator."[157]

The distinction between God and his creation is underscored by Torrance in his understanding of the unlimited freedom that characterises the being of the triune God, and the limited yet authentic freedom given to the whole universe. He cites approvingly the distinction made by Athanasius between the ontological dimension in God as *Father* and the cosmological dimension in God as *Creator*, arguing that God is always Father, but he is not always Creator: accordingly, "the creation of the world out of nothing is something *new even for God*. God was always Father, but he *became* Creator."[158] The new, decisive acts of God in creation, incarnation and Pentecost are indicative of the absolute and unlimited freedom of God to be other than he always has been. In ecstatic and generous love, God is neither the 'unmoved mover' of classical Aristotelian theology, nor the 'moved unmover'[159] of process theology, but the *Self-moved God* who is ever open to his creation. His immutability is expressed in terms of his freedom to love, not by virtue of the static, abstract attributes implicit in classical theism. For Torrance, God is immutable because of his constancy as the ever self-living and ever self-moving Being. In ecstatic love he graces his creation with a reality and freedom of its own, authentic yet contingent upon God's own unlimited freedom.

That authenticity is guaranteed by the activity of the Holy Spirit whereby creation is "creatively upheld and sustained in its existence beyond its own power in an *open-ended relation* toward God in whom its true end and purpose as creature are lodged."[160] The Spirit is therefore the eschatological 'perfecting' Spirit who holds the whole created order – animate and inanimate, human and non-human, personal and non-personal – in the freedom of divine love. Indeed, he is not only sustainer, but also, in a dynamic sense, the energising agent in what Gunton calls the 'forward movement of the cosmos': he is "the divine energy releasing the energies of the world, enabling the world to realize its dynamic relatedness."[161]

At times Torrance and Gunton employ the language of *perichoresis* as a helpful concept in their discussion of the dynamic interrelatedness of the

---

[156] Torrance, Thomas F., *Divine and Contingent Order*, Oxford: Oxford University Press, 1981: viiff.

[157] Torrance, *The Christian Doctrine of God*: 222.

[158] *Ibid*: 208, author's italics.

[159] The term 'Moved Unmover' is an expression that Torrance attributes to Colin Gunton (*ibid*: 239, fn. 16).

[160] *Ibid*: 217, author's italics.

[161] Gunton, "Relation and Relativity": 108.

cosmos. In his elaboration of the doctrine of God as Sovereign Creator,[162] Torrance pursues the idea of the 'dynamic three-way reciprocity' between Father, Son and Spirit in what he calls "the perichoretic coactivity of the Holy Trinity."[163] Gunton suggests that the character of the universe may be expressed as a "*perichoresis* of interrelated systems."[164] These intimations of a cosmic *perichoresis* will be explored more fully in Chapter 5. Here we note that it is precisely because God embraces creation's "frail contingent reality within the everlasting power of his divine presence"[165] that we should expect trinitarian theology to offer a cogent *analogia relationis* between the creator and his creation. God's own ecstatic perichoretic life finds expression in the creation that he has brought into being, the creation that he unchangeably and unconditionally loves and blesses. Creation is open precisely because God himself is open; it is free – in the contingent sense – precisely because God is free; alive and surprising because God is inexhaustibly living and creative in his inner being. The dynamic perichoretic freedom of the triune God overlaps and intersects with the contingent freedom of the cosmos in such a way as to "give rise to refined and subtle patterns of order in the on-going spatio-temporal universe which we cannot anticipate but which constantly takes us by surprise."[166]

The notion of a cosmic *perichoresis* implicit in the writings of recent trinitarian theologians, and articulated more precisely in Colin Gunton's 1992 Bampton Lectures[167], represents the culmination of more than half a century of trinitarian reflection and debate since Karl Barth re-opened the door in his biblically-based presentation of the doctrine of the Trinity. As indicated earlier, Barth's understanding of *perichoresis* was conspicuously static and therefore limited in its contribution to a full appreciation of God's relational involvement with his creation. No doubt this was in large part due to his rather abstract 'revelation model' of the Trinity which allowed little room for the dynamically interactive interpretations favoured by later theologians. Having already introduced the concept of *perichoresis* at various points in this chapter, it would be helpful at this stage to trace the origins, development and interpretations of the concept since it was first introduced in the literature of the early church Fathers.

---

[162] Torrance, *The Christian Doctrine of God*: 203-234.
[163] *Ibid*: 198.
[164] Gunton, "Relation and Relativity": 106.
[165] Torrance, *The Christian Doctrine of God*: 218.
[166] *Ibid*: 222.
[167] Published under the title *The One, the Three and the Many*: see especially pp. 155-179, in which Gunton proposes a theology of relatedness, presenting the concept of *perichoresis* as a helpful way to map the eternal dynamic of deity.

The Doctrine of *Perichoresis*

The term *perichoresis*, though implicit in the theological formulations of the Cappadocian Fathers, who needed to defend themselves against charges of tritheism, was neither specifically identified nor clarified theologically as a trinitarian concept until a few centuries later, when tritheism became a major problem in the life of the church. Prestige cautions us against minimising the dependence of the Cappadocians on the insights of Athanasius, whose understanding of the co-inherence of the three persons led him to remark that

> the Son is omnipresent, because he is in the Father, and the Father is in Him; the case is different with creatures, which are only to be found in separate determinate localities; but the Spirit who fills all things clearly is exempt from such limitation, and must therefore be God, and is in the Son as the Son is in the Father.[168]

Athanasius' reference to 'creatures' is important: arguing that *perichoresis* refers to the reciprocal *interiority* of the divine persons, Miroslav Volf rightly observes that, in a strict sense, "there can be no correspondence to the interiority of the divine persons at a human level. Another human self cannot be internal to my own self as subject of action. Human persons are always external to one another as *subjects*."[169] So the indwelling of other persons is an exclusive prerogative of God. However, we might maintain, with Volf, that *perichoresis* is constructive at the ecclesial level with respect to the *interiority of personal characteristics*.[170]

Athanasius' primary concern, however, was not so much trinitarian as christological in his opposition to the Arian insistence that Christ was a created being, thus denying the co-inherence of two natures, divine and human. Beyond this early christological appropriation of the word, the richness of the term *perichoresis* may be appreciated when we consider that, throughout the history of Christian thought, it "provides a way of attempting to express how unity and distinction are combined in the Trinity, in the incarnate Logos and in creation as reunited with God."[171] In the fourth century Gregory of Nazianzus employed the Greek verb *perichoreo* to refer to the process whereby life and death, though they appear to differ greatly from one another, "yet 'reciprocate' and resolve themselves into one another."[172] In his first letter to Cledonius the

---

[168] Quoted in Prestige, *God in Patristic Thought*: 284, referring to *Epist. 4 ad Serap. episc. Thmuitanum* (356-362 A.D.).

[169] See Volf, Miroslav, *After Our Likeness: The Church as the Image of the Trinity*, Grand Rapids: Eerdmans, 1998: 208-213.

[170] The idea of *perichoresis* in the context of human sociality – i.e. as an *anthropological* metaphor – is developed further later in this section, and more fully in Chapter 4.

[171] Harrison, Verna, "Perichoresis in the Greek Fathers" in *St Vladimir's Theological Quarterly*, Vol. 35, No. 1, 1991: 53-65.

[172] Prestige, *God in Patristic Thought*: 291.

Presbyter, Gregory gives christological significance to the verb. Referring to the two natures of Christ, he writes: "Just as the natures are blended so too are the titles which mutually transfer by the principle of their natural togetherness."[173] Whether Gregory was referring to the static notion of 'coinherence', or mutual indwelling, or the more dynamic process of interpenetration, is open to question.[174]

The noun *perichoresis* was not technically in circulation until much later. Maximus Confessor, the seventh-century Greek theologian and monk from Constantinople, drew from Gregory's christological use of *perichoreo* and ascribed to it dynamic rather than static significance, so that "it was used to portray the reciprocity and exchange of the divine and human *actions* in the one person of Christ."[175] Thunberg argues that Maximus was the first Christian writer to give to the term *perichoresis* a central position within orthodox Christology,[176] and it is of more than passing interest that Maximus attributed anthropological and cosmological significance to the concept, to the extent that the idea of coinherence was, for him, a characteristic of every level of reality – human, divine and cosmic. The idea of *theosis*, or participation in the divine, is implicit in Maximus' theology, embracing a soteriological interpenetration of the believer with the object of belief. At the cosmological level, Maximus proposed the idea that perichoretic coinherence was built into the structure of the created natural world, a proposition which has gained currency in the dynamic relationality of such contemporary trinitarian theologians as Pannenberg, Moltmann, Torrance and Gunton.

---

[173] St. Gregory of Nazianzus, "Epistle 101 – The First Letter to Cledonius the Presbyter" in *On God and Christ*, Crestwood NY: St. Vladimir's Seminary Press, 2002: 158.

[174] For a discussion of Prestige's preference for *perichoreo* to mean 'to reciprocate' or 'to interchange' rather than 'to interpenetrate', see *ibid*: 53-57. Harrison prefers to ascribe a more dynamic and energetic understanding of *perichoreo* to Gregory, anticipating the exchange of names, titles, activities and attributes (*communicatio idiomatum*) in the later vocabulary of Maximus Confessor and John of Damascus. On the word 'coinherence', Gunton notes its Latin origin, which is static in meaning rather than dynamic, preferring the Greek term *perichoresis* as the more satisfactory of the two terms. In his discussion of the static and dynamic nuances in the term *perichoresis*, Baxter Kruger maintains that both are "eternally true in God. The 'static' perichoretic mutual indwelling of the Father, Son and Spirit is the ontological reality of God, and it is an ontological reality which eternally and dynamically expresses itself in an unspeakable fellowship of love. Both the fact of perichoresis and its living expression in the love of the Father, Son and Spirit are eternally true in the being of God." (Kruger, C. Baxter, *Recovering the Trinity and Perichoresis and Their Significance for the 3rd Christian Millennium*, Adelaide; unpublished Perichoresis Lectures 2002: 63).

[175] Fiddes, Paul S., *Participating in God: A Pastoral Doctrine of the Trinity*, London: Darton, Longman & Todd, 2000: 73, author's italics.

[176] Thunberg, Lars, *Microcosm and Mediator: The Theological Anthropology of Maximus the Confessor*, Chicago and La Salle ILL: Open Court Publishing, 1995: 26.

Trinitarian – as distinct from christological – application of the *perichoresis* concept has its origin in Pseudo-Cyril in the sixth century, though it was developed more thoroughly and consistently by John of Damascus in *De fide orthodoxa*. Translation from the Greek into Latin generated two meanings, static and active. *Circuminsessio* derived from the Latin *circum-in-sedere*, meaning to sit around, and was therefore appropriated by those who preferred to adopt a more passive interpretation of trinitarian relatedness, such as Thomas Aquinas. Others opted for the Latin *circumincessio*, derived from *circum-incedere*, which means to move around, a state of doing rather than a state of being.

A number of analogies have been suggested to convey the mutuality and interdependence implicit in the notion of *perichoresis*, such as the light of lamps which permeate one another in undifferentiated light, perfume sprayed into the air, or the three dimensionality of physical objects. However, as LaCugna points out, these analogies "do not convey the dynamic and creative energy, the eternal and perpetual movement, the mutual and reciprocal permeation of each person with and in and through and by the other persons."[177] They are also impersonal, which is why she supports the image of the 'divine dance' as an effective metaphor and, moreover, an intriguing and suggestive play on words: the Greek *perichoreuo*, meaning to 'dance around' (derived from the word *choreia*, or 'dance'), closely resembles *perichoreo*, which means to 'encircle' or 'encompass'.

For Fiddes, the image of the divine dance is "not so much about dancers as about the patterns of the dance itself, an interweaving of ecstatic movements."[178] This reflects his conviction that it makes "perfectly good grammatical sense to speak of a perichoresis of *movements*, though the theological tradition has referred to a perichoresis of divine subjects."[179] However, Fiddes' emphasis on relations, and the dynamic activity which underlies the diversity of divine actions, could be interpreted as a diminution of distinct hypostatic identity, a danger of which he is aware. The possibility of collapsing persons into relations parallels Gunton's concern – at the levels of human, cosmic and divine reality – to reinforce the particularity of the one against the plurality of the many.[180] For Gunton, ontology and relation are not opposites, but complementary: they stand or fall together. People and things, like God, have substantiality, particularity and distinctiveness "*by virtue of and*

---

[177] LaCugna, *God For Us*: 271.
[178] Fiddes, *Participating in God*: 72.
[179] *Ibid*: 73.
[180] Gunton, *The One, the Three and the Many*, especially Chapters 2 and 7, in which the author laments the homogeneity characteristic of Western culture, representing what Václav Havel describes as 'a mirror image' of the repressive ideologies of communist East Europe. Gunton's book is an attempt to reinstate the necessity for distinctiveness and particularity in society, without degenerating into individualism; he claims that "almost everywhere there operates a strong Platonist drive to turn particularities into abstractions, variety into homogeneity." (*Ibid*: 44).

not in face of their relationality to the other."[181] *Perichoresis* is therefore the foe and not the agent of homogeneity. Because uniqueness is as much the object of God's loving concern as oneness, the Spirit – whose distinctive mode of action, for Gunton, is perhaps the constitution of particularity even as the Son is the one in whom all things hold together – gives shape to all that exists, directing each person and thing until it reaches ultimate eschatological perfection.

In their discussion of the inner life of the Trinity, both Volf and Thomas Torrance share Gunton's disquiet with regard to any implied separation between ontology and relation.[182] Volf's specific concern is ecclesial: to emphasise relations at the expense of persons not only runs the risk of persons being absorbed into one undifferentiated 'substance', but jeopardises the notion of 'personal rights', which may result in sanctioning the abuse of power within a hierarchical structure of relationships. In his preference for the more 'participatory' language of relations rather than the 'observational' language of persons, Fiddes gets round this problem by transmuting Pannenberg's three 'living realizations of separate centres of action' into "three living realisations of movements or directions of action", arguing that these can equally be conceived as distinguishing themselves from each other. In this way, Fiddes maintains hypostatic distinctiveness, which is essentially a particularity of *action* by which the divine persons are reckoned distinct from each other.[183] This perspective is consistent with his view that God is 'an event of relationships', a 'perichoresis of *movements*', into which human beings are drawn as active participants, and not just observers.

In the revised text of a sermon preached in Great St Mary's, Cambridge, in 1985, Bishop Kallistos Ware refers to the perichoretic coinherence of Father, Son and Holy Spirit as "an unceasing movement of mutual love – the 'round dance' of the Trinity."[184] The feminist theologian Patricia Wilson-Kastner adopts the 'round dance' metaphor, but, as LaCugna has shown, her re-interpretation of *perichoresis* as *perichoreusis*, though commendable, is methodologically suspect: she places her model of the triune God within the intradivine life rather than locating it in the economy of salvation. Only the latter context, for LaCugna, is adequate to convey the dynamic choreography of the divine dance, in which human beings are drawn in as beloved partners

---

[181] *Ibid*: 194, author's italics.

[182] See Torrance, *The Christian Doctrine of God*: 194ff., where the author understands the concept of *perichoresis* "as essentially active in its basic significance without any split in its wholeness between ontological and dynamic aspects"; and Volf: "The constitution of the persons and their relations are, of course, not to be conceived as two temporally sequential steps, but rather as two dimensions of the eternal life of the triune God" (Volf, *After Our Likeness*: 216-217).

[183] Fiddes, *Participating in God*: 81ff.

[184] +Kallistos of Diokleia, "The human person as an icon of the Trinity" in *Sobornost*, Vol.8 No.2, 1986: 6-23.

(John 17:20-21).[185]

Moltmann, too, embraces the language of dancing in his understanding of perichoretic life. One evening he was reading a passage from Augustine's *Confessions* which led him to respond with an eagerness to participate in what he calls an 'unconditional Yes to life':

> When I love God I love the beauty of bodies, the rhythm of movements, the shining of eyes, the feelings, the scents, the sounds of all this protean creation. When I love you, my God, I want to embrace it all for I love you with all my senses in the creations of your love.[186]

The circulatory character of dance – expressed as a "fluid motion of encircling, encompassing, permeating, enveloping, outstretching"[187] – is what it means for God to be intensely alive and vibrantly active in the eternity of his love. Trinitarian *perichoresis*, in which Father, Son and Spirit are united precisely because of their engagement in mutual, reciprocal and dynamic self-giving love, is, for Moltmann, a process of most perfect and intense empathy[188]: it is a process whereby unity within the divine life derives intrinsically from its own inner circulation.

Though *perichoresis* has a valid ontological interpretation in the notion of coinherence, in the sense that the three persons of the Trinity coinhere in *being* as well as in act, the understanding depicted in the preceding paragraphs is inherently dynamic and relational. There is a three-way reciprocity which is so profound, so ineffable, that the Western 'doctrine of appropriation', which conveys the idea that each person of the Trinity is assigned particular attributes appropriate to his being,

> falls completely away as an idea that is both otiose and damaging to the intrinsic truth of Christ who, as the Word and only begotten Son of God, constitutes the *one* revelation of the Father and the *one* way by

---

[185] LaCugna, *God For Us*: 272-275. See also Wilson-Kastner, Patricia, *Faith, Feminism and the Christ*, Philadelphia: Fortress Press, 1983.

[186] Moltmann, Jürgen, *The Source of Life: The Holy Spirit and the Theology of Life*, London: SCM Press, 1997: 88.

[187] LaCugna, *God For Us*: 272.

[188] Moltmann, *The Trinity and the Kingdom of God*: 175. So Torrance: "Since God is Spirit, we must understand the περιχώρησις between the Father, the Son and the Holy Spirit within the One Being of God in a wholly spiritual and intensely personal way, not in a static, but in a dynamic yet ontological way, as the eternal movement of Communion which the Triune God ever is within himself and in his active relations toward us through the Holy Spirit." Like Moltmann and LaCugna, Torrance interprets this communion *ad intra* as a dynamic reality between the three divine persons "in which their differentiating properties instead of separating them actually serve their oneness with one another." (Torrance, Thomas F. *Trinitarian Perspectives: Toward Doctrinal Agreement*, Edinburgh: T. & T. Clark, 1994: 141).

which we can go to the Father.[189]

For Torrance, all of God's acts have behind them the full weight of the Trinity whilst simultaneously each person of the Trinity retains his own distinct identity: this interpretation of the concept of *perichoresis* implies that the doctrine of appropriation need not have arisen at all as a response to the Augustinian bias towards the one divine essence as the starting place for an understanding of God.

For the Catholic theologian Thomas Weinandy, who essays a strictly ontological 'reconception' of the Trinity, this *"perichoresis* of *action* on the part of all three persons completely revolutionizes the *perichoresis* of the East and the circumincession of the West."[190] Whilst his focus is on the Trinity *ad intra*, Weinandy claims to have recovered what he describes as 'an unprecedented dynamism' within the perichoretic divine life by attributing activity to all three persons of the Trinity in spiration and begetting. Noticeably, the Spirit is conceived as the one who makes this mutual coinherence of action possible and intelligible, a view which contradicts the strict linearity – and hierarchy – implicit in the Orthodox understanding of the monarchy of the Father, from whom both Son and Spirit proceed.[191] The reciprocal interaction between Father, Son and Spirit proposed by Weinandy replaces this linearity with a symmetrical coinherence which simultaneously negates the passivity of the Augustinian presentation of the Spirit as impersonal 'bond of love'. Despite Weinandy's limited *ad intra* ontological orientation, his trinitarian reconception accommodates a helpful re-evaluation of the role of the Spirit in active *perichoresis*.

---

[189] Torrance, *The Christian Doctrine of God*: 200, author's italics. See also Athanasius, *Ad Serapionem*, 1.28 and 30-31, where the early church theologian advances the idea that "the Father does all things through the Word and in the Spirit." However, Torrance acknowledges that "In every creative and redemptive act the Father, the Son and the Holy Spirit operate together in fellowship with one another but nevertheless in ways peculiar to each of them. It is not possible for us to spell that out in terms of any demarcations between their distinctive operations, if only because within the coactivity of the three divine Persons those operations perichoretically contain one another and pass over into one another while remaining what they distinctively are in themselves." (Torrance, *The Christian Doctrine of God*: 198).

[190] Weinandy, *The Father's Spirit of Sonship*: 79, author's italics. Weinandy's 'reconception' of the Trinity is based on the thesis is that "if we, who are Christians, are conformed into sons of the Father by the Spirit through whom we are empowered to cry out in the same words as Jesus, then the eternal Son himself must have been begotten and conformed to be Son in the same Spirit in whom he eternally cries out 'Abba!'" (*Ibid*: ix-x).

[191] In this regard, Weinandy's discussion centres on the ecumenical obstacle of the *filioque* controversy.

The notion of triangularity as a *necessary* presupposition of triune love *ad intra* was explored by Richard of St. Victor in the twelfth century. In his *De Trinitate* he argues that genuine love needs to be not only mutual but *shared*, if it is to exist in all its fullness. This requires a third person: "Shared love is properly said to exist when a third person is loved by two persons harmoniously and in community, and the affection of the two persons is fused into one affection by the flame of love for a third."[192] For Richard, this third person in the case of God was the Holy Spirit, the *condilectus* or 'co-beloved'. More recently, David Miller has suggested the need for a *ménage à trois* in matters of ultimate love, both divine and human, maintaining that a "threatening fantasy lurks in the trinitarian image: *the necessity of the third in love.*"[193] His approach follows that of Augustine's search for *vestigia trinitatis* within human nature, together with his notion of the lover, the beloved and the love that unites the two. Though he was not attempting to derive an insight into the nature of the Trinity from the concept of love, Miller's analogical methodology cannot take us very far in our understanding of trinitarian interrelatedness. Pannenberg rightly points out that, in order to find a basis for the doctrine of the Trinity "we must begin with the way in which Father, Son, and Spirit come on the scene and relate to one another *in the event of revelation.*"[194]

This event of revelation is, as Moltmann and others have demonstrated most forcefully, summed up in the cross: "The cross stands at the heart of the trinitarian being of God; it divides and conjoins the persons in their relationships to each other and portrays them in a specific way."[195] The perichoretic love that resides within the divine life is at the same time both ecstatic and sacrificial. This most central of all interpretations of perichoretic life is expressed powerfully in Andrei Rublev's fifteenth-century icon representing the visit of the three angels to Abraham (Genesis 18).[196] The icon portrays the three angels in a circular pattern, suggestive of the 'round dance'

---

[192] Richard of St. Victor, *De Trinitate* III. 19 in Zinn, Grover A. (trans), *Richard of St. Victor*, New York: Paulist Press: 1979: 392.

[193] Miller, David L., *Three Faces of God: Traces of the Trinity in Literature and Life*, Philadelphia: Fortress Press, 1986: 44, author's italics. Miller's thesis is not very convincing: in his desire to press his point that 'every dyad turns out to be a triad' (after the contemporary theologian Tom Driver) he tends towards impersonality in some of his examples.

[194] Pannenberg, *Systematic Theology*, Vol. I: 299, my italics. Drawing from the biblical statement that God *is* love (1 John 4:8), Pannenberg points out that "[e]ven if we presuppose a plurality of persons in a relationship of love, the persons are related to one another by something else, i.e. love, which is not itself thought of as a third, as the third person." (*Ibid*: 297).

[195] Moltmann, *The Crucified God*: 207.

[196] The insights that follow are drawn from +Kallistos of Diokleia, "The human person as an icon of the Trinity": 18-20, in which the author refers to Evdokimov, Paul, *L'Orthodoxie*, Neuchâtel/Paris, 1959: 233-238.

or *perichoresis* of the Trinity. The three figures, with head inclined, are turned towards each other, as if in dialogue. The circle is not closed but open, indicative of the ecstatic love of the Trinity, a love that, in sovereign divine freedom, creates the world. In Rublev's icon, the three angels each point towards a chalice that is positioned in the centre of a cube-shaped table, resembling an altar, on which they are seated; in this chalice there is the head of an animal. The Genesis 18 story of Abraham's willingness to sacrifice Isaac is the foil for the greater story of the triune God's self-sacrificing love, and so we are invited to ponder the deeper meaning of Rublev's icon:

> It tells us that the mutual, outgoing love of the Trinity, expressed in the creation of the human person, is at the same time a sacrificial love. In total solidarity with the world, God the Trinity takes responsibility for all the consequences of the act of creation.[197]

This is the language of *kenosis*, of suffering and ecstatic love, expressed in terms of trinitarian *perichoresis*.

Taking a pneumatological perspective on *kenosis*, a doctrine which was originally conceived christologically, Moltmann argues that the Spirit who accompanies Jesus throughout his life and in his passion, and who is therefore his *companion* in suffering, is the Spirit of condescension who experiences progressive *kenosis*.[198] In defence of 'Spirit Christology', Clark Pinnock writes about the Spirit as the one who "prepares, constitutes and communicates the mystery of the incarnation." Ultimately, the Son's death and resurrection "is a trinitarian event in which the three Persons experience the mutuality and reciprocity characteristic of the triune God."[199] The cross is therefore an intratrinitarian drama, a dynamic *perichoresis* of suffering love for the sake of the whole world, an event in which Father, Son and Holy Spirit are all intimately, necessarily, *perichoretically* involved: "God was in Christ reconciling the world to himself" (2 Corinthians 5:9).

Perichoresis and the Nature of Reality

Earlier we noted Moltmann's theology of the Spirit as 'the power of futurity' acting in dynamic perichoretic power, embodying an eschatological vision of hope for the whole of creation. Seeking a perichoretic understanding of the relation of God to creation, he exegetes Acts 17:28 – "In him we live, move and have our being" – in terms of a panentheistic coexistence of 'God in creation'

---

[197] +Kallistos of Diokleia, "The human person as an icon of the Trinity": 20.

[198] Moltmann, *The Spirit of Life*: 60-65.

[199] Pinnock, *Flame of Love*: 92-93. Pinnock cautions against a liberal interpretation of the phrase 'Spirit Christology' where Spirit is used to refer to the divine element in Jesus rather than trinitarian person. His use of the term preserves trinitarian distinctives in order to emphasise the perichoretic role of the Spirit in the economy of salvation.

and 'creation in God':

> Always to stress only the distinction between God and the world and God's transcendence over the world in the doctrine of creation is to adopt a one-sided approach and a theology of secularization imitating the secularizing of the world.[200]

In a tribute to the sixteenth-century philosopher and scholar, Giordano Bruno, who was burnt alive for heresy, Moltmann hails him as a prophet of our times, "the herald of a 'new paradigm' for a world in which human beings can survive in organic harmony with the Spirit of the universe."[201] Eschewing the mechanistic universe of Galileo and Newton, Moltmann endorses Bruno's embrace of the old Stoic doctrine of the world-soul which gives all things life and movement in the divine dynamic of the universe.

Moltmann's implicit use of the language of *perichoresis* in his vision of a creation which is moving under the impulse of the Spirit towards its eschatological consummation, is made explicit by Gunton in his discussion of the concept as a dynamism of relatedness at all levels of reality. Seeking a postmodern response to the failure of modernity – manifested in the fragmentation of culture, destructive individualism, naturalistic philosophies and the deification of meaninglessness – he articulates the concept of *perichoresis* as an appropriate construct for interpreting human existence in God's creation[202]: "The dynamism of mutual constitutiveness derives from the world's being a dynamic order that is summoned into being and directed

---

[200] Moltmann, *History and the Triune God*: 133. Anticipating possible confusion between pantheism and panentheism, Moltmann points out that his pneumatological doctrine of creation is predicated on the assertion that the Spirit lives in eternal perichoretic unity with the Son and the Father, and therefore "there cannot be a dissolution of God in the world, as theologians fear, nor the divinization of evolution which some new age scientists (E. Jantsch, F. Capra) want." (*Ibid*: 133).

[201] *Ibid*: 164. For a fascinating fictionalised account of Giordano Bruno's life, see West, Morris, *The Last Confession*, Sydney: HarperCollins*Publishers*, 2000: in this book, his last (he died in its final stages of writing), the author recreates Bruno's story, in which the Dominican monk and philosopher (through West's creative, yet historically accurate, imagination) defends his beliefs over a two-week period whilst in prison in Rome, where he was incarcerated by the Catholic authorities for seven years on charges of heresy; rather than recant, Bruno was burnt at the stake on 17 February, 1600. See also Moltmann's evaluation of Bruno's cosmological theses in Moltmann, Jürgen, "'From the Closed World to the Infinite Universe': The Case of Giordano Bruno" in *Science and Wisdom*, Minneapolis: Fortress Press, 2003: 158-171 (previously published in Häring, H. and Kuschel, K. J. (eds), *Gegenentwürfe. 24 Lebensläufe für eine andere Theologie. Festschrift für Hans Küng zum 60. Geburtstag*, Munich, 1998: 157-167).

[202] Gunton, *The One, the Three and the Many*: 163-179. Recognising that the orientation of being is distorted and delayed – but not removed – by sin and evil, Gunton invokes the incarnation and the redeeming agency of the Spirit as the means by which all things return to perfection.

towards its perfection by the free creativity of Father, Son and Holy Spirit."[203] Gunton therefore advocates a perspective on the world that is ultimately perichoretic in that everything in creation contributes in some way to the being of everything else. To speak thus is to acknowledge movement, recurrence and interpenetration as defining characteristics of a creation which reflects, within the constraints of an admittedly human rational construct, the nature of its Creator, as Paul declares in Romans 1:20.[204] Gunton's proposal may therefore be viewed as an attempt to integrate all levels of reality – divine, human and cosmic – within the construct of *perichoresis* in order to offer a more coherent paradigm conspicuously absent in modernity.

Earlier, we noted Volf's suggestion that the idea of *perichoresis* has ecclesial relevance; in other words, at the human level there is a similarity between the unity of the church and the unity of the triune God.[205] It is the Spirit of God who makes this unity a concrete reality within the life of the local church:

> Each person gives of himself or herself to others, and each person in a unique way takes up others into himself or herself. This is the process of the mutual internalization of personal characteristics occurring in the church through the Holy Spirit indwelling Christians. The Spirit opens them to one another and allows them to become *catholic persons* in their uniqueness. It is here that they, in a creaturely way, correspond to the catholicity of the divine persons.[206]

However, when *perichoresis* is applied to the Christian community of faith, it is important to recognise that human beings are not interior to the Spirit in the same way that the Spirit is interior to human beings. Volf insists that personal

---

[203] *Ibid*: 166.

[204] Romans 1:20: 'For since the creation of the world God's invisible qualities – his eternal power and divine nature – have been clearly seen, being understood from what has been made, so that men are without excuse.'

[205] Volf's exegesis of John 17:21 leads him to resist the idea that human perichoretic unity is *identical* to divine perichoretic unity: "It is not the mutual perichoresis of human beings, but rather the indwelling of the Spirit common to everyone that makes the church into a communion corresponding to the Trinity, a communion in which personhood and sociality are equiprimal." (Volf, *After Our Likeness*: 213).

[206] *Ibid*: 211-212, author's italics. Volf's understanding of catholicity has personal, ecclesial and *inter*ecclesial application: "Just as every church is a catholic church because the whole Christ is present in it through the Holy Spirit, so also is every believer a catholic person because the whole Christ indwells everyone through the Holy Spirit." (*Ibid*: 279). The interecclesial relevance of the *perichoresis* of the divine persons is revealed as local churches, absorbing the unique identifying characteristics of their local context, transmit these characteristics to other churches. "By opening up to one another both diachronically and synchronically, local churches should enrich one another, thereby increasingly becoming catholic churches." (*Ibid*: 213).

interiority is one-sided.[207] Human beings participate in the perichoretic life of God in a distinctively different way to that which reflects the interiority of trinitarian divine life: the Spirit indwells human persons, but humans do not indwell the *person* of the Spirit in the same way that the Father and Son indwell him in divine *perichoresis*. We might note here LaCugna's rejection of a divine *perichoresis* which is distinct from a human *perichoresis*: consistent with her vision to focus the doctrine of the Trinity on the communion between God and *ourselves*, rather than on the nature of the innertrinitarian life, she insists – contra Volf – that there is only one *perichoresis*, implicit in Jesus' high-priestly prayer in John 17:20-21. LaCugna critiques the methodology of the feminist theologian, Patricia Wilson-Kastner, who seeks to model the equality of human persons on trinitarian *perichoresis*, with its characteristics of inclusiveness, community and freedom. LaCugna prefers to ground her vision of egalitarian human community in the economy of salvation and "the revelation of the concrete forms of human community proclaimed by Jesus as characteristic of the reign of God."[208]

What is clear, irrespective of the precise nature of the theological correspondence between divine and human *perichoresis* contemplated by LaCugna, Volf, Fiddes, Gunton and others, is that the mutuality and reciprocity implicit in the intradivine life is, for all of them, normative as the ontological ground for all human interactions. And because *all* human beings are caught up with one another in the complex reality of our total environment, what Gunton picturesquely calls the "bundle of life",[209] then it is appropriate to apply the perichoretic analogy inclusively rather than exclusively: it is not to be confined to the Christian community, but is relevant for all human beings.

Furthermore, the richness of the language of *perichoresis* with respect to human community lies not only in the mutuality and reciprocity of giving and receiving, but also in its insistence that particularity is not diminished, but rather enhanced.[210] So, as Gunton argues consistently, the concept enables 'the one and the many' in dynamic interrelations to be sustained without loss to either the particularity of the one or the plurality of the many. In short, it offers us a window into both our understanding of God as triune being, *unitas in trinitate* and *trinitas in unitate*, and also our own self-understanding as unique creatures who have been created to live in communal solidarity in his world.

We might now ask, with Gunton, "Is it right to speak of perichoresis in the

---

[207] *Ibid*: 211.

[208] LaCugna, *God For Us*: 274.

[209] Gunton, *The One, the Three and the Many*: 170.

[210] The sociologist Clifford Geertz emphasises the particular in our dealings with one another: "We must, in short, descend into detail, past the misleading tags, past the metaphysical types, past the empty similarities to grasp firmly the essential character of not only the various cultures but the various sorts of individuals within each culture, if we wish to encounter humanity face to face." (Geertz, Clifford C., *The Interpretation of Cultures*, New York: Basic Books, 1973: 53).

impersonal world also?"²¹¹ Already, we have noted hints at a cosmic *perichoresis* in the writings of a number of contemporary theologians, and, as we shall see in Chapter 5, which is devoted to the examination of *perichoresis* as a principle of cosmological unity, modern physics offers a persuasive argument in favour of the proposition that the universe created by God is perichoretic in character. Commenting on the orderliness and complex reproductive genius discernible in creation, Pinnock maintains that a "power of creativity is at work in the universe, which can be viewed as a creaturely perichoresis of dynamic systems echoing the trinitarian mystery."²¹² Advances in science invite us to view the universe as a system of interrelated parts, in which the behaviour of the whole is more significant than detailed examination of the fragments that constitute the system.

It is this insight which Guiseppe Del Re, an Italian theoretical chemist, translates into the cosmological metaphor of the 'Great Dance', reflecting the instinctive human longing for a model of coherence that holds everything together.²¹³ In his foreword to Del Re's book, Thomas Torrance observes that the author uses the 'Great Dance Image'

> to give meaningful expression to the dynamical order of the universe as a coherent, evolving pattern in which all things participate as if in a dance or a ballet, combining general harmony and coherence with evolution, randomness, irreversibility.²¹⁴

The notion of contingence which we identified in the writings of both Gunton and Torrance reflects the freedom and openness implicit in the dance metaphor embraced by Del Re. In Greek thought as well as in early Christian reflection, dance was a widespread image for the participation of all created beings in God.²¹⁵ Before its appearance in recent scientific thinking, motivated in part by the search for a coherent *Weltanschauung* – or overall cosmic perspective – the metaphor of dance can be traced back to Platonic and medieval interpretations of the meaning and purpose of life. Plotinus, the third-century Neoplatonist moral and religious teacher, sustains the cosmic dance image in his description of the vitality of the stars in the universe, employing at times the language of 'dance-play': so

> we may take the comparison of the movement of the heavenly bodies to a choral dance; if we think of it as a dance which comes to rest at

---

[211] Gunton, *The One, the Three and the Many*: 171.
[212] Pinnock, *Flame of Love*: 67.
[213] Del Re, Guiseppe, *The Cosmic Dance: Science Discovers the Mysterious Harmony of the Universe*, Radnor PA: Templeton Foundation Press, 2000.
[214] *Ibid*: x.
[215] Fiddes, *Participating in God*: 73, where the author refers to the 'never-ending dance' of the angels around the throne of God, and the 'hierarchy of dancing celestial choirs' envisaged by the Neoplatonist Denys the Areopagite.

> some given period, the entire dance, accomplished from beginning to end, will be perfect while at each partial stage it was imperfect: but if the dance is a thing of eternity, it is in eternal perfection.[216]

Plotinus' reference to rest, alongside his allusion to eternal perfection, seems to reflect here the Platonic idea of God as the still, unmoving and perfect centre of the dance. Fiddes suggests that perhaps the image of the dance as a metaphor for the inner participation of the triune God did not take hold of the Christian imagination precisely because the notion of God as a motionless or immoveable deity, as portrayed in conventional theism, did not sit well with the ecstasy and dynamism implicit in the vocabulary of choreography.[217] But with the recovery of an understanding of trinitarian life that emphasises dynamic relationality and mutual reciprocity in the place of Thomist notions of immutability and impassibility, the language of dance is now theologically permissible. It has captured the imagination not only of theologians intent on restoring the Trinity to its rightful place at the center of Christian life and doctrine, but also of a number of scientists who espouse a vision of the universe as a dynamic cosmic theatre displaying the harmony and coherence characteristic of the dance metaphor.

Without detracting in any way from the Barthian insistence on revelation, specifically God's self-revelation in the historical person of Jesus Christ in the economy of salvation, as the bedrock of trinitarian discourse, 'Trinity talk' has broadened over the last half-century to incorporate insights ranging from the philosophical anthropology of John Macmurray to the cosmological theories of those who are working at the cutting edge of the science-theology interface. This chapter has traced the significant theological movements from a revelation-based but relatively static interpretation of the Trinity to one that is characterised by a dynamic eschatologically-oriented *perichoresis*. In the process, the notion of *perichoresis* has been presented as an appropriate integrative construct at the levels of divine, human/social and cosmic reality, a construct which highlights the activity of the Spirit as the eschatological power of God at work in all creation, enabling all that exists – personal and non-personal – to fully and finally become itself in the freedom of divine love. So the Holy Spirit may be understood as "the power that transcends and operates within nature, guiding it to its destiny,"[218] and "the ecstasy of divine life, the overabundance of joy, that gives birth to the universe and ever works to bring about a fullness of unity."[219] It remains to spell out more specifically in the next

---

[216] Plotinus, *Enneads* (Fourth Ennead, Fourth Tractate), 4.4.8; see also 4.4.33.

[217] Fiddes, *Participating in God*: 74. Stillness at the centre of some form of cosmic dance is implicit in the thought of the twentieth-century poet T. S Eliot: "At the still point of the turning world ... there the dance is ... Except for the point, the still point, there would be no dance, and there is only the dance." (Eliot, T.S., 'Burnt Norton' I (Four Quartets) in *Collected Poems*, London: Faber & Faber, 1963: 191).

[218] Pinnock, *Flame of Love*: 67.

[219] *Ibid*: 48.

two chapters the contours of *perichoresis* as a pneumatologically-oriented dialogical construct at the level of pastoral practice and as a principle of cosmological unity, before proposing how these insights might be synthesised into a model of pastoral and scientific coherence.

CHAPTER 4

Redressing the 'Failure of Nerve' – Perichoresis as a Dialogical Construct at the Level of Pastoral Practice

There are several dimensions to the central theme permeating this chapter, which has to do with the pastoral significance of *perichoresis*. When we speak of 'pastoral' in the context of Christian ministry we are concerned with the way in which the community of faith orders and conducts itself, not only ontologically and functionally, but also inwardly and outwardly. In other words, we need to address not only the inner life of the community of faith as both fact and dynamic expression of the inner life of the Trinity, but also its outward orientation, or *ekstasis*, through which God opens up his triune life to all people, and through which the community of faith discovers its intrinsic God-ordained humanness in relation to the whole created order. Earlier we noted LaCugna's description of a person as "not an individual but an open and ecstatic reality, referred to others for his or her existence. The actualization of personhood takes place in self-transcendence, the movement of freedom toward communion with other persons."[1] Similarly, the church is identified as such not only in its catholicity[2] – its openness to others *intra muros ecclesiae* – but also in its witness to the triune God as it lives out his life in the arena of the world. In its calling, asks Kruger rhetorically, "does the Church not become a player in the real saga of the human race?"[3]

Having established the trinitarian structure of God's ministry as the basis for all ministry, we focus in this chapter on the *practice* of ministry, in order to elucidate the contours of *perichoresis* as a pneumatologically-oriented dialogical construct at the level of pastoral practice. As we proceed, we shall affirm what many ecclesiologists assert, that "continual conversion to God's triune *communio* is the central condition for continual reform of our own

---

[1] LaCugna, Catherine Mowry, *God For Us: The Trinity and Christian Life*, San Francisco: HarperCollins, 1991: 260.
[2] For a discussion of the catholicity of the church, with a clear eschatological perspective, see Volf, Miroslav, *After Our Likeness: The Church as the Image of the Trinity*, Grand Rapids: Eerdmans, 1998: 259-282.
[3] Kruger, C. Baxter, *Recovering the Trinity and Perichoresis and Their Significance for the 3rd Christian Millennium*, Adelaide; unpublished Perichoresis Lectures 2002: 69.

churches,"[4] an axiom which has its origin in the distinctive work of the Holy Spirit. In the process, we will eschew abstract, speculative trinitarian debate and, in particular, highlight the concrete reality of the Spirit who is, in the words of the Nicene Creed, the 'giver of life.'

Particularity – Contexts and Persons

In Chapter 3 we noted that because uniqueness is as much the object of God's loving concern as oneness, the Spirit gives shape to all that exists, directing each person and thing until it reaches ultimate eschatological perfection. This emphasis on the uniqueness of both persons and communities of faith argues for an approach to pastoral practice which recognises the operation of the Spirit within the particularity of specific lives and specific contexts: "'the Spirit of life' is only there as the Spirit of this or that particular life. The experience of God's Spirit is as specific as the living beings who experience him, and as varied as the living beings who experience him are varied."[5] The Spirit is therefore, in David Cunningham's phrase, 'a witness to particularity', an expression that he fleshes out in the context of the pastoral work of evangelism and preaching, and the manifestation of *charismata* within the community of faith: so "the one Spirit is manifested in different ways among different Christian believers".[6] In preaching, for example, Scott Black Johnston asks, "Who listens?", to which he replies: "Particular people with particular histories in particular churches. To preach faithfully requires that we take these particularities into account."[7]

The particularity to which Johnston refers has to do with the specific cultural, psychological, economic and social contexts (micro-anthropology) that define an audience, as distinct from the universal characteristics of listeners (macro-anthropology). Whilst it is manifestly impossible for preachers to speak into the unique circumstances of every listener's life simultaneously, it is clearly advantageous for them to contextualise their message within a micro-

---

[4] Buckley, James J., 'The Wounded Body: The Spirit's Ecumenical Work on Divisions among Christians', in Buckley, James J. and Yeago, David S (eds), *Knowing the Triune God: The Work of the Spirit in the Practices of the Church*, Grand Rapids: Eerdmans, 2001: 223.

[5] Moltmann, Jürgen, *The Spirit of Life: A Universal Affirmation*, Minneapolis: Fortress Press, 1992: 180.

[6] Cunningham, David S., *These Three Are One: The Practice of Trinitarian Theology*, Oxford: Blackwell, 1998: 204-207.

[7] Johnston, Scott Black, "Modes of Discourse for the Sermon in the Postmodern World" in Allen, R. J., Blaisdell, B. S. and Johnston, S. B., *Theology for Preaching: Authority, Truth and Knowledge of God in a Postmodern Ethos*, Nashville: Abingdon Press, 1997: 175. Johnston points out, though, that preachers need to attend to both the faithful language of the church and the way in which particular communities talk in concrete contexts: "Relativism is not the answer; relevance is!" (*ibid*: 177).

anthropological framework. It is then the privilege and gift of the Spirit to take that which we offer, not only in preaching but in every dimension of pastoral ministry, and give it practical application in the unique lives of particular people.

It is precisely because life is specific and not general, everywhere different, never the same, that Moltmann speaks of the vitalising energies of the Spirit that both unite the community of faith and distinguish its members one from the other. Buckley and Yeago make a similar claim regarding the concrete action of the triune God: "trinitarian doctrine *codifies the knowledge of God given in Christian particularity*: in the movement of the stories of Israel, in the patterns of the Church's prayer and liturgy, in the logic of mission and ministry."[8] So the Spirit may be described as the particularising agent of life within specific personal and ecclesial contexts. The central role of the Spirit in the ministry of the church is emphasised by Zizioulas, whose identification of the ministry of the church with that of Christ is predicated on Christology being conditioned pneumatologically: "What, therefore, the Spirit does through the ministry is to constitute the Body of Christ *here and now* by *realizing* Christ's ministry *as* the Church's ministry."[9]

Our earlier discussion of the nature of pastoral ministry highlighted its relational – as distinct from functional – composition. Ministry, more than anything else, "renders the Church a *relational* reality, i.e. a mystery of love, reflecting here and now the very life of the trinitarian God."[10] For Zizioulas, the relational character of ministry[11] – which can only be brought about by the *koinonia* of the Spirit – is expressed as a double movement of the church, both *ad intra* and *ad extra*. For example, issues of ecclesial authority, reflecting the life of the Trinity *ad intra*, derive from relationship rather than power; and the mission of the church *ad extra* is profoundly soteriological, in which the trinitarian mystery of love is given incarnational expression as an organic part of the relational life of the concrete local (and for Zizioulas, *eucharistic*) community.[12]

In his volume dealing with the practice of trinitarian theology, Cunningham argues that the doctrine of the Trinity is not just something that Christians think – it is also something they do, profoundly shaping the way life should be

---

[8] Buckley, James J. and Yeago, David S, "Introduction: A Catholic and Evangelical Theology?" in Buckley and Yeago, (eds), *Knowing the Triune God*: 15, authors' italics.

[9] Zizioulas, John D., *Being as Communion: Studies in Personhood and the Church*, London: Darton, Longman & Todd, 1985: 211, author's italics.

[10] *Ibid*: 220, author's italics.

[11] Zizioulas posits a "fundamental *interdependence between the ministry and the concrete community of the Church*" through the agency of the Spirit, who is the Spirit of community (*ibid*: 212).

[12] Zizioulas interprets the incarnational imperative of ministry in relational terms by asserting that the "nature of mission is not to be found in the Church's *addressing* the world but in its being fully in *com-passion* with it" (*ibid*: 224, author's italics).

lived.[13] As Lindbeck has pointed out, doctrines are intrinsically practical because they are "communally authoritative teachings regarding beliefs and practices that are considered essential to the identity or welfare of the group."[14] This echoes Barth who, whilst acknowledging that the *mysterium trinitatis* must remain a mystery, warns of the danger of irrelevant speculation unless the doctrine of the Trinity is seen as 'belonging to the Church'. LaCugna's collapse of the Trinity *ad intra* into *ad extra* seeks to eliminate the notion of mystery altogether in a passionate attempt to articulate a practical doctrine with radical consequences for Christian life:

> The doctrine of the Trinity does more than set out criteria for orthodoxy. It is also the framework for reflecting on the nature of the human person, on the relationship between humankind and all other creatures of the earth, on the relationship between ourselves and God. In short, *all theological reflection*, whether conducted under the rubric of ethics, sacramental theology, ecclesiology, or spirituality, is potentially a mode of trinitarian theology.[15]

However, argues Cunningham, it is far easier to endorse a practical theology of the Trinity than to articulate one. His own text is an attempt to redress what he calls a 'failure of nerve' on the part of most trinitarian theologians to attend to the diverse concrete particularities implicit in fleshing out what LaCugna calls a 'living trinitarian faith'.[16] Not only is it risky to align oneself with a particular viewpoint – in, for example, the arenas of human sexuality, ecclesial authority, community life, political action, violence and suffering – but it is considerably more difficult to attend to "precisely what we ought to do differently in order to 'enact' or 'perform' the Christian doctrine of God."[17] A recent attempt to correct this deficiency (subsequent to Cunningham's work) can be found in Paul Fiddes' *Participating in God*, subtitled *A Pastoral Doctrine of the Trinity*, in which the author connects trinitarian theology with

---

[13] Cunningham, *These Three Are One*, in which the author cites approvingly a number of theologians who have demonstrated, at the least, an awareness of the need to relate the doctrine of the Trinity to Christian life, notably Catherine LaCugna, Leonardo Boff and Jürgen Moltmann (*ibid*: 29-30).

[14] Lindbeck, George, *The Nature of Doctrine: Religion and Theology in a Postliberal Age* (Philadelphia: Westminster, 1984: 74.

[15] LaCugna, *God For Us*: 380.

[16] Cunningham is particularly critical of LaCugna's failure to address specific concrete issues in spite of her allusion to a 'living trinitarian faith' as the necessary outcome of her theological discourse; see Cunningham, *These Three Are One*: 41-45. He also rebukes (*ibid*: 44) Alan Torrance for his empty – and ultimately irrelevant – 'banal observation' that a trinitarian understanding of persons in communion is "neither a form of 'praxis' nor a mode of *doing*, but a dynamic in which we find ourselves" (see Torrance, Alan J., *Persons in Communion: An Essay on Trinitarian Description and Human Participation*, Edinburgh: T. & T. Clark, 1996: 320, author's italics).

[17] Cunningham, *These Three Are One*: 42.

the discipline of practical theology in an "imaginative 'interplay between idea and action'."[18] Even more recent is Buckley and Yeago's edited series of essays based on the premise that "knowing the triune God is inseparable from participating in a particular community and its practices – a participation which is the work of God's Holy Spirit."[19]

More broadly, Cunningham's own exposition of the practical implications of trinitarian thinking directs us into a perichoretic experience of life that challenges the modern cult of the individual, focusing instead on "complex webs of mutuality and participation" which have ramifications not only anthropologically but also cosmologically.[20] We shall note in a number of places that his treatise is helpfully practical at the level of pastoral ministry because, mindful of his own critique, it concentrates on specific contexts and outcomes rather than abstract speculation.

For example, Cunningham explores the 'trinitarian virtue' of particularity, in which he critiques the celebration of autonomy in contemporary Western culture.[21] His emphasis on two other trinitarian virtues – polyphony and participation (to be discussed later in this chapter) – should not be construed as implying a diminishment of particularity and difference: "Because God is Three, particularity is necessarily a trinitarian virtue; and yet, because God is also One, we are called to construe this particularity in an anti-individualistic way."[22]

---

[18] See Fiddes, Paul S., *Participating in God: A Pastoral Doctrine of the Trinity*, London: Darton, Longman & Todd, 2000; the quotation is cited from Campbell, Alistair, "The Nature of Practical Theology" in Woodward, James and Pattison, Stephen (eds), *The Blackwell Reader in Pastoral and Practical Theology*, Oxford: Blackwell, 2000: 85.

[19] Buckley and Yeago, "Introduction: A Catholic and Evangelical Theology?": 1.

[20] Cunningham, *These Three Are One*: 8. Alluding to the threefold witness in the disputed text of 1 John 5:7, Cunningham comments rhetorically on both the figurative richness and the cosmic scope of the Johannine language, in which the words 'spirit', 'water' and 'blood' "evoke a wide range of biblical and theological motifs, both triumphant and tragic: the creation of the world, the birth of children, the sacrifice of animals, the murder of human beings, the freeing of slaves, the conquest of lands, and the warnings of prophets" (*ibid*: 9-10). So Cunningham infers from these 'three earthly witnesses' that trinitarian theology speaks not only into the practice of the church (as in baptism and the eucharist) but also into wider issues related to public life and the created order. Whilst the present chapter of this book gives paramount consideration to the pastoral practice of the church as a human community, Chapter 5 explores the wider, cosmic implications of trinitarian perichoretic thinking.

[21] The phrase 'trinitarian virtues' reflect "dispositions that *God has by nature*, and in which *we participate by grace*" (*ibid*: 123, author's italics); they are essentially *relational* in character, formed in human beings in the context of divine-human relationship – in other words, Cunningham eschews an interpretation of 'virtue' as either a moral position attainable by our own effort or a divine work in which human beings are merely passive receptors.

[22] *Ibid*: 198; the previous chapter in this book examined in some detail the relationship between the Three and the One in classical trinitarian theology, in which we noted that

In order to appreciate Cunningham's emphasis on particularity as distinct from *individuation* – a vital distinction that he claims some theologians have overlooked[23] – it is helpful to summarise his understanding of the process of human communication, a dimension of relational life intrinsic to many aspects of pastoral ministry. He develops an example of what he calls *rhetorical invention* as a 'triune mark',[24] arguing that the most helpful way of describing the process of a person preparing a speech is to imagine this in terms of two 'processions'[25] – the production of language, and the construction of the audience. Persuasion takes place through some form of communication, so focusing us on the way language operates and attending to those who will be hearing what is communicated. This leads to an emphasis not so much on substantive terms (speaker, argument and audience) as on relations – of language, *speaking* and *being spoken*; of the audience, *constructing* and *being constructed*. To emphasise the substantive – or individuating – terms is to be in danger of treating them as independent entities: losing any one of them can

---

the starting-point for Eastern trinitarian theology was a redefined *hypostasis* with relational attributes, in contrast to the Western emphasis on the unity, or oneness, of God. God's being *ad intra* is relationally structured: relationality, or *self-relatedness*, is ontologically characteristic of God himself: there is therefore differentiation within the divine life. For the Cappadocian Fathers the concept of person was not individualistic, but relational.

[23] See, for example, his remonstration against Colin Gunton's way of putting the matter (*ibid*: 201). On the other hand, it may be reasonably argued that Gunton is seeking to reinstate the necessity for distinctiveness and particularity in society, without degenerating into individualism: see Gunton, Colin E., *The One, The Three and the Many: God, Creation and the Culture of Modernity*, Cambridge: Cambridge UP, 1993, especially Chapters 2 and 7.

[24] Cunningham argues that because we know by revelation something of the triunity of God we can offer accounts that describe the creation as reflecting this triunity. That is, we can construct parallels between Christian doctrine and certain elements of the created order. These 'triune marks' (*vestigia trinitatis*) are not defined as 'embedded' in nature – rather they represent human construals which clarify doctrinal affirmations of triunity. Cunningham helpfully critiques Barth's suspicion of *vestigia trinitatis* expressed as natural theology (*ibid*: 98-106), and summarises by stating that Christ, by his incarnate example, "teaches us to 'read' the triune marks of the created order." So we can appropriate the best of the *vestigia* tradition whilst avoiding its dangers. Especially we can appropriate the narratives of God's 'production' of the world through Israel, Christ and the church and not allow them to fade into the background. Because God is ever about the business of 'producing' the world, everything in the world reflects the glory of God ... so it is legitimate for human beings to parallel the trinitarian being of God by searching for *vestigia* in the created order.

[25] This language of 'processions' is, of course, reminiscent of the terminology adopted by early trinitarian theologians in describing the relationships between Father, Son and Holy Spirit.

demolish the entire process of persuasion.[26]

Human communication is therefore "a fluctuating and highly unstable process, in which various actions are always being displaced by new events."[27] The personal pronouns – 'you' and 'I' in communicative relations – are not static entities, distinguishing individuals from the rest of the world. Rather, they represent, as McFadyen points out, "the contribution and engagement of people in a particular network of communication."[28] Particularity, therefore, does not render us into isolated individuals – our particularity derives from the very interactions in which we are historically and necessarily involved as human beings whose lives are embedded in community. Cunningham illustrates this with reference to his own artistic preferences, shaped – 'particularised' – by a range of experiences and exposures throughout his life: "The starkly individualistic claim that 'my tastes are purely my own' can survive only in a radically decontextualized account of my life."[29]

Perichoretic Themes in Pastoral Life

Earlier, we observed that the richness of the language of *perichoresis* with respect to human community lies not only in the mutuality and reciprocity of giving and receiving, but also in its insistence that particularity is enhanced rather than diminished. We also concluded that the mutuality and reciprocity implicit in the perichoretic life of the Trinity is normative as the ontological ground for all human interactions. Having demonstrated the need to attend to particularity in pastoral practice, we are now ready to identify specific dimensions of pastoral ministry and show how they display nuances or layers of perichoretic reality. As we proceed, the necessity for contextual particularity will be reinforced, for the Spirit at work in human community – especially, though not exclusively, Christian community – is, as we have seen, the 'witness to particularity'.

In our earlier discussion of the *perichoresis* construct we were reminded of Miroslav Volf's insight that the term refers to the reciprocal *interiority* of the trinitarian persons. Father, Son and Holy Spirit are not only enveloped in a dynamic, reciprocal life of self-giving love, but – at a structural level – they interpenetrate each other in a totally unique and unrepeatable way without losing their distinctiveness as persons. Strictly speaking, perichoretic life in the

---

[26] Cunningham, *These Three Are One*: 108-111.

[27] *Ibid*: 200-201.

[28] McFadyen, Alistair I., *The Call to Personhood: A Christian Theory of the Individual in Social Relationships*, New York: Cambridge University Press, 1990: 81; consider also the personalist philosophy of John Macmurray (*Persons in Relation*, London: Faber, 1970) for whom true personhood emerges only within the context of community, and apart from which persons do not exist at all.

[29] Cunningham, *These Three Are One*: 202.

sense that *God* has it is unavailable to human beings. Fiddes endorses this interpretation on the grounds that the notion of 'mutual interiority' between human and divine would, technically, open up the possibility of human and divine actions becoming mutually attributable, which not only is in danger of dissolving the distinction between divine and human, but also carries horrifying ethical implications: who ultimately is responsible for human atrocities?

However, Fiddes is keen to maintain the full strength of Christ's prayer in John 17:20-21 – "I pray also for those who will believe in me … that all of them may be one, Father, just as you are in me and I am in you." Accordingly he suggests that although human *subjects* cannot indwell divine *subjects* they can "dwell in the places opened out within the interweaving relationships of God; they dwell, we might say, not in 'spaces of subjectivity' but in 'relational spaces'."[30] We might suggest, therefore, an *analogous* correspondence between divine perichoretic life and *perichoresis* on the human plane: if finite creatures cannot love perichoretically in the exact way that God does within the divine communion, at least we might want to say that "we participate in a sort of availability analogous to that which the trinitarian persons enjoy for one another."[31] This is, as Fiddes states, the language of participation, a theme developed at some length in this book in Chapter 2 in the context of our participation in the ministry of Christ in the world, and intimated in Chapter 3 in terms of human participation in the divine life. How, then, might we interpret perichoretic participation at the level of pastoral practice? We can discern at least three 'perichoretic themes', which I have labelled *community formation*, *community realisation* and *community operation*.

Firstly, the circulatory life of the Trinity suggests a structure of communion that patterns itself at the human level after the intense dynamic reciprocity of the Three, giving shape to the community of faith. So, one expression of perichoretic life at the human level refers to *community formation*.[32] If God is 'pure mutual participation', or 'without remainder relational',[33] and Father, Son and Spirit indwell each other such that they are indivisible, then our

---

[30] Fiddes, *Participating in God*: 50. The author's reference to 'spaces of subjectivity' draws from the work of the philosopher Calvin Schrag, cited by Cunningham in his book *These Three Are One*; although Fiddes acknowledges the ideas of Schrag and Cunningham in tempering Enlightenment arrogance concerning the human 'I', he expresses unease about the way both draw parallels between human persons and the triune God (*ibid*: 48-49).

[31] Rogers, Eugene F., Jr., "The Stranger as Blessing" in Buckley and Yeago, (eds), *Knowing the Triune God*: 271.

[32] The phrase 'community formation' as developed in this chapter should not be confused with the same term adopted by Poling and Miller in their discussion of practical theology: see Poling, James N. and Miller, Donald E., *Foundations for a Practical Theology of Ministry*, Nashville: Abingdon, 1985.

[33] See Gunton, Colin E., "Relation and Relativity: The Trinity and the Created World" in Schwobel, Christoph (ed), *Trinitarian Theology Today: Essays on Divine Being and Act*, Edinburgh: T. & T. Clark, 1995: 92-112.

participation in this life may be viewed as an indwelling which actually constitutes us as human beings. Or, to use Volf's pneumatologically biased phrase, we indwell "*the life-giving ambience of the Spirit*, not the person of the Spirit."[34] We cannot indwell God as subjects, nor can we indwell one another as human beings; on what grounds, then, can our indwelling be regarded as perichoretic? Fiddes envisions this in a dynamic sense in terms of an indwelling of divine 'relational spaces', in which human beings are drawn into a *perichoresis* of movements, or relations. Volf's interpretation of perichoretic reality is less dynamic, as evidenced by his use of such terms as 'interiority', 'indwelling' and 'catholicity' to describe the structure of trinitarian and ecclesial relations. He writes:

> Because the Son indwells human beings through the Spirit ... *the unity of the church is grounded in the interiority of the Spirit* – and with the Spirit also in the interiority of the other divine persons – *in Christians* ... It is not the mutual perichoresis of human beings, but rather the indwelling of the Spirit common to everyone that makes the church into a communion corresponding to the Trinity, a communion in which personhood and sociality are equiprimal.[35]

It is instructive to note that the earliest usage of the word *perichoresis* related to the two natures of Christ. Cunningham suggests that "the significance of the incarnation is precisely its revelation of a more intimate relationship between God and human beings than was ordinarily thought possible."[36] This leads him to assert that the formation of the community of faith is predicated on what he calls "a profound mutual participation between God and human beings."[37] However, since human beings do not possess the capacity to indwell, it is more appropriate to posit an asymmetrical relationship between God and humanity – but a relationship, nonetheless, which is intensely alive, creatively dynamic and as mutually reciprocal as the divine-human distinction is able to offer. The shape and life of the pastoral community, therefore, derives from the initiative of the triune God of grace, who has chosen human beings to participate in his dynamic, perichoretic self-giving life of love. As we shall see, this has important implications for the way in which power in the faith-community is perceived and how decisions are made and authority exercised, as well as helping us to understand the diverse nature of the Christian community. Germane to these practical concerns is the so-called 'gender debate', to which some attention will also be given because of the feminist protest against patriarchalism in ecclesial life.

---

[34] Volf, *After Our Likeness*: 211, author's italics; Volf's context has to do with the relation between God and human beings, in which he articulates an interiority which is one-sided, i.e. the Spirit indwells human beings, but not vice versa.
[35] *Ibid*: 213, author's italics.
[36] Cunningham, *These Three Are One*: 182.
[37] *Ibid*: 181.

The second 'perichoretic theme' – *community realisation* – is an extension of the motif of 'community formation'. Our participation in the life of God determines our participation in *each other*. Given that personal interiority is solely an intradivine attribute, we refer here to a way of life that approximates as closely as possible the hospitable life of the Trinity. The notion of hospitality is a characteristic feature of God, who creates space for human beings to experience in the fullest sense possible what it means to 'feel at home'. Closely linked to this is the idea of 'receptivity', which means that "I invite the other to 'be at home' with me."[38] Pembroke cites the dialogical philosopher Gabriel Marcel: "to provide hospitality is truly to communicate something of oneself to the other,"[39] noting that for Marcel being present for another person is a grace, not a skill to be learned. A key word in Marcel's vocabulary is *disponibilité*, which Pembroke translates as availability, or disposability, which conveys the virtues of openness, fidelity and belonging: "in freely disposing of myself for the other I am liberated."[40]

Volf understands ecclesial giving and receiving in terms of *the interiority of personal characteristics*, corresponding to – but not imitating exactly – the interiority of the divine persons. In this mutual internalisation of personal characteristics

> we give to others not only something, but also a piece of ourselves, something of that which we have made of ourselves in communion with others; and from others we take not only something, but also a piece of them. Each person gives of himself or herself to others, and each person in a unique way takes up others into himself or herself.[41]

Though Volf is wary of describing this communion of persons in perichoretic language, it is evident that a form of *perichoresis* is apparent in this experience of mutual giving and receiving. It is a way of life that corresponds to Alistair McFadyen's theory of personhood: "we are properly centred as persons only by being directed towards the true reality of other personal centres: we become truly ourselves when we are truly for others."[42]

The last of our three 'perichoretic themes' within the church has to do with ecclesial practice in its many and various forms. Mindful that the *praxis* of ministry has to do with 'truth in *action*', a necessary 'doing' in which theory

---

[38] Pembroke, Neil, *The Art of Listening: Dialogue, Shame, and Pastoral Care*, Grand Rapids: Eerdmans, 2002: 21.
[39] Marcel, Gabriel, *Creative Fidelity*, translated by R. Rosthal, New York: The Noonday Press, 1964: 91.
[40] Pembroke, *The Art of Listening*: 13; on "Presence as Grace and Availability", see *ibid*: 13-30. Marcel may at times seem to be advocating a submission to exploitation, but Pembroke notes that he develops his ideas within the context of a *mutual commitment* to belonging; self-valuing is an important aspect of Marcel's concept of *disponibilité*.
[41] Volf, *After Our Likeness*: 211.
[42] McFadyen, *The Call to Personhood*: 151.

and practice intersect in such a way as to generate transformative influence both within and outside the walls of the church, we might tentatively label this *community operation*.[43] In Chapter 2 we noted a number of different emphases given to the discipline of pastoral ministry, including ministry as compassion, reconciliation, and community formation. In a recent attempt to summarise the visible dimensions of Christian ministry under the rubric of participation in the ministry of Christ, I articulated three broad areas of ministry: worship, mission, and compassion (expressed in terms of pastoral care within and beyond the community of faith).[44] When we speak of 'community operation', therefore, we are addressing the characteristically visible dimensions of pastoral practice to which these three broad areas refer, and in which important strands of perichoretic reality may be discerned. Rowan Williams reminds us that these dimensions of activity in the world, particularly compassion and mission, reflect the characteristics of what early theologians called *theosis*, otherwise known as 'deification' or divinisation'.[45] *Theosis* has less to do with an assumption of divine attributes than with participation in the life of God to such a degree that God's life and energy are expressed through believers, who become, in Luther's phrase, 'little Christs'.

Community Formation – Difference and Diversity

In this section we address a number of issues that relate to the way internal ontological shape may be attributed to the local community of faith. Paul Fiddes points out that the purpose of trinitarian language is not to provide us with an example to copy at the human level, "but to draw us into participation in God, out of which human life can be transformed."[46] Ultimately, he asserts, the language of Trinity is about interdependence, not domination, having more to do with such concepts as diversity, difference and mutuality than with oneness as a source of power. We noted in Chapter 3 that Lacugna's vision of trinitarianism repudiates every conceivable form of subordination among persons. She alleges that the 'theological defeat of the doctrine of the Trinity'

---

[43] 'Tentative', because of the ever-present tendencies in pastoral ministry to steer towards pragmatic models of ministry which focus on functional performance rather than a relationally-oriented interpretation (as discussed in Chapter 2).

[44] Buxton, Graham, *Dancing in the Dark: The Privilege of Participating in the Ministry of Christ*, Carlisle: Paternoster, 2001, especially Part Two: 'Some Implications for Ministry Practice': 115-236.

[45] Williams, Rowan, "Deification' in Wakefield, G. S. (ed), *The Westminster Dictionary of Christian Spirituality*, Philadelphia: Westminster Press, 1983: 106.

[46] Fiddes, *Participating in God*: 66; the author begins his treatment of this theme by critiquing the Emperor Constantine's understanding of what came to be called in the Middle Ages 'the divine right of kings': Constantine's theology was based on an absolute monotheism which interpreted power as the desire to unify, to place oneness and universality above diversity and difference (*ibid*: 62-65).

in the post-Cappadocian era – predicated on the claim that "the one God, even if *internally* triune, appears externally to us as *one*"[47] – opened the door to confusion between God's benevolent Fatherhood and all kinds of dominating hierarchies, religious, moral, political and sexual.

The Catholic ecclesiology of Joseph Ratzinger, now Pope Benedict XVI, is one example of how contemporary theological monarchianism may be construed as determining the hierarchical structure of authority within the church. Critiquing the notion of pure relationality on the grounds that Father, Son and Holy Spirit coincide in "pure unity",[48] Ratzinger swings the pendulum firmly towards *homoousion* and posits the priority of substance over relations within the intradivine life. This leads him to interpret the *structures* of ecclesial life within the same monistic framework. As Volf concedes, Ratzinger is willing to maintain that

> the 'indivisible unity of the church' is better illustrated in the perichoresis of the three divine persons, in this 'perpetual, dynamic intertwining and mutual interpenetration of spirit to spirit, love to love,' than in the image of the one divine monarchy[49]

but in his ecclesiology, the relations between divine persons are able to shape ecclesial spirituality only, not ecclesial structures. For example, in a more recent series of ecclesiological essays, Ratzinger intriguingly quotes Hilary of Poitiers, who "beseeches the divine mercy 'that you will want to fill the outstretched sail of our faith and acknowledgement with the breath of your Spirit'."[50] Ratzinger applies Hilary's endorsement of the Spirit not to the way in which the community of faith is given form or shape as a charismatic organism, but to the limits and dangers of activism amongst those already in authority. His concession to the Spirit is limited to the possibility that by "doing far too much ourselves and running things far too much ourselves, we could perhaps get in the way of the leadership of the Holy Spirit and set our work up against him."[51]

The structural hierarchy proposed by Ratzinger operates within both the

---

[47] LaCugna, *God For Us*: 392, author's italics.

[48] Ratzinger, Joseph, *Introduction to Christianity*, London: Burns & Oates, 1969: 135.

[49] Volf, *After Our Likeness*: 71, citing Ratzinger, Joseph, *Das neue Volk Gottes: Entwürfe zur Ekklesiologie*, Düsseldorf: Patmos, 1969: 214. For Ratzinger, the primacy of substance is clearly worked out in his ecclesiology, even though he maintains some form of symmetry between substance and relations in his trinitarian thinking. For a more complete discussion of Ratzinger's correspondence between the Trinity and ecclesiology, see *ibid*: 67-72, 200-201.

[50] Ratzinger, Joseph, *Church, Ecumenism and Politics: New Essays in Ecclesiology*, Slough: St Paul Publications, 1988: 60, quoting Hilary of Poitiers, *De Trinitate* 1:37, *Corpus Christianorum* LXII: 35.

[51] Ratzinger, *Church, Ecumenism and Politics*: 60.

universal church and each local congregation: at the universal level, the Pope is the visible head of the church, with bishops as local heads. This ecclesiology draws directly from his insistence that the one substance of God is the focus for unity in the church, whereas other ecclesiologists – such as John Zizioulas – prefer to locate unity within the communion of the triune God. Because ontology and relation within the Trinity are not opposites, but complementary, Fiddes' conception of a *perichoresis* of movements *ad intra* retains both hypostatic identity and dynamic, relational activity.[52] These two characteristics – identity and activity – are fundamental not only to the nature of the divine life, but also to the life of the church. For example,

> The multiple actions of God within the triune communion are expressed outwardly in a diversity of action in the world, which is manifested in turn in the multiplicity of spiritual gifts – *charismata* – in the local assembly of believers, and in the diversity of local congregations among themselves.[53]

The pastoral ministry of the local church is presented here in terms of perichoretic movements of grace and love, an entering into the flow of life and divine activity within the triune being of God. Such an understanding of local – and translocal[54] – ecclesiology challenges the hierarchical model of church structure which many fear would open the door to the dominating role of a priest or bishop at the expense of a diminishment of the life of the local community of believers. Ultimately, the local congregation is, in Moltmann's phrase, the 'lived out' Trinity. To pursue the sequence 'one God, one Christ, one bishop, one community' is to obtain unity, but it also "ties the Spirit to the ministry, so that an intrinsically charismatic community can hardly develop because the community remains passive: it is a recipient of the actions of the church's ministry."[55] So the lived-out unity of the charismatic community is

---

[52] In Chapter 3, we noted that Fiddes' transmutes Pannenberg's three 'living realizations of separate centres of action' into 'three living realisations of movements or directions of action', arguing that these can equally be conceived as distinguishing themselves from each other. In this way, Fiddes maintains hypostatic distinctiveness, which is essentially a particularity of *action* by which the divine persons are reckoned distinct from each other.

[53] Fiddes, *Participating in God*: 85.

[54] Whilst Ratzinger and Zizioulas differ with regard to their basic ecclesiological models, they both acknowledge the existence of the universal church – for Ratzinger, the local congregation is a 'church' only to the extent that it submits to the authority of the one universal church; for Zizioulas, each local church is *in itself* the universal church in its particular concrete location: for a thorough critique of the two theologians' interpretation of the relationship between the Trinity and ecclesiology , see Volf, *After Our Likeness*: 29-123.

[55] Moltmann, Jürgen, *History and the Triune God: Contributions to Trinitarian Theology*, London: SCM Press, 1991: 63; this is tantamount to "the reduction of the 'charismatic community' to the charisma of the one ministry" (*ibid*: 63).

expressed in the mutual love and care amongst "a fellowship of men and women without superiors or inferiors, a fellowship of men and women freed through love."[56]

The Brazilian Franciscan priest Leonardo Boff identifies four interlocking characteristics of the Trinity, expressed in the language of 'communion-perichoresis'. They may be summarised as follows: the existence of *difference*, or distinction, in the Trinity without thereby "multiplying God and falling into tritheism or polytheism"; the *irreducibility* of Father, Son and Spirit, who "are not just different from one another; they are also irreducible one to another ... [so] each is unique and non-interchangeable"; the eternal *communion* of the three divine Persons (the divine names themselves denote relationships, notes Boff); and the existence of a scriptural *order* in these relationships, which Boff interprets as a descriptive device to indicate the differences and simultaneous reciprocity between the three Persons.[57]

Boff examines the implications of this for ecclesiology, using a cosmic analogy: the "solar mystery of perichoretic communion in the Trinity sheds light on the lunar mystery of the church."[58] His 'communion-perichoresis' vision of the Trinity leads to "a vision of a church that is more communion than hierarchy, more service than power, more circular than pyramidal, more loving embrace than bending the knee before authority."[59] Human beings tend to frame

---

[56] *Ibid*: 64.

[57] Boff, Leonardo, *Trinity and Society*, Tunbridge Wells: Burns & Oates, 1988: 140-141; the book was conceived and written during Boff's year of silence following his criticism by the Vatican for teaching 'errors' in his book *Church: Charism and Power*, published in 1981.

[58] *Ibid*: 153.

[59] *Ibid*: 154; noticeably, Boff eschews any 'causal process' or dependence within the Trinity, claiming that the relationship between the three divine Persons "is one of reciprocal participation rather than hypostatic derivation, of correlation and communion rather than production and procession" (ibid: 146). Migliore comments that to speak of God as triune "is to set all of our prior understandings of what is divine in question. God is not a solitary monad but free self communicating love. God is not the supreme will-to-power over others but the supreme will-to-community in which power and life are shared. To speak of God as that ultimate power whose being is in giving, receiving and sharing love, who gives life to others and wills to live in community, is to turn upside down our understandings of both divine and human power. The reign of the triune God is the rule of sovereign love rather than the rule of force. A revolution in our understanding of the true power of God and of fruitful human power is thus implied when God is described as triune. God is *not* absolute power, *not* infinite ego-centrism, *not* majestic solitariness. The power of the triune God is not coercive but creative, sacrificial, and empowering love; and the glory of the triune God consists not in dominating others but in sharing life with others. In this sense confession of the triune God is the only understanding of God that is appropriate to and consistent with the New Testament declaration that God is love (1 John 4:8)." (Migliore, Daniel, *Faith Seeking Understanding: An Introduction to Christian Theology*, Grand Rapids: Eerdmans, 1991: 63-64).

things in terms of hierarchy: instead of viewing A in *relation* to B, we often prefer to view A in *comparison* to B, from which perspective we derive description, direction and purpose. Reverting to hierarchical views, we find ourselves attributing greater value to some ministries than others, which can easily lead to the devaluation of some people, whilst others are given an exalted status.[60] In contrast, the more the church seeks to eliminate destructive comparisons between Christians, and the more it advocates – and cultivates – co-operative, rather than competitive or hierarchical, ministries, the more it reflects the shared trinitarian life of co-existence in diversity. For Boff, the moral imperative implicit in this ecclesial model is expressed not just *intra muros ecclesiae*, but more particularly in terms of social liberation.

Robin Greenwood, an Anglican pastoral theologian and parish priest, argues that we should not get caught up in the 'threeness' of a trinitarian paradigm. Rather, we should interpret the Trinity primarily as a communion of difference that points to the dynamic interrelation of a number of persons, places and roles that together constitute a rich wholeness. The ecclesiological significance of this has to do with what he calls 'the subversive character of the Church', which is "to continue reshaping itself in order to show society its true life, through making creative connections between the worlds of work, home and faith,"[61] worlds that have traditionally been compartmentalised, with potentially conflicting allegiances. Greenwood's vision of the local Christian community is perichoretically inspired, kenotically motivated and eschatologically shaped. It is "an agent of change, becoming, however partially, a sign and foretaste of God's passionate desire for the fulfilment of all creation in justice, reconciliation, and kaleidoscopic harmony."[62] Just as the church is to draw its identity and shape from the Trinity, seeking to image the communion life of God in its structure and practices, so it is to offer society a transforming way of life and living that embraces peace, justice and hope:

> This calls for a reconstruction of ecclesiology in such a way that it can draw into dynamic interaction worship, spirituality, the building up of a faith community and an engagement with the world with an expectation of calling out one another in love to be what God intends.[63]

---

[60] I am grateful to Elizabeth Smith, a graduate student in my Summer 2003 class on "Participation in the Ministry of Christ" at Fuller Theological Seminary, for this insight: she writes in an unpublished class assignment that "this paradigm is not without its use within specific contexts and parameters, but, expanded beyond the limits of its design, it can be demeaning and destructive."

[61] Greenwood, R., "Ordering the church for working with God's life in the world: Equal and differing callings" (see http://ministry.ireland.anglican.org/articles/greenwood.pdf, accessed on 10.10.03).

[62] *Ibid*: 14.

[63] *Ibid*: 11. For a Wesleyan perspective on this, see Runyon, Theodore, *The New Creation: John Wesley's Theology Today*, Nashville: Abingdon, 1998, in which the

The preceding comments assume that hierarchy as a structural paradigm is interpreted pyramidically. However, if hierarchy is construed not as a pyramid but, more constructively, as a series of concentric circles with those in authority exercising a unifying ministry from the centre – reflecting an Orthodox understanding of the Trinity, in which *monarche* and equality co-exist in harmony – then perhaps hierarchy may be viewed as a valid expression of ecclesial life. If human beings – especially in Western societies – inevitably tend towards hierarchy in their social organisation,[64] the question arises: will the abolition of traditional and contemporary hierarchical structures preclude the emergence of alternative hierarchical forms in ecclesial life? More fundamentally, must hierarchy always be viewed negatively? Perhaps if hierarchy and humility are viewed as two sides of the same coin, hierarchy need not be disparaged as it assumes a more acceptable face.

The traditional hierarchical model of ecclesial life has given rise to two related topics that have generated much heat in recent years: patriarchy and subordinationism. LaCugna is passionate in her insistence that patriarchy, "the rule of the *pater*, the father, is based on a nontrinitarian and ultimately non-Christian conception of God."[65] The emerging feminist consciousness has been characterised in some quarters by a powerful liberationist thrust to combat sexism, defined in explicit terms as patriarchal domination of women by men. At the moderate biblical end of the feminist spectrum[66] the emphasis is on genuine equality between the sexes, involving a hermeneutical approach to the biblical text that encourages women to find their place within the total life of the church. In contrast, Rosemary Ruether and Elisabeth Schussler Fiorenza are two forthright critics of patriarchalism within the theological tradition, and their writings are 'revisionist' in an attempt to reinterpret the Christian tradition within a more liberal and radical pro-feminist framework.[67]

The revisionist critique of the Christian tradition identifies androcentrism and patriarchy as evils which are ingrained within the fabric of Western

---

author argues that human beings are called "not only to mirror God in their own lives but to reflect the grace which they received into the world, and thus to mediate the life of God to the rest of creation" (*ibid*: 13).

[64] For a defence of this argument within the context of managing human resources for effective leadership and supervision, see Sayles, Leonard R. and Strauss, George, *Human Behavior in Organizations*, Englewood Cliffs NJ: Prentice-Hall, 1966: 347-392, in which the authors claim that "it is easy to understand the emergence of a pyramidical structure when the efforts of more than a small number of people must be coordinated" (*ibid*: 348).

[65] LaCugna, *God For Us*: 393.

[66] See, for example, the evangelical perspectives of Elaine Storkey in *What's Right with Feminism*, Grand Rapids: Eerdmans, 1985.

[67] See, in particular, Ruether, Rosemary Radford, *Sexism and God-Talk: Toward a Feminist Theology*: London, SCM Press, 1983; Fiorenza, Elisabeth Schussler, *In Memory of Her: A Feminist Reconstruction of Christian Origins*, London, SCM Press, 1983.

Christian culture, the practical result of which is "a deeprooted misogyny or hatred of women ... Feminist theologians believe that the sin of misogyny is manifested throughout the Bible and church history in the suppression of the roles of women among the people of God and in identification of sin with femaleness."[68] Their solution is to liberate the biblical text from its patriarchal straitjacket by rediscovering the equality between men and women that was lost in the early Christian accommodation to the prevailing culture. The gospel emphasis on servanthood has strong pastoral overtones, as Oden reminds us. Significantly, this shepherding imagery is gender-inclusive: "We are well served by a central image of ministry that is nurturant, life-enabling, and non-combative except in extreme emergency, when the sheep are endangered. Modern stereotypes that portray shepherds always as males fail to grasp the fact that in primitive pastoral societies, women as often as men were active in caring for valued animals, the source of wealth in nomadic families."[69] The suggestion of a nurturing, even parenting, dimension in ministry within the context of community lends itself as much to women as to men.

These observations, of course, are welcome grist to the feminist mill. However, when feminist theologians espouse a strongly ideological and radical stance, assuming for women the very dominance despised within patriarchy, and losing sight not only of biblical authority but also of the Christian call to servanthood, then it does a great disservice to the cause of women's rightful place within the ministry of the church. Ruether rightly reminds us that ministry does not dispense with the notion of power: rather "ministry means exercising power in a new way, as a means of liberation of one another ... Ministry overcomes competitive one-up, one-down relationships and generates relations of mutual empowerment."[70] When men think otherwise and hold to an exclusive masculine priesthood, then it is time to confront what may be the tip of a patriarchal iceberg, hidden for too long. But when women reinterpret the biblical text in order to wrest power from men, the pendulum is in danger of swinging away from servanthood and into the very territory for which men have been indicted.[71]

---

[68] Grenz, Stanley J. and Olson, Roger E., *20th Century Theology: God and the World in a Transitional Age*, Downers Grove, IVP, 1992: 228.

[69] Oden, Thomas C., *Pastoral Theology: Essentials of Ministry*, San Francisco: Harper & Row, 1983: 52.

[70] Ruether, *Sexism and God-Talk*: 207.

[71] We must surely welcome, albeit cautiously, these corrective adjustments to the injustices and dehumanising tendencies within the history of the church. However, the espousal of any theological method that denies Scripture its authoritative role within the Christian tradition is a far more serious matter. Although the feminist agenda seeks to re-interpret the Bible primarily through a corresponding re-reading of the text, some exponents stray at times into more radical territory when they challenge ultimate biblical authority. Mary Daly is an early example of 'post-Christian feminists' who have lost their anchor in the revealed Word of God and who see no hope of remaining within the church as it is constituted today (see Daly, Mary, *Beyond God the Father: Toward a*

This necessary perception of Christian authority as servanthood, demonstrating a critical correspondence between *kenosis* and *perichoresis*, is explored by Alan Lewis in his understanding of Christian vocation as that which takes place within a theology of the cross (*theologia crucis*).[72] In our earlier discussion of Rublev's icon we concluded that the event of the cross is an intratrinitarian drama, a dynamic *perichoresis* of suffering love for the sake of the whole world, an event in which Father, Son and Holy Spirit are all intimately, necessarily, *perichoretically* involved. So the language of *kenosis*, of suffering and ecstatic love, is expressed in terms of trinitarian *perichoresis*. Lewis' essay needs to be read in the light not only of this understanding of the mutual, outgoing, *kenotic* love of the Trinity, but also of Anderson's corresponding assumption that "the church exists as a community of self-emptying, or kenotic presence, in the world."[73]

In his exposition of the way of *ecclesia crucis*, Lewis exposes the church's capitulation to secularisation in a number of key areas under the umbrella idolatry of a theology that bypasses the centrality of the cross. His major thesis is that only when the church has recovered a *theologia crucis* can vocation be truly reflective of the vocation of Christ. In similar vein to Hall's critique of North American Christianity[74], Lewis expounds the doctrine of *kenosis* with vigour, arguing that only in self-emptiness can the church, like Christ, discover its fullness: only in an other-centred commitment can the church reflect the

---

Philosophy of Women's Liberation, Boston, Beacon, 1973). The radical wing of feminist theology is guilty of promoting such a strong ideological line that its adherents fall into the same trap as those whom they criticise. In fact, ideological extremism is discernible in feminist theology in three areas that ironically correspond to its critique of traditional (patriarchal) theological method. Firstly, in their generalising assumption that *all* biblical texts are androcentric, radical feminist theologians are carelessly indiscriminate, a charge that they lay at the door of their 'male oppressors' who, they claim, stereotype women and universalise male language within the biblical text. Secondly, the polarisation that accompanies their own distancing of men from women echoes their condemnation of similar tendencies in patriarchy, especially in their assertion that men are regarded as ontologically superior to women. Thirdly, feminist theologians accuse men of treating women as objects to advance their own ends rather than real characters of worth. This utilisation of women by men is paralleled by feminist theology's imaginative reinterpretation of key motifs to promote a feminist perspective, in which masculine gives way to feminine: for example, Ruether's revision of the historical Jesus leads her to maintain that "the Jesus of the synoptic Gospels can be recognized as a figure remarkably compatible with feminism."(Ruether, *Sexism and God-Talk*: 135).

[72] Lewis, Alan E., "Unmasking Idolatries: Vocation in the *Ecclesia Crucis*" in Kettler, Christian D. and Speidell, Todd H. (eds), *Incarnational Ministry: The Presence of Christ in Church, Society and Family*, Colorado Springs, CO: Helmers and Howard, 1990: 110-128.

[73] Anderson, Ray S., *The Shape of Practical Theology: Empowering Ministry with Theological Praxis*, Downers Grove: IVP, 2001: 116.

[74] Especially evident in Hall, Douglas John, *Thinking the Faith*, Minneapolis: Fortress Press, 1991.

ministry of Christ. In the words of Bishop Kallistos Ware, "Without *kenosis* and cross-bearing, without the exchange of substituted love and all the voluntary suffering which this involves, there can be no genuine likeness to the Trinity."[75]

However, claims Lewis, the church has indulged itself in a "self-destroying imitation of the world's success and plenitude."[76] Quoting a Presbyterian Statement of Reformed Faith, he affirms the role of the Spirit in giving us the courage we need "to unmask idolatries in church and culture."[77] In particular, theology itself is criticised for its failure to divest itself of a lust for power and glory. In the light of this critique, Lewis turns his attention to his central concern, the secularisation of vocation. One measure of a rededication to servanthood is how we view the 'call' to ministry. Here, Lewis argues passionately for identification between vocation and cross: "they are the same reality."[78] Jesus' words in John 15:16, "You did not choose me, but I chose you", challenge the idolatry of "volunteerism and free choice" in our perception of Christian vocation, a calling which needs to be re-interpreted as kenotic self-renouncing ministry.

Lewis argues that authority and rule have been severed from servanthood and suffering in the history of clericalism. This secularisation of vocation is considered by Lewis under five headings, through which he suggests the church has modelled itself on patterns of vocation which have more to do with 'Gentile' models of power and wisdom rather than with Christ. Lewis' five clerical 'idolatries' are *perfectionism, power, permanence, professionalism* and *privatism*.

Renouncing these, men and women who are called out of secular employment into 'full-time' Christian ministry need to willingly embrace the following vulnerable features associated with their vocation: an acceptance of weakness, for God calls us in spite of our failings, not because of our manifest strengths and abilities; a renewed understanding of power that resides not in privilege and position but in the Spirit of Christ crucified ("My grace is sufficient for you," the Lord reminded Paul, "for my power is made perfect in weakness" - 2 Corinthians 12:9); the possibility that God may sovereignly call someone *out* of ministry as well as *into* ministry, enabling welcome transitions in ministry to occur; an acknowledgment that excellence in Christian ministry is not the same as ascending the ladder of a successful career; and the recognition that all ministry takes place within the context of community.

These dimensions of vulnerability in Christian vocation, which correspond to the life of the trinitarian God – whose love has been expressed by Vanstone

---

[75] Kallistos of Diokleia, "The human person as an icon of the Trinity" in *Sobornost*, Vol.8 No.2, 1986: 20.
[76] Lewis, "Unmasking Idolatries": 112.
[77] *Ibid*: 113.
[78] *Ibid*: 113.

as limitless, precarious and vulnerable[79] – lie at the heart of all pastoral ministry. In particular, Lewis' final insistence that "the individual's 'call' is not discrete and separate; it has truly *occurred* only when heard and confirmed by the community"[80] represents a challenge to all interpretations of 'call' which focus on grandiose claims to power and glory grounded in hierarchical models of ecclesial life. It is instructive to note that the apostle Paul, convinced though he was that God had called him, nevertheless presented himself before the Jerusalem leadership, so that his ministry might be seen to be in partnership with theirs. Commenting on Galatians 2:2, Ridderbos observes that "it was necessary that everybody should not be going his own way. This was a communal matter."[81]

The following quote from LaCugna demonstrates her conviction that when men and women live their lives in close and inclusive interrelationship, giving and receiving without separateness, subordination or division, the church is 'an icon of the Trinity':

> The trinitarian doctrine of God, as the basis for a trinitarian ecclesiology, might not specify the exact forms of structure and community appropriate to the church, but it does provide the critical principle against which we can measure present institutional arrangements. Very simply, we may ask whether our institutions, rituals, and administrative practices foster elitism, discrimination, competition, or any of several 'archisms', or whether the church is run like God's household: a domain of inclusiveness, interdependence, and cooperation, structured according to the model of *perichoresis* among persons.[82]

Moltmann suggests that the idea of the Motherhood of the Holy Spirit may help to overcome patriarchy in the image of God and the domination of men in the church.[83] The femininity of the Spirit has been explored by a number of other theologians,[84] but the primary objection to patriarchy has, of course, to do

---

[79] See Chapter 2 for a brief discussion of Vanstone's theology of *kenosis*, developed in Vanstone, W.H., *Love's Endeavour, Love's Expense: The Response of Being to the Love of God*, London: Darton, Longman & Todd, 1977: 39-54.

[80] Lewis, "Unmasking Idolatries": 126, author's italics.

[81] Ridderbos, Herman N., *The Epistle of Paul to the Churches of Galatia*, Grand Rapids, Eerdmans, 1953: 81.

[82] LaCugna, *God For Us*: 402.

[83] Moltmann, Jürgen, *The Source of Life: The Holy Spirit and the Theology of Life*, London: SCM Press, 1997: 35-37.

[84] A brief, but helpful, discussion may be found in Pinnock, Clark H., *Flame of Love: A Theology of the Holy Spirit*, Downers Grove: IVP, 1996: 15-17. For a more general treatment of the problem of language in 'naming' God, see Soskice, Janet Martin, *Metaphor and Religious Language*, Oxford: Clarendon Press, 1985; Duck, Ruth C., *Gender and the Name of God: The Trinitarian Baptismal Formula*, Cleveland, Ohio: The Pilgrim Press, 1991.

with the designation of God as 'Father'. In response to the claim that few scholars have adequately tackled this thorny issue, Cunningham argues that a word's 'meaning' is not determined by the intention of the writer or speaker: "it is a rhetorical construct, and its content is, at least in part, in the hands of its hearers and readers."[85] He suggests that the problem may arise because of the very need to use names to identify the Three as distinct individuals, whereas a focus on *relations* within the Trinity would obviate that need, at least to some extent.

Human language, of course, is a fragile – and at times misleading – vehicle for conveying the truth about God, though various metaphors may go some way towards alleviating some of the concerns expressed by those who feel 'oppressed' or demeaned by the term 'Father'. The linguistic problem has been recognised by Barth, who emphasises *relational* attributes and *processions* within the Trinity when he writes of Father, Son and Spirit:

> If these three names ... are really in their threeness the one name of the one God, then it follows in this one God there is primarily at least – let us put it cautiously – something like fatherhood and sonship, and therefore something like begetting and being begotten.[86]

It is not the purpose of this book to examine in depth alternative designations for Father, Son and Holy Spirit, but Cunningham's triad of *Source, Wellspring* and *Living Water* is suggestive as an experiment in the practice of trinitarian theology. The formulations convey the ideas of motion and relation, avoid the perennial difficulty of masculine language, and utilise an image (a spring of water) that has a rich trinitarian history. Cunningham's proposal has merit in complementing rather than dispensing with the traditional forms of naming three – after all, as Jenson notes, that Jesus called on God with 'father' rather than with 'mother' "is a fact about the historic person Jesus that we can no more change by decree than we can decree that he was not Jewish, or a wandering rabbi, or unpopular with the Sanhedrin."[87] Furthermore, in the context of subordinationism, Cunningham's designations offer an opportunity to retain radical intradivine equality, whilst avoiding some sort of temporal order often attributed to the Three:

---

[85] Cunningham, *These Three Are One*: 50.
[86] Barth, Karl, *Church Dogmatics* 1/1, Edinburgh: T. & T. Clark, 1936: 363.
[87] Jenson, Robert, "The Father, He ..." in Kimel, Alvin F. (ed), *Speaking the Christian God: The Holy Trinity and the Challenge of Feminism*, Grand Rapids: Eerdmans, 1992: 104. In the same vein, as Thomas Oden has persuasively observed, "Jesus was male and not female. But he was also Jewish and not gentile, born in Palestine and not Norway. He is also of Davidic descent and not of some other family descent." (Oden, *Pastoral Theology*: 45).

> The Source is the cause of the Wellspring and the Living Water; but the Wellspring is also the cause of the Source (which must be source of something) *and* the cause of the Living Water (causing it to flow forth). Finally, the Living Water is the cause of the Source and the Wellspring, bringing them into full life and providing a vehicle through which they can act upon the world.[88]

As we have noted throughout our study to date, the *perichoresis* construct reflects the radical, relational co-equality implicit in Cunningham's triad, celebrating difference and diversity within the framework of mutual interdependence. These same themes of difference and diversity are characteristic of the community of believers participating in a life of true communion with each other. In the context of ecclesial politics, for example, those who contend that God has set men over women in the home and in the church may be guilty of using the word 'difference' as a code word[89] – or, as Vanhoozer puts it, language used in the service of ideology: "Ideology legitimates ruling-class domination by making its ideas and norms appear natural, just and universal."[90]

In his helpful assessment of the concept of subordinationism within the Trinity, and its derivative implications for the gender debate in ecclesiology, Kevin Giles affirms that men and women "are differentiated by God's creative initiative, but this differentiation exists within their shared humanity."[91] It is their God-given sexual identity to which the concept of 'difference' alludes: it "does not imply or necessitate the subordination of one party."[92] As a rejoinder to those who espouse a rigid androcentric interpretation of ecclesial authority, we may quote Barth: "The summons to both man and woman to be true to themselves may take completely unforeseen forms right outside the systems in which we like to think."[93] Gunton is equally forthcoming:

> If ... the attribution of particular positions to particular groups or orders is to be replaced by a pattern more reflective of the free personal relations which constitute the deity, should we not consciously move

---

[88] Cunningham, *These Three Are One*: 113. But why do we still *think* in terms of *appropriation* rather than the indivisible action of God? Ultimately, suggests Cunningham, such appropriation functions pragmatically: it aids us in understanding better, believing more firmly and articulating more persuasively.

[89] As suggested in Giles, Kevin, *The Trinity and Subordinationism: The Doctrine of God and the Contemporary Gender Debate*, Downers Grove: IVP, 2002: 186.

[90] Vanhoozer, Kevin J., *Is There a Meaning in the Text?: The Bible, the Reader and the Morality of Literary Knowledge*, Grand Rapids: Zondervan, 1998: 173 (cited in Giles, *The Trinity and Subordinationism*: 187).

[91] Giles, *The Trinity and Subordinationism*: 188.

[92] *Ibid*: 186.

[93] Barth, Karl, *Church Dogmatics* 3/4, Edinburgh: T. & T. Clark, 1961: 151.

towards an ecclesiology of perichoresis: in which there is no permanent structure of subordination, but in which there are overlapping patterns of relationships, so that the same person will be sometimes 'subordinate' and sometimes 'superordinate' according to the gifts and graces being exercised?[94]

Gunton's perichoretic ecclesiology is essentially charismatic at heart: the community of faith is constituted in its internal ordering by the Spirit of life, who is the agent of diversity.[95] Likewise for Moltmann, the charismatic community is "a *unity in diversity* and a *diversity in unity*."[96] He cites the apostle Paul's teaching about *charismata*, maintaining that the "acceptance of other people in their difference and their particularity is constitutive for the community of Christ."[97] The Spirit is always at work in the church to facilitate this trinitarian way of life, orchestrating his manifold gifts and graces in a symphony of hope, for ultimately we are all "members of a church on the way toward the full realization of God's life; communion is an eschatological hope."[98] Moltmann's interpretation of authority exercised within the charismatic community is therefore expressly pneumatological. The Spirit must be given full freedom to reign within the community of the church, distributing his authority through the individual and through the community as a whole. Consequently, there can be no fixed pattern by which the will of God is accomplished within each community. This does not mean, of course, that there are no norms for community life: Moltmann specifically identifies *kerygma*, *koinonia* and *diakonia* as essential elements of all that the church is called to be. But in the performance of these essential 'commissions of the community', we must acknowledge the inventiveness and ingenuity of the Spirit, who alone 'constitutes' the church, to use the terminology of John Zizioulas.[99]

---

[94] Gunton, Colin E., *The Promise of Trinitarian Theology*, Edinburgh: T. & T. Clark, 1991: 80.

[95] Zizioulas argues that the vitality of the church is dependent upon the creative ministry of the Spirit, who 'constitutes' the church as communion in the sense that, as the Spirit of *koinonia*, he transcends all distinctions and not only enables the church to come alive but actually causes it to come into existence: so "pneumatology does not refer to the well-being but to the very being of the church." (Zizioulas, *Being as Communion*: 132).

[96] Moltmann, *The Spirit of Life*: 193, author's italics.

[97] *Ibid*: 184.

[98] LaCugna, *God For Us*: 403.

[99] Moltmann sums up the matter well in his discussion of the relationship between the 'assignments', or callings, of individual people and the calling of the community as a whole. Commenting on those who function in the church in their assigned tasks, he points out that their commission "does not separate them from the people and does not set them above the people either, for it is exercised in fellowship with and by commission of the whole people and in the name of that people's commissioning. But the thing for which the people are commissioned does not come from them themselves; it comes from their God, in whose name they speak and act." (Moltmann, Jürgen, *The Church in the Power of the Spirit*, London, SCM Press, 1977: 303). What Moltmann is

This simultaneous exercise of authority can only take place if all members of the community recognise their dependence not only on one another but also on the Holy Spirit. Only the Spirit has the wisdom and power to orchestrate a diverse community of individuals in such a way as to mediate divine authority in the service of the Kingdom of God. In an intriguing exploration of the musical term *polyphony* – which refers to multiple tones and sequences played simultaneously, overlapping each other in such a way that no one note is so dominant that it renders another mute – Cunningham links the concept to trinitarian theology, suggesting that

> Christianity proclaims a polyphonic understanding of God – one in which *difference* provides an alternative to a monolithic homogeneity, yet without becoming a source of confusion. Attention to any one of the Three does not imply a diminished role for the others; all three have their distinctive melodies, and all are 'played' and 'heard' simultaneously without damage to God's unity.[100]

For Cunningham, "the communion that informs and underwrites our common bond of humanity" is an expression of "the perfect, polyphonic communion of the inner life of God."[101] He traces the way music has been explored in the writings of three theologians – Bonhoeffer, von Balthasar and Milbank – observing that, for Milbank, the Christian concept of community recognises the same sort of 'non-exclusionary difference' that is exemplified in polyphonic music. Listening to music "takes place within the context of an interpretive community"[102] – similarly, Christians within the community of faith listen and learn together, participating in a 'common language' defined by Cunningham as common practices, such as worship, education, and care for others. He develops one such practice, baptism, showing how the water imagery associated with baptism reflects the contours of a specifically trinitarian polyphony, encouraging us to see ourselves as being polyphonically incorporated into the 'symphony of the Church'.

---

emphasising here is a simultaneous outworking of divine authority through the gathered community and through individuals, which he defines as a *genetic connection*. "The Spirit leads men and women into the fellowship of the messianic people, at the same time giving everyone his own place and his particular charge." (*Ibid*: 306).

[100] Cunningham, *These Three Are One*: 129; the parallel between the metaphors of symphony and dance is suggestive, for both convey a sense of movement, vitality, heterogeneity and consensus.

[101] *Ibid*: 164. In a similar vein, Jenson explores the perichoretic harmony of the Trinity with reference to music, suggesting that we might understand God as a 'melody' that is fugued; a fugue is a polyphonic composition, usually with a single main theme, in which melodic voices interweave imitatively. Declaring that there is nothing so capacious as a fugue, Jenson closes his exposition of the doctrine of God with the remarkable statement that "God is a great *fugue*." (Jenson, Robert W., *Systematic Theology*, Vol I - *The Triune God*, New York: Oxford University Press, 1997: 236, author's italics).

[102] *Ibid*: 134.

Community Realisation – Love

Cunningham identifies Paul's teaching about the Body of Christ (1 Cor. 12:14-27) as emblematic of the polyphony of the triune God in terms of "the importance of difference, the appropriateness of homogenization, and the radical equality of the members of the body."[103] These elements of the life of the church reflect a mutually-determinative interconnectedness that he explores more fully in a chapter devoted to the 'trinitarian virtue' of participation, which deals with the essential *character* of the relations within God, and, by extension, within the community of faith. We suggested the phrase 'community realisation' as a succinct expression of this degree of participation at the ecclesial level.

Volf's concept of the 'interiority of personal characteristics' – proposed as a measure of ecclesial perichoretic reality – may be likened to the giving and receiving of pieces of a jigsaw puzzle, as suggested by the rabbi Lawrence Kushner:

> Each lifetime is the pieces of a jigsaw puzzle.
> For some there are more pieces.
> For others the puzzle is more difficult to assemble.
>
> Some seem to be born with a nearly completed puzzle ...
> ... But know this. No one has within themselves
> All the pieces to their puzzle ...
>
> ... Everyone carries with them at least one and probably
> Many pieces to someone else's puzzle.
> Sometimes they know it.
> Sometimes they don't.
>
> And when you present your piece ...
> ... To another, whether you know it or not,
> Whether they know it or not,
> You are a messenger from the Most High.[104]

In our call to live ethically in the church and in the world, we actually need one another because we are created for relationship and can only realise our full humanity in communion with God and with each other. This communal life in the Spirit is what Anderson calls a 'lived transcendence', which assumes a

---

[103] *Ibid*: 155.
[104] Kushner, Lawrence, *Honey from the Rock: Visions of Jewish Mystical Renewal*, New York: Harper and Row, 1977. "It's rarely the author or featured speaker who has your puzzle pieces," observes Kushner; "it's usually someone who has a bit part in your life whose name is not recorded in the program" (from an interview with Lawrence Kushner published in *Personal Transformation*, "Being a Joyful Servant", http://www.personal transformation.com/Kushner.html, accessed on 15.10.03).

number of forms: the life of a kenotic and 'ek-static' community; a reality of life in solidarity with the world; and an eschatological life in God.[105] Taking the first two, he argues that the Spirit is continuously at work re-forming us into the *real* form of our intrinsic nature as the image of God. Kenotic community is not something we strive to achieve, but is the goal of our existence as we receive one another in love. If *kenosis* relates to our movement towards one another in communion with the incarnate Word, then *ekstasis* designates our movement towards transcendent life in the Spirit.

The motif of community is a profoundly theological one. At a number of places throughout this study we have traced its source to the Trinity, which is the prototype for the life of the church on earth: it follows that the defining characteristic of human community as God intended it to be is love. Here we are talking about a quality of love that starts from within the life of the community of faith as the result of each member's personal communion with God. The following illustration may help. Imagine a circle, similar to the wheel of a bicycle, around the rim of which individual people are situated. As each person moves along a spoke towards the hub of the wheel, there is a growing closeness between them. So it is in community: as we seek to draw closer to God in our own personal Christian walk, we discover that Christian community becomes more of a reality. That which God has given to us as gift becomes real amongst us. The actuality of community life is not something that we have to engineer or manipulate, though it certainly demands our co-operation and energies.

When we realise the truth that our love for God has this capacity to radiate out to embrace others, we are released into a new freedom to love. We no longer strive to love, but rest in the love that is in God himself. When we truly come to know this God who is pure love, and begin to rejoice in his gracious acceptance of us, we discover that we can accept others, however different they may be from us. Writing of this love that flows from the heart, Jean Vanier observes that "the more impossible it is in human terms, the more of a sign it is that their love comes from God and that Jesus is living."[106] However, this must not be interpreted as a recipe for passivity in community. Far from it: Christians are called to vibrant participation in the Christian life. This begins in the heart, for "a community is only a community when the majority of its members is making the transition from 'the community for myself' to 'myself for the community'."[107] In contemporary Western society, marked not only by individualism and narcissism but also by increasing social mobility, there is a danger that the deep longings in the human heart to belong will be translated into selfish interpretations of 'community for myself'. The task facing the Christian community is how to live in such a way as to be both attractive to

---

[105] Anderson, Ray S., *Historical Transcendence and the Reality of God*, London: Geoffrey Chapman, 1975: 227-251.

[106] Vanier, Jean, *Community and Growth*, Homebush NSW: Society of St Paul, 1979: 34.

[107] *Ibid*: 22.

those who belong as well as an authentic reflection of the life of God ... and therefore attractive to those as yet outside its boundaries.

The foundational reality of community is suggestive for a more complete understanding of the *imago Dei*, for in the final analysis "the *imago dei* is not merely relational; it is not simply the I-Thou relationship of two persons standing face-to-face. Instead, it is ultimately *communal*."[108] Grenz draws this conclusion from a thorough study of human sexuality, which articulates at the human level the quest for completeness that draws humans out of isolation into bonded relationships. More fundamentally, however, and all the more because "sexuality is not eradicated en route to eternity,"[109] sexuality reflects the eternal reality that human beings have been created to belong to one another, expressing a freedom – the freedom to be for another – that mirrors the freedom that resides within God himself. Drawing especially from the insights of Bonhoeffer and Barth, Grenz takes an ultimately eschatological – and polyphonous – perspective, asserting that the role of sexuality is of primary importance in bringing humans into community with Christ and with his disciples in the fellowship of his church:

> ... it is this connection that will eternally draw humankind into participation in the very life of the triune God, as the Spirit molds humans into one great chorus of praise to the Father through the Son, which in turn will mark the Father's eternal glorification of the new humanity in the Son.[110]

The significance of human sexuality may be articulated at three levels. In the context of the triune life, the 'quest for completeness' reflected in sexual differentiation and consummation is analogous to the polarity and complementarity of being within the Trinity.[111] At a second level, the consummation of love through sexual encounter is proleptic as it mirrors – albeit imperfectly – eschatological life for those who are 'in Christ', expressed in the language of participation, or *theosis*.[112] Thirdly, the profound experience of sexual intimacy directs us to an understanding of ecclesial life characterised

---

[108] Grenz, Stanley J., *The Social God and the Relational Self: A Trinitarian Theology of the Imago Dei*, Louisville: Westminster John Knox Press, 2001: 303, my italics.

[109] *Ibid*: 301; or, as Ray Anderson puts it, "Creaturely sexuality, even as human sexuality, exists as a penultimate form of essential sexuality" (Anderson, Ray S., *On Being Human: Essays in Theological Anthropology*, Eerdmans: Grand Rapids, 1982: 117).

[110] Grenz, *The Social God and the Relational Self*: 303.

[111] For a discussion of human sexuality as a 'sign' of the fundamental polarity of being which is constituted by the *imago Dei*, see Anderson, *On Being Human*: 104-129.

[112] On *theosis*, see Rakestraw, Robert V., "Becoming Like God: An Evangelical Doctrine of Theosis" in *Journal of the Evangelical Society* (September 1994): 365-379; Clendenin, Daniel B., "Partakers of Divinity: The Orthodox Doctrine of Theosis" in *Journal of the Evangelical Society* 40 (July 1997): 257-269.

by intense mutual giving and receiving in order that each person may find completion in communal, rather than just relational, life. Sexuality "is a continual reminder that we are persons designed for union with other persons ... it is the capacity for relationship, for ecstasis, and for self-transcendence."[113] And, as LaCugna further reminds us, although sexual desire tends to manifest itself in exclusivity, "exclusivity must transcend itself toward inclusivity – for example, openness to a new child or hospitality to the stranger."[114]

Within the Christian biblical and historical traditions, hospitality relates most particularly to the welcoming of strangers, and attention will be given to this dimension of inclusivity in the next section of this chapter. But it is instructive to note here that for the early Christian community, the practice of hospitality has a divine precedent. Citing the perennial demands on our own life and resources, as well as our own personal – and often pressing – problems, as barriers to the exercise of hospitality, Amy Oden asks why we should bother with the practice of hospitality and its attendant risks. To which she replies: "Because we are overwhelmed by the power of God's hospitable grace in our lives and cannot do otherwise."[115] For the early Christians, seeking to live out the trinitarian life, hospitality was not so much a gospel command as an expression of what it means to be made *imago Dei*. Boersma quotes the words of Reinhard Hütter, for whom the church's practice of hospitality is "both a reflection and an extension of God's own hospitality – God's sharing of the love of the triune life with those who are dust."[116] As the triune God is *ekstatic*

---

[113] LaCugna, *God For Us*: 406-407.

[114] *Ibid*: 407. We might note here that marriage has both exclusive and inclusive dimensions. Its exclusive nature is, of course, reflected in the intimacy implicit in the covenant between husband and wife. But the institution of marriage is also a central element in the fabric of society, with a vital outward orientation – the Anglican marriage service contains the following words: "In marriage husband and wife belong to one another, and they begin a new life together *in the community*" (my italics).

[115] Oden, Amy G. (ed), *And You Welcomed Me: A Sourcebook on Hospitality in Early Christianity*, Nashville: Abingdon Press, 2001: 87, to which further attention will be given later in this chapter in the context of the mission orientation that is implicit in the trinitarian shape of the community of faith.

[116] Hütter, Reinhard, "Hospitality and Truth: The Disclosure of Practices in Worship and Doctrine" in Volf, Miroslav and Bass, Dorothy C. (eds), *Practising Theology: Beliefs and Practices in Christian Life*, Grand Rapids: Eerdmans, 2002: 219, quoted in Boersma, Hans, "Liturgical Hospitality: Theological Reflections on Sharing in Grace" in *Journal for Christian Theological Research* 8 (2003): 67-77 – see http://home.apu.edu/~CTRF/articles/2003_articles/1_multipart_xF8FF_6_JTRFBoersma.pdf, accessed on 05.02.04. Boersma presents a framework of liturgical hospitality that embraces evangelical, baptismal, eucharistic and penitential dimensions, insisting that whilst hospitality is necessarily both welcoming and inclusive, it is not boundary-less: for example, the hospitality of baptism "implies the necessary exclusion of everything that does not belong to the Church of Jesus Christ" (*ibid*: 71), and penitence is "one of the means of guarding the hospitable character of the community of the Church" (*ibid*: 76). For a helpful discussion of hospitality as a Christian virtue see Pohl, Christine D.,

in orientation, his eternal life spilling out in creative love and freedom, seeking companions in communion and love,[117] so human beings are created with "an orientation that attends to otherness, listening and learning, valuing and honoring."[118]

Moltmann suggests that the notion of *perichoresis* conveys the offering of life-space to one another within the Trinity's own communion of being: the divine persons are 'habitable' for one another.[119] In emptying themselves into one another, the perichoretic community can also be seen as a kenotic community, enabling all creatures – and ultimately the whole new creation – to find their home in God, who is an *ekstatic*, open community of love. This "open Trinity", which Moltmann explicitly sets against the traditional figures of a closed, circular or triangular Trinity, establishes the basis of the unity of the disciples for which Jesus prays in John 17:21. But the church is not only a human community analogous to the divine perichoretic community: it is also "a community *in* the divine community of the triune God so that 'they [may] also be in us'."[120]

It is clear from the discussion above that the essential thread running through ecclesial life is love: "Spirit-evoked ecclesial solidarity entails living out the unity of the triune God."[121] This way of living binds believers together in what Cunningham describes as quite profound ways: "indeed, their lives implicate and are implicated by one another."[122] He offers the analogy of a family, suggesting that family members are fundamentally constitutive of who each member is; taking the analogy further, he argues that 'mother' and 'child' participate in one another to such a degree that no clear line can be drawn between them: what happens to one happens to the other. As it is in the shared life of the trinitarian God, "we too are called to live lives of mutual participation, in which our relationships are not just something we 'have', but

---

Making Room: Recovering Hospitality as a Christian Tradition, Grand Rapids: Eerdmans, 1999.

[117] See, on this, Boff, *Trinity and Society*: 220-222, where the author argues that "[c]reation arose from this wish of the three divine Persons to meet others (created by them) so as to include them in their eternal communion".

[118] Oden (ed), *And You Welcomed Me*: 14.

[119] Moltmann, Jürgen, "Perichoresis: An Old Magic Word for a New Trinitarian Theology" in Meeks, M. Douglas (ed), *Trinity, Community, and Power: Mapping Trajectories in Wesleyan Theology*, Nashville: Kingswood Books, an imprint of Abingdon Press, 2000: 115.

[120] *Ibid*: 121.

[121] Grenz, *The Social God and the Relational Self*: 335; Moltmann writes: "*Love* is another word for this community of mutual indwelling. Those who love are not in themselves but in others; those who are loved give others free space to live in them." (Moltmann, "Perichoresis: An Old Magic Word for a New Trinitarian Theology": 122).

[122] Cunningham, *These Three Are One*: 168.

are what constitute us as human beings."[123]

Cunningham illustrates this with reference to the mutual life of the first disciples of Jesus in Acts 2:42-47, observing that the community "that undertakes to share its meals and its money, as well as less tangible goods (e.g., its processes of education), is a community in which real 'participation' is possible."[124] Sherlock interprets this way of life as 'God on the inside', "who is both the pattern and the possibility for our living in community."[125] But, as we discussed above, the nature of the triune life implies that this ecclesial radical life of mutual love and care is not to be lived in a privatised ghetto, but outside in the wider community: "The distinction of the Persons means there is already 'otherness' *in* the divine self. God on the inside includes the possibility of God on the outside. God as triune allows for the coming into being of what is other *to* God."[126] So the community of faith is called to live out this life in God 'on the outside'.

There are several words that are helpful in describing the quality of love that the Spirit of God seeks to reproduce in the community of faith. Earlier, we noted the virtues of openness, fidelity and belonging within the philosopher Gabriel Marcel's interpretation of availability or *disponibilité*. Implicit in Marcel's ideas is a deeper form of participation than is often experienced in community life, a depth of 'togetherness' "that is so intimate and all-involving that one's very being is defined by the participation."[127] This demands a level of contemplation without which no genuine meeting can take place. It is evident that the virtues proposed by Marcel presuppose a degree of *agape*-love that closely reflects the perichoretic life of the triune God.

In his discussion of the divine life as the dynamic of *agape*, Grenz summarises C. S. Lewis's classic love quadrilateral of *storge* (affection, especially familial), *philia* (friendship), *eros* (desire, especially with reference to sexual love) and *agape* (self-giving love), acknowledging the predominance of *agape* in describing the character of the triune God, not only *ad intra*, but also by virtue of his saving actions in history. The first three types of love have traditionally been regarded as 'natural loves', but Grenz suggests that it is possible to find "overtones of *storge*, *philia*, and even *eros* within the biblical

---

[123] *Ibid*: 169. For a discussion of the analogical relationship between God and humanity provided by the *perichoretic* paradigm, in which the triune God "shares his divine life of communion with humans so that humans may live as a union of persons in communion with God and with one another," see Speidell, Todd H., "A Trinitarian Ontology of Persons in Society," in *The Scottish Journal of Theology* 43 (1994): 283-300.

[124] Cunningham, *These Three Are One*: 186.

[125] Sherlock, Charles, *God on the Inside: Trinitarian Spirituality*, Wanniassa, ACT: Acorn Press, 1991: 204.

[126] *Ibid*: 203; however, whilst rightly affirming co-operation over competition, Sherlock warns of the danger of so over-emphasising our corporate solidarity that we end up visualising ourselves as 'mere lumps in an undifferentiated mass.'

[127] Pembroke, *The Art of Listening*: 15.

narrative of the saving God."¹²⁸ This leads him to propose an ecclesial life characterised by an *agape*-love infused by the Spirit with compassionate familial concern, an inclination to enjoy the friendship of others and a desire for true communion with one another:

> In this manner, the Spirit brings the ecclesial community to fulfill the divinely given mandate to be the prolepsis of the new humanity as the *imago dei*, which is the goal of the biblical salvation-historical drama. As this occurs, the church serves as a community of salvation.[129]

Of particular interest is Moltmann's perspective on *philia*-friendship, grounded in an acceptance of each other's differences. Accepted as friends by God, believers discover that "the friendship of the 'Wholly Other' God which comes to meet us makes open friendship with people who are 'other' not merely possible but also interesting, in a profoundly human sense."[130] There is an *ekstatic* dimension to this type of friendship, in which the doors are thrown wide open for others to enter in and participate in the joy of the divine dance. It is an 'open friendship', a 'vulnerable atmosphere of life', which is based on the virtues of affection and respect: affection, for Moltmann, has to do with liking people for themselves, without making any demands on them, whereas respect has to do with their freedom. "Friends throw open the free spaces of life for one another, and accompany one another in sympathy and immense interest."[131]

Moltmann insists that the community of love is also an *erotic community*.[132] Not only in the patriarchal era, but also in more recent times, the word *eros* has been robbed of its original meaning, which has to do with 'passionate participation in the beautiful'. This type of love is motivated by the desire to seek union at the deepest and most intimate level: it is therefore a most appropriate term to describe our desire for God and for one another. God's self-sufficiency raises the question of whether or not we can speak of God desiring us, in the classical sense of *eros*. LaCugna insists that divine self-sufficiency is

---

[128] Grenz, *The Social God and the Relational Self*: 319; Grenz quotes Paul Tillich, who asserts that the other types of love remain ambiguous unless they are infused by *agape*: "In the holy community the *agape* quality of love cuts into the *libido*, *eros* and *philia* qualities of love and elevates them beyond the ambiguities of their self-centredness." (Tillich, Paul, *Love, Power and Justice: Ontological Analysis and Ethical Applications*, New York: Oxford, 1960: 116). The primary text from which many draw for inspiration is Lewis, C.S., *The Four Loves*, London: Collins Fontana Books, 1960, in which the author – defining *agape* as Charity, or Divine Love – argues that "Divine Love does not *substitute* itself for the natural – as if we had to throw away our silver to make room for the gold. The natural loves are summoned to become modes of Charity while also remaining the natural loves they were" (*ibid*: 122, author's italics).

[129] Grenz, *The Social God and the Relational Self*: 335.

[130] Moltmann, *The Spirit of Life*: 259.

[131] *Ibid*: 256.

[132] *Ibid*: 261-263.

a 'philosophical myth': when personhood is ultimate, as in the case of God, then "Eros can be thought of as arising out of plenitude not need, because it is out of fullness not emptiness that the lover wishes to give himself or herself to another."[133] At the human level, however, the context is not plenitude, but a 'never to be satisfied' dimension which lies at the heart of both mystical and sexual union: as human beings created *imago Dei*, we are forever reaching outwards, seeking ecstasy.[134] Modern distortions of erotic love, however, have attributed to *eros* allusions to domination and the desire to possess, especially sexually, reinforced by the (not necessarily improper) presence of 'need-love' in human relationships.[135] What has been lost here is the intense joy of mutual participation in one another, a generous desire to give to the other from within the very depths of one's being in order to experience the ecstasy of oneness.

This 'quest for completeness' has a spiritual dimension. Earlier, we referred to human spirituality as that which is grounded in an awareness and appreciation of the wonder and mystery of creation as 'sacramental reality.' Moltmann distinguishes between the deadly 'spirituality' of a 'not-of-this-

---

[133] LaCugna, *God For Us*: 352: so "[t]*he life of God does not belong to God alone*" (*ibid*: 354, author's italics). In this connection, Fiddes suggests that there might be a sense in which God has freely decided to be God *with us*, implying that he has *chosen* to need us, thus preserving his own freedom. Fiddes appears to be stretching the notion of erotic love here, bracketing it with the active language of 'willing', 'deciding' and 'choosing' (see Fiddes, *Participating in God*: 210-215). Cunningham notes that the "poetry of some mystical theologians traces the convergences between God's innertrinitraian love and erotic desire in some striking ways." He cites some verse from Hadewijch:
> When he takes possession of the loved soul in every way,
> Love drinks in these kisses and tastes them to the end.
> As soon as love thus touches the soul
> She eats its flesh and drinks its blood.
> Love that thus dissolves the loved soul
> Sweetly leads them both
> To the indivisible kiss –
> That same kiss which fully unites
> The Three Persons in one sole Being.

(from Hadewijch, Poems in Couplets, 16, in *Hadewijch: The Complete Works*, translated by Columba Hart, O.S.B., Classics of Western Spirituality, New York: Paulist Press, 1980: 350, cited in Cunningham, *These Three Are One*: 301).

[134] See LaCugna, *God For Us*: 350-356, where the author sustains her thesis that because desire lies at the foundation of what it means to be a human being, as we experience union our longing for the other increases and deepens.

[135] C. S. Lewis observes that "our whole being by its very nature is one vast need; incomplete, preparatory, empty yet cluttered, crying out for Him who can untie things that are now knotted together and tie up things that are still dangling loose." So, in the gospel, God in his grace addresses our 'Need-love' – for one another, for "it is not good that man should be alone", and for God, from whom "we implore forgiveness for our sins or support in our tribulations" (Lewis, *The Four Loves*: 9).

world' life *in* God, which divides spirituality from everyday life, and the vitality of a creative life *out of* God. Quoting Isaiah 58:6-8, he points out that "the weekly sabbath and the recurring sabbath years are the biblical foundations for the spirituality of the body and the spirituality of the earth, without which there can be no spirituality of the soul that gives life and health."[136] Spirituality is therefore not only personal and social, but also intrinsically ecological.

Benner identifies a number of distinctive characteristics of Christian spirituality, amongst which he includes "participation in God's Kingdom plan for the restoration of the totality of his creation."[137] This embraces response to such global concerns as pollution, overpopulation, resource scarcity and biological depletion, converging in an environmental ethic that highlights peace and wholeness within the natural world as well as amongst human beings. Following a similar line, David Tacey defines spirituality as "a feeling of being connected to a greater or larger whole, and an awareness that in the part or fragment, the radiance of the whole shines forth."[138] As an example of this sense of 'connectedness' he cites the experience of Aboriginal spirituality, which is a spirituality of 'deep seeing and deep listening'.[139]

Another example may be found in Celtic spirituality. Davies and Bowie observe that "the distinctive tenor of Celtic Christianity is one of a life-affirming integration which finds its theological centre in the vision of God as divine creativity and community, which is the Christian doctrine of the Trinity."[140] But there is more to Celtic Christianity than creativity and community. Other significant emphases are a holistic approach to life, in which body, soul and spirit are viewed as interrelated aspects of humanity; an openness to the direction of the Holy Spirit in all of life, in which a listening silence is central; a simplicity of lifestyle based upon the gifts of God's good creation; the importance of symbols, ritual and liturgy in worship; a deep respect for human life and the dignity of the individual; an understanding that all of life is sacramental, including the natural world; an awareness of life as a pilgrimage, expressed both spiritually and literally; the centrality of prayer and the disciplined life within a natural rhythm of work and rest; and a missionary zeal, embracing a concern not only for the soul but for the whole person. The symbol of the knot reflects the passionate Celtic belief in the trinitarian God, whose communal life is the basis for all human life: only in community with God, with each other and with the natural order of things can human beings discover their true identity and purpose. The interconnectedness between the

---

[136] Moltmann, *The Spirit of Life*: 96.

[137] Benner, David, *Care of Souls: Revisioning Christian Nurture and Counsel*, Grand Rapids: Baker Books, 1998: 106.

[138] Tacey, David, *ReEnchantment: The New Australian Spirituality*, Sydney: Harper-Collins*Publishers*, 2000: 20.

[139] *Ibid*: 113-117.

[140] Davies, Oliver and Bowie, Fiona, *Celtic Christian Spirituality*, London: SPCK, 1995: 21.

divine, the human and the physical is apparent in this spiritually motivated 'quest for completeness', which embraces not only a desire for union with God and with one another but also a desire to be more 'at home' in God's physical creation.

Community Operation – Worship

We now turn to the third of our three 'perichoretic themes', which is concerned with the visible dimensions of pastoral practice, and to which we have given the label 'community operation'. In our discussion of the first theme – community formation – we identified difference and diversity as fundamental characteristics of the ontological shape of the community of faith, and explored the language of 'polyphony' as an expression of the Spirit-inspired structure of the charismatic community, modelled on the polyphonic communion of the inner life of the triune God. In the process, the language of hierarchy and subordinationism was eschewed in favour of servanthood and equality. Subsequently, we suggested that the community of faith can only come into being, or be 'realised', as an authentic image of the Trinity insofar as it displays the essential characteristic of love; this was presented as a way of life that approximates as closely as possible the richly-contoured *agape*-love intrinsic to the hospitable life of the Trinity. This love is inclusive in its *ekstatic* orientation, and communal – rather than just relational – in its ultimate eschatological realisation.

The theme of 'community operation' directs us to ecclesial life in terms of ministry *praxis*, focusing on worship, mission and compassion. There is a delightful story of a little girl who was learning to play the piano, and whose musical skills were still very limited. One day she was playing some notes on the keyboard whilst staying with her family in a hotel in Norway. There was little to appreciate in her playing, and several guests found her "plink ... plonk ... plink ... plonk" intensely annoying. After a while, a man came and sat beside the girl, and started to play alongside her. The result was astounding - wonderful music from the two of them, the little girl playing as before, with the man supplying all the other notes. The man was the girl's father, the nineteenth-century Russian composer Alexander Borodin.[141] When we speak of participating in the ministry of Christ, we are talking about an engagement between God and ourselves which may be likened to the communion between Borodin and his daughter in that hotel in Norway.

In the same way that the great composer welcomed the playing of his little girl, embracing it and transforming it into something beautiful, so Christ receives all that we offer God, in thanksgiving, in worship and in service, and converts it in himself and presents it as something perfect and wholly acceptable to his Father, who is our Father. This is what the writer of the epistle

---

[141] This anecdote is related in Buxton, *Dancing in the Dark*: 117.

to the Hebrews conveys in his presentation of Jesus as our great high priest.[142] The theology of the incarnation reminds us that all humanity has been caught up in Christ's ascended and glorified humanity, so making it possible for us to participate by the Spirit in the Son's perfect communion with his Father.

Our discussion of worship is therefore predicated on the realisation that in Christ, our great high priest, our imperfect worship is converted by the Spirit into that which is holy and acceptable to the Father. True worship may be defined as a participation in the Son's worship of the Father, in which prayer, and the sacraments of baptism and the eucharist have a central place. There is a powerful trinitarian structure here, as James Torrance has shown. Christian worship, he writes, is trinitarian in three main ways: we pray to the Father, through the Son, in the Spirit; but we also pray to each of the three divine persons; thirdly, we glorify the one God, as expressed in the doxological formulation at the end of the liturgical singing of the psalms.[143]

---

[142] The epistle to the Hebrews is the most helpful New Testament book in formulating an acceptable theology of worship. There the writer spells out the superiority of Christ's fully effective priesthood over the limited priesthood of human intermediaries. Hebrews 9 draws out this distinction quite clearly in the context of worship; the sin-offerings in the tabernacle worship were unable to cleanse the conscience. This could only be accomplished by the blood of Christ, whose once and for all offering of himself has opened the way for us to now "draw near to God with a sincere heart in full assurance of faith" (Hebrews 10:22). This is the gospel of grace. Jesus Christ is the mediator of a new and better covenant, foreshadowed by the Levitical priesthood. His perfect sacrifice means that he has now entered heaven on our behalf as a man for all humanity, "now to appear for us in God's presence" (Hebrews 9:24). He has done what no human being can ever have done, and as a faithful high priest in heaven his perfect and acceptable ministry continues on behalf of all humanity. He is our advocate, our intercessor, forever receiving our imperfect worship, concentrating it in himself and presenting it as a fragrant offering to the Father. For a thorough exposition of this theme, see von Allmen, J.-J., *Worship: Its Theology and Practice*, London: Lutterworth Press, 1965: Allmen insists that the one who leads us in our worship is none other than the Lord himself: "God, Father, Son and Holy Ghost, is both the subject and the object of Christian worship, He who serves and is served by the cult, He who commands and He who welcomes the service, He who speaks and He who listens, He whom we implore and He who grants our requests" (*ibid*: 184).

[143] See Torrance, James B., *Worship, Community, and the Triune God of Grace*, Carlisle: Paternoster Press, 1996: 6-31. David Cunningham suggests that the eucharist underwrites the trinitarian virtue of 'peacemaking' in five ways: we offer one another a sign of peace before the eucharist commences; we retell the salvation narrative, reminding us that peace is at the heart of God's being; in the *epiclesis*, we pledge to be a people of peace as we call upon the Spirit to descend upon the eucharistic elements; we participate in one another's lives in a profound way as we re-enact 'table-fellowship'; and, finally, we orient our lives outwards towards the world, that we might live peaceable and peacemaking lives (see Cunningham, *These Three Are One*: 237-269).

If "worship is where most people internalise their theology"[144], then a trinitarian grammar informing Christian doxology and prayer "will mould congregations who will think about God in Trinitarian ways and relate to God in Trinitarian ways *even if they have never had a doctrine of the trinity formally explained to them.*"[145] Certainly a trinitarian structure to worship may be overdue in many Christian congregations.[146] But, as Parry recognises, trinitarian worship is more than the incorporation of doctrinally correct formulations that ascribe appropriate references to Father, Son and Holy Spirit in Christians songs and hymns, and in the way Christians pray: a full-orbed trinitarian structure to worship has to do with *participation* in the worship that takes place within the triune life.[147]

Torrance presents our participation by the Spirit in the Son's worship of the Father as a 'double movement of grace that is "grounded in the very perichoretic being of God."[148] Drawing from the insights of Michael Polanyi, for whom religious ritual, or worship, is "the highest degree of indwelling that is conceivable"[149], we may interpret this 'indwelling' nature of worship as a form of participatory knowledge, "a world in which the interplay of elements mutually inhere and cohere in such a way that each part derives its meaning from the whole at the same time that it contributes to the meaning of the whole."[150]

This is particularly evident in the sacrament of the eucharist, a pastoral practice which "provides one of the most important sites for our formation in the trinitarian virtue of participation."[151] Cunningham interprets the invocation of God's presence in the eucharistic rite as a focal expression not only of our participation in God's life, but also of God's participation in our lives, in which believers are drawn into a greater awareness of and contact with God. More suggestive, however, is his exposition of Feuerbach's declaration that "You are what you eat." Maintaining that the eucharist "has become such a ritualized or

---

[144] White, Susan, *Whatever Happened to the Father? The Jesus Heresy in Modern Worship*: 23, cited in Parry, Robin, "Putting the Trinity Back into Charismatic Spirituality", unpublished paper presented at Salt and Light Theological Forum (September 2003).

[145] Parry, "Putting the Trinity Back into Charismatic Spirituality", author's italics.

[146] A premise that is fundamental to White's thesis in *Whatever Happened to the Father?*

[147] Parry is ultimately concerned to see worship leading to an *encounter* with God as Trinity: for a fuller development of this theme, see Parry, Robin, *Worshipping Trinity: Coming Back to the Heart of Worship*, Milton Keynes: Paternoster, 2005.

[148] Torrance, *Worship, Community, and the Triune God of Grace*: 32.

[149] Polanyi, Michael, *Personal Knowledge*, Chicago: University of Chicago Press, 1958: 198.

[150] Wood, Susan K., "Participatory Knowledge of God in the Liturgy" in Buckley and Yeago, (eds), *Knowing the Triune God*: 102.

[151] Cunningham, *These Three Are One*: 172.

sentimentalized event that its profundity has evaporated"[152], he suggests that to deliberately conjure up different elements involved in bringing food to our table is, *ipso facto*, to acknowledge that eating something actually brings us into relationship with it – its history enters our lives in a deeply participative way. Likewise, in the eucharist, we mysteriously take Christ's body into ours, with the result that Jesus' prayer in John 17:20-23 becomes the language of mutual participation.

If the history of what we eat is incorporated into our lives in the way Feuerbach suggests, the eucharist represents a powerful appropriation of the saving acts of the triune God as we physically receive the elements of bread and wine into our bodies. *Heilsgeschichte* is the action of God as Trinity, or, as Moltmann puts it, "this trinitarian history is nothing other than the eternal perichoresis of Father, Son and Holy Spirit in their dispensation of salvation."[153] The eucharist is certainly a rehearsal of the triune history of salvation, but it is a rehearsal which is more than *anamnesis*. In a mysterious and compelling way, the sacrament powerfully draws past, present and future together in the life of the faith-community. If remembrance brings the past alive, then the present is evident in the eucharist as proclamation, participation and fellowship; the future is clearly implied in the anticipation of the heavenly banquet. The theme of thanksgiving is also a central motif in the celebration of the sacrament. These six words – remembrance, proclamation, participation, fellowship, anticipation and thanksgiving – offer a rich and profound interpretation of the eucharist, though they do not, and cannot, contain its full mystery or theological significance.

A similar emphasis on the drama of the trinitarian history of salvation is apparent in Augustine's ancient baptismal practices in North Africa in the late fourth and early fifth century. Gregory Jones traces what he describes as a dramatic journey of conversion involving four stages,[154] which can be summarised as initial instructional preparation, an intensive period of formation, baptismal immersion, and post-baptismal 'homecoming' celebrations. In particular, Jones suggests that these ancient practices offer "a *comprehensively theological focus for human life, directed towards the*

---

[152] *Ibid*: 176.

[153] Moltmann, Jürgen, *The Trinity and the Kingdom of God: The Doctrine of God*, London: SCM Press, 1981: 157; Moltmann's theology of the eucharist is more fully developed in *The Church in the Power of the Spirit*: 242-260.

[154] Jones, L. Gregory, "Baptism: A Dramatic Journey into God's Dazzling Light: Baptismal Catechesis and the Shaping of Christian Practical Wisdom" in Buckley and Yeago, (eds), *Knowing the Triune God*: 147-177, in which Jones draws substantially from two major sources: Finn, Thomas M., "It Happened one Saturday Night: Ritual and Conversion in Augustine's North Africa" in *Journal of the American Academy of Religion* 58, No. 4 (Winter 1990): 589-616; and Harmless, William, S.J., *Augustine and the Catechumenate*, Collegeville: The Liturgical Press, 1995.

eschatological consummation of fellowship with the triune God."¹⁵⁵ In this light, baptism is understood not simply as a rite of passage, but as a sacrament of participation in the life of the triune God. It is, in LaCugna's words, "the sacramental and ontological act that transforms solitariness and separateness into communion",¹⁵⁶ an act that is more a journey of communion with God and communion with others. Baptism is participation in what von Balthasar calls the great *theo-drama*, in which God is simultaneously author, primary actor and director – so reinforcing the undivided actions of Father, Son and Spirit in the history of salvation¹⁵⁷ – and in which all the baptised have a vital role to play.

This rich interpretation of eucharistic – and baptismal – practices within the church should provoke true thanksgiving in the faith-community: "the intention of God's works is not that they should happen, but that they should awaken joy and thanksgiving, and the song of praise that returns to God."¹⁵⁸ As Barth declares,

> *Charis* always demands the answer of *eucharistia* [i.e., grace always demands the answer of gratitude]. Grace and gratitude belong together like heaven and earth. Grace evokes gratitude like the voice of an echo. Gratitude follows grace like thunder [follows] lightning.¹⁵⁹

In the eucharist, the three pastoral dimensions of worship, mission and compassion converge in a powerful way, for there the Christian community participates in what Fiddes describes as 'interweaving currents' in the history of the triune God – not only with thanksgiving, but also as we experience pain over the suffering in this world. In the eucharist we share in the drama of death and resurrection which is happening in the heart of God, for God still suffers in the midst of the pain and brutality of this world. Moltmann has rightly called the question of theodicy "*the open wound of life* in this world."¹⁶⁰ Alongside Fiddes' colourful interpretation of the sacraments as "pieces of earthly stuff that are meeting places with this God who exists in ecstatic movements of love"¹⁶¹, we might remember that we also meet with an open Trinity who feels the pain of his creation, and whose seeking Spirit is ever at work to bring healing and hope to the suffering and the oppressed. It is precisely because the eucharist is

---

¹⁵⁵ *Ibid*: 162, author's italics.

¹⁵⁶ LaCugna, *God For Us*: 404; interpreting baptism as a rite of participation for the whole community of faith, Moltmann argues that the "one baptism of men and women constitutes the church-community, not one single office' (Moltmann, "Perichoresis: An Old Magic Word for a New Trinitarian Theology": 123).

¹⁵⁷ On von Balthasar's development of *theo-drama* as a trinitarian construct, see Cunningham, *These Three Are One*: 78-80, citing von Balthasar, Hans Urs, *Theo-Drama: Theological Dramatic Theory* (5 vols.), San Francisco: Ignatius, 1988-1998.

¹⁵⁸ Moltmann, *The Spirit of Life*: 299.

¹⁵⁹ Barth, Karl *Church Dogmatics*, 4/1, Edinburgh: T. & T. Clark Ltd., 1956: 41.

¹⁶⁰ Moltmann, *The Trinity and the Kingdom of God*: 49.

¹⁶¹ Fiddes, *Participating in God*: 281.

inclusive as a catholic sacrament that we interpret it proleptically as a sign of the Kingdom: "[d]iscerning the body of Christ in the breaking of the bread enables us to discern him through the broken bodies of the prisoners, the thirsty and the hungry."[162] Our participation in the life of God naturally and necessarily impels us out into the world in other-centred service:

> When we withdraw from the world and on behalf of the world worship the Father in the name of Christ, we are not making some pietist escape from the world and the needs and claims of the world ... So we call upon the world to participate with us in our participation in the death and resurrection of Christ, to participate with us in our participation in the New Humanity, and to look with us beyond death to the fulfilment of God's purposes for all creation in resurrection.[163]

The communal meal as the central expression of the worshipping life of the church reminds us that the church is not a collection of individuals who happen to come together at certain times, but is "that community within the world which in her worship anticipates the perfect community of the Kingdom, waiting for the marriage feast of the Lamb."[164] In our worship we anticipate the ultimate eschatological community. We do not participate in isolation, but in solidarity with each other, and in communion with the heavenly company of angels and perfected saints. Our community life on earth, a life of mutual encouragement and of participation in Christ's mission in and for the world, derives from and is in fact an expression of our participation in the worship that characterises the life of the triune God. In our worship and in our calling to serve God in the world we are a redeemed community, reflecting the loving trinitarian communion into which the Spirit has drawn us.

In prayer, we participate in the 'conversation of heaven' as we dwell in the triune God who is ever interceding for us and for the world. "To be true and serious, to be the prayer which is heard by God, it must first and last be the

---

[162] *Ibid*: 283.

[163] Torrance, James B., "The Place of Jesus Christ in Worship" in Anderson, Ray S. (ed), *Theological Foundations for Ministry*, Edinburgh: T. & T. Clark Ltd., 1979: 358. The liturgies of the church also insist upon an integral link between worship and service, as expressed in one of the Anglican post-communion prayers:
> Almighty God,
> We thank you for feeding us
> With the body and blood of your Son Jesus Christ.
> Through him we offer you our souls and bodies
> To be a living sacrifice.
> Send us out
> In the power of your Spirit
> To live and work
> To your praise and glory. Amen.

(*The Alternative Service Book 1980*, London: Hodder & Stoughton, 1980).

[164] Torrance, "The Place of Jesus Christ in Worship": 365.

prayer of the One who as the true Son has the authority and power truly to address him as Father."[165] Prayer therefore has to do with our listening before our speaking: it is an expression of our relationship with God, into whose life we are privileged to participate. Jenson's insistence that God's triune life is in actuality a life with us is given expression in his understanding of the prayer life of the church:

> When the church prays to the Father in the Son's name, she is taken into the obedient response of the Son to what the Father tells him. As the church speaks and hears the gospel and as the church responds in prayer and confession, the church's life is a great conversation, and this conversation is none other than our participation in the converse of the Father and Son in the Spirit.[166]

We discover in prayer that God is for us and for all humanity: in his perfect love he knows our needs and the needs of the whole world before we ask. This is liberating, for we are thus free to come before God knowing, as Barth reminds us, that we are only creatures and not the Creator.

However, this insight should not cause us to have a fatalistic view of prayer, as if our praying were unable to make a difference. Fiddes is firm in his insistence that prayer is not just some existential phenomenon in which we are changed rather than the objects of our praying. Scientifically, we have moved beyond the image of nature as a clockwork mechanism, closed to human influence and simply ticking away as God intended in a closed web of cause and effect. Chaos theory, quantum mechanics and the relativity of time and space all point to an open system, in which humans have a part to play. In Chapter 2, we noted Fiddes' suggestion that God works persuasively by his Spirit within the whole of nature, calling out response from it. He suggests that we should be sympathetic to an openness in nature that enables us to visualise the universe as being open to God:

> If we *are* immersed more deeply into the interconnectedness of all things in God, and are more engaged in God's interrelational life, it would seem odd if we did not also have an effect upon other people and other things through our prayers. If *we* are being transformed by being drawn more deeply into community, it seems that the community in the world which God embraces should be changed by our involvement.[167]

Fiddes' cosmic perspective invites us to conceive of the universe as an organic community of natural processes, human relations and divine action, characterised by all kinds of connections of which we are unaware. Somehow through prayer we are drawn into what he calls a 'zone of interconnection', in which we become intensely aware of others in the Spirit – in intercession we

---

[165] Macquarrie, John, *Principles of Christian Theology*, London: SCM Press, 1966: 440.
[166] Jenson, *Systematic Theology,* Vol I - *The Triune God*: 228
[167] Fiddes, *Participating in God*: 125-126.

meet others in the *perichoresis*, the divine dance of Father, Son and Holy Spirit. This relational and mutual expression of prayer thus stands against other interpretations of prayer, such as the hierarchical 'two-cause' model,[168] suggesting that prayer is essentially relational, trinitarian and participatory. Such a perspective influences how we might pray with respect to the world of nature, and – at a more general pastoral level – offers the church a rich trinitarian framework within which to engage in prayer.

Community Operation - Mission

Mission, as we have already insisted, is at the heart of the trinitarian life of God. "Because God is triune, God can bless us. Because God blesses the other in God, God can bless the other without. Because God reaches out to another already within, God is not contained by the Trinity's inner life, but can reach out also to us."[169] And precisely because Christians participate in the divine life, mission is at the heart of the church, recalling our earlier reference to what Edward Farley describes as the world-transforming nature of 'ecclesial redemptive presence'. Richard Gollings, who was involved for many years in church planting in Mexico City and Tijuana, tells the story of two yearly migrants to the urban construction industry who were welcomed by a local pastor to share his dinner, and given a free room in the *templo* where his family lived. The notion of hospitality, which informed our understanding of the inner life both of the Trinity and of the community of faith, is evident here in the missionary heart of the local pastor: so the local church is called into being as a 'covenantal community', including and enabling "community obligations to strangers and outsiders."[170]

To participate in the mission of Christ is to enter into the reconciling ministry of the Spirit, who is continuously at work in the world in both hidden and improbable ways, with creative innovation and resourceful ingenuity, and with concern for the particularity of context. Whenever the Christian church ties the Spirit of mission down to its own specific programs, failing to recognise these essential characteristics, it has lost sight of what it means to

---

[168] This model argues that there is an immediate cause and an ultimate cause of events that happen in the world – or, as Aquinas put it, a *primary* and a *secondary* cause. Fiddes suggests that the 'two-cause' theory is important in its emphasis on the primacy of God and the way of grace, but perhaps this may be better expressed as grace coming through nature in a process of mutual contribution. For a discussion of difficulties with the 'two-cause' view, and some proposals for a way forward within the context of a God who acts and the point of intercessory prayer, see *ibid*: 115-151.
[169] Rogers, "The Stranger as Blessing": 271.
[170] Gollings, Richard, "Planting Covenant Communities of Faith in the City" in van Engen, Charles and Tiersma, Jude (eds), *God So Loves the City: Seeking a Theology for Urban Mission*, Monrovia CA: MARC, 1994: 129.

participate effectively in the mission of Christ, which is at the same time participation in the world. The mission of the church is the kerygmatic proclamation, in word and deed, of a freedom that permeates many different dimensions of social disruption and disease; yet it is a freedom that "can only be a single and a common freedom. It is the freedom for fellowship with God, man and nature."[171]

Mission,[172] however, is something that not only *creates* fellowship in all its richness: rightly understood, it *derives* from the faith-community's fellowship with the triune God. John Taylor argues that the church that will make a difference in society will be characterised by "the quickening of compassion and the kindling of awareness by the Spirit of Jesus through the scriptures, worship and fellowship of the church."[173] The role of the church is to be present in the world, because that is the arena of the Spirit's activity.[174] The Spirit, who is the Spirit of fellowship, leading men and women into vital union with each other within the community-of-being of God himself, creates the very context within which mission takes place.

Whilst we must avoid the trap of insisting that everything is mission – for then, as Neill has reminded us, "nothing is mission"[175] – the church is perhaps

---

[171] Moltmann, *The Church in the Power of the Spirit*: 17.

[172] The eminent missiologist David Bosch proposes a distinction between 'mission' and '*missions*': "The first refers primarily to the *missio Dei* (God's mission), that is, God's self-revelation as the One who loves the world, God's involvement in and with the world, the nature and activity of God, which embraces both the church and the world, and in which the church is privileged to participate. Missions ... refer to the particular forms, related to specific times, places, or needs, of participation in the *missio Dei*." (Bosch, David J., *Transforming Mission: Paradigm Shifts in Theology of Mission*, Maryknoll: Orbis Books, 1991: 10, author's italics). Mission is, ontologically, a defining characteristic of the church, for it expresses the inner impulse of the triune God to reveal himself through his church in the midst of the world. God delights to make himself known, and the church is both a sign of his kingdom, pointing to the reality of his rule of compassionate love, and a sacrament - a dynamic event of grace, in which he is present by his Spirit. Functionally, however, the community of faith gives form and shape to that impulse under the inspiration of the Spirit through appropriate missionary strategies. Each faith-community is privileged to participate in the mission of Christ in the world, but each will be involved in that mission in its own unique way.

[173] Taylor, John V., *The Go-Between God: The Holy Spirit and the Christian Mission*, London: SCM Press, 1972: 147.

[174] For example, the first few days of the New Testament church were marked by groups of believers "who broke bread in their homes and ate together with glad and sincere hearts, praising God and enjoying the favour of the people": and the result was that "the Lord added to their number daily those who were being saved" (Acts 2:46-47). Believers were *visible* in the world, living out their trinitarian faith as 'ecclesial redemptive presence'.

[175] Neill, Stephen, *Creative Tension*, London: Edinburgh House Press, 1959: 81.

in more danger of delineating mission too narrowly than too widely. We would do well to heed the words of Bosch, who describes mission as "a multifaceted ministry, in respect of witness, service, justice, healing, reconciliation, liberation, peace, evangelism, fellowship, church planting, contextualization, and much more."[176] The breadth of activity encompassed by this description challenges those who are inclined to reduce mission to having occasional guest services, inviting a visiting evangelist to 'conduct a mission' in the locality, or running introductory courses on Christianity at the church.

Taylor also points us away from a restricted interpretation of mission. He offers a perspective that is wide-ranging in its scope rather than narrow and reductionist, and invites us to reflect on the enormous breadth and range of the mission of the Creator Spirit.[177] In order to participate in that mission, we need both the courage to look beyond our narrow evangelical and ecclesiological boundaries and also the wisdom to discern where the Spirit is at work, often in the unlikeliest places and in the most improbable ways.[178]

Commenting on the concept of *perichoresis* as an interpretive construct for innertrinitarian 'onto-relations', Thomas Torrance suggests that

> While these onto-relations apply to our understanding of the Triunity of God in a unique and transcendent way, they also apply in quite another way to the interrelations of human persons whom God has created for communion with himself, and which in their created way reflect the uncreated relations within himself.[179]

---

[176] Bosch, *Transforming Mission*: 512.

[177] For Taylor, mission "embraces the plant-geneticist breeding a new strain of wheat, the World Health Organization team combating bilharzia, the reconstruction company throwing a bridge across a river barrier, the political pressure group campaigning for the downfall of a corrupt city council, the amateur dramatics group in the new cultural centre, the team on the new oil-rig, the parents' committee fighting for de-segregated schools in the inner city. The missionaries of the Holy Spirit include the probation officer and the literacy worker, the research chemist and the worn-out school teacher in a remote village, the psychiatrist and the designer, the famine-relief worker and the computer operator, the pastor and the astronaut. Our theology of mission will be all wrong unless we start with a song of praise about this surging diversity of creative and redemptive initiative." (Taylor, *The Go-Between God*: 38). In order to avoid the criticism that such an inclusive perspective is inadequately anchored to the gospel story, Bosch presents us with six christological themes that need to remain central to Christian mission in order to avoid the communication of what he calls "a truncated gospel": these are the incarnation, the cross, the resurrection, the ascension, Pentecost and the *parousia* (see Bosch, *Transforming Mission*: 512-519).

[178] For a brief exposition of the inclusive scope of mission, with a number of examples of the Spirit's improbable and surprising reconciling activity in the world, see Buxton, *Dancing in the Dark*: 164-173.

[179] Torrance, Thomas F., "The Distinctive Character of the Reformed Tradition" (a paper presented as the Donnell Lecture given at Dubuque Theological Seminary on 6 October 1988) in Kettler and Speidell, (eds), *Incarnational Ministry*: 9.

In the light of the preceding discussion regarding the reconciling mission of the Spirit *throughout the world*, and not just within the community of faith, Torrance's statement clearly cannot be limited to a reformed doctrine of the church, which is its original context. It is relevant within the wider context of society, for the body of Christ "must not only be present in the world, but also in solidarity with it."[180]

Boff takes this notion of solidarity to its ultimate expression, arguing that if churches take "the preferential option for the poor seriously" they will be engaging in a liberating pastoral mission which would be what he calls 'a sacrament of the Trinity': "Human society has been eternally willed by God to be the sacrament of trinitarian communion in history."[181] But Boff goes further: solidarity with the poor and the oppressed, with those who are 'strangers', helps us in our *understanding* of the communion of the Trinity.[182] To live a life of other-centred concern and action in the world is to plumb the depths of trinitarian life, for "trinitarian unity is integrating and inclusive; its end is the full glorification of all creation in the triune God, healing what is sick, freeing what is captive, forgiving what offends divine communion."[183]

Since the greatness of trinitarian communion "consists precisely in its being a communion of three *different* beings"[184], "the paradigm or perfect case of otherness"[185], a mission orientation predicated on welcome of the stranger and availability to all people (implicit in the notion of hospitality discussed above) reflects a celebration of otherness in all its diversity and richness, patterning the triune life of God. We begin to understand God in his triune glory as we participate in his other-centred love for all people. Worship is where most people internalise their theology: may we not reach the same conclusion with regard to mission? A trinitarian grammar informing Christian mission is likely to shape the way congregations think about and relate to the God who welcomes difference into his midst precisely because he is *in se* the God who is constituted by difference.

As Moltmann has shown, worship and mission are drawn intimately together in the eucharist: whilst the mystery of the supper serves to separate the initiated

---

[180] Pannell, William J., "Evangelism: Solidarity and Reconciliation" in Kettler and Speidell, (eds), *Incarnational Ministry*: 202.
[181] Boff, *Trinity and Society*: 24.
[182] *Ibid*: 13.
[183] *Ibid*: 148; on this, see also Speidell, Todd H., "The Humanity of God and the Healing of Humanity: The Trinity, Community, and Society" in Speidell, Todd H. (ed), *On Being Christian ... and Human: Essays in Celebration of Ray S. Anderson*, Eugene OR: Wipf and Stock Publishers, 2002: 195-205, where the author explores a number of concrete implications of what he calls 'a trinitarian-incarnational theology of Christian community in society'.
[184] Boff, *Trinity and Society*: 150, my italics.
[185] Rogers, "The Stranger as Blessing": 268.

from the rest of the world, "Christ's messianic feast makes its participants one with the physically and spiritually hungry all over the world."[186] This has important trinitarian significance, for the feast is supremely the thanksgiving sacrament of the church for all that the triune God has done – and continues to do in the power of the Spirit – in perichoretic activity to reconcile the world to himself. *Heilsgeschichte* is rehearsed as believers share in the eucharistic thanksgiving, for they are reminded that they are participating proleptically in the great messianic banquet, to which *all* are invited, especially the poor, the crippled and the blind (Luke 14:7-24), and to which *Heilsgeschichte* testifies.

In her collection of early Christian texts regarding hospitality and its practice, Oden traces the theme of vulnerability in five groups of people – the sick, the poor, travellers and pilgrims, widows and orphans, and slaves and prisoners. Her wide selection of texts is drawn from the first eight centuries of the Christian church and geographically covers virtually all the early Christian world. She concludes that "[t]he pervasive character of hospitality in early Christian writing demonstrates a lack of self-consciousness, a matter-of-factness, that suggests it is simply a given part of life, not the stuff of esoteric treatise."[187] So for the church today: to participate in the mission of the triune God in the world is to be willing to have our eyes opened by the Spirit of God so that we may see others "as brothers and sisters created by the same God and living as mutual guests in the same house provided by the same divine host."[188]

In the fifth century Gerontius recorded the life of a wealthy Roman citizen, Melania, who, with her husband Pinianus, sold their ample possessions and embarked on a life of charity. In Gerontius' words, they went around

> to simply all who were sick, visiting them in order to attend to them. They lodged strangers who were passing through, and cheering them with abundant supplies for their journey, sent them on their way. They lavishly assisted all the poor and needy. They went about to all the prisons, places of exile, and mines, setting free those who were held because of debt and providing them with money. Like Job, the blessed servant of the Lord, their door stood open to any of the helpless.[189]

---

[186] Moltmann, *The Church in the Power of the Spirit*: 258. "The fellowship of the table," writes Moltmann, "is the visible sign of the church's catholicity. But because this catholicity is messianically open for the uniting of mankind in the presence of God, the fellowship of the table is open to the world too" (*ibid*: 258).

[187] Oden (ed), *And You Welcomed Me*: 27; the author argues that the stranger motif is at the heart of Christian identity, grounded in the history of Israel: "Do not oppress an alien; you yourselves know how it feels to be aliens, because you were aliens in Egypt" (Exodus 23:9). For a moral perspective on hospitality in relation to those 'on the outside', see Ogletree, Thomas W., *Hospitality to the Stranger: Dimensions of Moral Understanding*, Philadelphia: Fortress Press, 1985.

[188] Oden (ed), *And You Welcomed Me*: 52.

[189] Gerontius, *The Life of Melania the Younger*, translated by Elizabeth A. Clark, in *Studies in Women in Religion*, Volume 14, New York: Edwin Mellen Press, 1984: 33, cited in Oden, *And You Welcomed Me*: 176.

The life of hospitality to which these two Roman citizens devoted themselves is reminiscent of the words of Jesus, who commenced his ministry in Nazareth by reading from the scroll of Isaiah, thus establishing the foundation upon which his mission to the human race was constituted. The gospel parable of the sheep and goats (Matthew 25:31-46) recapitulates this foundational core of ministry, reminding the church that to feed the hungry, to welcome the stranger, to clothe the naked, to care for the sick, and to visit those in prison, are not optional ecclesial extras. They strike at the very heart of what it means to love as God loves. Pohl reminds us that hospitality "reflects God's greater hospitality that welcomes the undeserving, provides the lonely with a home, and sets a banquet table for the hungry."[190] In these acts of love the church participates in the Trinity's open communion, embracing the 'other', welcoming difference, and contradicting life-denying exclusivism. Only the "participation and communion of all in everything can justifiably claim to be an image and likeness (albeit pale) of the Trinity, the foundation and resting place of the universe."[191]

Community Operation – Compassion

The framework within which genuine care and compassion can take place may be helpfully illustrated by contrasting two models of offering succour to a person who is struggling. Benner traces the shift during the twentieth century from the care of souls (*cura animarum*) to the cure of minds, arguing that the rise of modern psychology has been a major contributory factor in the professionalisation of therapy, within as well as outside the church.[192] The notion of soul care embraces not only nurture and support but also healing and restoration. But the primary thrust in contemporary therapeutic practice has more to do with *clinical* approaches that seek to apply psychological insights than the *pastoral* care of troubled people. The result is that nurture and support have given way to a greater focus on pragmatic solution-based psycho-therapeutic methods.

In Chapter 2 we noted the ascendancy of what Benner calls the 'therapeutic culture', dominated by Rogerian client-centred therapy, Freudian psychoanalysis, the growth and group therapies of the human potential movement, and a wide range of interpersonal therapies. Intrinsic to this new direction in therapeutic practice are reliance upon techniques and methodologies, and the

---

[190] Pohl, Christine D. *Making Room*, Grand Rapids, Eerdmans: 1999: 16, cited in Boersma, "Liturgical Hospitality: Theological Reflections on Sharing in Grace": 67.

[191] Boff, *Trinity and Society*: 151.

[192] Benner, *Care of Souls*: 35-50; prior to the growth of psychology in the twentieth century, we may also cite the increasing dominance of science in the seventeenth and eighteenth centuries, which markedly influenced the perception, and role, of religion as a major player in the traditional practice of 'soul care'. See also Oden, Thomas C., "Recovering Pastoral Care's Lost Identity" in Aden, Leroy and Ellens, J. Harold (eds), *The Church and Pastoral Care*, Grand Rapids: Baker, 1988: 17-32.

increasing role of the 'expert'. This 'professional' model, however, is in danger of paying too much attention to the latest fashions in the behavioural sciences, and too little to the journey that each person is travelling with his or her God. In a passionate defence of Christian pastoral care, Peterson waxes eloquently against present-day healing and helping disciplines, which "are like the River Platte as described by Mark Twain, a mile wide and an inch deep."[193]

Whilst many people have been concerned that the Christian community has been too ready to embrace the insights of secular psychology in its desire to help hurting people back into wholeness, psychological insights should not be summarily dismissed as if they were inimical to Christian truth. Both counselling and psychology are concerned with "constructive change and the central nature of the helping relationship."[194] We must beware the trap of putting Christianity and psychology into separate boxes, as if they had nothing to do with each other. But the danger of capitulating to the seductive pragmatism of secular therapies remains: as the philosophical theologian James Olthuis declares, the goal of all therapy "is not decisive conclusions or valid interpretation, but transformed connections, changed lives, the surge of mercy, a drawing nearer to each other, and to God. Not: 'Have I mastered the technique?' But: 'Has the person been seen, heard, and blessed?'"[195]

At the beginning of this chapter we affirmed the importance of attending to the particular in pastoral ministry. It is altogether too tempting to treat people as a homogeneous clump rather than as a diverse and colourful multitude of unique individuals, each with their own history, hopes and fears. To participate in the compassion of Christ is to "listen to the singular *who*" and seek to multiply differences.[196] Accordingly, the second model of pastoral therapy is based on the notion of two people travelling on a journey together, in which the one offering care and the one in need of care experience the grace of God as they both open themselves up to the Spirit: "we can lay down our lives when we make our faith, hopes and fears available to others as a means of *together* getting in touch with the Lord of Life."[197]

In this model, the emphasis is on mutual interaction and sharing, in which the space between them is perceived not as something that needs to be bridged by the application of a particular technique or therapeutic strategy that guarantees a solution, but as a risky and unpredictable "spiritual field of

---

[193] Peterson, Eugene H., *Five Smooth Stones for Pastoral Work*, Grand Rapids: Eerdmans, 1980: 3.

[194] Hurding, Roger, *The Bible and Counselling*, London: Hodder & Stoughton, 1992: 67.

[195] Olthuis, James H., "Dancing Together in the Wild Spaces of Love: Postmodernism, Psychotherapy, and the Spirit of God" in *Journal of Psychology and Christianity* 1999, Vol 18, No 2: 147.

[196] *Ibid*: 145.

[197] Nouwen, Henri, *In the Name of Jesus*, New York: CrossRoads, 1989: 43, my italics; Benner also develops the idea of 'journeying together' as the only way to effect personal

meeting."¹⁹⁸ Those who are privileged to journey as care-givers are called to participate in the healing process as a spontaneous journey of faith and adventure, recapitulating the motif of dance: "It is a sojourning together, a lingering in stages and phases, a sometimes struggle, sometimes dance, always adventure, on the way to renewed and deepened connections and reconnections with self and others."¹⁹⁹

Olthuis develops this thesis with reference to postmodern philosophy, suggesting that "deconstructive postmodernism is not only haunted by the multitudes of disconnections that surround us, but is perplexed and captivated by its desire to be open to the other, hospitable and forgiving."²⁰⁰ His metaphor of therapy as a 'dance of blessing' corresponds to the perichoretic life of the Trinity in its embodiment of movements of love that eschew domination and alienation. He interprets God's love as a passion, a dynamic that is open and caring, always delighting in the other. It is 'com-passion' because it is the rhythmic, pulsing surge of God's life within us that is oriented towards wholeness, connecting us back together with God, with each other and with all creation:

> The people we work with are strugglers, stragglers, wounded, just like all of us – their wounds bearing/baring (carrying and exposing) the evidence of their stories' truth and power – who need to be received, seen, heard, held, and accompanied in all their suffering. In brief, they need blessing: an attitude of deep respect, affirmation, and openness to the other which evokes a prayerful hope that God's love may surprise and surround, empower and convict, encourage, redeem, and heal. This transforms therapy into a dance of blessing which recognizes that we are all in this together, brothers and sisters in the skin, gifted and vulnerable, reaching out and drawing back, expectant and wary.²⁰¹

For Olthuis, the nature of Christian therapy needs to be understood as care rather than cure, as art rather than science, as adventure rather than treatment, and as spiritual process rather than psychology-plus-prayer.

---

transformation: see Benner, David, *Sacred Companions: The Gift of Spiritual Friendship and Direction*, Downers Grove: IVP, 2002: 39-41.

[198] Olthuis, "Dancing Together in the Wild Spaces of Love": 150.

[199] *Ibid*: 148.

[200] *Ibid*: 145.

[201] *Ibid*: 147. Olthuis does not argue that techniques and methods should be dismissed: they are valuable so long as they are used flexibly and are not allowed to take over: "The difference between a focus on method and a focus on persons which integrates methods is like the difference between conquering the water by powerboat, and flowing with the current in a canoe or catching the wind in a sailboat. Interestingly enough, going with the current or catching the wind demands a much higher level of technique than driving a powerboat, particularly in running rapids, navigating storms, and waiting out doldrums" (*ibid*: 148).

In his commentary on the different ways in which Christians demonstrate their love for each other, Moltmann observes that "[i]f God, the quickening Spirit, is love, then human experiences of love belong within the open spaces of this experience of God; and the experiences of God will intensify the experience of human love."[202] The demonstration of Christian compassion may therefore be likened to a participation in what Fiddes describes as 'relational spaces'. Rogers rightly observes that human beings, in their finitude, "cannot love perichoretically, as God does, as if by interpenetration. Rather their spatial boundaries first make love possible for them."[203] So God, in his patience and grace, grants space – and time – to human beings "as appropriate correlates to the trinitarian love-in-freedom"[204]: he gives us bodies and a history through which we might participate in his own divine *perichoresis*. Human beings participate in the triune life of compassion as they enter into mutually enriching compassionate relationships, characterised by openness, vulnerability and availability.

In his discussion of the essential components of effective pastoral care, Pembroke explores compassion and substitution as significant dimensions of his central theme of availability. If compassion implies taking "the hurt and sorrow of the other into one's home-space", substitution "is the willingness to *substitute* the other's freedom for one's own."[205] He outlines a number of concepts that are intimately related to the theme of substitution, notably generosity of spirit, trust, mutuality and servanthood. These themes are not only appropriate expressions of the innertrinitarian life, but they reflect the way in which God identifies with human beings in their suffering, and offer us a model for pastoral care within the community of faith.

In a chapter on the vulnerability of God in the face of human suffering, Fiddes develops his proposal regarding the movements that take place within the spaces within and between the interweaving currents of relational love in God. His discussion is based on his presentation of God as an 'event of relationships' or, better, 'three movements of relationship subsisting in one event.' He interprets the Father's eternal generation of the Son as a movement of self-giving 'like a father sending forth a son', in which human beings are invited to participate. Similarly, when we pray to God as Father, we are participating in a movement like that of a son's response to a father, echoing – albeit faintly – the Son's obedient 'yes' to the Father. Fiddes' third direction of movement within the Trinity incorporates the Spirit, whose procession from the Father through the Son (according to the Eastern view[206]) may be interpreted as

---

[202] Moltmann, *The Spirit of Life*: 267.
[203] Rogers, "The Stranger as Blessing: 271; see also Volf, *After Our Likeness:* 210-211.
[204] Rogers, "The Stranger as Blessing: 271.
[205] Pembroke, *The Art of Listening*: 61, author's italics.
[206] Fiddes suggests that the Western addition of *filioque* to the Nicene Creed confuses the direction of movements within the Trinity: "to say that the Spirit proceeds eternally 'from the Father and the Son' makes the Son the same kind of source as the Father, obscuring the unique direction of 'sending' within the communion of God ... As Boff

an opening up of new depths of relationship and new possibilities of the future. This third relational current involves the creative expansion of God's life, an opening up of spaces within the interweaving relationships of God in which human beings are privileged to participate.

Drawing from von Balthasar's *Theo-drama*, Fiddes suggests that the experience of human suffering is taken up by God into himself: as self-giving Father, he suffers *with* his children, even though they may have resisted his love in causing that suffering. In the movement of sonship, God suffers not just 'with' but *as* human beings do, "bearing the 'no' of created beings within the 'yes' to the Father …taking all those movements of resistance up into the pattern of the dance."[207] In the third movement of 'deepening relations' God as Spirit enters into the human story in the most profound ways, suffering *in* us – and in creation's groaning in the pains of childbirth. Fiddes' understanding of divine perichoretic suffering has a twofold counterpart at the human level. In our Christian lives, and especially through prayer, we can participate in the suffering that God experiences in all three movements identified above, drawing us closer into the divine life (*theosis*). Secondly, we may find ourselves paralleling the divine pattern in ecclesial life, seeking to identify with one another in similar relational movements of love and compassion. If, as Moltmann insists, "God and suffering belong together"[208], then we must insist that humanity and suffering cannot be separated either:

> the experience of the risen 'Christ in us' is to be found not merely in the heights of spiritual contemplation, and not only for the first time in the depths of death, but already in the little experiences of suffering that is sustained and transformed. Anyone who loves dies many deaths.[209]

Because the fullness of human suffering is necessarily located within the interweaving currents of divine love, we may agree with Fiddes, that the "drama of human life can only take place within the greater drama of the divine life."[210] Our discussion in this section has been confined to the problem of suffering, but in many other pastorally sensitive areas, such as the threat of death, contemporary ethical concerns related to the sanctity of life, and the ever-present mystery of healing, we may discern similar contours of perichoretic life.[211] It is evident that the interpretation of pastoral care outlined above is predicated primarily on the spontaneous ministry of the Spirit rather than organised therapeutic programs that are often divorced from the vulnerable

---

points out, the reciprocal fellowship of God comes 'from' all three persons, so that the conjunction 'and' is everywhere (including *spirituque*)" (Fiddes, *Participating in God*: 80).

[207] *Ibid*: 185.
[208] Moltmann, *The Trinity and the Kingdom of God*: 49.
[209] Moltmann, *The Spirit of Life*: 211.
[210] Fiddes, *Participating in God*: 184.
[211] See, for example, Fiddes' discussions on forgiveness and death (*ibid*: 191-250).

real world of hurting people. As a paradigm of pastoral care and compassion, "[d]ancing in the wild spaces of love opens us up to the free play of grace, to the surprises of the spirit, to the indwelling of the Spirit, to the miracles of love."[212] In its reinforcement of the reciprocity of mutual giving and receiving, and in its enhancement of difference and particularity, the paradigm resonates effectively with the trinitarian experience of *perichoresis*.

This analogous correspondence between divine and human perichoretic life in the practice of ecclesial life in its worship, mission and pastoral care parallels similar insights with regard to the formation and realisation of the community of faith, demonstrating the robustness of the *perichoresis* construct in the pastoral life of the church. The next chapter takes this exploration a step further by considering the extent to which the physical universe reveals patterns of connectedness that may be likened to the perichoretic life of the God who has created all things *ex nihilo* as an expression of his own relational nature.

---

[212] Olthuis, "Dancing Together in the Wild Spaces of Love": 151.

CHAPTER 5

Probing the 'Web of Life' – Perichoresis as a Principle of Cosmological Unity

If, in the words of Gerard Manley Hopkins, the world "is charged with the grandeur of God", how might we express that grandeur? Woven throughout this book is the hypothesis that relationality is a critical – even essential – dimension of the divine imprint on creation. In earlier chapters we have explored the theme of relationality within the innertrinitarian life of God, and outlined the theological doctrine of *perichoresis* as a helpful construct in articulating the dynamic, interpenetrating *ad intra* communion between Father, Son and Holy Spirit. Within a Christian pastoral context the construct is also valuable in delineating how human beings might relate to each other as a community of faith, seeking to recapitulate the perichoretic life of the Trinity not only *intra muros ecclesiae* but also in their outward orientation, embracing neighbour, stranger and outcast. But we can go further: if, as we have consistently maintained, God is intimately involved in his creation – immanent as well as transcendent – then we might reasonably expect that his perichoretic life spills over into everything 'other' that he has brought into being, offering a richer view of creation itself as "a *perichoresis* of interrelated systems."[1]

A number of words immediately come to mind when pursuing this relational line of thought: they include, for example, interconnectedness, coherence, holism and harmony. These are themes that correlate powerfully with new insights in contemporary physics and biology, which emphasise that everything in the universe is bound up with everything else – all things are what they are because they are related to everything else.[2] Moltmann refers to this as the

---

[1] Gunton, Colin E., "Relation and Relativity: The Trinity and the Created World" in Schwobel, Christoph (ed), *Trinitarian Theology Today: Essays on Divine Being and Act*, Edinburgh: T. & T. Clark, 1995: 108.

[2] "Major conceptual advances in science now require that we recover a view of the universe in which every single thing or event is in fact related to everything else" (Del Re, Guiseppe, *The Cosmic Dance: Science Discovers the Mysterious Harmony of the Universe*, Radnor PA: Templeton Foundation Press, 2000: 15). Del Re cites the American mathematician Norbert Weiner, founder of cybernetics, and the Belgian physical chemist Ilya Prigogine, discoverer of the importance of steady-state systems, as the two scientists most representative of the new interest in and application of a holistic

'creation-community', a community of both creatures and environments contributing to a 'web of life on earth'. In his theology of nature, he argues that we need "a new integration of human culture in the nature of the earth if we want to survive, because we are dependent upon the nature of the earth, but nature is not dependent on us."[3] His concept of 'creation-community' is explicitly perichoretic in his notion of an inclusive Trinity that is "so wide open that the whole world can find room and rest and eternal life within it."[4]

Similarly, Boff extends his insights concerning innertrinitarian *perichoresis* to the physical universe, quoting Fritjof Capra: "In the new world-view, the universe is seen as a dynamic web of interrelated events ... All natural phenomena are ultimately interconnected, and in order to explain any one of them we need to understand all the others."[5] Although Capra wrote these words within a strongly Taoist and Buddhist view of reality, presenting physics as a spiritual path to be followed alongside other pathways within a New Age paradigm, his ideas have been influential in promoting an understanding of life as fundamentally relational. In particular, Capra's emphasis on 'systems thinking' has challenged the traditional Newtonian paradigm of the universe as a clockwork mechanism.

Whilst caution needs to be exercised in interpreting Capra's ideas in terms of his speculative links between physics and oriental spirituality, his systems approach – drawing together key themes in contemporary physics, such as quantum mechanics, chaos and complexity, emergence and self-organisation – alerts us to the value of interpreting the physical universe as an integrated and interconnected reality. His ideas are helpful as 'stepping-stones'[6] in

---

systems approach. Prigogine applied eight central concepts to the whole universe as well as to objects in it: coherence, emergence of information, and irreversibility (three general concepts); and information, order, interaction, organisation, and feedback (five specific concepts).

[3] Moltmann, Jürgen, "Perichoresis: An Old Magic Word for a New Trinitarian Theology" in Meeks, M. Douglas (ed), *Trinity, Community, and Power: Mapping Trajectories in Wesleyan Theology*, Nashville: Kingswood Books, an imprint of Abingdon Press, 2000: 125.

[4] *Ibid*: 117; see also Jenson, Robert W., *Systematic Theology, Vol I - The Triune God*, New York: Oxford University Press, 1997: 226, where the triune God is described as '*roomy*' in the sense of making room within himself for creation.

[5] Boff, Leonardo, *Holy Trinity, Perfect Community*, Maryknoll NY: Orbis Books, 2000: 15-16, quoting from Capra, Fritjof, *The Tao of Physics*, London: Collins Fontana, 1976.

[6] The metaphor of 'stepping-stones' is taken from John Taylor, who concedes that "if these mystical ideas are used as an entrée into modern physics they have value, but only if used as stepping stones to the greater precision of the real thing" (Taylor, John G., writing in Chapter 7 of Davies, P.C.W. and Brown, J.R. (eds), *The Ghost in the Atom: A Discussion of the Mysteries of Quantum Physics*, Cambridge: Cambridge University Press, 1991: 114-115, and quoted in Southgate, Christopher *et al.*, *God, Humanity and the Cosmos: A Textbook in Science and Religion*, Edinburgh: T & T Clark, 1999: 230). For a helpful assessment of Capra within a discussion of some resources for thinking

understanding, from a Christian perspective, the relationship between the real world which science describes and the God who has brought that world into being and who sustains it by his Spirit. In this chapter we will briefly survey some of the major developments in quantum theory, chaos theory and self-organising systems, and discuss the growing awareness within the scientific community that the universe is best appreciated not in reductionist terms, but *holistically*. This shift from reductionism to holism has been summarised by Guiseppe Del Re in the statement that "the concept of system has changed its reference model from a collection of loosely coupled subsystems or particles to a tightly integrated whole, such as an organism."[7] Perhaps this new consciousness is most evident in the field of quantum mechanics.

Quantum Theory and Holistic Non-Locality

At the beginning of the twentieth century Einstein outlined his Special Theory of Relativity (STR), in which he argued, as others had before him, that the laws of physics are the same in all frames of reference where the velocity is constant: this is why a ball continues to drop vertically when tossed up in the back of a car travelling at any speed – both ball and thrower are travelling at the same speed. The second postulate of the STR is that the speed of light is constant, regardless of the velocity of the source of light or of the observers. These postulates led Einstein to formulate the principle of 'time dilation', which states that we can no longer consider time to be an absolute quantity: whether two events occur simultaneously depends on the reference frame in which they are observed. For example, scientists have shown that an atomic clock travelling at high speed in a jet plane ticks more slowly relative to its stationary counterpart.

In 1915, his General Theory of Relativity, which took into account the curvature of space-time, gravitational force and acceleration, gave rise to a set of equations that established the geometry of space-time, and led to the discovery that the universe was not static, but expanding. If Einstein was disturbed by the implications of this conclusion – he introduced the idea of a 'cosmological constant' into his equations to sustain the principle of a static universe, but later acknowledged this as 'the greatest blunder of my life' – he was even more disturbed by quantum theory. Whilst Einstein's theories of

---

about the relationship between God and creation from the perspective of Eastern religious and spiritual paradigms, see Southgate *et al.*, *God, Humanity and the Cosmos*: 226-243; see also Barbour, Ian G., *When Science Meets Religion: Enemies, Strangers or Partners?*, San Francisco: HarperCollins, 2000: 84-86, where Barbour argues that Capra has overstressed the similarities between physics and Eastern thought and virtually ignored the differences between them. For a searching critique of Capra's narrative within the context of the history of science, see Brooke, John and Cantor, Geoffrey, *Reconstructing Nature: The Engagement of Science and Religion* (1995-6 Gifford lectures), Edinburgh: T. & T. Clark, 1998: 75-105.

[7] Del Re, *The Cosmic Dance*: 41.

relativity were pivotal in the collapse of the Newtonian worldview, they did not shake his deterministic outlook. Faced with the uncertainties implicit in quantum mechanics, he famously observed that "God does not play dice with the world." But this is precisely what quantum theory seemed to imply, with its inherent probabilistic structure.

Quantum theory represents one of the theoretical bases of modern physics, and was first formulated in the 1920s, based upon the work of the German physicist Max Planck, who suggested that energy exists in individual packets or units, called *quanta* – in the same way that matter does – rather than as a continuous unquantifiable electromagnetic wave. Besides his inherent dislike of uncertainty in physics, Einstein was averse to quantum mechanics because the theory suggested that information between particles habitually travelled faster than the speed of light (technically referred to as non-locality), thus undermining his own theory of relativity – he is reputed to have referred to the phenomenon as 'spooky [or 'ghostly'] action-at-a-distance'.[8] The non-locality implicit in the information flows between particles is one of the more remarkable features of the atomic and subatomic world of protons, electrons and photons, and relates to the concept of 'entanglement', to which we will return below. But what radically transformed the scientific world was the way in which quantum mechanics "swept away many deeply entrenched assumptions about the nature of reality, and demanded a more abstract vision of the world."[9]

In the macroscopic world we are used to seeing things in either one place or another; the quantum world, however, behaves very differently. Thomas Young's well-known two-slit experiment clearly demonstrates that elementary particles of energy or matter, depending on the conditions, may behave like particles or waves, or both simultaneously. In this experiment, a beam of light is aimed at a barrier with two vertical slits. The light passes through the slits and the results are recorded on a photographic plate. The result is that an interference pattern is recorded, demonstrating that photons and electrons and other subatomic particles manifest both wave and particle effects. In fact, in order to obtain such a pattern, it is necessary for the particle to travel through both slits *at the same time*, with interference taking place between the waves/particles going through the slits. Each particle not only goes through both slits, but simultaneously takes every possible trajectory on its way to the target. But as soon as an attempt is made to observe this quantum phenomenon, the trajectories are disrupted and revert to the predictable two lines of light, aligned

---

[8] Max Jammer notes the appearance of the phrase in a remark made by Einstein's friend Paul Ehrenfest in 1932: "If we recall what an *uncanny theory of action-at-a-distance* [*unheimliche Fernwirkungstheorie*] is represented by Schrödinger's wave mechanics, we shall preserve a healthy nostalgia for a four-dimensional theory of contact-action [*Nahwirkungstheorie*]!" in Jammer, Max, *The Philosophy of Quantum Mechanics: The Interpretations of Quantum Mechanics in Historical Perspective*, Chichester NY: Wiley, 1974: 117, author's italics.

[9] Davies, Paul, *The Cosmic Blueprint*, London: Unwin, 1989: 165.

with the slits. The experiment shows conclusively that each particle of light moves simultaneously in what is called a *superposition* of possible trajectories, so long as no measurement takes place. In other words, the particle exists in all possible states at the same time, superimposed on each other.

Wave-particle duality, originally discovered by the aristocratic French physicist Louis de Broglie in 1924, led to the development of the theory of quantum mechanics, with which Erwin Schrödinger and Werner Heisenberg are most closely associated. Underlying the theory is Heisenberg's 'uncertainty principle', which states that precise, simultaneous measurement of two complementary values – such as the position and momentum of a subatomic particle – is impossible: for example, the more exactly we can measure a particle's position, the less exactly are we able to determine its momentum.[10] All we can do is to generate a range of possible results within a probability distribution, which implies that quantum mechanics is inherently statistical, challenging the deterministic view of reality implicit in classical Newtonian physics. Schrödinger, a physicist and mathematician, formulated his wave equation to explain the behaviour of particles at the quantum level, enabling the calculation of the probability of finding a particle at a certain position when an observation is made.[11] The act of measuring actually 'collapses' the wave, so that only one of the superimposed states results.

This phenomenon of quantum mechanics – the idea that an atom can exist simultaneously in both a decayed and a non-decayed state – has been illustrated by the well-known paradox of 'Schrödinger's cat'. In this thought experiment, a (hypothetical!) cat is sealed in a box, with a device inserted which has a 50:50 probability of releasing cyanide into the box. As long as no observation is made, the cat is, according to quantum theory, "in a complex linear combination of dead and alive"[12] when the cyanide gas is released. It is in a hybrid, or superimposed, state of being both-dead-and-alive at the same time. As soon as an observer intrudes upon the scene, superposition is lost and the cat is evidently *either* dead *or* alive. The principle underlying this interpretation of quantum theory is that objective reality, though it exists, is not determined or settled until our very act of observing brings it into being – the so-called 'Copenhagen interpretation', with which the Danish physicist Niels Bohr is associated.[13] This is the 'measurement problem' of quantum mechanics, which

---

[10] Similarly, other pairs, such as time and energy, are subject to the uncertainty principle.

[11] The wave equation was so-called because the probability distribution of the outcomes has the mathematical form of a wave. As Barbour notes, the equation "portrays a complex pattern of probability waves that are accurately correlated with a large set of observations but not with an individual observation" (Barbour, *When Science Meets Religion*: 66).

[12] Penrose, Roger, "Big Bangs, Black Holes and 'Time's Arrow'" in Flood, R. aand Lockwood, M., (eds), *The Nature of Time*, Cambridge, Mass.: Basil Blackwell, 1965: 60.

[13] Worthing comments that Schrödinger's attempt in his thought experiment to relate the uncertainty involved in radioactive decay to large-scale structures has not been satisfactorily resolved: "In essence, we are left with two systems, one predictable, the

remains unresolved in spite of a number of ingenious theories, such as Wigner's consciousness thesis that "it is the entry of information into the mind of the observer that collapses the quantum wave and abruptly converts a schizophrenic, hybrid, ghost state into a sharp and definite state of concrete reality."[14] A particular difficulty here, of course, is that the brain is itself composed of atoms that behave in a quantum way,[15] although the problem may have more to do with our ignorance of the mind-brain relationship. According to Davies, Wigner's ideas "suggest that the solution of the mind-body problem may be closely connected with the solution of the quantum measurement problem, whatever that will eventually be."[16]

Bohr coined his 'principle of complementarity' to describe mutually exclusive modes of description within the quantum world. His resolution of the wave/particle duality was to assert that each quantum state represents an aspect of a hybrid reality, in which each state interferes with the others to produce the resultant pattern.[17] But how can an electron or photon be both a particle and a wave at the same time? Paul Davies appeals to the 'principle of complementarity':

> How can the mind be both thoughts and neural impulses? How can a

---

other unpredictable, one deterministic, the other indeterministic, one describing the large-scale macro-systems of the universe, the other the quantum micro-systems. Both, however, exist within the same interconnected physical universe and, according to the Christian confession, are subject to the same divine providence." (Worthing, Mark W., *God, Creation, and Contemporary Physics*, Minneapolis: Fortress, 1998: 133).

[14] Davies, Paul, *God and the New Physics*, London: Penguin Books, 1984: 115. Barbour remains unconvinced about such an observer-dependent universe: "Surely it is not mind as such that affects observations, but the process of *interaction* between the detection apparatus and the microsystem. The experimental results might be recorded on film or on a computer printout that no one looks at for a year. How could looking at the film or printout alter the outcome of an experiment that has been recorded for a year?" (Barbour, *When Science Meets Religion*: 80, author's italics).

[15] The same objection may be made with regard to measuring instruments, which consist of atoms that exhibit quantum behaviour.

[16] Davies, *God and the New Physics*: 115; later in this chapter, we note the increasing attention being paid by scientists to the topic of human consciousness, and consider the thesis proposed by David Bohm that "matter and consciousness have the implicate order in common" (Bohm, David, *Wholeness and the Implicate Order*, New York: Routledge and Kegan Paul, 1980: 197). More bizarre is Hugh Everett III's many-worlds (or multiverse) interpretation, which posits a series of parallel universes equal to the number of possible superimposed states, and between which there is unfettered access. This theory is, by definition, speculative and untestable since we have no access to other universes parallel to our own, and few scientists are willing to endorse it as it represents "the antithesis of the quest of physics to look for the simplest explanation" (Wilkinson, David, *God, the Big Bang and Stephen Hawking*, Tunbridge Wells: Monarch, 1993: 66).

[17] For a full exposition of his understanding of quantum theory, see Bohr, Niels, *Atomic Theory and the Description of Nature*, Cambridge: Cambridge University Press, 1934.

> novel be both a story and a collection of words? Wave-particle duality is another software-hardware dichotomy. The particle aspect is the hardware face of atoms – little balls rattling about. The wave aspect corresponds to software, or mind, or information, for the quantum wave is not like any other sort of wave anybody has ever encountered … It is a wave that tells us what can be known about the atom, not a wave of the atom itself.[18]

In summary, the quantum view of the world departs from classical assumptions in a number of important ways.[19] Firstly, the deterministic paradigm has given way to an emphasis on probabilities, such that uncertainty and probability are inherent features of quantum reality, rather than being an observational limitation. We should remember here that we are dealing with subatomic reality, so that we cannot immediately translate quantum insights, which are significant at the submicroscopic level, into the macroscopic world. The desk at which I am sitting as I type these words is still a desk, a concrete reality in the macroworld of my experience. Nonetheless, in the quantum context, it is also a ferment of interacting subatomic particles. The lesson to be learned is that we cannot dismiss the fact that our "commonsense view of the world, in terms of objects that really exist 'out there' independently of our observations, totally collapses in the face of the quantum factor."[20] Secondly, the reductionist perspective has given way to a more holistic understanding and approach to physical reality. In modern physics,

> the image of the universe as a machine has been transcended by the alternative perception of an indivisible, dynamic whole whose parts are essentially related and can be understood only as patterns of a cosmic process. At a subatomic level, the interrelations and interactions between the parts of the whole are more fundamental than the parts themselves.[21]

---

[18] Davies, *God and the New Physics*: 107.

[19] These summary points are made in Southgate *et al., God, Humanity and the Cosmos*: 114; for the purposes of our discussion, we will not develop the fourth and final point made by Southgate, even though it is a fundamental premise underlying the quantum view of the world, which is that "the classical assumptions of continuity and divisibility (that between any two points there is an infinite number of intermediate values) have given way to *quantisation* – for certain physical quantities, the range of permissible values is severely restricted" (*ibid*: 114).

[20] Davies, *God and the New Physics*: 107; Davies may be overstating the case here, as our view of reality only *seems* to collapse – our 'commonsense' perspective may be more robust than Davies suggests. Until we know how quantum mechanics and classical physics work together in some unified theory, it is premature to be dogmatic about a 'total collapse'.

[21] Ó Murchú, Diarmuid, *Quantum Theology: Spiritual Implications of the New Physics*: New York: Crossroad, 1997: 35-36.

In his critique of Wigner's human consciousness theory – as well as of ideas proposed by John Wheeler that we live in an observer-created universe in which the key feature is not consciousness but communication – Barbour comments that "the lesson to be learned is that phenomena in the world are interdependent and interconnected, not that they are mental in character or intrinsically dependent on the human mind."[22] This emphasis on the interconnectedness of parts such that *wholeness* is the primary reality rather than the reductionist's passion for microscopic units led David Bohm to develop his theory of implicate/explicate order.[23] Bohm gives priority to the 'implicate' order "which exists 'folded up' in nature and gradually unfolds as the universe evolves, enabling organization to emerge."[24] We will develop this idea in the context of emergence and self-organisation in a later section of this chapter, but it has relevance to our discussion of quantum mechanics because of the property of 'non-locality', a third significant departure from the assumptions of classical physics.

'Locality' may be defined as "the condition that two events at spatially separated locations are entirely independent of each other, provided that the time interval between the events is less than that required for a light signal to travel from one location to the other."[25] In effect, it denies 'action-at-a-distance'. Bohm was troubled by the limitations of locality for his understanding of human life and the nature of reality. He doubted the theory that subatomic particles had no objective existence and took on definite properties only when physicists tried to observe and measure them. He began to suspect that there was a deeper order underlying the complex behaviour of particles, giving rise to his theory of an 'implicate order' in the universe, an 'undivided wholeness' that governs all reality. He theorised that there was a 'guiding wave', or 'quantum potential', that determined the motion of particles, so that they obeyed the implicate order which was etched deeply within the universe. In his 1959 experiments with Aharonov in quantum interconnectedness he discovered that in certain circumstances electrons are able to 'feel' the presence of a nearby magnetic field even though they are travelling in regions of space where the field strength is zero, suggesting the presence of non-locality as an underlying characteristic of the quantum world.

Earlier, Einstein had collaborated with two colleagues in Princeton, Podolsky and Rosen, to challenge two basic quantum assumptions: that individual subatomic particles had no real properties until they were observed; and that particles interacted with each other even though they may be separated by vast distances. Their thought experiment – dubbed the EPR Paradox, after the names of the researchers – involved separating a two-proton particle, and measuring

---

[22] Barbour, *When Science Meets Religion*: 80.
[23] See Bohm, *Wholeness and the Implicate Order*, especially pp. 172-213.
[24] Davies, *The Cosmic Blueprint*: 176.
[25] Parker, Sybil P. (ed), *McGraw-Hill Dictionary of Scientific and Technical Terms*, New York: McGraw Hill, 1994, 5th ed., under 'locality'.

the spin of one proton. They concluded that, according to quantum theory, the consequent 'collapse' of the wave function necessarily and instantaneously determines the counterbalancing spin (in the opposite direction) of the other proton, even though the protons may be isolated from each other by a great distance, even light years apart.[26] Because these findings contradicted his own philosophical objections to the measurement problem' and non-locality, Einstein concluded that quantum theory was incomplete: there must be 'hidden variables' in the separated particles that explained what was happening.

One of Bohm's supporters, John Bell, a physicist at the CERN laboratory near Geneva, tested the determinateness of the EPR hypothesis[27], and showed that quantum mechanics "predicts a significantly greater degree of correlation than can possibly be accounted for by any theory that treats the particles as independently real and subject to locality."[28] In 1982 a team of French research scientists, led by the physicist Alain Aspect, undertook a laboratory experiment of quantum interconnectedness that confirmed the inequalities between quantum theory and locality implicit in Bell's theorem. The theories and experiments summarised above highlight the need for further explanation of the physical processes at work; at one level, they might seem to support Bohm's proposal of an implicate order as the basis for all reality. For Bohm,

> the whole universe can be thought of as a kind of giant, flowing hologram, or *holomovement,* in which a total order is contained, in some implicit sense, in each region of space and time. The explicate order is a projection from higher dimensional levels of reality, and the apparent stability and solidity of the objects and entities composing it are generated and sustained by a ceaseless process of enfoldment and unfoldment, for subatomic particles are constantly dissolving into the implicate order and then recrystallizing.[29]

The priest and social psychologist Diarmuid Ó Murchú draws from the work

---

[26] Einstein, Albert, Podolsky, Boris and Rosen, Nathan, "Can Quantum-Mechanical Description of Physical Reality Be Considered Complete?" in *Physical Review* 47 (1935): 777-780.

[27] The test was conducted theoretically through equations rather than in a laboratory.

[28] Davies, *The Cosmic Blueprint*: 177; he continues: "It is almost as if the two particles engage in a conspiracy to cooperate when measurements are performed on them independently, even when these measurements are made simultaneously" (*ibid*: 177). See Bell, John, "On the Einstein-Podolsky-Rosen Paradox" in *Physics* 1:3 (1964): 195-200; his theorem is named 'Bell's Inequality' because Bell demonstrated "a mathematical inequality that unavoidably arises if the locality of classical physics is applied to quantum theory" (Worthing, *God, Creation, and Contemporary Physics*: 127).

[29] Pratt, David, "David Bohm and the Implicate Order," first published in *Sunrise*, Feb./March 1993 (see http://ourworld.compuserve.com/homepages/dp5/bohm.htm, accessed on 10.11.03); Pratt comments that "It was his hope that one day people would come to recognize the essential interrelatedness of all things and would join together to build a more holistic and harmonious world."

of Bohm and others to establish one of his tenets of 'quantum theology', which is that, in seeking to understand life, we need to begin with the whole rather than with the parts.[30] In other words, rather than adopting a reductionist, 'bottom-up' approach, we recognise the presence of 'top-down causation', a methodology with which Arthur Peacocke has been particularly associated – although, as we noted in Chapter 1, Peacocke has shifted away from the language of causation, preferring to think in terms of 'whole-part influence' in order to accommodate a more holistic systems-based understanding of the relationship between God and the world.[31] Whilst Bohm was not making any explicit theological statement, it is evident that 'top-down causation' correlates well with his 'hidden variables' approach to understanding how particles behave. In other words, "Bohm's implicate order is similar to field theory in its potential as a metaphor for the contingency of the physical cosmos on the

---

[30] Diarmuid, *Quantum Theology*: 56-58. Ó Murchú maintains that the search for community "is not merely a pursuit of security and intimacy to obviate our loneliness in an anonymous and impersonal world. It is much more than that. It is the expression – however haphazardly and imperfectly made – of a yearning from deep within the created order itself, a groaning arising from the heart of creation (to paraphrase St. Paul), seeking reciprocity and mutuality. The very fabric of creation and the very nature of God sing in unison a song of love" (*ibid*: 89). Ó Murchú's 'quantum theology' is at times a confusingly eclectic blend of pantheistic monism, religious syncretism (for example, Buddhist reincarnation nestles alongside the Christian resurrection-motif) and process theology, wrapped up in the language of quantum physics and the contemporary human 'search for enlightenment'. His starting point is not God, but human experience of the world as perceived with the quantum imagination: "When we try to understand how the parts [of the universe] interact and function for the sake of the whole, then the mystery begins to unfold, and we confront questions of ultimate meaning that concern theological discourse" (*ibid*: 49). The result of his theological method is that he embraces pantheistic interpretations of a 'God' who is at one with his creation, reflecting a strong desire to demolish all dualistic undercurrents that lead to perceptions that God is either inside or outside the created order. For Ó Murchú, the notion of pantheism may be a troubling one for humans, but "it is unlikely to be of any consequence to the creative life force which impregnates and enlivens our world with prodigious resourcefulness" (*ibid*: 50). The difficulty here is that in his decision to eschew any formal or traditional 'God-language' – Ó Murchú prefers such phrases as 'creative life force' and 'divine energy', though it is noticeable that *Quantum Theology* still abounds in references to God – the author fails to give sufficient emphasis to the essential 'otherness' of God, resulting in an enigmatic confusion of divine transcendence and immanence. Traditional theology loses out further in his reduction of 'sin' to humanity's failure to care for creation: this 'collusion between people and systems' leads him to argue that "systems, rather than individual people, become the instigators of immoral and irresponsible behaviour" (*ibid*: 200). In spite of these serious theological concerns, Ó Murchú's proposals are nonetheless highly suggestive and illuminating for an understanding of the universe as a relational and interactive reality.

[31] This shift also reflects Peacocke's inclination towards a more process-theological orientation.

continuing sustenance of God."[32] Indeed, as Davies points out, some physicists have speculated about the existence of a wave function for the whole universe, in which "the fate of any given particle is inseparably linked to the fate of the cosmos as a whole ... because its very reality is interwoven with that of the rest of the universe."[33]

Quantum Mechanics, Entanglement and the Doctrine of *Perichoresis*

Caution needs to be exercised in translating the quantum insights in the preceding section into explicit expressions of perichoretic life in the universe. Earlier, we noted Miroslav Volf's definition of *perichoresis* as an *ad intra* trinitarian construct, in which he refers to the reciprocal interiority of the divine persons in their mutual indwelling of each other. The question we face here relates to the validity of transferring this intrinsic divine characteristic to the created order. As finite human beings, we have no way of probing into the essential mystery of God's inner being. Yet the doctrine of *perichoresis*, as a trinitarian concept of divine unity, is uniquely appropriate because it "combines threeness and oneness without reducing the three to one or the one to three, and avoids the dangers of modalism as well as tritheism."[34] Furthermore, the doctrine conveys the dynamic vitality of a God who is immanently involved in his creation, and whose life in the history of the world is constitutive of his essential being *ad intra*. We are, I suggest, on secure theological ground in proposing *perichoresis* as an inclusive concept that directs us into the essential nature of God's inner being of community and dynamic relationality, whose energies are not contained within his innertrinitarian being, but reach out in other-centred love to all creation.

We have argued at various points in this book that we should expect a God who is an 'open' Trinity of love – and whose primary characteristic is relational, in the important sense that it is the relations between the divine persons which constitute the unity of God – to bring into being a creation that expresses his own ecstatic perichoretic life, a creation that he unchangeably and unconditionally loves and blesses. The concept of non-locality, pivotal in our brief review of the major features of quantum mechanics, reflects a radical interconnectedness that points towards an underlying order in the universe. In

---

[32] Worthing, *God, Creation, and Contemporary Physics*: 129; for a discussion of field theory in physics and its relevance to theology, see *ibid*: 117-124, in which Worthing notes the way in which some theologians, notably Thomas Torrance and Wolfhart Pannenberg, have utilised the insights of field theory as a metaphor for the energies of the Holy Spirit in creation (though Worthing is especially critical of Pannenberg's theological application of the field concept). Ways in which the Spirit might be interpreted as active agent in an evolving, indeterminate and 'open' universe are explored further in Chapter 6.
[33] Davies, *The Cosmic Blueprint*: 177.
[34] Moltmann, "Perichoresis: An Old Magic Word for a New Trinitarian Theology": 117.

his book *The Mind of God* Paul Davies reflects deeply on what he calls the 'uncanny' tuning of the human mind to the scientific workings of nature, and finds it remarkable that human beings have the mental capacity to "make a passable attempt at completing nature's 'cryptic crossword'."[35] He remarks at the end of the book that "the existence of mind in some organism on some planet in the universe is surely a fact of fundamental significance ... We are truly meant to be here."[36]

This allusion to some sort of mystical experience offering a holistic vision of reality is evident in the later writings of David Bohm,[37] who was convinced that metaphysical realities need to be embraced in our understanding of quantum non-locality. Bohm's own metaphysical inclinations are discernible in his remark that the implicate domain "could equally well be called idealism, spirit, consciousness. The separation of the two – matter and spirit – is an abstraction. The ground is always one."[38] Whilst Worthing cautions us against drawing too many theological conclusions from his writings[39], affirming Polkinghorne's observation that quantum theory "is not itself a sufficient basis for a universal metaphysics"[40], his additional concerns about an unwarranted drift into metaphysical speculation need not weaken the force of Bohm's holistic understanding of reality; in fact, at the scientific level, they "open the way for the operation of non-local correlations, downward causation and new organizing principles."[41]

The non-locality principle embedded in quantum mechanics is therefore highly suggestive of a universe that is a holistically interconnected reality, in which – at the quantum level – particles interact interdependently according to some guiding principle, or 'hidden variable'. In his study of the quantum concept of 'entanglement' – the technical term describing the way energy and matter particles interact at the quantum level, entangling with one another so

---

[35] Davies, Paul, *The Mind of God: Science and the Search for Ultimate Meaning*, London: Penguin, 1993: 148.

[36] *Ibid*: 232.

[37] See, especially, Bohm, *Wholeness and the Implicate Order*; Bohm, David and Peat, F. David, *Science, Order and Creativity*, New York: Bantam Books, 1988.

[38] Weber, Renee, *Dialogues with Scientists and Sages: The Search for Unity*, New York: Routledge & Kegan Paul, 1986: 101.

[39] Worthing, *God, Creation, and Contemporary Physics*: 129-130; for example, for large-scale systems "Bohm recognizes the validity of dividing systems into independent subsystems in a way compatible with classical physics" because of the particular conditions associated with the application of connectedness derived from the EPR experiment.

[40] Polkinghorne, John, "The Quantum World" in Russell, Robert J., Stoeger, William R. and Coyne, George V. (eds), *Physics, Philosophy and Theology: A Common Quest for Understanding*, Vatican City State: Vatican Observatory Publications, 198: 340.

[41] Davies, *The Cosmic Blueprint*: 182.

that they become intimately linked, or correlated[42], regardless of their distance from each other – Kirk Wegter-McNelly states that "the universe, at least from the point of view of quantum theory, manifests characteristics which indicate that it is an interconnected, relational whole."[43] Linking the concept of 'entanglement' synonymously with *perichoresis*, he suggests that there is "a certain plausibility to the idea that an entangled God who creates an entangled world (entangled in the scientific sense of quantum entanglement) would be entangled with the world God has chosen to create."[44] God is described as an 'entangled' God, in the sense that the Spirit acts as the 'go-between' who entangles the Father and the Son in their mutual relationship of love: the three divine persons are irreducibly unique, yet dynamically alive as a relational whole, reflecting a primary characteristic of quantum entanglement.

The notion of quantum entanglement – as for chaos, complexity and chance – should not be interpreted in terms of disorder: on the contrary, it directs us to a view of reality which, at the ultimate level, is remarkably *un*fragmented. The idea of God being entangled with his creation is another way of speaking about divine action in the world. At the end of Chapter 3 we referred to the activity of the Spirit as the eschatological power of God at work in all creation, enabling all that exists – personal and non-personal – to fully and finally become itself in the freedom of divine love. This is the language of *kenosis*, as God freely allows his creation to become what he has purposed it to be, neither distancing himself deistically from his creation nor overruling those free, natural processes that determine the unfolding of the universe through a creative interplay between chance and law. For Wegter-McNelly, the Spirit's activity in the world manifests God's 'loving entanglement' with the world. The concepts of *kenosis*, entanglement and pneumatology are brought together – might we suggest 'entangled'? – by Simmons, whose central thesis is that "divine kenosis is a form of entanglement with the world in which the Spirit is present in the world as sanctifying agapic love."[45]

---

[42] Erwin Altewischer and his research team at Leiden University in the Netherlands have recently shown that pairs of photons linked by the quantum effect of entanglement can pass through sheets of metal without the entanglement being destroyed, proving that the quantum linking of particles is far more robust than scientists had previously thought (refer to http://www.newscientist.com/hottopics/quantum/quantum.jsp?id=ns99992564, accessed on 11.11.03, citing a report in *Nature* Vol 418: 304).

[43] Wegter-McNelly, Kirk, *The World, Entanglement, and God: Quantum Theory and the Christian Doctrine of Creation*, unpublished doctoral dissertation, Berkeley CA: Graduate Theological Union, April 2003: 1.2.

[44] *Ibid*: 6.4.3; Wegter-McNelly's suggestion of *synonymity* appears to posit a link between entanglement and *perichoresis* that transcends the idea of *analogy* as the most appropriate expression of that relationship, and runs the risk of blurring the radical distinction between finite and infinite.

[45] *Ibid*: 136, referring to Simmons, Ernest L., "Toward a Kenotic Pneumatology: Quantum Field Theory and the Theology of the Cross" in *CTNS Bulletin* 19, No. 2 (Spring 1999): 11-16.

Drawing from our earlier trinitarian insights, it is important to emphasise that the concept of *perichoresis* was understood throughout the history of Christian thought as a way of showing how unity and distinction could be combined within the inner life of the Trinity. It enabled theologians to hold on to the essential oneness of God without sacrificing the uniqueness of each divine person. Might we not tentatively suggest here that the concept, expressed in the physical language of entanglement, similarly enables us to hold together the holistic behaviour of the universe as the unique creation of God and the distinctive behaviour of the particles that interact so uniquely at the quantum level? In other words, the 'undivided wholeness' that Bohm understood to govern all reality, may be viewed as analogous to the ultimate divine reality of an undivided – and indivisible – trinitarian God.

Similarly, at the quantum level, interactions in which atoms not only are located simultaneously in two separate places in a state of superposition but also *move through each other* may be understood as corresponding to the interweaving currents of energy and love that Fiddes interprets as a 'perichoresis of *movements*' within the divine life – in which Father, Son and Holy Spirit *indwell each other* in divine *perichoresis*. Note the italicised emphasis given to the phrases 'move through each other' and 'indwell each other'. The perspective I am presenting here is that the phenomenon of quantum entanglement, as an expression of the behaviour of matter at the subatomic level, reflects in a remarkable way the perichoretic reality of the Creator God.

In 1996 researchers at the laboratories of the National Institute of Standards and Technology in Boulder, Colorado, conducted an experiment in which they isolated a single beryllium ion (with one of its two outer electrons stripped away) in an electromagnetic trap, and cooled it to almost absolute zero with precisely tuned laser beams; they then coaxed it into two distinct internal quantum states at the same time. The atom started out in two widely separated places at the same time, rather like a marble that is somehow simultaneously located on opposite slopes of a large, shallow, round-bottomed bowl. As time progressed, it moved 'through itself' to the bottom of the 'bowl', then split to return to opposite sides of the 'bowl'.[46] Although the experiment involved only a single atom rather than the macroscopic world of concrete, visible objects, it spurred the researchers to further experimentation in order to cross the bridge between quantum mechanics and the macroscopic world. Four years later, in a report in *Nature*, another NIST team, including some of the original 1996 team, found that when the hypothetical 'bowl' is shaken, even minimally, the dual position of the atom ceases and it ends up on only one side of the 'bowl'.[47] In

---

[46] The experiment was conducted by Christopher Monroe, Dawn Meekhof, Brian King and David Wineland, and written up in Monroe, C., "A 'Schrödinger cat' superposition state of an atom" in *Science* 272 (24 May 1996): 1131 – for further details, see http://www.sciencenews.org/sn_arch/5_25_96/fob1.htm , accessed on 17.11.03.

[47] See Myatt, C.J., King, B.E., Turchette, Q.A., Sackett, C.A., Kielpinski, D., Itano, W.M., Monroe, C. and Wineland, D.J., "Decoherence of quantum superpositions through coupling to engineered reservoirs" in *Nature* 403 (20 January 2000): 269-273.

other words, environmental influences, represented by the 'shaking of the bowl', terminate superposition.

Although these experiments reflect the impracticability of applying the phenomenon of non-local quantum superposition to the empirical world of macroscopic objects, they do direct Christians towards a Creator whose presence operates at a level that is beyond the senses. This is a thesis taken up by the Catholic theologian Daniel Liderbach, who proposes an analogous relationship between the presence of the kingdom of God and the dynamics of the physical world realised through contemporary physics.[48] Furthermore, his study has significant ramifications for anthropology, since "the expanded knowledge of the physical world available from contemporary physics alters the manner in which humans relate to the world."[49] Following a comprehensive discussion of Einstein and his theories of relativity, in which he endorses the great German physicist's 'imaginative refashioning of the fundamental significance of the physical world', Liderbach turns his attention to quantum mechanics. Appreciative of Einstein's openness to new models of thinking about reality, he explores the quantum world, concluding that "there are within the world [of our senses] presences that suggest that the Presence of the kingdom is at least plausible for Christian believers who are sympathetic to physical science."[50] Liderbach's thesis connects with Bohm's 'implicate order' proposal in affirming that

> quantum physics has discovered that behind the world of common sense, behind the world of the senses, and even behind the world of logical consistency, there is present a world that had always existed, but that has only come to human awareness in the twentieth century.[51]

For example, whilst physicists acknowledge the existence of Planck's constant as a mathematical measurement of the separation between discrete energy *quanta*, it remains an unidentifiable field – or presence – that lies beyond the realm of the senses. The language of 'field' is important here, as many physicists are persuaded that the most fundamental physical entities are not particles, but fields, or 'fields of force'. In physics, a field is the region in which a particular type of force can be observed – for example, a gravity field, electromagnetic field, electric field or nuclear field; the laws of physics suggest that a field can also transmit energy and momentum. As Del Re points out, a field is not "a property of the points of a certain region of space; it is an entity in

---

[48] Liderbach, Daniel, *The Numinous Universe*, New York: Paulist Press, 1989.

[49] *Ibid*: 4; in Chapter 6 the anthropological significance of new insights in the field of contemporary physics is reviewed within the framework of the theological doctrine of *imago Dei*, a theme that is not taken up explicitly by Liderbach.

[50] *Ibid*: 68.

[51] *Ibid*: 79.

its own right, which reveals itself through properties of the points of space."[52]

Michael Faraday introduced the idea of field theory in the nineteenth century, hoping that ultimately all the fields of force could be incorporated into a final all-encompassing unified field. Over the years the field concept has been adapted alongside developments in classical and contemporary physics. In theology, the foremost proponent of field theory has been Wolfhart Pannenberg, who dates the idea back to pre-Socratic metaphysics, opening the way for him to integrate his doctrine of the Spirit with the Stoic doctrine of the divine *pneuma*, which was "a very fine stuff that permeates all things, that holds all things in the cosmos together by its tension (*tonos*), and that gives rise to the different qualities and movement of things."[53] Worthing critiques Pannenberg's incorporation of field theory into his theological formulation of a 'field of divine essence' – in which the dynamic activity of the Holy Spirit represents a part[54] – preferring to interpret field theory as "a metaphor for God's continuing sustenance of the universe" and acknowledging its potential usefulness in influencing the way in which "theology confesses this continuing 'presence' of God in creation."[55]

This confession of God's 'presence' in creation is, according to Liderbach, a plausible consequence of contemporary insights in quantum mechanics, even though it may be (or precisely because it is!) non-sensory, ultra-rational and beyond comprehension: "there are experiences of a Presence within human consciousness that are as far removed from ordinary human experiences as occurrences of the micro-world are removed from the motions of the macro-world."[56] As an example of what he calls traces of the kingdom within the

---

[52] Del Re, *The Cosmic Dance*: 176, drawing from Einstein's statement that 'electro-magnetic fields are not states of a medium but independent realities, which cannot be reduced to terms of anything else and are bound by no substratum" (in Einstein A., *Mein Welbild* (*The World as I See It*), Frankfurt: Ullstein Materialien, 1934, and quoted by T. F. Torrance in his introduction to his edited publication of Maxwell, J. C., *A Dynamical Theory of the Electromagnetic Field (1864), with an Appreciation by A. Einstein*, Edinburgh: Scottish Academic Press: 1982: ix-27).

[53] Pannenberg, Wolfhart, "The Nature of Creation" in *Systematic Theology*, Vol. II, Grand Rapids: Eerdmans, 1994: 81; Pannenberg credits Max Jammer with the idea of the Stoic doctrine of the divine *pneuma* as the direct precursor of the modern field concept.

[54] Taking an eschatological perspective, Pannenberg writes: "We are thus to think of the dynamic of the divine Spirit as a working field linked to time and space – to time by the power of the future that gives creatures their own present and duration, and to space by the simultaneity of creatures in their duration" (*ibid*: 102); earlier, he comments that "[w]hether or not we can describe the priority of the field over every kind of material manifestation is a matter that we may leave to advances in physics" (*ibid*: 101).

[55] Worthing, *God, Creation, and Contemporary Physics*: 124.

[56] Liderbach, *The Numinous Universe*: 89.

cosmos, Liderbach cites the example of 'tunneling'[57], which refers to the exit of elementary subatomic particles from a location in which they had been apparently inescapably enclosed. The phenomenon of entanglement, discussed above, is another clear example drawn from the world of quantum mechanics. These amongst many other examples may be interpreted as *vestigia trinitatis*[58]: they plausibly reflect the unseen presence of a relational God at work by his Spirit in his creation.

We noted earlier that Barth's major criticism of *vestigia trinitatis* was that they do not display the indissoluble unity and the indestructible distinction implicit in the biblical revelation of the divine Trinity. Given the unity implicit in the quantum concepts of non-locality and holistic interconnectedness, it is not too far a step to acknowledge the presence of traces of perichoretic life at the quantum level which point towards an underlying relational reality that is not immediately apparent in the macro-world of human experience and observation. This is given further support when we examine the astonishing geometry of the physical world.

Fractals and Holograms

Philosophically, the idea of a 'real world' beyond Bohm's 'explicate order' has a Platonic ring to it, reminiscent of Plato's Theory of Forms. However, whilst Plato's entire philosophical enterprise was based on the dualistic separation between the higher world of unchanging, timeless reality and the lower physical world of creaturely existence, such a premise was anathema to Bohm. His concept of an implicate/explicate order postulates a tacit convergence, rather than a rigid separation, between the seen and the unseen, an unfolding of the unity of that which *is* at the most fundamental, elemental level. This idea of convergence between the seen and the unseen articulates the contemporary interest in dialogue between science and religion. When scientists begin to think about the inanimate world with a sense of wonder and mystery, and when theologians exhibit a growing awareness of the natural world and humanity's place in the cosmos, the doorway is opened even more widely for new understandings of the physical world in which we live. In particular, both scientists and theologians are beginning to appreciate the extraordinary beauty and elegance of the universe.

Two ideas that have intrigued physicists in recent decades are the geometric figures associated with the 'Mandelbrot set' and the structure of holograms. The former is named after the IBM computer scientist Benoit Mandelbrot, who

---

[57] *Ibid*: 86, 136.

[58] We noted in Chapter 3 Barth's reluctance to acknowledge the existence of *vestigia trinitatis* in the physical world, though he did acknowledge their presence in a number of specific ways (see Barth, Karl, *Church Dogmatics* 1/1, Edinburgh: T. & T. Clark, 1936: 336-338).

discovered a geometric form known as a 'fractal', a word which he coined in 1975, derived from the Latin verb *frangere*, meaning 'to break'. Einstein had added to three-dimensional space a fourth dimension, time. Mandelbrot discovered that there existed space – fractional space – *between* the dimensions, leading to the idea of fractal dimensions. This opened up the way for the world of nature to be described in mathematical terms. An important principle underlying fractal geometry is that, again and again, the world displays a 'regular irregularity', a reality previously unnoticed by scientists until Mandelbrot developed some mathematical tools for describing the remarkably consistent patterns inherent in such physical phenomena as coastlines, snowflakes, mountains and clouds.

Traditional geometry is Euclidian in its measurement of length, depth and thickness; it deals with straight lines, smooth curves and symmetrical shapes. But the real world is, of course, more complex, and Mandelbrot's response to the question 'How long is the coast of Britain?' was that any coastline is, in a mathematically rigorous sense, infinitely long. As you decrease the scale of measurement, the measured length "rises without limit, bays and peninsulas revealing ever smaller subbays and subpeninsulas – at least down to atomic scales, where the process does finally come to an end. Perhaps."[59] Computer simulation of the coastline, reducing the map into successively more detailed images, reveals small-scale details similar to the large-scale characteristics. Though the details are random, the degree of irregularity looks very much the same irrespective of the degree of magnification.

In 1979, Mandelbrot was working on some mathematical iterations on the computer when he discovered a geometrical form which generated an extraordinarily complex structure, capable of an infinite number of magnifications. The resultant images are "breathtaking in their variety, complexity and beauty. One sees an astonishingly elaborate tracery of tendrils, flames, whorls and filigrees. As each feature is magnified and remagnified, more structure within structure appears, with new shapes erupting on every scale."[60] Although the Mandelbrot set is self-similar at magnified scales, the small-scale details are not *identical* to the whole. The set is infinitely elaborate, yet the extraordinary complexity derives from the simplest of mapping equations, requiring a remarkably compact computer program to reproduce the complete set. The English mathematician – and Platonist – Roger Penrose declared that the Mandelbrot set "is not an invention of the human mind: it was a discovery. Like Mount Everest, the Mandelbrot set is just there!"[61]

The Mandelbrot set demonstrates that "simple procedures can be the source

---

[59] Gleick, James, *Chaos: Making a New Science*, New York: Penguin Books, 1987: 96.
[60] Davies, *The Cosmic Blueprint*: 63.
[61] Penrose, Roger, *The Emperor's New Mind: Concerning Computers, Minds and the Laws of Physics*, Oxford: Oxford University Press, 1989: 95. See Mandelbrot, Benoit, *The Fractal Geometry of Nature*, San Francisco: W. H. Freeman & Co., 1977; for an introduction to Mandelbrot's background and groundbreaking work in fractal geometry, see Gleick, *Chaos*: 83-118.

of almost limitless variety and complexity,"[62] leading to at least three important conclusions. Firstly, the amazing beauty of these mathematical works of art is richly suggestive of the beauty inherent in the created order: we can now "decode the symmetries of nature, unearthing a symbolic content that is not readily apparent to someone observing the physical system itself."[63] Secondly, consistent with Mandelbrot's own philosophy that "simplicity breeds complexity"[64], we are encouraged to believe that the complexity apparent in the natural world derives from basic laws which themselves may not be complex. We will see below how significant this point is with regard to the concept of 'emergence'. Thirdly, the fact that the universe can be described in elegant mathematical forms and equations leads one to believe, as does Penrose, that there must be "some deep underlying reason for the accord between mathematics and physics"[65]; so mathematicians are discovering *what is already there*, rather than constructing an elaborate human edifice based upon empirically derived data drawn from the real world.[66] Del Re draws these three points together in his comment that "[t]he universe disclosed to us by science appears to be the most beautiful and glorious thing imaginable, endowed with an internal mysterious order reminiscent of fractals, an eerie by-product of the mathematics of complexity."[67]

Mandelbrot's pioneering research into fractal geometry reveals symmetries in its mathematical representation of nature that demonstrate a coherence permeating the physical world. A similar conclusion with perhaps more startling metaphysical implications may be made with regard to Bohm's theory of wholeness and the implicate order, especially with reference to his understanding of the universe as a hologram. Many physicists have rejected the more speculative aspects of Bohm's theories, regarding them as too metaphysical to be of any scientific value. In this book I have deliberately highlighted the work of Bohm because his model of reality reflects a profound ecological concern allied to a deep spirituality, which correlates with my conviction – developed further in Chapter 6 – that ecology and spirituality are critical dimensions of the perichoretic structure of the created order. The mathematician and philosopher of religion Kevin Sharpe, whose research interests focus on the nexus of science and spirit, and who has a particular interest in the theories of David Bohm, reminds us that

> [t]he physics of Bohm and others demonstrate that religion can attempt to contribute to the knowledge of the "hardest" of the empirical sciences, physics. It can do this in two positive ways at

---

[62] Davies, *The Cosmic Blueprint*: 63.
[63] Ó Murchú, *Quantum Theology*: 47.
[64] Gleick, *Chaos*: 222.
[65] Penrose, *The Emperor's New Mind*: 430.
[66] The notion of 'what is already there' corresponds to Bohm's concept of the 'holomovement' as the most fundamental expression of *what is*, as discussed below.
[67] Del Re, *The Cosmic Dance*: 19.

least: by providing a store of concepts, hypotheses and metaphysical approaches, and by providing the motivation to bring these to physics and to try upholding their empirical worth. Many religions, including Christianity, have much to say concerning the nature and direction of the physical world; *they should not be afraid of bringing these ideas, in appropriate forms, to the sciences*. As hypotheses, they are still open to the strictures of empirical verification or falsification, but unless this bridging attempt is made, our secular-scientific society and religion with its needed values will probably drift further and further apart.[68]

The growing awareness that science cannot evade questions of ultimate meaning has generated new interest in Bohm's ideas. Whilst Sharpe's caution regarding the hypothetical nature of metaphysical paradigms of reality needs to be acknowledged, the growing intensity of dialogue between science and religion obligates an openness – though not uncritical – to the sort of proposals put forward and defended by Bohm with characteristic energy and conviction. He was a passionate visionary and his model of reality presents an intriguing challenge to conventional approaches to physics. In order to appreciate more fully the value of his contribution to the contemporary science-religion debate, we now examine Bohm's incorporation of the hologram concept as an illustration of his theory of 'undivided wholeness'.

As discussed earlier, quantum mechanics is associated with the notion of interference patterns, as demonstrated in the two-slit experiment in which subatomic particles simultaneously traverse every possible trajectory en route to the photographic plate on the other side. This phenomenon of interference lies behind the concept of the hologram, developed in 1947 by the mathematician Dennis Gabor.[69] If an object is bathed in the light of a laser beam and a second laser beam is bounced off the reflected light of the first, the resultant photographic record is a meaningless pattern of swirls, a blur of light and dark lines. However, as soon as the film is illuminated by another light beam, the original wave pattern is regenerated as the original three-dimensional object.[70] From the properties inherent in the hologram flows Bohm's radical conception of primary reality, which "is not the external, visible, sensory world, but the

---

[68] Sharpe, Kevin, "David Bohm's Physics and Religion" (http://www.ksharpe.com/word/BM03.htm, accessed on 21.11.03), my italics; see also Sharpe, Kevin, *David Bohm's World: New Physics and New Religion*, Lewisburg, PA: Bucknell University Press, 1993; Sharpe, Kevin, "Relating the Physics and Religion of David Bohm" in *Zygon: Journal of Religion and Science* Vol. 25, No. 1 (March, 1990): 105-122.

[69] Gabor, D., "Microscopy by reconstructed wave fronts" in *Proceedings of the Royal Society* (1949) A157: 457-487.

[70] For a discussion of Bohm's understanding of holography at both the physical and metaphysical level, see Sharpe, Kevin, "David Bohm's Physics and Religion"; for a more complete introduction to the physical process of holography, see Abramson, Nils, *The Making and Evaluation of Holograms*, London: Academic Press, 1981.

invisible, enfolded realm of potential and possibility."[71] Bohm is suggesting a new notion of order here, which has nothing to do with the regular arrangement of objects or events; rather, "a *total order* is contained, in some *implicit* sense, in each region of space and time."[72] As an example, Bohm invites us to consider the experience of looking at the night sky, in which structures covering immense stretches of space and time are in some sense contained, or enfolded, in the tiny space encompassed by the eye.[73] However, there is a further element of Bohm's understanding of reality that derives from the nature of the hologram as a three-dimensional image. If a section of a holographic image is sliced off, that section contains all the information found in the whole image: remarkably, however small a section is cut off, that part will still contain a picture of the whole. Rather than obtaining individual pieces that make up the whole, what we get each time is smaller wholes. This is the 'undivided totality' or 'wholeness' aspect of Bohm's implicate order model of reality:

In terms of the implicate order one may say that everything is enfolded into everything. This contrasts with the *explicate* order now dominant in physics in which things are *unfolded* in the sense that each thing lies only in its own particular region of space (and time) and outside the regions belonging to other things.[74] This process of enfoldment and unfoldment takes place in force fields that obey the laws of quantum mechanics, which means that they reflect the quantum properties of non-continuity, non-causality and non-locality. This unbroken and undivided totality of movement is given the name 'holomovement' by Bohm: "[r]ather than something essentially static, activity is the basic form of the holomovement."[75] What we perceive, therefore, "is not a

---

[71] Ó Murchú, *Quantum Theology*: 57.

[72] Bohm, *Wholeness and the Implicate Order*: 149, author's italics.

[73] Bohm gives a more striking analogy of implicate order, involving a laboratory demonstration "with a transparent container full of a very viscous liquid, such as treacle, and equipped with a mechanical rotator that can 'stir' the fluid very slowly but very thoroughly. If an insoluble droplet of ink is placed in the fluid and the stirring device is set in motion, the ink drop is gradually transformed into a thread that extends over the whole fluid. The latter now appears to be distributed more or less at 'random' so that it is seen as some shade of grey. But if the mechanical stirring device is now turned in the opposite direction, the transformation is reversed, and the droplet of dye suddenly appears, reconstituted" (*ibid*: 149; see also pp. 179-180).

[74] *Ibid*: 177.

[75] Sharpe, "David Bohm's Physics and Religion"; Sharpe points out that "Bohm refers to a variety of psychological and neurological research that suggests that the notion of an object is an abstraction we learn from early childhood; the idea of a fixed object is not fundamental psychology. There is a more primitive level of perception, that of movement, or change, a break in the regular orders of arrangement. Objects that we perceive to be relatively fixed or slowly moving are built up from the mass of fundamental perceptions of movement. But our common-sense descriptions, which are mirrored in classical physics, are abstractions we are conditioned to regard as fundamental" (see his section on "The Holomovement Concept"). It is important to note

landscape of facts or objects, but one of *events*, of process, movement and energy."[76] In other words, at its most fundamental level, reality is not objective or tangible at all, but exists as a seamless flow of particles interacting, flowing, fluctuating as waves of quantum energy, and forming interference patterns that represent Bohm's implicate order of things. Initially, the idea of an interference pattern may seem to be a negative one, but in quantum mechanics such an interpretation should be resisted. Benthall encourages us to develop what he calls a 'finer sensitivity to interference patterning':

> We talk already of being on the same 'wavelength' as someone, of liking the 'tempo' of a metropolis, of absorbing the 'rhythms' of the countryside, and of getting 'good vibrations' from a situation or a person – as if the universe were an immense hologram of interfering wavefronts.[77]

In fact, the notion of the universe as one 'immense hologram' is precisely where Bohm is leading us. In his reversal of the Cartesian paradigm, which seeks to describe the explicate order, Bohm's work is an attempt to "reformulate the laws of physics so that their primary reference is to the implicate rather than to the explicate order, to the whole rather than to individual particles."[78] The classical (mechanistic) approach to science starts with elements, like fields and

---

that, for Bohm, the 'holomovement' is both undefinable and immeasurable, though from its (unknowable) laws one may abstract "relatively autonomous or independent sub-totalities of movement (e.g., fields, particles, etc.) having a certain recurrence and stability of their basic patterns of order and measure" (Bohm, *Wholeness and the Implicate Order*: 178).

[76] Ó Murchú, *Quantum Theology*: 57, author's italics; the idea of reality as a process dates back to Heraclitus, the Greek philosopher of 'eternal change', expressed in analogical terms as the continuous flow of a river which always renews itself. Whereas Parmenides taught a philosophical system that is grounded in the unity of *being*, Heraclitus emphasised a system that focuses on a multitude of phenomena in a state of *becoming*; these two philosophers greatly influenced Plato in his search for a constant, unchanging principle, above and beyond the material world, which gives some sort of order and meaning to the changing restlessness of the known world (for a succinct presentation of Plato's philosophy, see Hare, R. M., *Plato*, Oxford: Oxford University Press, 1983).

[77] Benthall, Jonathan, *Science and Technology in Art Today*, Praeger World of Art Series, 1972: 94-98 (see http://www.holography.demon.co.uk/reviews/rebenth2.htm, accessed on 21.11.03), where the author alludes to the poets, notably Gerard Manley Hopkins (*Pied Beauty*) and T. S. Eliot (*Four Quartets*), as examples of those whose work illuminates the concept of interference – Hopkins in celebrating the "interpenetration of wavefronts as a fundamental principle of life" and Eliot's "often obscure but always insistent imagery of vibration and flickering, circulation and patterning."

[78] Sharpe, "David Bohm's Physics and Religion".

particles, and seeks to derive an understanding of the whole through the interaction of the parts. The implicate order model of prime reality reverses the process by *starting with the undivided wholeness of the universe*, so that the task of science is then

> to derive the parts through abstraction from the whole, explaining them as approximately separable, stable and recurrent, but externally related elements making up relatively autonomous sub-totalities, which are to be described in terms of an explicate order.[79]

Bohm's theory of the implicate/explicate order is a creative and scientifically plausible interpretation of reality that correlates with the relational dynamism implicit in the theological concept of *perichoresis*. Earlier, in Chapter 3, we noted Paul Fiddes' proposal that the innertrinitarian life may be interpreted as a '*perichoresis*' of movements', transmuting Pannenberg's three 'living realizations of separate centres of action' into "three living realisations of movements or directions of action".[80] In other words, it is more appropriate to think of the divine life of the Trinity as an event of 'relationships', consistent with our emphasis on dynamic, mutual reciprocity at the heart of the relationship between Father, Son and Holy Spirit.[81] The significance of the concept of 'holomovement' as an expression of dynamic perichoretic activity should not be lost on us. Inherent in Bohm's thesis is that everything interpenetrates everything else: the 'holomovement', that which *is* as the most fundamental expression of reality, "is always a totality of ensembles, all present together, in an orderly series of stages of enfoldment and unfoldment, which *intermingle and inter-penetrate each other* in principle throughout the whole of space."[82] Consistent with his underlying premise that everything is enfolded into everything, Bohm suggests that reality may be represented as a sort of 'superhologram' in which past, present and future flow together in simultaneous co-existence. Time, like space, is therefore to be regarded as a secondary, rather than a primary, order, derived from the multidimensional reality of the

---

[79] Bohm, *Wholeness and the Implicate Order*: 179; note that "[d]espite the apparent separateness of things at the explicate level, everything is a seamless extension of everything else, and ultimately the implicate and explicate orders blend into each other" (Ó Murchú, *Quantum Theology*: 58).

[80] Fiddes, Paul S., *Participating in God: A Pastoral Doctrine of the Trinity*, London: Darton, Longman & Todd, 2000: 81ff.

[81] Fiddes is aware that an emphasis on patterns of relating may be seen as effectively downplaying the divine persons; accordingly, he notes that "understanding the persons in God as relationships precisely recognises their 'concrete particularity' (*ibid*: 83). It is in their unique active movements that "the *hypostases* distinguish themselves from each other" (*ibid*: 85), so affirming their hypostatic particularity: so, for Fiddes, an emphasis on relationships actually promotes and intensifies personhood.

[82] Bohm, *Wholeness and the Implicate Order*: 184, my italics.

'holomovement'.[83]

The metaphysical – indeed religious or spiritual – implications of Bohm's ideas are apparent in his concluding comment that his overall approach has "brought together questions of the nature of the cosmos, of matter in general, of life, and of consciousness."[84] The incorporation not only of matter – animate and inanimate – but also of *consciousness* into his theory of the implicate order is significant in the search for a relationship between matter and consciousness.[85] In his work on the mind-brain relationship, the neurophysiologist Karl Pribram draws from the insights of Gabor in proposing a neural holographic hypothesis as a "plausible mechanism for understanding phenomenal experience."[86] Seeking to understand how memories are stored in the brain, Pribram's research led him to the conclusion that they are encoded not in neurons, or groups of neurons, in specific locations but in quantum wave patterns distributed throughout the brain, similar to the way that interference patterns are created in holographic images. The trillions of connections between brain cells, the amazing memory capacity of the human brain, and our exceptional ability to retrieve information stored in the brain's memory bank led Pribram to suggest that the brain is a remarkably cross-correlated holographic system. One has only to consider, for example, how the brain instantly and automatically makes a wide range of mental associations, or recalls and re-images events and details from the distant past when prompted by a particular word or image, in order to appreciate the plausibility of this hypothesis: "[w]hat better mechanism can be operating than the associative recall provided by the holographic process?"[87], asks Pribram.

However, it is important to acknowledge his caveats with regard to the holographic hypothesis, such as the lack of quantitative data needed to specify

---

[83] Bohm summarises his thoughts on time in relationship to the total order of matter and consciousness at the end of his book as a prelude to a final comment on the implications of his proposals at the level of metaphysics: see *ibid*: 210-212.

[84] *Ibid*: 212.

[85] Consciousness is a topic of increasing importance amongst scientists; as a representative comment, the mathematician-physicist Roger Penrose points out that consciousness "is the phenomenon whereby the universe's very existence is made known" (Penrose, *The Emperor's New Mind*: 577); for a helpful discussion of consciousness as a contemporary issue see Jeeves, Malcolm A., *Human Nature at the Millennium: Reflections on the Integration of Psychology and Christianity*, Grand Rapids: Baker Books, 1997: 173-211; on the science of consciousness, see Crick, Francis H., *The Astonishing Hypothesis: The Scientific Search for the Soul*, London: Simon and Schuster, 1994.

[86] Pribram, Karl, *Languages of the Brain: Experimental Paradoxes and Principles in Neuropsychology*, Englewood Cliffs NJ: Prentice-Hall, 1971: 166; for a fuller discussion of Pribram's holographic hypothesis in relation to brain functioning, see *ibid*: 140-166.

[87] *Ibid*: 162.

the information processing capacity of the neural holographic process.[88] Pribram concludes his analysis by observing that, despite these limitations, "many hitherto paradoxical findings regarding brain function in perception become understandable when the holographic analogy is taken seriously."[89] More important, he maintains,

> the holographic hypothesis does not upset classical neurophysiological conceptions; it enriches them by a shift in emphasis from axonal nerve impulses to the slow potential microstructure that develops in post-synaptic, dendritic networks. At the same time, the holographic hypothesis enriches psychology by providing a plausible mechanism for understanding phenomenal experience.[90]

A number of scientists have drawn inspiration from Bohm's (and, at a later stage, Pribram's) endorsement of the universe as a giant hologram, in particular those with an interest in such phenomena as altered states of consciousness, mystical feelings of cosmic oneness, extra-sensory perception, out-of-body experiences, near-death experiences and even UFOs. Many of these have been documented by Michael Talbot in his book *The Holographic Universe*[91]: however, as the author makes clear in his introduction, many of the views and conclusions presented in the book go beyond those expressed by Bohm and Pribram, even though these two have played a major part in the development of the holographic paradigm. As is often the case with texts that purport to demonstrate the validity of paranormal phenomena, some of Talbot's material has been discredited. [92] Whilst this in itself should not lead us to invalidate the important insights developed by Bohm and Pribram with regard to the universe as a dynamically interconnected reality with holographic features, it serves as a

---

[88] Pribram notes that "there is considerable doubt whether 'brain waves' as presently recorded form the substrate of any meaningful interference pattern organization for information processing, although they may be indicative that some such process is taking place. Because of their wave length these wave forms can carry only very small amounts of information – even in the form of spatially interfering holographic patterns. By contrast, the holographic hypothesis pursued here emphasizes the role of junctional slow potential 'microwave' structures in brain function" (*ibid*: 165). Nor is he proposing that all brain functions or problems of perception be reduced to holographic analysis, acknowledging memory mechanisms other than those that fit the holographic analogy.
[89] *Ibid*: 165.
[90] *Ibid*: 166.
[91] Talbot, Michael, *The Holographic Universe: A Remarkable New Theory of Reality*, New York: Perennial/HarperCollins Publishers, 1991.
[92] Talbot's text specifically focuses on paranormal phenomena, and are presented as the cornerstone of 'Quanta-Gaia' (the quest to better understand the cosmos and our role in it). Talbot also relies on some dubious examples – for example the claims of the Hindu guru Sathya Sai Baba (such as his divinity, his multiple reincarnations and his miraculous powers) have been wholly discredited, yet Talbot takes the Indian 'avatar' quite seriously.

cautionary warning not to extrapolate too readily from the holographic analogy.

Notwithstanding this caveat, the combination of Bohm's theory of the implicate/explicate order as a model of cosmic reality and Pribram's holographic model of the brain challenges the conventional idea of nature as objective reality. It also points us towards an understanding of the universe – microscopically as well as macroscopically – that is fundamentally and indivisibly interconnected and, moreover, in a state of creative movement. Rigidly mechanical and deterministic models of the universe thus give way to a cosmology in which human beings are integrally connected to a natural world that is itself a 'restless adventure', always unfolding, a universe that is moving towards the new creation of Christian eschatology[93]. Haught argues that "for us to embrace the universe means that we must also welcome its inherent restlessness."[94]

Bohm was a critical realist, and insisted that his proposal "is not to be taken as an *assumption* about what the final truth is supposed to be, and still less as a *conclusion* concerning the nature of such truth."[95] There is, he maintains, a 'truth' that is deeper than the implicate order, which he calls the 'true profundity'[96] – this is the domain of the sacred, the source of all compassion, wisdom and love. Bohm's own religious orientation was towards Eastern mysticism, and whilst it is appropriate to question the extent to which his physics may have been influenced by his religious beliefs[97] – suggesting the possibility of pantheistic models of the divine presence in the universe – we should not underestimate the richness of his proposals for an understanding of

---

[93] In Chapter 1, the point was made that "Christians should be stimulated about the sort of future that science might propose, without losing sight of the biblical hope of the *eschaton*. It follows, therefore, that orthodox Christian faith must critique evolutionary models that postulate the gradual creation of perfected persons into a final state that is ultimately 'this-worldly'. Christian eschatology anticipates a new creation that *transcends* the possibilities of this world, demanding that we think in terms of radical newness. Openness to the scientific endeavour must not destroy Christian hope in God's radical intervention to bring about the new creation." These ideas should not detract from the essential point being developed in this chapter, that until such time as a new creation is brought about by divine act, human beings are privileged to participate in the still unfolding story of the universe.

[94] Haught, John, *Science and Religion: From Conflict to Conversation*, New York: Paulist, 1995: 191.

[95] Bohm, *Wholeness and the Implicate Order*: 213.

[96] See Bohm, David and Weber, Renee, "The Enfolding-Unfolding Universe: A Conversation with David Bohm" in *Re-Vision* 1 (3/4) 1978: 24-51.

[97] See, for example, the reservations expressed in Sharpe, "David Bohm's Physics and Religion", in which the author cites – though he does not necessarily support – the acerbic retort of Stephen Hawking: "I think it is absolute rubbish ... The universe of Eastern mysticism is an illusion ... A physicist who attempts to link it with his own work has abandoned physics" (Boslough, John, *Stephen Hawking's Universe*, New York: William Morrow & Co.: 127).

the relationship between God and his creation within a Christian framework.[98] In particular, the notions of indivisible wholeness and the totality of movement of enfoldment and unfoldment correlate suggestively with the interweaving currents of trinitarian love and energy consistent with the theology of the *perichoresis* construct. The quantum concepts of field theory and non-locality, central to Bohm's proposal of an implicate order, are, as argued above, indicative of a quantum entanglement that is perichoretic in character.

Bohm adopts a rather Gnostic-sounding perspective in giving credit to 'ever-changing forms of insight'[99] for a new awareness of the 'true profundity' underlying the implicate order. In contrast, orthodox Christian belief, enlightened by the science of quantum mechanics, points to divine revelation as the basis of a believer's faith in God as the triune Creator of all that exists, a God who creates, and continues to create, as an expression of his triune nature.[100] Denis Edwards has articulated and amplified this in the form of a statement: "The trinitarian God works in and through the process of the universe, through laws and boundary conditions, through regularities and chance, through chaotic systems and the capacity for self-organization."[101] It is to this capacity for self-organisation that we now turn in our examination of the perichoretic nature of the universe.

Chaos, Complexity and Self-Organisation

To speak of the universe in the language of a 'restless adventure' is to address its inherently self-organising character. In Chapter 1 we noted that a number of scientists and theologians have recently begun to take seriously the idea of God as the intelligent creator of an amazingly complex system, a universe which has been given freedom to develop within God-given built-in self-organising capacities. Central to this idea is the concept of *emergence*, which is a term that describes what happens when an interconnected system of relatively simple

---

[98] Note also that although *Languages of the Brain* is concerned exclusively with the science of the 'brain-behaviour endeavour' Pribram makes subsequent allusions to the spiritual dimensions implicit in the holographic paradigm; for example, see Pribram's interview with Jeffrey Mishlove, "The Holographic Brain" (http://twm.co.nz/pribram.htm, accessed on 21.11.03).

[99] Bohm, *Wholeness and the Implicate Order*: 17.

[100] Similarly, for Bohm, 'the deep structure of self-deception' replaces the Christian notions of sin and the fall (see Bohm, David, "On Self-Deception in the Individual" in Kellerman, Henry (ed), *Group Cohesion: Theoretical and Clinical Perspectives*, New York: Grune and Stratton, 1981: 429-439, cited in Sharpe, "David Bohm's Physics and Religion").

[101] Edwards, Denis, "The Discovery of Chaos and the Retrieval of the Trinity" in Russell, Robert J., Murphy, Nancey and Peacocke, Arthur R. (eds), *Chaos and Complexity: Scientific Perspectives on Divine Action*, Vatican City State: Vatican Observatory Publications, 1995: 170.

elements self-organises to form more intelligent, more adaptive and complex higher-level behaviour.[102] At the most basic level of understanding, emergence may be described as a 'bottom-up' process that represents "a movement from low-level rules to higher-level sophistication."[103] Fuller offers three simple examples in which emergent properties arise: water, a cell and a human brain. Water molecules are not in themselves wet, yet combined with many others they produce 'wetness'; proteins, nucleic acids and other chemicals are themselves not alive, but combined into a cell they become a living organism; finally, a neuron is not conscious, but acting together with other neurons it produces consciousness.[104] Fuller argues that emergence is an *anti*reductionist phenomenon, though that need not always be the case: for example, Del Re suggests that the difference between reductionism and emergence may be expressed in terms of the "gap between a fragmentary sort of description based on a system's parts [such as a man having two legs and arms and a brain, etc.] and the reality emerging from the cooperation of those parts to form a whole [a man is capable of both love and terrible atrocities]."[105]

Closely related to the concept of emergence are the notions of *complexity* and *chaos*. When scientists talk about complexity, they refer to intricate self-organising patterns of cells, organisms, neural networks in the brain, ecosystems … indeed the whole cosmos. Chaos theory refers not to total disorder, but to unaccountable natural processes in which extraordinarily complex patterns arise unpredictably out of turbulence. This occurs when the heat is turned on under a pan of soup: molecules move around all over the place in a dramatic frenzy of activity, and then, when the conditions are right, hexagonally shaped convection cells form as the liquid gets hotter. This is a classic example of emergence, a higher-level order arising out of disorder. Other common examples include the sudden appearance of a vortex in the disordered turbulence of a flowing river, and the remarkable emergence of six-sided crystalline snowflakes from randomly moving water vapour molecules.

Such processes seem to contradict the well-known Second Law of Thermodynamics, in which energy in a system tends to flow into lower levels of availability until disorder prevails. The argument that the second law will not permit order to arise from disorder with unpredictable spontaneity reinforces the idea that all processes manifest a tendency towards decay and disintegration (or entropy, which measures the degree of thermodynamic disorder or randomness). However, the second law acknowledges that entropy *can* decrease in one sub-system at the expense of an increase in another sub-system: it is only the *overall* entropy of a complete or *closed* system that must increase when

---

[102] For a helpful non-scientific introduction to the concept of emergence, see Johnson, Steven, *Emergence: The Connected Lives of Ants, Brains, Cities, and Software*, New York: Scribner, 2001.
[103] *Ibid*: 18.
[104] Fuller, Michael, *Atoms and Icons: A Discussion of the Relationships Between Science and Theology*, London: Mowbray, 1995: 32.
[105] Del Re, *The Cosmic Dance*: 19.

spontaneous change occurs. The Belgian physical chemist Ilya Prigogine coined the phrase 'dissipative structures' to describe those systems that *openly* relate to their environment, dissipating energy in order to evolve into new forms of order and organisation.[106]

Challenging classical physicists' obsession with equilibrium, Prigogine proposed that the universe was a far-from-equilibrium system, characterised by irreversible processes that have the capacity to generate coherent behaviour. At the same time, the British scientist James Lovelock noted that the chemical constitution of Earth – 77% nitrogen, 21% oxygen and only minor traces of carbon dioxide, methane and argon – represented a mixture that was chemically far from equilibrium, proving that the planet was alive in the sense of being an active bio-system with a living, dynamic atmosphere: "The rocks, the air, the oceans, and all life are an inseparable system that functions to keep the planet livable. I now believe that life can exist *only* on a planetary scale."[107] Living organisms are clear examples of non-equilibrium systems, interacting continuously with their environment, consuming energy and radiating heat. A classic example is the human body, which reflects the process of higher levels of order arising through self-organising systems as the result of a continuous energy exchange with their environment.

According to Gaia thinking – a name suggested by Lovelock's friend William Golding, author of *Lord of the Flies*, after the Greek goddess of Earth and nature – human beings have a symbiotic relationship with everything else that makes up planet Earth, a perspective that, for Lovelock, is a scientific hypothesis rather than a religious proposition. However, as Snyder points out, the obviously spiritual overtones of Gaia – represented within mainstream ecologically-aware Christianity, in a wide range of neopaganist belief systems, such as Earth-goddess worship and New Age consciousness, and in contemporary ecofeminist perspectives – is "evidence of the shift in global consciousness from the subject/object split to an awareness of the 'subjective' –

---

[106] See Prigogine, Ilya and Stengers, Isabelle, *Order Out of Chaos*, New York: Bantam Books, 1984. In applying the new insights of quantum theory, complexity and chaos theory to the field of human organisation and management, Margaret Wheatley describes life as "open systems that engage with their environment and continue to grow and evolve." (Wheatley, Margaret J., *Leadership and the New Science: Learning about Organization from an Orderly Universe*, San Francisco: Berrett-Koehler Publishers, 1999: 77). Wheatley suggests that organisations that regard themselves as open systems, avoiding the rigidity that accompanies an over-reliance upon structures and adapting to their environments in fluid, flexible ways, are more likely to sustain themselves: "in the world of self-organizing structures, we learn that useful boundaries develop through openness to the environment. As the process of exchange continues between system and environment, the system, paradoxically, develops greater freedom from the demands of its environment" (*ibid*: 93).

[107] Attributed to Lovelock and cited in Joseph, Lawrence E., *Gaia: The Growth of an Idea*, New York: St. Martin's Press, 1990: 3, author's italics.

or better, *personal* – nature of all knowledge."[108] Whilst the Gaia hypothesis both stimulated and reinforced pantheistic notions of Earth-worship and other mystical, neopaganist paradigms – which orthodox Christians resist on the theological grounds that the distinction between Creator and creation is dissolved – and though it has its limitations as an ultimately purposeful and comprehensive worldview,[109] it offers a richly rewarding relational perspective. "Every human life is connected with every other, organically and ecologically. The same principles, in fact, run through all earthly existence. Human life is linked organically, interdependently, to everything else on earth."[110]

Indeed, as ably demonstrated by Lovelock in his writings, there has existed over time a remarkably coherent pattern of self-regulating behaviour governing the evolution of planet Earth, so that, in spite of major environmental disruptions that would appear *a priori* to generate collapse and disintegration, the planet has survived intact, its temperature maintained by its own internal self-regulating mechanism.[111] Lovelock's thesis accords with Del Re's cosmological metaphor of the Great Dance, which points to, first of all, "the existence of a general, common pattern to which all objects, systems, and organisms conform."[112] What matters to Del Re in his discussion is the notion of coherence: the mechanistic *Weltanschauung* is reductionist in its attempt to explain reality in terms of its constituent *parts*. What marks out coherence is its emphasis on *relationality* within the system and the behaviour of the system as a whole, rather than on the parts that constitute the system.

The Gaia hypothesis focuses on the place of Earth within the solar system; it does not specifically address either the submicroscopic world of quantum physics or the cosmic macroworld. The English scientist and theologian Celia Deane-Drummond critiques Gaia for being too pessimistic because it places

---

[108] Snyder, Howard A., *EarthCurrents: The Struggle for the World's Soul*, Nashville: Abingdon Press, 1995: 182; see the informative chapter in his book entitled "Life on a Living Planet: The Gaia Worldview" (*ibid*: 177-185).

[109] For a discussion of Gaia's limitations, see *ibid*: 184-185.

[110] *Ibid*: 183.

[111] See Lovelock, James, E., "Hands Up for the Gaia Hypothesis" in *Nature* 344 (1990): 100-102; also Lovelock, James E., *The Ages of Gaia: A Biography of Our Living Earth*, New York: Bantam Books, 1990; Lovelock, James E., *Gaia: A New Look at Life on Earth*, Oxford: Oxford University Press, 1995. Davies comments that "Gaia provides a nice illustration of how a highly complex feedback system can display stable modes of activity in the face of drastic external perturbations. We see once again how individual components and sub-processes are guided by the system as a whole to conform to a coherent pattern of behaviour" (Davies, *The Cosmic Blueprint*: 132) – a fine example of emergence. Del Re points out that Lovelock's reference to Gaia – the Greek name for the goddess earth – should not be construed as suggesting that the earth is a living organism, exhibiting a sort of homeostasis akin to that characteristic of living organisms, such as a whale or a mosquito: similarity, he observes, does not mean identity: for a summary of Del Re's argument, see Del Re, *The Cosmic Dance*: 21-22.

[112] Del Re, *The Cosmic Dance*: 11.

planet Earth above the future of humankind, offers no 'moral responsibility' to preserve the human race, and therefore displays an inherently 'malevolent face of nature towards humanity': "Gaia needs to be 'tamed' if she is not to become 'too big for her boots'."[113] However, notwithstanding these valid criticisms, Gaia – when combined with the insights of quantum non-locality and entanglement, the elegant symmetries of nature revealed in the geometry of fractal dimensionality, and the coherence inherent in notions of an 'implicate order' and a multidimensional 'holomovement' underscoring all reality – confronts the reductionist inclinations of modern science and contributes to a cumulatively compelling argument for the presence of some form of perichoretic activity threading through all reality.

In Chapter 3, we noted Barth's opinion that the doctrine of *perichoresis* may be interpreted as the final sum of the doctrine of *unitas in trinitate* and *trinitas in unitate*. The trinitarian God of Christian faith is dynamically and ecstatically relational as Father, Son and Holy Spirit ('the many'), yet also indivisibly whole ('the one'). The central hypothesis in this chapter is that this God, as the Creator of all that exists *ex nihilo*, has not only brought into being a universe that reflects his perichoretic nature but is also involved in his creation in ways that express that nature. The scientific evidence of interconnectedness implicit in a quantum mechanical view of the universe corresponds to the dynamic perichoretic interactions that characterise the life of the triune God. The Trinity's essential indivisibility finds expression in the notions of coherence, 'undivided wholeness' and ecological symbiosis discovered by scientists working in the disciplines of mathematics, computer science, physics and biology. Gunton's proposal that creation displays the features of a *'perichoresis of interrelated systems'*, corresponding to 'the one and the many' nature of the Trinity, is therefore well supported.

Evolutionary Emergence

Earlier we referred to God's 'loving entanglement' with the world in terms of the kenotic love of a God who freely allows his creation to become what he has purposed it to be. In Chapter 2, we suggested that, as the author of creativity, God makes room for unpredictable novelty in the emerging of the potential of the natural world alongside the predictability of 'laws of nature'. In this section, we examine briefly the concept of emergence as it relates to the activity and presence of God, in which the idea of God's self-limitation, or *kenosis*, is developed. The matter has been succinctly articulated by Gregersen: "How could one from an informed Christian perspective think consistently about

---

[113] See Deane-Drummond, Celia, "God and Gaia: Myth or Reality?" in *Theology* 95, 766 (1992), especially pp. 280-284; for further discussion by Deane-Drummond on Gaia, see *Gaia and Green Ethics: Implications of Ecological Theology*, Grove Ethical Studies No. 88, Bramcote: Grove, 1993; "*Gaia* as Science made Myth: Implications for Environmental Ethics" in *Studies in Christian Ethics*, Vol. 9 No. 2: 1-15.

God's relation to a universe that seems to be self-organizing, if not self-creative?"[114] This is important for the purposes of this study, since the idea of a God who allows his creation to unfold, or emerge, according to an inherent capacity for self-organisation points us towards a crucial relationship between *kenosis* and *perichoresis* in the doctrine of creation.

Polanyi sums up the essence of emergence in his statement that it is as meaningless to represent life in terms of physics and chemistry as it would be to interpret a grandfather clock or a Shakespeare sonnet in the same terms. But this does not imply that lower levels do not have a bearing on higher levels: *"they define the conditions of their success and account for their failures, but they cannot account for their success, for they cannot even define it."*[115] This is particularly apparent when we consider the process by which the universe came into being following the 'big bang'. How did the features of cosmic space take shape? What 'invisible hand' guided the formation of planets? The unusual, even mysterious, degree of order governing the planetary orbits suggests that either this is a coincidence, "or some as yet unknown physical mechanism has operated to organize the solar system in this way."[116] In this connection, we referred at the beginning of this book to the anthropic principle, which states that the whole cosmos, right from the very beginning, was 'fine-tuned' in such a way that life as we know it today would not have been possible if conditions had been ever so slightly different.

In his discussion of emergence, Johnson refers to the behaviour of ant colonies: remarkably, there is no command structure telling the ant what to do. In a quite extraordinary way ants participate in the life of the colony in a coordinated fashion not because they are carrying out orders from a leader, but because they respond at the immediate, local level to all that is going on around them. They do not have a 'big picture' available in order to determine their behaviour.[117] This is a classic example of what scientists call 'bottom-up' emergence. The human body makes an even more fascinating case study in emergence: how is it that 75 trillion cells can emerge into the complexity that is the human body? In a remarkable way, individual cells, with no bird's eye view of the final outcome, self-organise on the basis not only of the DNA encoded within them, but also as they relate to the other cells around them.

---

[114] See Gregersen, Niels Henrik, "The Creation of Creativity and the Flourishing of Creation" in *Currents in Theology and Mission* 28:3-4 (June/August 2001): 400-410.

[115] Polanyi, Michael, *Personal Knowledge*, Chicago: University of Chicago Press, 1958: 382, author's italics.

[116] Davies, *The Cosmic Blueprint*: 130.

[117] For a biblical insight on this, see Proverbs 6:9:
> Go to the ant, you sluggard; Consider its ways and be wise!
> It has no commander, No overseer or ruler,
> Yet it stores its provisions in summer
> And gathers its food at harvest.
> How long will you lie there, you sluggard!
> When will you get up from your sleep?

The classic interpretation of emergence is that it is essentially a 'bottom-up' phenomenon, on the basis of inherent laws, or autonomy, present within natural processes.[118] However, Arthur Peacocke reminds us that we need to acknowledge the possibility of the joint operation of 'causation' in both 'bottom-up' and 'top-down' directions, particularly in the case of complex living systems. For example, "conscious brain states could be 'top-down' causes at the 'lower' levels of neurones."[119] Gregersen has written extensively in recent years on the reconciliation of 'bottom-up' emergence with theistic (specifically Christian) causation. He asks: "Could it be that God has so created the material world that it has an innate ability to form life out of matter and thus give rise to new emergent phenomena such as perception, feeling and consciousness?"[120]

At this point we need to recognise an important distinction between emergence as a property of natural processes – as, for example, in the growth of crystals or in fluid dynamics – and emergence as a characteristic in *biological evolution*. In a recent book Samuel Powell refers to the "vast increase in complexity as we move from the physical universe to the living world and to the consequent need to broaden the scope of scientific explanation."[121] Following Karl Popper's notion of 'propensity' – which may be defined as an inherent tendency for a sequence of events to realise a particular possibility[122] – Peacocke suggests that there are propensities in evolution towards the possession of certain characteristics, "propensities that are inherently built into an evolutionary process based on natural selection of the best procreators."[123]

---

[118] For a persuasive presentation of this argument, see Clayton, Philip, "The Emergence of Spirit" in *CTNS Bulletin* 20.4 (Fall 2000): 3-20.

[119] Peacocke, Arthur R, *Theology for a Scientific Age: Being and Becoming – Natural, Divine and Human*, Minneapolis: Fortress Press, 1993: 158.

[120] Gregersen, "The Creation of Creativity and the Flourishing of Creation": 400; see also Gregersen, Niels Henrik, "From Anthropic Design to Self-Organized Complexity" in Gregersen, Niels Henrik (ed), *From Complexity to Life: On the Emergence of Life and Meaning*, New York: Oxford University Press, 2002: 204-234.

[121] Powell, Samuel M., *Participating in God: Creation and Trinity*, Minneapolis: Fortress Press, 2003: 109.

[122] Popper first presented his propensity theory in a paper read for him in Bristol, in his absence, by his pupil Paul K. Feyerabend (see Popper, Karl R., *Realism and the Aim of Science* Totowa NJ: Rowman and Littlefield, 1983: 282, fn.; see *ibid*: 348-361, where Popper argues his case for his propensity interpretation of probability. He defines a propensity in physics as a property "of the *whole situation* and sometimes even of the particular way in which the situation changes. And the same holds of the propensities in chemistry, in biochemistry, and in biology." (Popper, Karl, *A World of Propensities*, Bristol: Thoemmes, 1990: 17, author's italics).

[123] Peacocke, Arthur, "Biological Evolution – A Positive Theological Appraisal" in Russell, Robert John, Stoeger, William R. and Ayala, Francisco J. (eds), *Evolutionary and Molecular Biology: Scientific Perspectives on Divine Action*, Vatican City State: Vatican Observatory, 1998: 365.

Describing emergence, in general terms, as "the denomination of something new which could not be predicted from the elements constituting the preceding condition", Emmeche, Køppe and Stjernfelt argue that "what is needed is an ontological non-reductionist theory of levels of reality which includes a concept of emergence, and which can support an evolutionary account of the origin of levels."[124]

The idea of 'levels of reality' is implicit in the concept of graded ontological hierarchies. Barbour identifies various hierarchies of levels, such as the structural hierarchy ranging from quarks through to ecosystems, the functional hierarchies of reproduction (gene, genome, organism, population) and neural activity (molecule, synapse, neuron, neural network, brain, body), and the many social/cultural hierarchies that describe human behaviour.[125] Methodological reductionism is a scientific procedure in which particular levels within a particular hierarchy are studied scientifically in order to understand them better. Metaphysical, or ontological, reductionism, however, asserts the primacy of science over any form of metaphysical interpretation of reality; it is a form of fundamentalist scientism in its attempt to reduce every single phenomenon to physics or chemistry. This form of reductionism, advocated by such writers as Richard Dawkins and Stephen Jay Gould, contradicts the sort of evolutionary emergence that Peacocke and Gregersen are proposing. Peacocke's theology of God's immanence in the world is emergent in his understanding of the 'intelligible continuity' of the processes at work in the world "in which the potentialities of its constituents are unfolded in forms of an ever-increasing complexity and organization."[126]

What is unique about evolutionary emergence – or 'emergent evolution'[127],

---

[124] Emmeche, C., Køppe, S. and Stjernfelt, F., "Explaining Emergence: Towards an Ontology of Levels" in *Journal for General Philosophy of Science* 28: 83-119 (1997), available online at http://www.nbi.dk/~emmeche/coPubl/97e.EKS/emerg.html (accessed on 09.02.04); the authors argue that "new developments in physics, biology, psychology, and crossdisciplinary fields such as cognitive science, artificial life, and the study of non-linear dynamical systems have focused strongly on the high level 'collective behaviour' of complex systems which is often said to be truly emergent, and the term is increasingly used to characterize such systems."

[125] Barbour, *When Science Meets Religion*: 108.

[126] Peacocke, *Theology for a Scientific Age*: 300; the idea of an unfolding of that which is already within is reminiscent of David Bohm's theory of an 'implicate order'.

[127] "Under what I call emergent evolution stress is laid on this incoming of the new. Salient examples are afforded in the advent of life, in the advent of mind, and in the advent of reflective thought. But in the physical world emergence is no less exemplified in the advent of each new kind of atom, and of each new kind of molecule. It is beyond the wit of man to number the instances of emergence. But if nothing new emerge – if there be only regrouping of pre-existing events and nothing more – then there is no emergent evolution." Morgan, Conwy Lloyd, *Emergent Evolution*, London: Williams and Norgate, 1923: 1-2.

as some have called it – is the emanation of something distinctly *new*, strictly 'emergent' rather than merely 'resultant'.[128] From a theistic perspective, two issues immediately arise that need to be examined: the first has to do with purpose: in what sense is it possible to speak of a God whose purposes are being fulfilled through the processes of evolutionary emergence? Secondly, if God is involved in shaping the direction of evolutionary processes, how do we account for the "ubiquity of pain, suffering and death"[129] in creation?

The question of purpose may be rephrased: in what sense can God be thought of as bringing forth newness if, in Jacques Monod's famous words, the 'stupendous edifice of evolution' is in fact grounded in the chance occurrences of biological evolution?[130] In response, we suggested in Chapter 1 that a coherent 'theology of nature' may reasonably reflect the wisdom of a God who has set in motion a process with a general direction and goal, but the realisation of that goal is left not only to the operation of the laws of nature but also to free choices, random events and other unpredictable interactions: in other words, chance, accident and competition are all parts of the evolutionary process, though – crucially – they are not the products of sheer chance. As Barbour observes, a "patient God could have endowed matter with diverse potentialities and let it create more complex forms on its own."[131] In fact, as demonstrated by Prigogine and Eigen, the combination of chance and law actually permits the creative emergence of new forms of life over time.[132]

In Chapter 2 we noted Polkinghorne's suggestion that when God created *ex nihilo* he brought into being "a universe which is free to exist 'on its own', in the ontological space made available to it by the divine kenotic act of allowing the existence of something wholly other."[133] The creative God respects the unfolding of his universe with its own inbuilt laws, initial conditions and potentialities, making room – as an act of divine *kenosis* – for unpredictable novelty in the emerging of the potential of the natural world alongside the predictability of 'laws of nature'.[134] In his pursuit of a doctrine of creation that

---

[128] The distinction is between properties which can be predicted (resultant) and properties which cannot (emergent): see Emmeche, Køppe and Stjernfelt, "Explaining Emergence: Towards an Ontology of Levels".

[129] The phrase is from Peacocke, "Biological Evolution – A Positive Theological Appraisal": 369.

[130] Monod, Jacques, *Chance and Necessity*, London: Collins, 1972. On the concept of 'natural purpose', see Cole-Turner, Ronald, *The New Genesis: Theology and the Genetic Revolution*, Louisville: Westminster/John Knox Press, 1993: 54-60.

[131] Barbour, *When Science Meets Religion*: 113.

[132] See Peacocke, *Theology for a Scientific Age*: 118, referring to Prigogine, Ilya, *From Being to Becoming*, San Francisco: W.H. Freeman, 1980; and Eigen, Manfred and Winkler, Ruthild, *The Laws of the Game*, New York: Knopf, 1981.

[133] Polkinghorne, John, *Science and Christian Belief*, London: SPCK, 1994: 167.

[134] Haught points us to the very heart of the doctrine of *kenosis* in drawing an analogy with human relations, in which "we are most responsive to others whose love takes the shape of a non-interference that gives us the slack to be ourselves. We feel most

is faithful to the concept of emergence as a phenomenon to be traced *all the way through*[135], Clayton follows the theological leanings of Peacocke in proposing a process-trinitarian theology of emergence that acknowledges *freedom* as the most appropriate expression of a form of Hegelian dialectic between the infinity and finiteness of God. Arguing that God has purposes that cannot be attributed to nature itself, Clayton offers "a theory of *purposiveness without purpose* in the emergence and behaviour of organisms, a middle distance between the nonpurposiveness of chemical emergence and the clearly purposive behaviour of intentional (self-purposive) agents."[136]

What Clayton is resisting is the notion of what he calls 'evolution with invisible strings'; for him, *kenosis* means eschewing all forms of personal action or cosmic purpose in the unfolding of the life of the biosphere. Criticising the atomism of reductionists like Richard Dawkins – who focuses exclusively on the *material* of evolution – and drawing from the insights of classical Platonic and Aristotelian philosophy, Clayton proposes a 'top-down' flow of informational form and structure guiding the behaviour of individual organisms. Distinguishing between the emergence of life (biological causality) and the emergence of spirit (mental causality), he argues that theories of biological emergence need not necessarily assume a faith dimension. However, in a passionate defence of purpose in the universe, the Cambridge palaeontologist Simon Conway Morris argues that evolution has metaphysical implications and that natural selection operates under narrow constraints built into the structure of reality. He interprets convergence as the recurrent tendency of biological organisation to arrive at the same 'solution' to a particular need. Much of his book is devoted to a detailed discussion of the basic chemistry of DNA, RNA and proteins, but none of these building blocks of life can help us to understand the origin of life. Ultimately, argues Morris, there is a higher purpose that controls nature, and he is trenchant in his critique of the 'genetic fundamentalism' of evolutionary scientists like Dawkins and Gould, chastising

---

liberated, and most alive, in the presence of those who risk letting us be ourselves, whereas we feel cramped by those who force their presence upon us. We tender our deepest devotion to those who by restraining their powers allow us to unfold our lives at our own pace, and we resent those who cannot curb their coercive impulses and are constantly running our lives. Unfortunately we often think of God as wielding this crude kind of might rather than bestowing *a love that is mighty precisely in its restraint*" (Haught, *Science and Religion*: 161, my italics).

[135] For Clayton, the issue of "how the traditional God of theism can be reconciled with the thermodynamics of dissipative systems or with the phenomena of self-organization" is a reconciliation which is "all too easy" and thus represents " too low a standard": see Clayton, "The Emergence of Spirit": 6.

[136] *Ibid*: 9; so "actual purposes can be predicated only of purposive beings; a colony of bacteria functions in a purposive manner without possessing actual purposes. The colony behaves *as if* it really desires to nourish itself and grow, but it does not desire growth in the conscious way that you now desire a glass of orange juice" (*ibid*: 16).

them for their failure to treat theology seriously.[137]

If, as Morris insists, life is not as ruthlessly purposeless as some scientists suggest, is there a place for God in Clayton's metaphysics? An answer may be found in his understanding of the emergence of 'spirit', which he defines in terms of the emergent levels of *consciousness*, such as intentionality, self-awareness, rational reflection and artistic creativity. This leaves open the possibility that God can influence the thoughts of conscious human beings within a panentheistic framework[138], suggesting a category of divine action that is neither interventionist nor occasionalist, but one based on *already existing* divine energies. In this proposal, human thought may be interpreted as an expression of the constant character of an all-pervading God.

At a different level, however, Clayton alludes to what he calls 'focal divine actions', in which he acknowledges that God may also, in principle, reconnect with the human mind "via the sphere of human/divine interaction we call the realm of the spirit, including personal religious experience, culture, art, philosophy, and theology itself."[139] The idea of 'focal divine actions' would appear to be similar to Gregersen's notion of God's 'superabundance', which is predicated on the grace of God who acts in special, generous ways to bless his creation beyond that which is already taking place as the result of the habitual operation of existing divine energies.[140] Not only do we conceive of the universe as a highly complex self-organising system, displaying an inherent creativity in which order triumphs over disorder – a thesis that is "remarkably

---

[137] See Morris, Simon Conway, *Life's Solution: Inevitable Humans in a Lonely Universe*, Cambridge: Cambridge University Press, 2003.

[138] We noted in Chapter 1 that a panentheistic interpretation of God's interactions with his creation differs from pantheism in holding together God's transcendence with his immanence *without confusing the two*. In other words, God's otherness is not compromised since he is continually interacting with the whole world system in a top down causative influence, culminating in events observed in the regularities and laws operative within the universe and explained by the natural sciences. This enables us to hold scientific theories about the universe in creative tension with fundamental Christian beliefs about the transcendent sovereignty of God. For a stimulating collection of papers on panentheism, see Clayton, Philip D. and Peacocke, Arthur R. (eds), *In Whom We Live and Move and Have Our Being: Panentheistic Reflections on God's Presence in a Scientific World*, Grand Rapids: Eerdmans, 2004.

[139] *Ibid*: 17.

[140] Drawing on the biblical concepts of creation and blessing, Gregersen argues that God is 'the generous creator of creativity'. Exploring the theological nature of divine blessing as *inclusive* (it spreads, widening its scope), *reciprocal* (as God blesses, so human beings reciprocate, blessing God), both *transcendent* and *immanent* (bestowed *on* humans, yet also working *within* them), and a combination of *fundamental sustenance* and *superabundance*, he proposes a more general hypothesis: "*God is the generous creator of self-organizing systems*" (Gregersen, "The Creation of Creativity and the Flourishing of Creation": 409, author's italics).

congruent with the basic outline of religious faith"[141] – but we are directed towards a theology that sees God at work in unexpected ways in his creation, and especially in his relationship with human beings.

Gunton, adopting an eschatological perspective, suggests that the doctrine of the Spirit enables us to more fully appreciate the contours of God's providential activity as both general and particular, for the Spirit is both 'the upholder of the everyday' in the human and non-human realms and also the one who, in transforming grace, is at work in specifically redemptive ways to restore the world back to all that it was created to be: "The Spirit thus both shapes the interacting fields of force that are the universe and is the one who realises those particular surges of divine activity which call created beings back from destruction and on to their course to perfection."[142] Gunton draws his theology of general providence and particular/special providence together in suggesting that

> God's action, as energy giving rise to energy variously organised, may be conceived to shape the day to day life of the world, even sometimes miraculously – in anticipation of its eschatological destiny – without violating that which is 'natural', because what is natural is that which enables the creation to achieve its promised destiny.[143]

What is significant here is the idea that what appears to be 'natural' and autonomous in the unfolding process of what we might term *purposive*

---

[141] Haught, *Science and Religion*: 155; the theme of faith's promise inherent in the sciences of chaos and complexity is spelled out further by Haught: "many processes in the natural world (a) begin with an amazing modesty and simplicity, (b) unfold into a turbulence or chaos, but then (c) eventually burst out into the richest and most beautiful of patterns" (*ibid*: 155).

[142] Gunton, Colin E., *The Triune Creator: A Historical and Systematic Study*, Grand Rapids: Eerdmans, 1998: 178; Gunton's use of the phrase 'fields of force' should not be confused with Pannenberg's 'field theory of the Spirit', a proposal which Peters admires for its 'scholarly courage', but which has been criticised, not only by Peters, as a speculative theory: "Historians of science are quick to point out the dangers of trying to float a theological assertion aboard a scientific ship, because the intellectual weather can change suddenly … How long will field theory stay afloat? If someday it should sink, will Pannenberg's theology of spirit sink with it?" (Peters, Ted, "Introduction" in Pannenberg, Wolfhart [Ted Peters (ed)], *Towards a Theology of Nature: Essays on Science and Faith*, Louisville: Westminster/John Knox, 1993: 14). Gunton employs the 'fields of force' concept to refer to the structure of the universe expressed in scientific language, rather than literally ascribing it to the Holy Spirit in a descriptive sense, as Pannenberg does.

[143] Gunton, *The Triune Creator*: 176; we noted in Chapter 3 Dalferth's insight that eschatology should be defined as that which expresses the *goal* of all creation, human and physical, rather than specific, identifiable *eschata* (see Dalferth, Ingolf U., "The Eschatological Roots of the Doctrine of the Trinity" in Schwobel, (ed), *Trinitarian Theology Today*: 147-170).

evolution should perhaps be interpreted as the inevitable consequence of a process set in motion and sustained by a trinitarian God who freely releases his creation to be itself. Gregersen points out that, from a theological perspective, "such an *auto*nomous process is at the same time a *theo*nomous process if God is the stimulating power of inspiration who elicits the most fruitful possibility spaces in which creatures try out their pathways, and who also restricts other possible possibility spaces."[144] So *all* processes, from general providence – in terms of the historic unfolding of creation from the moment of the 'big bang' onwards – to specific providential acts (which some interpret in interventionist language) may be elucidated in theonomous terms.

For Russell, however, the important question is whether or not we can construct a view of special providence in which we understand God's objective acts in nature and in history *in a non-interventionist manner consistent with science*.[145] Proceeding from the premise that quantum statistics[146] underlie and produce the fundamental properties of the *real* (classical) world, and not a different quantum world – for, ontologically, there is only one world seen through two different epistemologies, classical and quantum – Russell argues that "God creates the (classical) world not by reordering its structures ('order out of chaos') but by creating the quantum processes that produce the classical world."[147] So God's order in the classical world may be interpreted as 'the order of quantum chaos'[148] – just as the texture of wood is ultimately the statistical

---

[144] See Gregersen, Niels Henrik, "The Idea of Creation and the Theory of Autopoietic Processes" in *Zygon: Journal of Religion and Science* Vol. 33, No. 3 (September, 1998): 333-367, author's italics; for Gregersen, autopoietic systems are 'self-productive' systems that differ from other self-organising systems in their production of *new* internal components, thus continually creating *new* system-environment interactions.

[145] See, especially, Russell, Robert John, "Does the 'God Who Acts' Really Act in Nature?: New Approaches to Divine Action in Light of Science" in *Theology Today* (April 1997): 43-65.

[146] Specifically, the behaviour of particles such as protons, electrons and neutrons, which are described by Fermi-Dirac statistics, and particles such as photons and gravitons, which are described by Bose-Einstein statistics.

[147] *Ibid*: 59.

[148] See Russell, Robert John, "Quantum Physics in Philosophical and Theological Perspective" in Russell, Robert John, Stoeger, William R. and Coyne, George V. (eds), *Physics, Philosophy and Theology: A Common Quest for Understanding*, Vatican City State: Vatican Observatory, 1988: 343-368. For further discussions of divine action within the framework of contemporary physics, see Barbour, *When Science Meets Religion*: 150-180; Wiseman, James A., *Theology and Modern Science: Quest for Coherence*, New York & London: Continuum, 2002: 112-132; Polkinghorne, John, "The Laws of Nature and the Laws of Physics" in Russell, Robert John, Murphy, Nancey and Isham C.J. (eds), *Quantum Cosmology and the Laws of Nature: Scientific Perspectives on Divine Action*, Vatican City State: Vatican Observatory; Notre Dame: University of Notre Dame Press 1993: 437-448; Polkinghorne, John, "The Metaphysics of Divine Action" in Russell, Robert John, Murphy, Nancey and Peacocke, Arthur R. (eds), *Chaos and Complexity: Scientific Perspectives on Divine Action*, Vatican City State: Vatican

dance of electrons and protons, so quantum chance gives classical order its form and structure. By extension, evolutionary biology may be interpreted as God acting within the quantum mechanical processes underlying specific genetic mutations. Russell's proposal, shared by a number of contemporary Christian quantum physicists, challenges an exclusive dependence on 'top-down' thinking – implicit, for example, in Bohm's 'hidden variables' model – in its presentation of a strictly 'bottom-up' account of divine action.

Furthermore, an over-dependence on a form of 'whole-part influence' or 'top-down' model of causality presents some difficulties with respect to the impact of divine action on the lives of human beings, as Clayton has shown. How meaningful is it, he asks, to speak of God influencing or guiding individuals in a process that advances "from the universe-as-a-whole, down through superstrings and galaxies to our individual planet, and then through the history of biological evolution and countless billions of genetic mutations to one person existing today?"[149] Barbour suggests that 'bottom-up' emergence may be combined with a 'top-down' influence or causality, in which God is conceived as a 'determiner of indeterminacies', providentially controlling what seems to an outside observer as chance events; so "God does not have to intervene as a physical force pushing electrons around but instead actualizes one of the many potentialities already present – determining, for example, the instant at which a particular radioactive atom decays."[150] Whatever preference we have with regard to divine action, human understanding is fraught with uncertainty – after all, "there are ineluctable limitations on our ability to comprehend what it would mean to be a divine agent."[151] Polkinghorne is equally candid:

> I find it difficult to understand ... how God or synchronicity can be so effective in shaping the flux of physical events ... If we do not understand how we ourselves interact with the physical world (though we feel certain that we do and none of us treats himself as if he were a robot) then it is scarcely surprising that we do not understand how God might do so either.[152]

This insight leads Russell to point towards trinitarian theology, specifically the

---

Observatory; Berkeley: Center for Theology and the Natural Sciences, 1995: 147-156; Stoeger, William R., "Describing God's Action in the World in Light of Scientific Knowledge of Reality" in Russell, Murphy and Peacocke (eds), *Chaos and Complexity*: 239-262.

[149] Clayton, Philip D., *God and Contemporary Science*, Grand Rapids: Eerdmans, 1997: 194.

[150] Barbour, Ian G., *Religion and Science: Historical and Contemporary Issues*, London: SCM Press, 1988: 312.

[151] Wiseman, *Theology and Modern Science*, 131.

[152] Polkinghorne, John, *One World: The Interaction of Science and Theology*, London: SPCK, 1986: 73.

triune action and presence of God *in* the world, rather than God's interaction *with* the world, as the most appropriate framework within which to understand God's energies in directing his creation towards its ultimate goal.

The Ubiquity of Pain, Suffering and Death

The second issue raised earlier in connection with evolutionary emergence – the ubiquity of pain, suffering and death – is problematic for Christians whose faith rests in a God who is love. However, if we sustain the picture of a God who is "involved creatively in an open-ended process that involves both randomness and lawfulness"[153], then the idea of love assumes a more profound meaning. Love does not coerce, but encourages and nourishes; hence, "if the world is to be anything distinct from God it has to have some scope for meandering about and for experimenting with different ways of existing."[154] Furthermore, a finite universe requires the dissolution of the old to make way for the new: God in his love does not interfere even though pain and suffering are the inevitable result. This suggests that the evolutionary process is characterised by gains and losses as it travels towards its eschatological promise of a new creation. In this context, Russell helpfully distinguishes between pain and suffering, which derive directly from human sin and contaminate human life and the environment, and death and disease, which are the natural prerequisites for the evolution of life.[155]

For the Christian, the problem of natural evil is more problematic than that of moral evil. The traditional interpretation of moral evil is predicated on the 'free-will defence' argument: human beings have been created to respond freely to a kenotic God rather than to function as automatons, or 'puppets on a string'.[156] Polkinghorne suggests a variation of the 'free-will defence' with

---

[153] Edwards, Denis, *The God of Evolution: A Trinitarian Theology*, New York/Mahwah N.J.: Paulist Press: 50.

[154] Haught, *Science and Religion*: 61-62.

[155] Russell, Robert John, "Special Providence and Genetic Mutation: A New Defense of Theistic Evolution" in Russell, Stoeger and Ayala, (eds), *Evolutionary and Molecular Biology: Scientific Perspectives on Divine Action*: 222.

[156] The free-will defence position has been well articulated by the Christian philosopher Alvin Plantinga: "A world containing creatures who are significantly free (and freely perform more good than evil actions) is more valuable, all else being equal, than a world containing no free creatures at all. Now God can create free creatures, but He cannot *cause* or *determine* them to do only what is right. For if he does so, then they are not significantly free at all; they do not do what is right *freely*. To create creatures of *moral good*, therefore, He must create creatures capable of moral evil; and he cannot give these creatures the freedom to perform evil and at the same time prevent them from doing so. As it turned out, sadly enough, some of the free creatures God created went wrong in the exercise of their freedom; this is the source of moral evil. The fact that free creatures sometimes go wrong, however, counts neither against God's omnipotence nor against

regard to the presence of evil and suffering in the whole created order, in which God treats the processes of the world with the same respect as he does the actions of humanity. Through divine kenotic love, he argues, the principle of cosmic integrity is upheld. Ultimately, the freedom and flexibility given to the world's processes "affords the means by which the universe explores its own potentiality, humankind exercises its will, and God interacts with his creation."[157] But God does not watch all this, as the popular – but theologically misguided! – song goes, 'from a distance': he is intimately involved in the playing out of what von Balthasar describes as the great *theo-drama*, in which the divine Persons suffer in perichoretic vulnerability *with* their creation, epitomised supremely in the incarnation and the suffering of the Cross.

With regard to the natural world, Fiddes argues that our prayers are not limited to human personal life, but can have a real effect on the forming of patterns in nature: the triune God delights to draw us into his perichoretic energies at work in the physical world, so that we too can contribute to his 'pattern-making'. Why, then, are there so many catastrophic events, such as earthquakes, floods and droughts, which afflict planet Earth? Does not our participative intercession in God's interweaving and loving *perichoresis* make a difference? Why do we not experience more of the 'amplifying of God's Spirit' in creation through our prayers? One response is to maintain that there are 'hidden factors' at work, both in human life and in all creation "which for the moment the combined influences of divine and human love, united in prayer, cannot overcome."[158] These factors – social pressures, genetic defects, inheritance of the consequences of others' sins, and interactions between people 'below the surface' of what can be seen – combine to resist God's persuasive love. There may be blockages, deeply embedded in the world of nature, which somehow thwart God's purposes for the time being. [159]

Clearly, this does not go very far in responding to the problem of theodicy, even though we may agree philosophically with Leibniz that all evil, including natural evil, is consistent with the best possible world. There can be no

---

His goodness; for He could have forestalled the occurrence of moral evil only by removing the possibility of moral good." (Plantinga, Alvin C., *God, Freedom and Evil*, London: George Allen & Unwin, 1975: 30, author's italics).

[157] Polkinghorne, John, *Science and Providence: God's Interaction with the World*, London: SPCK, 1986: 67.

[158] Fiddes, *Participating in God: A Pastoral Doctrine of the Trinity*: 147.

[159] *Ibid*: 144-148; for more complete discussions of the role of prayer in relationship to divine action in the world, see Ward, Keith, *Divine Action*: London: Collins, 1990: 154-169; Wiles, Maurice, *God's Action in the World*, London: SCM Press, 1986 (representing the Bampton Lectures for 1986): 95-108; Polkinghorne, *Science and Providence*: 69-76; Fiddes, *Participating in God: A Pastoral Doctrine of the Trinity*: 115-151; and two thorough studies of the doctrine of divine providence and the place of prayer: Tiessen, Terrance, *Providence and Prayer: How Does God Work in the World?*, Downers Grove: IVP, 2000; Sanders, John, *The God Who Risks: A Theology of Providence*, Downers Grove: IVP, 1998.

thoroughly rational defence of God in a world in which there is so much human pain and physical devastation.[160] Indeed, the philosophical question persists: why did God create a world that requires life to evolve through death? Why create a world in which pain and suffering and disease so readily take root? Ultimately, those who argue that the moral development of human beings requires a world that is characterised by the presence of natural evil (the so-called 'vale of soul-making' argument) – valid though that might be in some individual experiences – cannot easily sustain that thesis as a general hypothesis unless they appeal to eschatology. So we might propose a theodicy that is predicated on an approach that looks *forward* to the outworking of God's final purposes, rather than *backward* to the origin and mystery of evil. Following Pannenberg, Russell suggests that theodicy and the problem of evil can only be addressed – though never 'resolved' – within the framework of a theology of redemption and new creation: "The long sweep of evolution may not only suggest an unfinished and continuing divine creation but even more radically a creation whose theological status as 'good' may be fully realized only in the eschatological future."[161]

Whilst theology and philosophy offer partial answers to the theodicy problem, perhaps the most helpful response to the problem of natural evil in the physical creation is one that takes into account the findings of modern physics, which, as we have seen in this chapter, present us with a picture of the universe that is characterised by the most remarkable mathematical elegance and relational interconnectedness. In such a universe, the quantum features of randomness, risk and unpredictability are necessary attributes of the emergent self-organising processes that are inherent in the very fabric of creation. In the light of all that we have discussed in this chapter, we may reasonably concur with Ward that contemporary physics at the very least allows us to conceive of a physical universe that 'lives by opposition':

> It is of the nature of the energy of which [the material universe] is constituted to destroy as well as to create, to renew itself precisely by destruction, and so generate the new by its own continual perishing ... Its vast energies continually interact and annihilate one another, yet generate new properties in the process. In such a world-system of many delicately balanced energies, held in an elegant mathematical web of rational principle, capable of generating emergent properties, including all the mental properties involved in the existence of a community of free rational wills, the creative originating Will can act to form and realize the structures of the physical order and bring its

---

[160] The great Lisbon earthquake of 1755, which killed tens of thousands of people, many of whom were worshipping in church at the time, radically challenged Leibniz' hypothesis (which was first published in 1710).
[161] Russell, "Special Providence and Genetic Mutation: A New Defense of Theistic Evolution": 223.

diversity into final unity with itself.[162]

So the universe in which we live and which science has opened up to us in such extraordinary detail – both macroscopically and microscopically – is a provisional universe in the sense that it is still reaching towards its goal.[163] Furthermore, from a critical realist perspective, our understanding of physical processes is also incomplete and provisional. In both senses of provisionality, therefore, we do well to remain open with regard to the question of theodicy in the natural realm. The presence of natural evil coheres with a picture of the universe as a 'world-system of delicately balanced energies' that destroy in order to create. Holmes Rolston III utilises the concept of 'travail' as a key to understanding natural evils, relating it to the root idea of birthing, of a woman in labour as she delivers her child, in which regeneration is coupled with suffering. So, "struggle is the principle of creation. Struggle is always going on, and it is this struggle in which life is regenerated. Nature is always giving birth, regenerating, always in travail."[164] But to focus on travail and suffering is to see "only the shadows, and there has to be light to cast shadows."[165] We also perceive the universe as an integrated web of rational order and creativity, a creation marked by the most surprising interconnectedness between its particular elements, in which God acts teleologically by his Spirit shaping and directing all that he has made.

God's Perichoretic Presence in Creation

Throughout this book, *perichoresis* has been presented as a helpful construct in understanding the *ad extra* activity of the Trinity in the world. How then might

---

[162] Ward, *Divine Action*: 65.

[163] How we correlate the final end of the Earth as a planet with the ultimate end of the universe is, of course, a theologically complex issue. Following Pannenberg, Worthing acknowledges the lack of congruence between biblical eschatology and scientific cosmology. Accordingly, the "oft-made assumption that the apocalyptic *parousia* of Christ and consummation of creation is to be equated with a much more radical end of the entire universe inn the remote future as predicted by physicists would seem unwarranted. It is entirely possible to understand biblical apocalyptic literature as speaking of a renewal or transformation of the world rather than its absolute destruction and subsequent re-creation." (Worthing, *God, Creation, and Contemporary Physics*: 178). This perspective identifies the problem of eternity as an underlying concern in the reconciliation of biblical and scientific eschatologies.

[164] Rolston, Holmes, III, "Does Nature Need to be Redeemed?" in *Zygon: Journal of Religion and Science*. Vol. 29, No. 2 (June, 1994): 213.

[165] *Ibid*: 213; on this, Rolston notes that nature is "orderly, prolific, efficient, selecting for adapted fit, exuberant, complex, diverse, regenerating life generation after generation" (*ibid*: 213).

we summarise divine action with reference to the twin doctrines of *kenosis* and *perichoresis* as presented in the preceding section? A number of conclusions are outlined below, which may be labelled *kenotic freedom*; *pneumatological presence*; *divine entanglement*; *eschatological consummation* and *intercessory participation*. Though we can usefully comment on each dimension of divine action in the world as a discrete feature in its own right, it is evident that there is a good deal of overlap between each of these five dimensions.

Firstly, when we speak of *kenotic freedom*, we mean that the only way that God's creation can realise its full potential is for its Creator to 'step back', not in a deistic sense of remote disinterest, but in kenotic love for that which he has brought into being *ex nihilo*, freeing his creation to emerge into its own internal coherence through the sort of perichoretic quantum interactions that we have described in this chapter. The character of God is revealed here, for "in the act of seeking intimacy with the universe, God forever preserves the difference and otherness of that beloved world."[166] This insight is consistent with the assertion made in Chapter 4 that God welcomes difference precisely because he is *in se* the God who is constituted perichoretically by difference. God's creation is not absorbed or dissolved into his being in some divine pantheistic *mélange*: it is an open universe in which God chooses to be 'entangled', not in a coercive, controlling way, but through the agency of the Spirit, who "graciously accompanies and celebrates every emerging form of life."[167]

Secondly, the notion of *pneumatological presence* underscores the role of the Spirit in divine action. Pinnock identifies the Spirit as "the perfecting source of the dynamism evident in the cosmos."[168] More specifically, the perichoretic themes of difference and diversity are clearly discernible in Stoeger's pneumatology, in which the "Spirit of God is sent forth to enable the Word to be spoken and realised in richly diverse ways – each with its own autonomy and integrity, and dynamism, but also with its own network of relations with other created beings and with God."[169] Moltmann has recently suggested that "God

---

[166] Haught, John F., *God After Darwin: A Theology of Evolution*, Boulder, Colo.: Westview Press, 2000: 114. For a thorough treatment of the relationship between the triune God and creation from the perspective of the world's participation in God, highlighting the trinitarian themes of identity and difference and drawing from both the natural and social sciences, see Powell, *Participating in God: Creation and Trinity*.

[167] Edwards, Denis, "Saving Grace and the Action of the Spirit outside the Church" in Reid, Duncan and Worthing, Mark (eds), *Sin and Salvation*, Hindmarsh SA: Adelaide Theological Forum, 2003: 221. For a fuller treatment of this theme, see Edwards, Denis, *Breath of Life: A Theology of the Creator Spirit*, Maryknoll: Orbis Books, 2004, especially pp. 112-116.

[168] Pinnock, Clark H., *Flame of Love: A Theology of the Holy Spirit*, Downers Grove: IVP, 1996: 68.

[169] Stoeger, William R., SJ, "Cosmology and a Theology of Creation" in Regan, Hilary D. and Worthing, Mark William (eds), *Interdisciplinary Perspectives on Cosmology and Biological Evolution*, Hindmarsh SA: Adelaide Theological Forum, 2002: 144. The idea of the Spirit as the eschatological presence and power of God at work in creation is, as

acts upon the world not so much through interventions or interactions, but rather through God's presence in all things and God's *perichoresis* with all things."[170] This echoes Russell's focus on trinitarian theology with its emphasis on the triune presence and activity of God in creation, rather than just his interaction with the world. Consistent with his earlier writings, Moltmann interprets this perichoretic 'mutual indwelling of God in the world *and* the world in God' pneumatologically, in which the "self-organization of matter and the self-transcendence of all that lives are the divine Spirit's signs of life in the world."[171]

Thirdly, the concept of *divine entanglement* is predicated on the premise that if quantum and classical worlds are ontologically identical – we just do not *see* them that way – then it follows that events in the universe may be interpreted as highly interconnected and complex networks of non-local correlations, encapsulated in the quantum concept of entanglement. The complexities of quantum mechanics have opened up to us one possible way in which to understand how the Spirit may be at work in creation, acting "whenever nature reaches ecstatically beyond itself in the unfolding of the universe and in the dynamic story of life."[172] Denis Edwards responds to the wonder such processes evoke in us by appealing to Rahner's conviction that God is 'unfathomable mystery', drawing us more deeply into an awareness of our creaturehood and God's mystery.[173] In the process, we come to realise afresh that we are somehow connected with the self-organising complexities associated with the creative emergence of life and consciousness.

Noting that *kenosis* marks the beginning of creation, the English theologian Keith Ward directs us to the promise of *theosis* as its consummation, which is the final purpose of God for creation. This leads us to a fourth dimension in our understanding of divine action, namely *eschatological consummation*. All creation, both human and non-human, will find fulfilment in perichoretic harmony within the trinitarian life of God (Ephesians 1:10), rather than terminating in an entropic emptiness.[174] Until then, through the actions of

---

we noted in Chapter 3, central to much contemporary trinitarian theology, especially that of Jenson, Moltmann, Torrance, Pannenberg and Gunton. In the final chapter, in drawing together some of the theses explored in this study, the possibility of interpreting the Holy Spirit as the *élan vital* permeating the cosmos will be discussed.

[170] Moltmann, Jürgen, "Reflections on Chaos and God's Interaction with the World from a Trinitarian Perspective" in Russell, Murphy and Peacocke (eds), *Chaos and Complexity*: 205-210.

[171] *Ibid*: 208.

[172] Edwards, Denis, "Ecology and the Holy Spirit" in Preece, Gordon and Pickard, Stephen (eds), *Starting with the Spirit*, Hindmarsh SA: Adelaide Theological Forum: 2001: 245.

[173] *Ibid*: 257-259.

[174] See Ward, Keith, "Cosmos and Kenosis" in Polkinghorne, John (ed), *The Work of Love: Creation as Kenosis*, Grand Rapids: Eerdmans, 2001: 152-166.

general and particular providence, God "enters with empathy into the experience of the world, and feels with pain the brokenness of its patterns and the alienation at their heart."[175] In ever-deepening *kenosis*, God's loving 'entanglement' with the world, mediated through the physical processes described by quantum mechanics at the subatomic level, invites all to participate in the divine dance of life.[176] This is the language of trinitarian creation, in which we understand creation not just as a single act at the moment of the 'big bang' (*creatio originalis*) but also as *creatio continua* and *creatio nova*. As Moltmann has pointed out, a fixation with *creatio originalis* at the expense of the associated doctrines of continuous creation and of the new creation still to be consummated only succeeds in "tying the picture of God's creation inexorably to the notions about the static cosmos which were current coin in the Christian middle ages."[177]

Fifthly, the principle of *intercessory participation* in divine action reminds us that if creation is a continuing process, open to new possibilities, and prayer is the means by which human beings are drawn into what Fiddes has called a 'zone of interconnection' (discussed in Chapter 4), then prayer should be understood as "part of the way in which God decrees that his creative and redemptive action in the world should be given a particular shape and form."[178] Whilst it is not possible in this book to examine in detail alternative interpretations of the relationship between prayer and divine action, we have already suggested earlier that prayer is the context within which we meet others in the *perichoresis* of Father, Son and Holy Spirit. There is freedom in God to work out his purposes in the way he chooses, yet also freedom for us to contribute in a way that fulfils us in special ways as we are drawn into his divine life. This is the language of participation. Human beings have been given the amazing privilege of working together with God, our prayers "augmenting and amplifying the urgings of God's Spirit."[179] So intercession "becomes the enfolding of someone in the interweaving currents of the love of God, and encouraging them to find the movements of health and healing that are already there."[180] Here Fiddes affirms God's sovereignty in taking the initiative, but not his unilateral activity. This approach invites us to see that though the end may always be purposed in God, the *route* to that end depends very much upon the

---

[175] Fiddes, Paul S., "Creation Out of Love" in Polkinghorne (ed), *The Work of Love*: 187.

[176] Fiddes' own preference for divine action is in terms of the *attractiveness* of love and the *movement* of persuasion (*Ibid*: 184-191); his view is that "the patterns of action and behaviour in human society and in the systems of the natural world are influenced by the patterns of God's own being" (*ibid*: 186).

[177] Moltmann, Jürgen, *God in Creation: A New Theology of Creation and the Spirit of God*, San Francisco: Harper & Row, 1985: 193; see also Astley, Jeff, Brown, David and Loades, Ann, (eds), *Creation: A Reader*, London and New York: T. & T. Clark, a Continuum imprint, 2003: 25-26.

[178] Ward, *Divine Action*: 169.

[179] Fiddes, *Participating in God: A Pastoral Doctrine of the Trinity*: 136.

[180] *Ibid*: 137.

choices we make – so there is something very open-ended about the way God's purposes are actually worked out in the world.

We can offer a theological summary of these five dimensions of kenotic freedom, pneumatological presence, divine entanglement, eschatological consummation and intercessory participation by appealing to Moltmann's doctrine of creation, which is thoroughly trinitarian in its grounding in an understanding of God as self-communicating love, self-limiting love and inner-trinitarian perichoretic love.[181] God cannot deny his own love, and he remains true to himself in self-communicating love in bringing into being a creation that is other than himself: for Moltmann, necessity and freedom axiomatically coincide in God. Divine self-limitation is expressed in terms of God making room *in himself* for creation: it is "only God's withdrawal into himself which gives that *nihil* the space in which God then becomes creatively active."[182] God, in trinitarian love, "opens up the space and the time and the freedom for that 'outwards' into which the Father utters himself creatively through the Son."[183] In other words, the "trinitarian relationship between the Father, the Son and the Holy Spirit is so wide that the whole creation can find space, time and freedom in it."[184] The dynamic perichoretic freedom of the triune God *in se* therefore finds ecstatic, kenotic expression "in the space God yielded up for it through his creative resolve."[185]

Moltmann proposes a 'trinitarian order' for his doctrine of creation from God in God: "*The Father* creates the world out of his eternal love through *the Son*, for the purpose of finding a response to his love in time, in the power of *the Holy Spirit*, which binds together what is in itself different."[186] This is no mere interpretation of the classical trinitarian doctrine of appropriation: creation is, in Moltmann's view, that which flows out of the depths of inner-trinitarian love. God creates because he is love, and he desires that all creation find fellowship in the free kingdom of his Son. It is *because of his love for his Son* that God creates, expressed by Moltmann in the language of emanation, or a 'pouring out', of the energies of the Holy Spirit. Because the triune God continually breathes the Spirit into his creation, everything that is "exists and lives in the

---

[181] For a succinct summary, see Moltmann, Jürgen, *The Trinity and the Kingdom of God: The Doctrine of God*, London: SCM Press, 1981: 105-114; for a more complete exposition of his doctrine of creation, see Moltmann, *God in Creation: A New Theology of Creation and the Spirit of God*, first presented as the 1984-1985 Gifford Lectures at Edinburgh, and written in response to the contemporary environmental crisis: in *God in Creation*, Moltmann also shapes his theology of creation in the light of the natural sciences.

[182] Moltmann, *God in Creation: A New Theology of Creation and the Spirit of God*: 109.

[183] *Ibid*: 109; so "[t]ime is an interval in eternity, finitude is a space in infinity, and freedom is a concession of the eternal love" (*ibid*: 111).

[184] *Ibid*: 109.

[185] Moltmann, *God in Creation: A New Theology of Creation and the Spirit of God*: 156.

[186] Moltmann, *The Trinity and the Kingdom of God*: 113-114, author's italics.

unceasing inflow of the energies and potentialities of the cosmic Spirit."[187] Citing Buber's remark that "in the beginning was relations", Moltmann amplifies as follows: "The patterns and the symmetries, the movements and the rhythms, the fields and the material conglomerations of cosmic energy all come into being out of the community, and in the community, of the divine Spirit."[188]

In her assessment and critique of Lovelock's Gaia hypothesis, Deane-Drummond advocates a trinitarian approach to the relationship between God and creation because it "prevents Gaia from assuming too great an importance over and beyond a scientific hypothesis" and reminds us of the unity of all creation implicit in the immanence of the Spirit in the universe.[189] The value of Gaia lies in its encouragement for us to conceive of the Earth in a globally ecological way, but we must be careful that we neither attribute divinity to the planet, as some Gaia-advocates do, nor ascribe to it the status of a self-sustaining and self-conscious organism. Trinitarian theology insists that "God created the entire natural order as a complex interrelated ecosystem that cannot exist in isolation from His sustaining influence."[190] In fact, as Moltmann asserts, the relational scope of the universe finds its source in trinitarian *perichoresis*, which is "at once the most intense excitement and the absolute rest of the love which is the wellspring of everything that lives, the keynote of all resonances, and the source of the rhythmically dancing and vibrating worlds."[191] The reciprocal indwelling and mutual interpenetration of *perichoresis* is the precise starting point of his relationally grounded thesis of God *in* the world and the world *in* God, an ecological doctrine of creation that eschews both monotheism and pantheism in its emphasis on *panentheism*.[192]

---

[187] Moltmann, *God in Creation: A New Theology of Creation and the Spirit of God*: 9.

[188] *Ibid*: 11; theology, therefore, "seeks to understand the evolving fruitfulness of the universe in terms of the patient and subtle operation of the Spirit *on the inside* of physical process" (The Doctrine Commission of the General Synod of the Church of England, *We Believe in the Holy Spirit*, London: Church House Publishing, 1991: 143, my italics).

[189] Deane-Drummond, "God and Gaia: Myth or Reality?": 283.

[190] Young, Richard A., *Healing the Earth: A Theocentric Perspective on Environmental Problems and their Solutions*, Nashville: Broadman & Holman, 1994: 62.

[191] Moltmann, *God in Creation: A New Theology of Creation and the Spirit of God*: 16.

[192] See fn. 123 in Chapter 1 for an extended comment on panentheism, especially the point that whilst panentheism maintains that God and the world are *not* identical (unlike pantheism, in which deity is *wholly* immanent), the term is, in fact, difficult to define with exactness, because the distinction between God as a *transcendent* Being and the reality included in God is notoriously imprecise. Just as there are different varieties of pantheism, so there appear to be different understandings of panentheism. We might also note here Deane-Drummond's helpful insight that the "spurious links between Gaia and mysticism are unhelpful both from the perspective of scientists, who then tend to reject Gaia altogether, and from the perspective of theologians, who revert to a form of pantheism under the guise of innovative science" (Deane-Drummond, "God and Gaia: Myth or Reality?": 284).

A pantheistic interpretation of God and the world fails to distinguish between God and his creation, dilutes difference as a feature of the universe, and – in its more extreme monist form – eschews the diversity that is self-evidently present in creation. Self-differentiation and individuation are characteristic features of a universe that has been brought into being by the God who is *in se* differentiated as Father, Son and Holy Spirit, the one God in eternal *perichoresis*. But even panentheism is insufficient as a final description of God's engagement with and in his creation: what is needed is a trinitarian theology of creation that not only holds transcendence and immanence together, distinguishing between Creator and creation, but also understands the universe as an emergent, self-organising and interconnected network of dynamic processes in which the Spirit is active as the preserver of both gloriously inventive difference and transcendent symbiotic harmony.

So, with Moltmann, we might interpret the Spirit in cosmic terms as the kenotic Spirit of *creativity*, the Spirit of *holism*, the Spirit of *individuation* and the Spirit of *openness*.[193] This pneumatological and eschatological perspective on the universe as perichoretic reality is foundational in the 'community of creation':

> It is not the elementary particles that are basic, as the mechanistic world view maintains, but the overriding harmony of the relations and of the self-transcending movements, in which the longing of the Spirit for a still unattained consummation finds expression.[194]

To discover that we, as human beings, belong in the 'creation-community' and to experience – at a deeply personal level – our own interconnectedness with creation is to be drawn into the very centre of the perichoretic life of God, where we find healing and wholeness for ourselves, and a renewed awareness of what the theologian David Tracy calls 'God's shattering otherness'.[195] To

---

[193] See Moltmann, *God in Creation: A New Theology of Creation and the Spirit of God*: 100.

[194] *Ibid*: 103.

[195] Tracy, David, "The Hidden God: The Divine Other of Liberation" in *Cross Currents* 46 (1996): 6; this theme is explored fully in Fox, Patricia A., ""God's Shattering Otherness: The Trinity and Earth's Healing" in Edwards, Denis (ed), *Earth Revealing –*

rediscover our place in God is to be fully human again; it is to realise afresh that God welcomes difference precisely because he is *in se* the God who is constituted perichoretically by difference; and it is to is to celebrate and value 'God's shattering otherness' in every corner of God's good and beautiful creation.

Earth Healing: Ecology and Christian Theology, Collegeville: The Liturgical Press, 2001: 85-103.

CHAPTER 6

Imaging the Perichoretic God – Towards a Model of Scientific and Pastoral Coherence

In his assessment of the Christian tradition's view of nature, Paul Santmire considers the theologies of two representative, yet strikingly dissimilar, twentieth-century thinkers, the confessional Protestant theologian Karl Barth and the Jesuit priest and theologian Pierre Teilhard de Chardin. He commends both Barth and Teilhard de Chardin for their adherence to a theology that makes universal claims – anchored in the revelation of God in Jesus Christ[1] – in a society characterised by secularisation and cultural disintegration. However, Santmire's appreciation is tempered by his charge that both theologians have yielded to the "nature-denying metaphor of ascent":

> For both Barth and Teilhard, the spiritual motif of the tradition has triumphed, in the form of a rigorous and thoroughgoing attention to personal being, at the expense of natural being. Notwithstanding significant countervailing trends, especially in Teilhard's thought, in both these theologies the ecological motif of the tradition has been pushed to the background, if not out of sight altogether.[2]

Santmire critiques Barth's theology of creation on the grounds that, for Barth, the world of nature is purely instrumental: although it is the *theatrum gloriae Dei* – through which, as Barth concedes, God may speak to a person – it is accorded theanthropocentric status as "merely the temporal setting for the

---

[1] In this respect, Santmire draws similar conclusions to my own regarding the place of revelation in the contrasting theologies of Barth and Tillich (see Chapter 2).

[2] Santmire, H. Paul, *The Travail of Nature: The Ambiguous Ecological Promise of Christian Theology*, Minneapolis: Fortress Press, 1985: 145-146. Although he regards Tillich as an important 'dialogue partner' in any debate about the Christian response to nature, Santmire does not include him in his critique – Tillich had developed a richly sacramental and theologically well-grounded appreciation of nature, but "his self-confessed romanticizing approach to nature simply did not elicit any visible following in the dominant schools of theology in his own time" (*ibid*: 141): more generally, Tillich "writes self-consciously 'on the boundary' of classical Christian thought" because of his refusal to think of God in personal terms (*ibid*: 252, fn.1).

really real",³ which is the drama between God and *humanity*. The fecundity of God – a theme that permeates the writings of Santmire and Denis Edwards, for example – is noticeably absent from Barth's theology of creation. In our discussion of the concept of emergence in self-organising systems in Chapter 5, we noted Gregersen's description of God as productively superabundant, "the generous creator of self-organizing systems."⁴ The intimation of biological fertility implicit in such a description is suggestive of a God for whom the natural world is more than "the construction of the space for the history of the covenant of grace."⁵ Drawing from Bonaventure's trinitarian theology, Edwards argues that *everything* within the created order reflects God's self-expression: "[e]very species, every ecosystem, the whole biosphere, every grain of sand and every galaxy, is a self-expression of the eternal Art of divine Wisdom."⁶ For Santmire, such a perspective radically contradicts Barth's "unconscious baptism of the modern secularization of nature."⁷

Teilhard de Chardin fares no better: Santmire notes his revival of the discredited concept of orthogenesis (the theory that trends in evolution constitute a driving force and continue under their own momentum) as a means of affirming the singular goal of the evolutionary process, which is the centrality and supremacy of humanity as it ascends to God. This necessarily puts him on a collision course with those who wish to assign to the created order a substantive and material eternal destiny. Teilhard was not anti-nature in this regard – he was in awe of the created order, and his understanding of evolution in Darwinian terms was explicit in his theology of nature. He would have approved of contemporary insights into emergentism and the self-organising complexity inherent in the unfolding of the universe through a creative interplay between law and chance. But his overriding personalist philosophy led him inexorably into an eschatological vision in which the physical ultimately yields to the human and the spiritual; so "all reality, even material reality, around each one of us, exists for our souls. Hence, all sensible reality around each one of us exists, through our souls, for God in our Lord."⁸ All is finally absorbed into spirit.

---

³ *Ibid*: 152. In theanthropocentrism everything revolves around God and humanity: so nature is merely the backdrop to salvation history; in its extreme evangelical form, theanthropocentric concern for the environment is justified on the grounds that caring for creation witnesses to the glory of God, so leading others to Christ. For a full discussion, see Young, Richard A., *Healing the Earth: A Theocentric Perspective on Environmental Problems and their Solutions*, Nashville: Broadman & Holman, 1994.
⁴ Gregersen, Niels Henrik, "The Creation of Creativity and the Flourishing of Creation" in *Currents in Theology and Mission* 28:3-4 (June/August 2001): 409.
⁵ Barth, Karl, *Church Dogmatics* 1/1, Edinburgh: T. & T. Clark, 1936: 44.
⁶ Edwards, Denis, *Jesus the Wisdom of God: An Ecological Theology*, Homebush NSW: St Pauls, 1995: 110.
⁷ Santmire, *The Travail of Nature*: 155.
⁸ Teilhard de Chardin, Pierre, *The Divine Milieu: An Essay on the Interior Life*, New York: Harper & Row, 1965: 56.

In an exposition of the theology of 'Père Teilhard', Henri de Lubac, a fellow-Jesuit and one of his close friends, quotes from a letter written by Teilhard in 1929:

> It seems to me that I have almost succeeded in formulating a sort of "Physics of the Spirit", which expresses more completely the suggestions sketched out in my note on the Phenomenon of man. It is a *sort of reduction of the Universe to the spiritual*, on the physical plane … that has for me the fortunate corollary of legitimizing the retention of persons (i.e. the "immortality" of souls) in the Universe.[9]

Two months after writing this, Teilhard wrote in another letter: "I find now that I can no longer envisage the World otherwise than in the form of an immense movement of Spirit."[10] For Teilhard, the universe was essentially a spiritual rather than a material reality, a 'personal Universe', or – to use one of his favourite phrases – a 'World of souls'.

However, Santmire's critique of Barth's 'humanity of God' and Teilhard's 'personalistic universe' as alternative stories of the whole of reality closes on a more positive note. Each, he suggests, contains the seeds of a more promising scenario, though neither theologian was able to paint such a picture as 'nature slips from their hands': that scenario is encapsulated in Santmire's root metaphors of fecundity and migration to a good land, both presented as alternatives to the dominating metaphor of ascent. He invites us to imagine that we are climbing a mountain. There are two alternatives that we are asked to consider as we make our way up the mountain: either we keep our gaze firmly fixed upwards, unaware of all around us as we journey towards the transcendent light above; on the other hand, we may choose to look around us as we make the journey, our eyes drinking in the beauty and glory of the mountain scenery.

The first perspective – the metaphor of ascent – is predicated on a form of spirituality that takes us not just towards God, but *away from* nature. The second metaphor, that of fecundity, invites us into an awareness and appreciation of the rich goodness of creation, which Santmire couples with his metaphor of migration to a good land, an eschatological vision of promise that offers inspiration and hope *in the midst of nature*. As Elaine Wainwright reminds us, the promise of a restored humanity in Isaiah 35:5-6 is framed by the promise of a restored world, in which the desert will rejoice as it blossoms like the crocus, the burning sand will become a pool and the thirsty ground bubbling springs: then will the blind see and the deaf hear – the two promises are

---

[9] de Lubac, Henri, S.J., *The Faith of Teilhard de Chardin*, London: Burns & Oates Ltd., 1965: 153, Lubac's italics; see, especially, the full chapter, "Polyvalence of the Cosmos" (*ibid*: 150-168) for an exploration of this theme within the framework of Teilhard's apologetics.

[10] Written to Léontine Zanta when Teilhard was in Peking (*ibid*: 153).

inextricably linked and are not to be pulled apart.[11]

Exploring Metaphors of Ecological Promise

The metaphor of ascent has been critiqued by the American spiritual writer Matthew Fox, who rejects all interpretations of spirituality that isolate the contemplative dimension from engagement in and with the world. He contrasts two types of spirituality, which he labels 'climbing Jacob's ladder' and 'dancing Sarah's circle'.[12] The ladder theme, claims Fox, has dominated the history of spirituality, with its (misinterpreted) implication of ascent to God and of various stages, or steps, which the Christian pilgrim must go through in order to reach God 'up there'. Fox suggests that Greek ideas, especially the Platonic notion of an upward progression from the concrete to the abstract, lie behind this narrow and unbiblical understanding of true spirituality. He contrasts this paradigm with the more authentic proposition that "God is not spatially up but in one's midst ... The question is not so much *where* God is as *when* will the people allow God to be among them?"[13] The earthiness and sheer celebration which is characteristic of Jewish spirituality is made explicit in Fox's allusion to God's promise of a child to Sarah, though she was past the age of child-bearing (Genesis 18:11-15): when that promise is fulfilled there is joy and laughter, for God has *come to* her in crazy, glorious and imaginative possibility.

One particular way in which Fox develops the contrast between a 'ladder-spirituality' and a 'dance-spirituality' is by insisting that the "proper dynamic of our spiritual lives is in/out and not up/down."[14] In the up/down schema there is the suggestion of individual escapism, whereas dancing with others is all about involvement and shared experiences. Ladder-climbing conveys the idea of strenuous effort and the fear that one might never reach the top; dancing invites us into an enterprise that stimulates and refreshes. The in/out paradigm is described by Fox in terms of mysticism and prophecy. Through mysticism we enter into the transcendent joys of life and living, encountering God, one another and all of creation in the innermost depths of our being: we are then equipped and motivated to re-enter the world in all its confusion and pain, speaking truth and life out of that which we have received. 'Dancing Sarah's

---

[11] See Wainwright, Elaine M., "A Transformative Struggle towards the Divine Dream: An Ecofeminist Reading of Matthew 11" in Habel, Norman C. (ed), *Readings from the Perspective of Earth*, Sheffield: Academic Press, 2000: 162-173.

[12] Fox, Matthew, *A Spirituality Named Compassion*, San Francisco: Harper, 1979: 36-67; these two paragraphs are drawn from Buxton, Graham, *Dancing in the Dark: The Privilege of Participating in the Ministry of Christ*, Carlisle: Paternoster, 2001: 289-290. For similar ideas expounded in the context of Luther's theology, see Forde, Gerhard O., *Where God Meets Man: Luther's Down-to-Earth Approach to the Gospel*, Minneapolis: Augsburg, 1972.

[13] Fox, *A Spirituality Named Compassion*: 41, author's italics.

[14] *Ibid*: 46.

circle' requires us to look around, so that we might express the energy of the divine life *amongst others* and so draw them into the dance.

The image presented here is one of celebration as an inclusive and holistic response to the gift of life. The 'in/out' dynamic suggested by Fox, vitalised by the image of dancing, has a strong perichoretic ring to it. We are encouraged to see life as a dynamically interweaving web of interactions at both the human and the non-human level. The image is taken up theologically by Santmire in his extensions of both Barth and Teilhard. He asks:

> Would it be anything but an enhancement of God's grace, from a Barthian perspective, not to begrudge the generosity of God, rather to confess that the creatures of nature also have an external determination, that God intends to have a history also with the galaxies and the dinosaurs and the birds of the air, that they also, in due proportion, along with our fellow human beings, are our "covenant partners"?[15]

In similar vein, he invites us to expand the Teilhardian vision of universal cosmic history, envisaging the confluence of "many lines of creaturely emergence, each with its own eschatological value."[16] Whilst the human line may be *primus inter pares*, might we not be enriched in our understanding of God's grace by embracing a vision of a 'commonwealth of creaturely being'? The metaphor of fecundity implicit in such a vision is apparent in Genesis 1:31: "God saw all that he had made, and it was very good." The different hierarchies of 'levels of reality' discussed in Chapter 5 reveal a divine Creator whose world "abundantly diversifies with a cornucopian fecundity in its 'becoming' in time."[17] Peacocke quotes the concluding passage of Darwin's *The Origin of Species*, echoed in Hopkins' *The Grandeur of God*, in order to illustrate this remarkable fruitfulness:

> It is interesting to contemplate a tangled bank, clothed with many plants of many kinds, with birds singing on the bushes, with various insects flitting about, and with worms crawling through the damp earth, and to reflect that these elaborately constructed forms, so different from each other, and dependent upon each other in so complex a manner, have all been produced by laws acting around us ... There is a grandeur in this view of life, with its several powers, having been originally breathed by the Creator into a few forms or into one; and that, whilst this planet has gone cycling on according to the fixed laws of gravity, from so simple a beginning endless forms

---

[15] Santmire, *The Travail of Nature*: 171-172.
[16] *Ibid*: 172.
[17] Peacocke, Arthur R., *God and Science: A Quest for Christian Credibility*, London: SCM Press, 1996: 14; see Darwin, Charles [1859], *The Origin of Species*, Baltimore: Penguin Books, 1968: 459-460.

most beautiful and most wonderful have been, and are being evolved.[18]

The grandeur of God lies not only in his sovereign glory as the Creator of all things, but also in the extraordinary diversity of his creation, unfolding over time in the human, animal and natural realms. Biologists teach us that there is an amazing branching network in the 'tree of life'. The millions of species that exist on planet Earth are not a haphazard jumble of animals and plants and other natural phenomena – rather, they share a nested relationship in the 'tree of life', each contributing to and drawing from unique ecosystems, which are themselves interdependent. This reinforces the idea, raised by Bohm and Lovelock and other scientists[19], that planet Earth is a complex global biosystem, characterised by remarkable biological diversity. "The natural world is not a single entity but a marvelously rich, multidimensional, diverse, and intricate collection of lifeforms and things."[20] God is glorified, Sallie McFague continues, "not by the denial of difference, but by its flourishing and fulfillment."[21]

Our brief study in the previous chapter of some of the central features of quantum mechanics, particularly with regard to the principles of non-locality and entanglement, highlighted the interactive behaviour of physical particles at the quantum level. In particular, we concluded from the quantum concept of entanglement that events in the universe may be interpreted perichoretically as expressions of the dynamic life and energy of the Spirit "who is present in every flower, bird, and human being, in every quasar and in every atomic particle, closer to them than they are themselves, enabling them to be and to become."[22] Because God is the God of the particular, the God who loves *all* that he has made, McFague encourages us to adopt a radical sacramental view of nature that celebrates every part of God's diverse creation in the metaphorical language of the 'body' of God. In her book, *The Body of God*, she captures the essence of ecological diversity and unity by tracing the particular features discernible in a tide pool and a rock face; as we pay attention to the detail we see a world that we had not seen before. We see "unbelievable individuality, diversity, and complexity combined with astonishing networks of

---

[18] *Ibid*: 15-16.
[19] See Chapter 5 for a discussion of David Bohm's concept of an 'implicate order' as the basis behind all reality, and James Lovelock's view that planet Earth may be understood as a global ecosystem (to which he gave the name 'Gaia').
[20] McFague, Sallie, *Super, Natural Christians: How We Should Love Nature*, Minneapolis: Fortress Press, 1997: 173.
[21] *Ibid*: 174.
[22] Edwards, Denis, "For Your Immortal Spirit Is in All Things: The Role of the Spirit in Creation" in Edwards, Denis (ed), *Earth Revealing – Earth Healing: Ecology and Christian Theology*, Collegeville: The Liturgical Press, 2001: 56.

interconnectedness and interdependence."[23] Then, adopting the language of *perichoresis*, she observes that the different species and individuals "live on top of, in between, and inside each other."[24] Such perichoretic interdependence is, argues McFague, characteristic of the whole created order, in which human beings are symbiotically intertwined with the life – and death – of all things.

We are invited, therefore, to *embrace* the physical creation as an expression of our God-given humanity, not – as in Teilhard's thinking, for example – to *reduce* it to the spiritual. The central tension in Santmire's thesis is that a person's "identity as a human being may be essentially rooted in the world of nature (the metaphor of fecundity) or it may not be (the metaphor of ascent)."[25] His affirmation of the metaphor of fecundity as a mark of what it means to be made *imago Dei* is reinforced by his statement that we are all essentially 'landed creatures': indeed, to be disconnected from the world of nature is to be stripped of our identity as human beings. Not only do we – as created beings – 'live and move and have our being' within the world of nature, but spiritual experience is itself located within the ecological context. To pull spirituality and ecology apart is to do violence to the very fabric of creation as God's gift of self-communicating, self-limiting, perichoretic love.

Moltmann's 'Ecological Concept of Space' – Pastoral Implications

In the previous chapter we noted Moltmann's proposal that the dynamic perichoretic freedom of the triune God *in se* finds ecstatic, kenotic expression "in the space God yielded up for it through his creative resolve."[26] He remarks that ever since Augustine there have been many theological meditations on time, but very rarely do we find any on *space*: with regard to time, theology has rightly focused on the importance of history, but space has been left to the scientists. In taking up the theological challenge,[27] Moltmann proposes an 'ecological concept of space', in which he eschews the idea of space as a *homogeneous* concept. He distinguishes between three things: the essential omnipresence of God, which he calls *absolute space*; the *space of creation* in the world-presence of God conceded to it – in creating the universe, God brings into being that which is distinct from the space of God (absolute space); and, thirdly, *relative places*, relationships and movements in the created world – so

---

[23] McFague, Sallie, *The Body of God: An Ecological Theology*, London: SCM Press, 1993: 62.
[24] *Ibid*: 63.
[25] Santmire, *The Travail of Nature*: 25.
[26] Moltmann, Jürgen, *God in Creation: A New Theology of Creation and the Spirit of God*, San Francisco: Harper & Row, 1985: 156.
[27] It is precisely because ecological theology is such a central feature of Moltmann's whole theological enterprise that particular attention is given to his insights in this chapter.

living things occupy a multiplicity of different ecological environments within God's created space-time world. Every living thing has its own world in which to live, a world to which it is adapted and which suits it. For Moltmann, space, as created reality, is primarily *living space* for the richness and variety of different forms of life. "Living spaces belong to life"[28]: the idea of uniquely appropriate ecological spaces is not a secondary reality, but something that is fundamental to Moltmann's thinking. The converse is also true: just as every life has its own living space, so every living space shapes its own living beings.

However, if creation is treated as an object to dominate, the particular environments created by God for the nourishment of unique living things are destroyed in the drive to create a homogeneous environment amenable to humanity's desire to dominate all things. The drive for uniformity (especially in today's highly-globalised culture) weakens and destabilises the rich diversity of God's creation. Everything becomes 'McDonaldised' in the contemporary consumer-driven culture. Things are valued for their usefulness to humanity rather than for what they are *as creations of God*. Douglas John Hall echoes Santmire's critique of the metaphor of ascent when he states that imaging God "is not rising above the earth, as if we were pure spirit ... we are bodies, and our imaging of God is inseparable from our imaging of the earth."[29] He suggests that human pride – a refusal to acknowledge our basic creaturehood – is responsible for our desire to rise above "this affinity with our earthly source and matrix."[30]

We may draw at least three important conclusions from these ecological insights, each of which has significant pastoral implications. They are the *invitation to adventure*, the *necessity of boundaries*, and the need for what McFague calls a *Christian nature spirituality*. The first two relate to Moltmann's own observation that both expanse and limitation characterise the way in which human beings experience their space. In a stimulating discussion of the impulse towards adventure that is God's gift to human beings, the Swiss doctor Paul Tournier reminds us that the word 'enthusiasm' literally means 'feeling God within oneself'. Specifically, he argues that an enthusiastic person is one who is captivated by the spirit of adventure, willing to embark on risky and perhaps dangerous pursuits. Tournier suggests that all of us are endowed intrinsically with this spirit of adventure because we are all made in the image of an adventurous God. This instinct "may be cloaked, smothered, and repressed, but it never disappears from the human personality. The timidest pen-pushing clerk will disclose under psychoanalysis, and particularly in the analysis of his dreams, a secret nostalgia for the adventure which he has sacrificed to security."[31]

---

[28] See Moltmann, Jürgen, "God and Space", a previously unpublished essay in Moltmann, Jürgen, *Science and Wisdom*, Minneapolis: Fortress Press, 2003, 111-126.
[29] Hall, Douglas John, *Imaging God: Dominion as Stewardship*, Grand Rapids: Eerdmans, 1986: 179.
[30] *Ibid*: 180.
[31] Tournier, Paul, *The Adventure of Living*, Crowborough: Highland Books, 1983: 5.

A sign at a roadside church once declared: "Some people never sing; they die with all their music still inside them." To be made *imago Dei* is to be enthused by the same spirit of adventure that animates the triune being of Father, Son and Holy Spirit.[32] God's music is the music of life, the music of adventure, the music of going on a journey full of anticipation and a sense of discovery. To be willing to take risks, to step out into the adventure of living, which is God's gift to all human beings, is to see life through new eyes, to discover that there is a whole new way of life available in God which has to do with enjoying our humanity and God's good gifts to us in his creation. To be truly human is to take life less seriously than we often do.[33] It is to sing the song that God has put into our lives, and not to drown it in the clamour of activism and busyness that often overwhelms us. The English mystic, Evelyn Underhill, writing at the beginning of the twentieth century, described many Christians as 'deaf people at a concert':

> They study the program carefully, believe every statement in it, speak respectfully of the quality of the music, but only really hear a phrase now and again. So they have no notion at all of the mighty symphony which fills the universe, to which our lives are destined to make their tiny contribution, and which is the self-expression of the Eternal God.[34]

The 'mighty symphony' to which Underhill alludes may be interpreted as the symphony of a creation that is replete with biological diversity and fecundity,

---

[32] The idea of an exuberant and adventurous God correlates with our earlier thoughts about God as an 'open Trinity' in which all creatures – and ultimately the whole new creation – find their home in God, who is an *ekstatic*, open community of love.

[33] Ted Engstrom relates the following homily composed by an old monk called Brother Jeremiah, who, reflecting on his many years, concluded that he had taken life too seriously. This is what he wrote: "If I had my life to live over again, I'd try to make more mistakes next time. I would relax. I would limber up. I would be sillier than I have been this trip. I know of very few things I would take seriously. I would take more trips. I would climb more mountains, swim more rivers, and watch more sunsets. I would do more walking and looking. I would eat more ice cream and less beans. I would have more actual troubles and less imaginary ones. You see, I am one of those people who live prophylactically and sensibly and sanely, hour after hour, day after day. Oh, I've had my moments, and if I had it to do over again, I'd have more of them. In fact, I'd try to have nothing else. Just moments, one after another, instead of living so many years ahead each day. I have been one of those people who never go anywhere without a thermometer, a hot water bottle, a gargle, a raincoat, aspirin, and a parachute. I would go places, do things, and travel lighter than I have. If I had my life to live over, I would start barefooted earlier in the spring and stay that way later in the fall. I would play more. I would ride on more merry-go-rounds. I'd pick more daisies" (Engstrom, Ted, *The Pursuit of Excellence*, Grand Rapids: Zondervan, 1982: 90).

[34] From the first of four broadcast talks by the English mystic Evelyn Underhill, subsequently published under the title *The Spiritual Life*, Harrisburg PA: Morehouse Publishing, 1997.

which is itself "the dynamic, exuberant overflow of the fecundity of trinitarian life."[35] To experience human life in all its fullness has to do with *paying attention* to this creation in such a way that we see it with new eyes, epitomised in the following well-known lines from *Aurora Leigh*, Elizabeth Barrett Browning's nineteenth-century verse-novel of contemporary early Victorian life in England:

> ... Earth's crammed with heaven,
> And every common bush afire with God:
> But only he who *sees*, takes off his shoes,
> The rest sit round it, and pluck blackberries ...[36]

To experience nature in this sacramental way is to begin to know our place in the space of God's creation, moving onwards and forwards, 'migrating to the good land' of God's new creation. It is to experience transformation not only as we discover afresh our basic humanity in solidarity with God's created order, but also as we recognise that the Christian mission is "an eschatological witness on behalf of the whole creation, as it groans in travail."[37] Santmire quotes the words of J. Christiaan Beker:

> Paul's church is not an aggregate of justified sinners or a sacramental institute or a means of private self-sanctification but the avant-garde of the new creation in a hostile world, creating beachheads in this world of God's dawning new world and yearning for the day of God's visible lordship over his creation."[38]

However, the necessary counterpart of expanse in human life is limitation. Moltmann develops the idea of personal bounded living-space not only geographically and ecologically, but also socially and morally. Geographically, we cannot live adventurously without at times putting down some roots, if only for a short time. Human beings need boundaries: we feel secure when we border ourselves in. Ecologically, we need our own personal dwelling place, "the home where we can escape the homelessness of the desert."[39] We like to create our

---

[35] Edwards, *Jesus the Wisdom of God*: 116. The implications of this are spelled out further by Edwards: " ...the rain forest of the Amazon is to be understood as the self-expression of the divine Trinity. It is a sacrament of God's presence. Its vitality and exuberance spring from the immanent presence of the Spirit, the giver of life. They express the trinitarian love of life. The rain forest, in its form, function and beauty as a harmonious biotic community is the work of art of divine Wisdom" (*ibid*: 117).
[36] Browning, Elizabeth Barrett, *Aurora Leigh*, London: J. Miller, 1864: 'Seventh Book', my italics.
[37] Santmire, *The Travail of Nature*: 210.
[38] Beker, J. Christiaan, *Paul the Apostle: The Triumph of God in Life and Thought*, Philadelphia: Fortress Press, 1980: 33.
[39] Moltmann, "God and Space": 114.

own environment within which we can feel, if not safe, at least 'at home' or at rest: only God, in his 'world-transcendence', is unrestricted.[40]

We examined the concept of *social* spaces in Chapter 4 in terms of a communal interpretation of *imago Dei*: in their 'quest for completeness', human beings discover their identity not just in narrow or exclusive I-Thou relationships, but as they participate freely in the interconnected web of giving and receiving that characterises the 'creation-community' of creatures and environments that inhabit planet Earth. As we enter a way of life that approximates as closely as possible the perichoretic life of the Trinity we are imbued with a radical new sense of social justice. We begin to recognise the unique part that we can play in our own ecological space. As finite creatures, our participation in these spaces is limited, but it inevitably assumes a *moral* dimension. The spaces we inhabit depend upon us, the decisions we make, and the decisions made by others before us. The consequences of self-centred anthropocentricism in our relationship with nature are primarily twofold: a deterioration in personal living-spaces, and environmental degradation, both of which are evident in human society today, such as in the poorest quarters of our cities or in marginalised rural communities. Moltmann interprets these social and moral living spaces perichoretically because

> their interaction – their warp and weft, their interlocking – goes beyond the simple subject-related ecological living-spaces. Every living thing has its space and home: *oikos*. Every living thing is a space for others: *perichoresis*. And it will be immediately clear that in saying this we are anticipating the doctrine of the Trinity.[41]

Limit is therefore as much a characteristic of human life as expanse: both experiences of space, however, are grounded perichoretically precisely because the triune God yields space within his own perichoretic being for the living-space of the whole world. God, as perichoretic reality, in whose triune life each person is at the same time "the space for the movement, life and dwelling of the two others"[42], is consistent in ceding to his creation both differentiation and movement. He respects the diversity and dynamism of his creation by granting to every particle and every plant, every creature and every ecosystem, its own freedom to be and to become within its own ecological living space, a space that is itself – perichoretically – a space for others. From the perspective of pastoral ministry, each human being is therefore open to creation for his or her own liberation, yet at the same time bounded within his or her own ecological space, within which that liberty is realised for human and non-human creation alike.

This experience of liberation, however, demands a spiritual framework if it is to be actualised in the life of each human being – and in the wider 'creation-

---

[40] *Ibid*: 114.
[41] *Ibid*: 115.
[42] *Ibid*: 118.

community', which is the ultimate goal of God's eschatological purposes. This framework – a 'Christian nature spirituality' – is offered by Sallie McFague as an incarnational love of nature that involves paying attention to 'what is', as highlighted in the earlier-quoted lines of Browning from *Aurora Leigh*. Interpreting this 'paying attention' as an awareness, even a celebration, of *difference*, she admits to the difficulty of really learning to see what is different to ourselves: "We can acknowledge a thing in its difference if it is important to us or useful to us, but realizing that something other than oneself is real, in itself, for itself, is difficult."[43]

Citing Emily Dickinson's insight that 'we cannot love what we do not know', McFague contrasts two ways of seeing. The first – what Marilyn Frye calls the 'loving eye'[44] – is an attention to detail that exalts "the specialness, the difference, the intricacy, the 'unutterable particularity' of each creature, event, or aspect of nature that calls forth wonder and delight – a knowing that calls forth love and a love that wants to know more."[45] The French mystic and philosopher Simone Weil suggests that to see in this way is tantamount to prayer. In her book *Waiting on God* she argues that when prayer is intense and pure enough for contact with God to be established, "the whole attention is turned towards God."[46] Concentrated attention is, for Weil, the pathway to truth:

> I have the everlasting conviction that any human being, even though practically devoid of natural faculties, can penetrate to the kingdom of truth reserved for genius, if only he or she longs for truth and perpetually concentrates all his/her attention upon its attainment.[47]

The second, and inferior, way of seeing – the 'arrogant eye' – is epitomised in the popular NASA poster of planet Earth as a swirling blue and white coloured marble floating in black space. Whilst such an image has immediate cosmetic and popular appeal,[48] McFague argues that it utterly fails to convey the rape and pillage, the environmental pollution and violence that take place on a

---

[43] McFague, *Super, Natural Christians*: 28.

[44] Frye, Marilyn, "In and Out of Harm's Way: Arrogance and Love" in *The Politics of Reality: Essays in Feminist Theory*, Freedom CA: Crossing Press: 1983: 53-83, esp. 72-76; note Frye's insight that the loving eye "knows the complexity of the other as something which will forever present new things to be known" (*ibid*: 76).

[45] McFague, *Super, Natural Christians*: 31.

[46] Weil, Simone, *Waiting on God*, London: Collins, 1963: 66.

[47] *Ibid*: 30-31; Weil's notion of truth lies at the deepest level of personal understanding, and yet it is also available at any place and at any time to anyone who desires it precisely because it is not learned but comes to us from outside, that is from God.

[48] For example, McFague found it a useful image to raise consciousness about the fragility of the planet; it also evokes a sense of wonder in calling to mind the inhospitable environments of all other planets known to humankind, reinforcing God's special creation of Earth, unique and 'fine-tuned' to provide just the right conditions for life to be sustained for billions of years.

daily basis in every part of the planet. As an image, it is remote and ultimately meaningless precisely because it fails to acknowledge and respect Earth as *subject*. As an alternative to the dominant 'subject-object' model, she proposes an ecological 'subject-subjects' model, on the analogy of friendship, which is predicated on the language of relationships: "respect, reciprocity, interest in the particular, openness, paying attention, care, concern."[49]

Moltmann expresses this friendship in terms of community: "if nature and humanity are to survive on this earth, they must find the way to a new community with each other. Human beings must integrate themselves once more into the earth's cosmic setting."[50] His theological foundation is both distinctively pneumatological and necessarily trinitarian. It is pneumatological in his insistence that through the Spirit's immanence in the world God calls all things into being: he is the Creator Spirit who is the giver and sustainer of life. He is, as we concluded in Chapter 3, the eschatological power of God at work in all creation, enabling all that exists – personal and non-personal – to fully and finally become itself in the freedom of divine love. Moltmann's cosmic theology is trinitarian because God, *as trinitarian Creator*, is also the 'Spirit of the Universe'. In other words, 'Spirit' as "the dynamic of self-organization on the diverse levels of the universe" is divine not because we choose to call this cosmic dynamic 'God', but precisely because God is differentiated *in se* as Father, Son and Spirit.[51]

Our discussion in this section has identified a number of significant dimensions of the Spirit's activity amongst human beings that flow from the concept of ecological space. Each of these dimensions has an important bearing on Christian pastoral ministry. Enthused by 'the Spirit of adventure', who animates the human spirit, we are encouraged to discover our place in God's creation, and to enter into a new awareness of our identity in relationship with created matter. Such symbiosis with nature is in stark contrast to the person who is so "caught up in the idolatries of tyrannical professionalism, and such pragmatism of spirit, that instead of seeing creation with a childlike and overwhelming delight" he or she sees it "only as data for the intellect, and as resources for consumption."[52] The Spirit of adventure leads us into an attentiveness to *everything* that God has made precisely because we are

---

[49] *Ibid*: 37.

[50] Moltmann, Jürgen, "'From the Closed World to the Infinite Universe': The Case of Giordano Bruno" in *Science and Wisdom*, Minneapolis: Fortress Press, 2003: 168-169 (previously published in Häring, H. and Kuschel, K. J. (eds), *Gegenentwürfe. 24 Lebensläufe für eine andere Theologie. Festschrift für Hans Küng zum 60. Geburtstag*, Munich, 1998: 157-167).

[51] *Ibid*: 170; for a full discussion of the relationship between creation and the triune God, particularly in the theologies of Colin Gunton and Thomas Torrance, see the section 'The Trinity and Creation' in Chapter 3.

[52] Houston, James M., *I Believe in the Creator*, London: Hodder & Stoughton, 1979: 215.

constrained by an ethic of love that respects the richness of God's creation as the self-expression of God's fecundity.

If to be a human being is to 'glorify God and enjoy Him for ever' – in the words of the Westminster Shorter Catechism – then living in God's image means enjoying all that God enjoys. This sort of enjoyment derives not from a cavalier 'spirit of adventure' that rides indifferently over the many ecological issues that confront us politically, economically and socially, but from an ethic that recognises God's love for his creation, and therefore *loves because he loves*. This perspective – what McFague refers to as 'a new lens for seeing' – focuses us on "*thinking differently* so that we might behave differently."[53]

The behaviour to which McFague alludes is intensely practical and urgent. Her list of issues includes prenatal and nutritional care of the young, experimental genetics, rape and sexual abuse, endangered species, AIDS, the homeless, clear-cut logging practices, affirmative action laws, taxation policies, pollution control and water rights, abortion and contraception availability, immigration laws, health insurance and care, and educational costs and opportunities. It is evident that, at a practical level, many of these concerns have local and contextual relevance. Whilst Christians are not to dissociate themselves from wider social issues – such as the long-term health of planet Earth – the pastoral ministry of the church operates primarily at the level of the particular, not the general. God calls us into particular social relationships and invites us to explore our humanity in the context of particular environments, often at great pain and cost. As Moltmann points out, we cannot be permanently 'open to the world', for that would destroy us "through the multiplicity of its impressions."[54] Ultimately, we depend for our identity on 'complex webs of mutuality and participation', which are primarily local rather than global. As we argued in Chapter 4, our identity derives from the very interactions in which we are historically and necessarily involved as human beings whose lives are embedded in local community.

Earlier, in Chapter 2, reference was made to the Australian theologian Denham Grierson, who has examined the characteristic features of local congregations, arguing that each faith-community is unique in its history and identity. 'Naming' those characteristics (signs of meaning in the local context) will help to determine purpose and direction in the church's ministry in the community. Grierson challenges the assumption that local churches are neat, tidy and generally civilised: "A particular congregation is never neat, sometimes barely Christian and only rarely civilised"![55] Accordingly, he

---

[53] McFague, *The Body of God*: 202; McFague delineates a wide range of concerns that derive from 'the relationship of an ecological theology of embodiment to concrete, nitty-gritty decisions on all sorts of difficult issues in our personal and private lives" (*ibid*: 203). Whilst her proposed paradigm – the world as God's body – does not offer clear answers to the issues raised, it is intended to offer a new shape for humanity and for the world that is based on a framework that transcends individualistic anthropocentricism.

[54] Moltmann, "God and Space": 114.

[55] Grierson, Denham, *Transforming a People of God*, Melbourne, JBCE, 1984: 18.

proposes six dimensions that 'name' a community of faith, which he defines as 'signs' of the hidden sources of meaning and significance which constitute the people as a community of faith. These dimensions are summarised as time, space, language, intimacy, consensus and circumstance.[56]

Time, the first dimension, has to do with a congregation's awareness of its past, present and future: memory, vision, expectation, being stuck in the past ... all relate to the 'time-sense' that pervades the life of a community of faith. Grierson's second 'sign', *space*, has to do with how the people indwell their environment: "The institutional order and organised arrangements people give to their way of being is capable of telling their hidden tale of their spiritual pilgrimage."[57] *Language* functions in circumscribing the people's reality: key words, phrases and images all contribute to language as a powerful instrument of self-consciousness. The total experience of a people's shared life is implicit in the closeness, depth and commitment involved in *intimacy*. *Consensus* defines what is commonly affirmed, reflecting the world view of the congregation: this involves such things as its common belief system, and the values and truths which are shared and thus shape the congregation. Finally, every congregation is located in a specific context, which Grierson defines as its *circumstance*; geography, economic issues, ethnicity, social background, deprivation or abundance. All these create both opportunity and limitation for a faith-community, reflecting Moltmann's insight that limit is as much a characteristic of human life as expanse.

The 'Spirit of particularity' therefore shapes human beings within particular ecological (and congregational) spaces, to which we are summoned to *pay attention* with 'loving eyes'. It is in this sense that we begin to recognise the unique part that we can play in our own ecological space, a limited space that both protects us for our sake and affords opportunity for concrete action for the sake of others and for the sake of the environment. We discover in our own personal dwelling space, which is at the same time the dwelling place of the Spirit, the possibility of being fully human. This is precisely the promise of a 'Christian nature spirituality' that celebrates detail and difference even as it honours the integrity of the cosmos as a unified and interconnected whole.

Nature as an Enchanted[58] and Interconnected Reality

Throughout this book we have had occasion to refer to God's creation in terms of beauty, a characteristic that reflects the nature of God himself. McGrath argues that to deny a transcendent dimension in nature is to "rob nature of its

---

[56] *Ibid*: 53-93.
[57] *Ibid*: 66.
[58] The adjective 'enchanted' is preferred to the more popular description of nature as 'sacred' in order to emphasise the Christian doctrine that nature bears the marks of its Creator, rather than being intrinsically divine. The term 'sacramental' may also be used, for a similar reason.

deepest meaning, and humanity of the hope that this signifies."[59] This suggests a critical link between the transcendent beauty of creation and the realm of the sacred, leading us into a richer experience of transcendence, wonder and divine glory. However, as Gilkey rightly reminds us, and as we have emphasised in our discussion of natural theology, "what is known of God in nature by no means represents the center of the knowledge of God for the Christian."[60] But a concentration on the centre, which is the person of Jesus Christ as the sum and fulfilment of the Christian revelation of God, should not devalue the sacramental significance of nature, for "to know nature truly is to know its mystery, its depth, and its ultimate value – it is to know nature as an image of the sacred, a visible sign of an invisible grace."[61]

In Chapter 5, we noted that the themes of eschatological consummation and the sanctification of creation are fittingly drawn together in Moltmann's theology of the sabbath as the 'feast of creation', for on the sabbath "the redemption of the world is celebrated in anticipation" – it is the "foretaste of the world to come."[62] So we are invited by God to set the sabbath apart, to enter in to his own sabbath rest, and so enter proleptically into an experience of the divine 'completion' of creation, anticipating the eschatological 'rest' of God in his creation:

> The end of all things is the cosmic Sabbath, that day in which the human creature as creation's steward will stand before God in worship and thanksgiving and praise and will thereby reflect God's image in the world, being and saying and doing what God is and says and does in God's creation.[63]

In sabbath stillness we acknowledge creation as sacramental – beauty "is not just a sort of froth on the surface of things. It is something very deep about the

---

[59] McGrath, Alister, *The Re-enchantment of Nature: Science, Religion and the Human Sense of Wonder*, London: Hodder & Stoughton, 2002: 19.

[60] Gilkey, Langdon, *Nature, Reality, and the Sacred: The Nexus of Science and Religion*, Minneapolis: Fortress Press, 1993: 195; Gilkey goes on to declare that "far more important for our tradition, as for its biblical roots, is the presence and activity of God within history and especially within the communities of the covenant, the Hebrew community and the community established around the person and work of Jesus Christ. If in nature the divine power, life, and order or law are disclosed through dim traces, and if the divine redemptive love is revealed only in ambiguous hints in and through the tragedy of suffering and death, it is in the life of Israel, in the life and death of Jesus, and in the historical pilgrimage of the peoples of God that all of this is disclosed in much greater certainty, clarity, and power" (*ibid*: 195).

[61] *Ibid*: 204.

[62] See, especially, "The Sabbath: The Feast of Creation" in Moltmann, *God in Creation: A New Theology of Creation and the Spirit of God*: 276-296.

[63] Dabney, D. Lyle, "The Nature of the Spirit: Creation as a Premonition of God" in Pickard, Stephen and Preece, Gordon, *Starting with the Spirit*, Hindmarsh SA: Australian Theological Forum, 2001: 110.

Imaging the Perichoretic God 263

world."[64]

The new discipline of ecotheology is burgeoning today as the result of a growing awareness of humanity's failure to look after God's good gift of creation. We argued in Chapter 2 that to live responsibly as human beings within the created order is to move beyond a purely utilitarian ethic and to embrace a spirituality that acknowledges the wonder and mystery of creation as 'sacramental reality.' However, jostling alongside concerned Christians are many others, amongst whom are those whose interest in the environment stems from neopagan roots, including a fascination with nature mysticism. This has been stimulated in part by the failure of the Christian church to demonstrate respect for and concerned involvement in nature, a neglect over the years that has prompted Sallie McFague to insert what she calls a 'deeply subversive' comma between 'super' and 'natural'. Her writings express a passionate desire to see Christians live not just 'supernatural' lives, but 'super, natural' lives, living "*in* the earth, and *for* the earth ... understanding ourselves as excessively, superlatively concerned with nature and its well-being."[65]

This final chapter is an attempt to integrate the notion of the enchantment of nature into a coherent model of dynamic, perichoretic reality, and to demonstrate the significance of the theological concept of *imago Dei* as a means of integrating human life and the natural order. In order to achieve this, we need to spell out more fully an understanding of nature as an enchanted and interconnected ecological reality. In his introduction to the first volume of the *Earth Bible* series, Norman Habel argues that many Christian traditions, especially in the West, have interpreted the biblical text in such a way as to devalue Earth.[66] The purpose of the 'Earth Bible Project' is to promote a renewed interest in creation as a central theological theme, not as a topic in the biblical text, nor as backdrop to human history, but critically concerned with "listening to Earth as a subject in the text."[67] Habel and his fellow-contributors argue that the thrust of biblical interpretation in the Western tradition has tended towards anthropocentricism, androcentricism and patriarchy, based on a reading of Genesis 1:26-28 that emphasises God's explicit directive to rule over every living thing and subdue the earth. The members of the Earth Bible team make a powerful plea for ecojustice in humanity's relationship to planet Earth. Eschewing Western hierarchical dualistic thinking that places human beings *above* nature, they advocate a policy of partnership that resists the violation and exploitation of nature.

Accordingly, six 'ecojustice principles' undergird the Earth Bible Project endeavour: they are the principles of intrinsic worth, interconnectedness, voice,

---

[64] Polkinghorne, John, *Serious Talk: Science and Religion in Dialogue*, Harrisburg PA: Trinity Press International, 1995: 1 (quoted earlier in Chapter 1).
[65] McFague, *Super, Natural Christians*: 5-6.
[66] Habel, Norman C. (ed), *Readings from the Perspective of Earth*, Sheffield: Academic Press, 2000: 25-37.
[67] *Ibid*: 29.

purpose, mutual custodianship and resistance. Each of these principles is addressed in the *Earth Bible* series. For example, in a study of Genesis 6:11-13, Gardner interprets the biblical text as a failure of God's creatures to respect the intrinsic worth of each other and of the earth.[68] Reid, in his exegesis of Revelation 21.1-22.5, identifies John's evident allusions to the 'this-worldly' vision in Isaiah 65: here we have no "earth-despising gnosticism" – in fact, heaven comes down to earth, not the reverse! So the earth, "turned into a place of God's absence by godless human beings, is to become once more the dwelling place of God."[69] Earth, once shamed and denuded, is replete with the glory of God. And from Genesis through to Revelation, the biblical text is perceived by the Earth Bible team as active subject rather than passive object: planet Earth has a voice to be heard, not silenced; it functions according to an in-built purpose; and it exists – human and non-human – as a complex and mutually-supportive community of interconnected living things.

In his commentary on Romans 8:18-22, the Jesuit New Testament scholar Brendan Byrne offers an ecojustice hermeneutic, arguing that the passage conveys "a strong sense of solidarity in both suffering and hope between non-human creation and the human world."[70] Human beings are neither above nor separate from the rest of creation; each person is a member of a complex ecosystem, a biotic community that embraces all living things. But an attitude of integrity *towards* creation must be accompanied by an appreciation of the integrity *of* creation. Aldo Leopold once famously wrote that a thing is right "when it tends to preserve the integrity, stability and beauty of the biotic community. It is wrong when it tends otherwise."[71] However, the concept of the integrity of creation is far more complex than we might imagine. The biologist Carolyn King argues that what is needed is one that "does justice to (a) the restless dynamism of the real natural world recognised by science, and to (b) the real conflicts of interests between individual and community at all levels of nature."[72]

We see here a very real tension in ecological ethics between the whole and

---

[68] See Gardner, Anne, "Ecojustice: A Study of Genesis 6.11-13" in Habel, Norman C. and Wurst, Shirley (eds), *The Earth Story in Genesis*, Sheffield: Academic Press, 2000: 117-129.

[69] See Reid, Duncan, "Setting Aside the Ladder to Heaven: Revelation 22.1-22.5 from the Perspective of Earth" in Habel and Wurst (eds), *The Earth Story in Genesis*: 232-245.

[70] See Byrne, Brendan, SJ, "Creation Groaning: An Earth Bible Reading of Romans 8.18-22" in Habel (ed), *Readings from the Perspective of Earth*: 193-203; Byrne acknowledges that "the clear distinction Paul makes between human beings and the rest of creation stands in some tension with the principle of interconnectedness" that "tends to reinforce a sense of duality between human beings and the rest of creation."

[71] Leopold, Aldo, *A Sand County Almanac: With Essays on Conservation from Round River*, New York: Ballantine Books, 1949: 262.

[72] King, Carolyn M., *Habitat of Grace: Biology, Christianity and the Global Environmental Crisis*, Hindmarsh SA: Australian Theological Forum, 2002: 136.

the parts, between the biotic community and the needs of the individual. A sacramental view of creation insists that all creation is to be valued for its own sake as the handiwork of God, not for its usefulness to human beings.[73] But on what basis are we to judge between conflicting claims within the ecosystem, such as the culling of animals when they are overpopulating a particular habitat, and in danger of causing severe ecological damage? Are some creatures more valuable than others, and how do we decide?[74] Developing ecological ethics is difficult precisely because of the community factor: "the community within which we live and to whom we are responsible does not stop with human beings but includes all the earth others."[75] McFague's ethic of care has a concern for the particular, for that which is different: it is based on the concept of friendship, in which solidarity supersedes survival, and the good of the whole is the ultimate goal.

In this model of care the physical is perceived as an intimation of the divine. Sacramental reality is expressed in the glory of natural forms, proclaimed in their particularity, their diversity, their thickness – in their unique '*it*ness'. McFague calls this 'horizontal Christian sacramentalism', focusing on the things themselves rather than their divine message.[76] In this view, nature is enchanted precisely because it is the creation of God, not because it points to the God of creation. This perspective takes us further than McGrath's observation that nature, "when rightly understood, points beyond itself, to a 'yonder' we shall one day know and inhabit."[77] Nature, then, is to be treasured for what it is, rather than just for what it does; though it speaks to us of God, it is, in its richness and variety, the 'body' of God in the sense that God is "*the* inspirited body of the entire universe, the animating, living spirit that produces, guides, and saves all that is."[78]

In his quest for a radical re-enchantment of nature, David Tacey argues that there needs to be a moral and ethical revolution in our hearts if we are to arrest the impoverishment of the earth caused by our exploitative abuse. Treating

---

[73] This is the first ecojustice principle expounded by the Earth Bible team: see Habel (ed), *Readings from the Perspective of Earth*: 42-44.

[74] For a discussion of the relationship between humanity and creation from the perspective of the integrity of creation and human discernment, see McFague, *Super, Natural Christians*: 150-175; Edwards, Denis, *Jesus the Wisdom of God*: 153-171; King, *Habitat of Grace*: 133-137. Edwards proposes the level of consciousness of the creatures involved as a suitable criterion for ethical discernment (Edwards, *Jesus and the Wisdom of God*: 161-163); others suggest the importance of rights and justice as a basis for the ethics of care, but faced with the question "does the wolf have the right to eat the lamb for dinner, or does the lamb have the right to survive?", then the notion of rights may prove to be inadequate when applied to the natural world (McFague, *Super, Natural Christians*: 157).

[75] McFague, *Super, Natural Christians*: 151.

[76] *Ibid*: 172-175.

[77] McGrath, *The Re-enchantment of Nature*: 188.

[78] McFague, Sallie, *The Body of God*: 20.

God's universe as a 'creation-community' may take us part of the way along the road. But there is a second revolution that Tacey insists must be experienced, a spiritual revolution that percolates deep within the human psyche: "[t]he truly ecological task is to repair not just our damage in the outer world but also the deep splits in our psychological make-up and dualistic world view."[79]

The Spirit as *Anima Mundi*, or Cosmic *Élan Vital*

Contemporary physics – especially the non-locality principle in quantum theory – reminds us that all of creation may be interpreted within a holistic frame of reference: in other words, the universe is a dynamic whole whose parts are essentially related. In the last chapter we suggested that the complexities of quantum mechanics have opened up one possible way in which to understand how the Spirit may be at work in creation: highly interconnected and complex networks of non-local correlations reflect the manifestation of God's 'loving entanglement' with the world. However, the Spirit has often been confined to personal piety and ecclesial activity, with little attention being given to his role in creation. Whilst there are only a few biblical texts that demonstrate the link between the Spirit and creation, their scarcity should not undermine their vital connection. Pinnock traces the scriptural evidence, concluding that the "Spirit is present and active in creation – in its inception, continuation and perfection."[80] He goes on to say that the Spirit "indwells creation and works on the inside of it by means of subtle operations."[81] How then might we interpret the Spirit's presence in creation?

Some theologians, notably Wolfhart Pannenberg, have utilised the insights of scientific field theory as a metaphor for the energies of the Holy Spirit in creation.[82] Pinnock follows a similar line in proposing that the Spirit is "the

---

[79] Tacey, David, *ReEnchantment: The New Australian Spirituality*, Sydney: HarperCollins*Publishers*, 2000: 177; notably, the trinitarian doctrine of *perichoresis* emerges as a central insight in Tacey's example of the Australian Aboriginal people, for whom land is an extension of themselves.

[80] Pinnock, Clark H., *Flame of Love: A Theology of the Holy Spirit*, Downers Grove: IVP, 1996: 52-55; Pinnock acknowledges the insights of some theologians, such as Calvin, who recognise the Spirit's cosmic functions; however, it is only in the second half of the twentieth century that theologians of the calibre of Moltmann, Torrance, Pannenberg and Gunton have articulated a comprehensive cosmic theology of the Spirit (as discussed in Chapter 3).

[81] *Ibid*: 66.

[82] See Chapter 5 for a brief discussion of field theory, with particular reference to Wolfhart Pannenberg ('Quantum mechanics, entanglement and the doctrine of *perichoresis*'). See also Thomas Torrance's contention that Maxwell's dynamical field theory was the most important development in physics between Newton and Einstein, in his introduction to his edited publication of Maxwell, J. C., *A Dynamical Theory of the*

field of creativity shaping the process" of *creatio continua*.[83] In the previous chapter, we concluded that the universe is an emergent, self-organising and interconnected network of dynamic processes in which the Spirit is active as the preserver of both gloriously inventive difference and transcendent symbiotic harmony. He is the "dynamic flow of divine power that sustains the universe, bringing forth life."[84] Taking an eschatological perspective, he is the perfecting Spirit, acting with perichoretic grace and love as he steers all creation towards its final goal. These expressions of Spirit life and energy are consistent with much contemporary thinking about the role of the Spirit in a cosmic context. However, a growing number of writers are beginning to think of the Spirit's activity with reference to the metaphysical language of 'soul'.

In *Science and Wisdom*, a collection of articles that explore the contemporary scientific quest from the perspective of Christian insights, Moltmann examines the case of the sixteenth-century Dominican monk and philosopher Giordano Bruno, who was condemned to death for heresy.[85] Amongst other things, Bruno was accused by the Catholic authorities of identifying the Spirit with the *anima mundi*, or 'world soul', a pure universal spirit regarded by ancient philosophers as the divine essence that enfolds and energises all life in the universe: the Stoic philosophers believed the *anima mundi* to be the only vital force in the universe. Plato was the first to suggest that the notion of 'world soul' held the same relation to the physical creation as the human soul did to the body in anthropology. The term 'world soul' – which conceptually is not too far from the theory of an 'implicate order' proposed by David Bohm – could be misleading as an expression of the life force of the universe because of its appropriation in Asian philosophical thinking and in Hindu religion, where it assumes a pantheistic significance. However, if the Spirit of God, *distinct* from creation, is understood to be the organising, orchestrating energy of the world, then it is logically possible to retain the idea of the Spirit as the divine pan*en*theistic *anima mundi* without dissolving God in the world or losing sight of his transcendence. Moltmann is clear on this point:

> The justifiable fear of pantheism ... must not lead to the destruction of the true pan-entheism, which we find in Bruno and Goethe. It is only if God remains God that his immanence in the world effects what is everywhere detectible: the self-transcendence of all open-life systems, their evolution, and their ever more complex warp and weft in relationships of community; for it is in this immanence that we find the

---

Electromagnetic Field (1864), with an Appreciation by A. Einstein, Edinburgh: Scottish Academic Press: 1982: ix-27.

[83] Pinnock, *Flame of Love*: 65.

[84] Johnson, Elizabeth, *Women, Earth, and Creator Spirit*, New York: Paulist Press, 1993: 42.

[85] Moltmann, "'From the Closed World to the Infinite Universe': The Case of Giordano Bruno": 158-171.

'more' which thrusts beyond every existing condition.[86]

Bruno was burnt at the stake in 1600, in spite of his defence that his ideas were those of a philosopher rather than a theologian. However, his advocacy of the Spirit as *anima mundi* – or 'soul-ecology', in the words of Thomas Moore[87] – lives on in contemporary thinking. Moltmann describes the Creator Spirit as a divine artist who pours his whole soul into his creation.[88] McFague is similarly inspired by the concept, which she defines as "a sensibility that sees other people, animals, mountains, and even city buildings as presenting themselves to us vividly, each in its own particularity, independence, and subjectivity."[89] An intriguing exchange between Phaedrus and his son John in Robert Pirsig's *Zen and the Art of Motorcycle Maintenance* suggests that we should not be too hasty in dispensing with such a concept:

> After a while [John] says, "Do you believe in ghosts?"
> "No", I say.
> "Why not?"
> "Because they are *un*-sci-en-*ti*-fic."
> The way I say this makes John smile. "They contain no matter," I continue, "and have no energy and therefore, according to the laws of science, do not exist except in people's minds."
> The whisky, the fatigue and the wind in the trees start mixing in my mind. "Of course," I add, "the laws of science contain no matter and have no energy either and therefore do not exist except in people's minds." [90]

Ultimately, "the pictures we draw, the systems we build, can never fully

---

[86] *Ibid*: 170. For a similar understanding of trinitarian panentheism in which divine transcendence and divine immanence are seen as mutually presupposing, see Edwards, Denis, *Breath of Life: A Theology of the Creator Spirit*, Maryknoll: Orbis Books, 2004, 130-142.

[87] Moore, Thomas, *Care of the Soul: A Guide for Cultivating Depth and Sacredness in Everyday Life*, New York: HarperCollins, 1992: 268.

[88] Moltmann, "'From the Closed World to the Infinite Universe': The Case of Giordano Bruno": 169.

[89] McFague, *Super, Natural Christians*: 112.

[90] Pirsig, Robert M., *Zen and the Art of Motorcycle Maintenance: An Inquiry into Values*, London: The Bodley Head, 1974: 38. And if the 1s and 0s of binary code are cited to support the proposal that information theory lies at the heart of physical laws, thereby grounding them in the material world, Johnson warns that "the price for banishing platonic mysticism may be a dizzying self-referential swirl: the laws of physics are made of information; information behaves according to the laws of physics. Everything begins to seem like ghosts" (Johnson, George, *Fire in the Mind: Science, Faith and the Search for Order*, London: Viking, 1996: 25).

embrace the richness and the unruliness of creation."[91] Or, as Thomas Torrance puts it, human beings "cannot pursue natural science scientifically without engaging at the same time in meta-scientific operations."[92]

It is apparent from our discussion above that the community of creation may be understood as a web of life inhabited and energised by the Holy Spirit. The creative and re-creative Spirit is the vitalising Spirit, active from the moment of the big bang, releasing life and possibility as creation unfolds and reaches towards its intended goal. This is consistent with the proposal sustained throughout this book that the activity of the Spirit is the eschatological power of God at work in all creation, enabling all that exists to fully and finally become itself in the freedom of divine love. All humanity is caught up in this eschatological drive towards fulfilment in God, who, as trinitarian love, welcomes and draws all creation – human and non-human – to himself through his Spirit. Susan Buckles picks up this theme, interpreting the Spirit as the life of creation: in bringing his gifts of life and freedom, "the Spirit's distinctive ministry is to complete God's purposes for human purposes and for all creation."[93]

A term popularised by the French philosopher Henri Bergson in the early twentieth century is *élan vital*, a metaphysical force thought to cause the evolution and development of organisms. 'Vitalisation' describes the process by which living things become more and more animated, ultimately expressed in terms of consciousness. At the pinnacle of the evolutionary chain, human beings are more vitalised than other organisms, more conscious and self-aware. The *élan vital* was therefore understood to be the source of life itself, permeating the cosmos and departing from us when we die.[94] *Élan vital* is Bergson's term for what he saw as a very conscious inner creative impulse, the antithesis to the analytical intellect. In similar vein, Tillich considers human beings to be "fully rational only on the foundation of, and in interdependence

---

[91] Johnson, *Fire in the Mind*: 28.

[92] Torrance, Thomas F., *Divine and Contingent Order*, Oxford: Oxford University Press, 1981: 3.

[93] See Buckles, Susan, "Life in the Spirit and the Spirit of Life" in Speidell, Todd H. (ed), *On Being Christian ... and Human: Essays in Celebration of Ray S. Anderson*, Eugene OR: Wipf and Stock Publishers, 2002: 128-146.

[94] Vitalism (or vitalisation) is an anti-reductionist philosophy, referring to the holistic idea that life is an emergent process that cannot be reduced to chemical processes that occur in the cell. The concept has been discarded by many at a purely scientific level with advances in biochemistry, although our understanding of the biochemical processes that distinguish living from non-living matter has become increasingly sophisticated, with the realisation that these fundamental processes are incredibly complicated. But the concept has significant philosophical currency in the context of our present discussion (see, on this, http://www.fact-index.com/v/vi/vitalism.html, accessed on 12.05.04).

with, nonrational factors."[95] Commenting on the victory of the nineteenth-century 'bourgeois revolution', which exalted utilitarianism as a philosophy of cultural and personal life, Tillich argues that the predominance of 'technical reason' – the sacrifice of reason as a principle of truth and justice, and its employment as a tool in the service of technical society – "evoked a reaction by the vital forces in man."[96]

These 'vital forces' are, for Tillich, powerful inner impulses that enable human beings to discover their purpose for living, empowering them with 'the courage to be'. Tillich defines the 'courage to be' as "the ethical act in which man affirms his own being in spite of those elements of his existence which conflict with his essential self-affirmation."[97] He was well aware that these forces could be expressed as a 'will to power' shaped by destructive political or cultural goals, as in the totalitarian Fascist and Soviet movements that arose during his lifetime. But, at a more profound level, they cause human beings to pursue a path of idealism and self-fulfilment, an enthusiasm and adventure for life to be experienced in full technicolour. In its most fruitful expression, *élan vital*, or vitality, is interpreted by Moltmann as 'an undreamt-of love for life':

> In this world, with its modern 'sickness unto death', true spirituality will be the restoration of the love for life – that is to say, *vitality*. The full and unreserved 'yes' to life, and the full and unreserved love for the living are the first experiences of God's Spirit, which is not for nothing called *fons vitae*, 'the well of life'.[98]

In the Hindu religion, the concept of vitality, or *élan vital*, may be likened – in its highest-ranking state – to Brahma, the stream of pure consciousness that unites human beings with nature in pantheistic bliss. Throughout the world in various belief systems and cultures, the concept has its equivalents, as in the Chinese life force 'Chi', and the Sanskrit 'Prana'. Within the Wisdom

---

[95] From "The World Situation", the opening chapter in a volume of collected essays and other writings by Paul Tillich in Thomas, J. Mark (ed), *The Spiritual Situation in Our Technical Society: Paul Tillich*, Macon: Mercer University Press, 1988: 12.

[96] *Ibid*: 12. Drawing from the insights of Hobbes and his theory of the absolute state, Tillich utilises the biblical symbol of Leviathan in his analysis of the crisis of contemporary world society. He argues that 'Leviathan' "swallows all elements of independent existence, political and economic, cultural and religious", but warns of the danger of falling into a form of liberal laissez-faire individualism as a reaction against totalitarian absolutism (*ibid*: 7-10).

[97] Tillich, Paul, *The Courage to Be*, London: Collins Fontana, 1952: 15. Tillich embodies in this book the substance of the 27th series of lectures delivered at Yale University in 1952 under the auspices of the Terry Foundation – the cardinal tenets of the Foundation are 'loyalty to the truth, lead where it will, and devotion to human welfare'.

[98] Moltmann, Jürgen, *The Spirit of Life: A Universal Affirmation*, Minneapolis: Fortress Press, 1992; the contrast between 'spirituality' and 'vitality' – and the need to integrate the two concepts in a new vitality of 'life against death' – is explored by Moltmann within the framework of the liberation of the body for its true health (*ibid*: 83-98).

Christology of the Christian tradition the *élan vital* is analogous to Sophia, the Wisdom of God, who, as Edwards has demonstrated, is "radically associated with creation and with all creatures, [and] who pitches a tent among us in Jesus of Nazareth."[99]

A distinctively *Christian* interpretation of *élan vital* therefore requires us to propose an identity between the creative, life-giving ecological Spirit of God and the redeeming Spirit of Christ. They are not separate or different in some way: they are one and the same. This is a crucial trinitarian insight: as Yahweh's creative *ruach*[100], the same creating Spirit of the Father is the redeeming Spirit of Christ. To speak of the Spirit as God's cosmic *élan vital* is therefore to posit a continuity between the Spirit who enlivens and sanctifies us in our relation to God and the Spirit who enlivens us in our relation to the created world. To deny this continuity is to polarise spirituality and vitality, isolate the soul from the body, and embrace a dualism that conflicts with the holism implicit in the biblical presentation of *imago Dei*.

Moltmann writes of the sensuousness of the divine Spirit, who stirs afresh in us a love of life and a love for the God who is the source and fullness of life. He is the Spirit who rekindles our senses so that we might experience the presence and life of God in all things and amongst those around us. Only this resounding 'yes' to life can contradict the crushing burden of death and our indifference to the pain and suffering around us. In his exposition of the 'cruciform creation', Holmes Rolston III alludes to a doctrine of providence in which all affliction is drawn into the divine will. "The world is not a paradise of hedonistic ease, but a theater where life is learned and earned by labor, a drama where even the evils drive us to make sense of things."[101] The 'genius' that makes alive and redeems from evil is, for Rolston, the Spirit of God, "the great divine yes hidden behind and within every no of crushing nature."[102] The Spirit who lures creation towards its eschatological goal is also the quickening Spirit who awakens us to a new love – a new love for God and all that finds its place in God:

> When I love God I love the beauty of bodies, the rhythm of movements, the shining of eyes, the embraces, the feelings, the scents, the sounds of all this protean creation. When I love you, my God, I want to embrace it all, for I love you with all my senses in the creations of your love.[103]

---

[99] Edwards, *Jesus the Wisdom of God*: 19.

[100] For a discussion of the continuity between the redemptive and creating Spirit, see Moltmann, *The Spirit of Life*: 8-10.

[101] Rolston, Holmes, III, "Does Nature Need to be Redeemed?" in *Zygon: Journal of Religion and Science*. Vol. 29, No. 2 (June, 1994): 219.

[102] *Ibid*: 220.

[103] Moltmann, Jürgen, *The Source of Life: The Holy Spirit and the Theology of Life*, London: SCM Press, 1997: 88 (cited also in Chapter 3).

The Integrating Concept of *Imago Dei*

The doctrine of *imago Dei* has been introduced at various stages throughout this study as a means of demonstrating the interconnectedness between a number of concepts that are central to the primary thesis. Acknowledging the growing awareness within the Christian community of the impact of science and technology on contemporary life, we noted in the first chapter that a comprehensive theology of *imago Dei* requires a healthy and positive interaction between human beings and their environment. This theme has been sustained in subsequent chapters, with particular recognition, in Douglas John Hall's words, that human spirituality is cheapened when it fastens on the divine in such a way as to exclude nature and even history from the realm of transcendent wonder. A pivotal affirmation is that human beings have been created for relationship, not just with God and each other, but also with the physical world, to the extent that the fate of humankind is inextricably linked to that of planet Earth.

A second major theme integral to the concept of *imago Dei* is that human beings are created not just for insular, exclusive relationships with one another but for richly-textured communal life together, mirroring the generosity of the Trinity in whose divine life in the world the ecclesial community participates. Because God's life is essentially *ekstatic*, reaching out to embrace all that he has created, the life of the Christian faith-community – defined by LaCugna as an 'icon of the Trinity' – is similarly inclusive in its welcoming, hospitable attention not only to those who confess the Christian faith, but also to those who are outside its borders. The divinely-ordained social structure of humanity means that human beings "exist first of all as co-humanity, in a polarity of relation through which the image and likeness of God is discerned as responsible love."[104] As Anderson points out, Cain's murder of Abel is "first of all an act against the *imago Dei* which cannot be destroyed in one without damaging the other."[105]

To live authentically in the image of God is therefore to acknowledge our essential interdependence, even as we acknowledge our individual uniqueness. In fact, as we noted in Chapter 4, our particularity derives from the very interactions in which we are historically and necessarily involved as human beings whose lives are embedded in community, not just within the pastoral community of faith but more widely in solidarity with all humanity, and within the whole 'creation-community' web of life. Tillich makes the same point in his understanding of the basic ontological structure of humanity. On the one hand, a human being's value "is a consequence of the ontological self-affirmation as an

---

[104] Anderson, Ray S., *On Being Human: Essays in Theological Anthropology*, Eerdmans: Grand Rapids, 1982: 154.

[105] *Ibid*: 154; this is because both Cain and Abel "bear the *imago Dei* as a concrete and social structure of their human existence."

indivisible, unexchangeable self."¹⁰⁶ On the other hand, "the self is only self because it has a world, a structured universe, to which it belongs and from which it is separated at the same time. Self and world are correlated and so are individualization and participation."¹⁰⁷

The problem of human existence, however, is that the essential interdependence between the 'courage to be oneself' and the 'courage to be as a part' – i.e. as a part of the world to which a human being belongs as a *participant* – has become 'existentially split' because of human finitude and estrangement. Tillich exegetes this existential split in *The Courage to Be*, arguing that true faith embraces both human striving for union with ultimate reality and personal encounter with God: it transcends both mystical participation and personal confidence. For Tillich, this transcendence is exemplified in the lives of Martin Luther, representing ecclesiastical Protestantism, and his great adversary Thomas Münzer, representing evangelical radicalism:

> Both men experienced the anxiety of meaninglessness and described it in terms which had been created by Christian mystics. But in doing so they transcended the courage of confidence which is based on a personal encounter with God. They had to receive elements from the courage to be which is based on mystical union.¹⁰⁸

Tillich's ontology of humanity is profoundly rich in its insistence that to be created *imago Dei* takes us beyond the experience of personal encounter with God into an awareness that we are embraced, even carried, by a transcendent power of being in which all things participate. This is expressed in his notion of the 'God above God', the 'ground of being' that both includes and transcends the type of theism that is epitomised in the divine-human 'I-Thou' personal encounter. Ultimately, Tillich's 'ground of being' theology is untestable precisely because, in our finite understanding, we are unable to fully comprehend who 'God above God' really is, let alone describe this God in any meaningful way. Any shift from the infinite to the finite (in Tillichian terms, from 'essence' to 'existence') necessarily corrupts our understanding of God. But Tillich's theological enterprise has value in pointing us towards a dialectical interpretation of participation, in which the world, or structured universe, "would not be what it is without *this* individual self."¹⁰⁹ In other words, his correlation of individualisation and participation affirms the essential

---

¹⁰⁶ Tillich, *The Courage to Be*: 90; Tillich calls this ontological self-affirmation 'the courage to be oneself' – he denounces "the bad theological usage of jumping with moral indignation on every word in which the syllable 'self' appears" (*ibid*: 90).
¹⁰⁷ *Ibid*: 90.
¹⁰⁸ *Ibid*: 166.
¹⁰⁹ *Ibid*: 91.

interdependence between human beings and the created world. We might term his understanding of *imago Dei* as an 'anthropological ontology of participation'.

Following a similar line, Hall expounds his 'Being=Being-With' equation with reference to the German word *Mitsein*, which literally means 'with-being'. The word – invented by Heidegger – resonates with many words that are common in everyday German speech, reflecting a world "in which all things interact, a world where mystery means the encounter of being-with-being (*Untereinandersein*), a world in which reality is discovered in reciprocity."[110] Hall further elucidates *Mitsein* in terms of the Hebrew concept of *shalom*, which articulates the mutuality of all that exists in a state of wholeness and well-being, incorporating the ideas of completeness, soundness, welfare and peace.[111] All three great monotheistic faiths – Christianity, Judaism and Islam – subscribe to the concept of *shalom* or *salam*. In the New Testament the Greek word 'eirene' has much the same meaning and usage as *shalom*, and draws from the Old Testament focus on inward peace and outward prosperity. The name of Islam is derived from the word 'salam', which literally means to be safe, secure, sound, wholesome, unharmed, unimpaired and intact, where every thing finds its fullness, glory and perfection. The state of 'salam' refers to the inner state of internal peace, characterised by symmetry and equilibrium.[112]

Shalom also resonates with *perichoresis* in its emphasis on the harmonious integration of all things whilst maintaining distinction. *Shalom* implies 'peace for all people', focusing on the notion of the individual-in-community, and the idea of 'completeness' suggests wholeness brought about by the coming together of different parts. Besides the commonly accepted theme of 'peace for all people', *shalom* conveys two further goals for life: liberation for creation and justice for humanity.[113] These themes are closely interrelated and overlap. In his book *Spirituality and Liberation*, Robert McAfee Brown expounds Micah 6:8, arguing that the verse is not about "*three different assertions* being made, but one assertion being made in *three different ways*." So we "cannot talk compellingly about any one of the three phrases until we have talked about all three of them." He expresses the logic of his argument in the form of three

---

[110] Hall, *Imaging God*: 118-119.

[111] See Brown, Francis *et al*, *The Brown-Driver-Briggs Hebrew and English Lexicon*, Peabody MA: Hendrickson, 2000: 1022-1023.

[112] Based on a discussion with Arthur Saniotis, following a paper, "Reflections on *TAWHID* (Divine Unity): Islam and Ecology", presented at a conference on 'Ecology and Biodiversity: Theological and Scientific Perspectives', Adelaide SA, 23-25 January 2004. See Saniotis, Arthur, "Nature as an Expression of *TAWHID* (Divine Unity): Islam and Ecology" in Edwards, Denis and Worthing, Mark (eds), *Biodiversity and Ecology as Interdisciplinary Challenge*, Adelaide: ATF Press, 2004: 101-108.

[113] As indicated in the full title, see Duchrow, Ulrich and Liedke, Gerhard, *Shalom: Biblical Perspectives on Creation, Justice and Peace*, Geneva: WCC Publications, 1989, for a complete exposition of these themes.

Imaging the Perichoretic God

equations: to *act justly* means to love tenderly and to walk humbly with God; to *love tenderly* means to walk humbly with God and to act justly; to *walk humbly with God* means to act justly and to love tenderly.[114]

The biblical notion of *imago Dei* integrates these three equations in its emphasis on the twin themes of ecojustice – caring for planet Earth – and social justice – caring for one another – within the overarching framework of a humble relationship with God. Hall cites Birch and Rassmussen, who draw from a wide range of Old Testament material, particularly the Wisdom Literature and the Genesis creation myths, for their perception of humanity's 'rootedness in creation' and 'shared finitude with all God's creation'.[115] God's eschatological purposes are then articulated in terms of a redemptive *shalom* for the whole of creation, involving the restoration of the relationship between God, humanity and nature, in which humanity finds its rightful place *within*, not *above*, nature:

> Is the redemptive activity of God and the redemptive work of Christ directed and limited to the human? Many would say so, but it hardly seems possible biblically. Unless we see human life lived in a vacuum, redemption must involve the rest of nature as well because redemption is precisely God's effort to restore the whole network of relationships that have been broken by sin.[116]

McAfee Brown's equations from Micah 6:8 may also be expressed negatively, as highlighted by Hall in his incisive critique of 'man against nature': "there can be no mastery of nature that does not finally disclose itself as the necessity of mastering *human* nature."[117] Hall traces this predicament to a predominant hierarchical view of creation, in which the endeavour to control assumes a destructive spiral affecting nature and humanity alike. The only way of escape is a renewed awareness of the holistic relational ontology that lies at the heart of *imago Dei*. "And for the human creature, to be *imago Dei* means also to be *imago mundi*."[118] As dust of the earth, we are in continuity with nature: "our imaging of God is inseparable from our imaging of the earth."[119] This insight derives not only from the biblical affirmation of human creatureliness but also from the expanded knowledge of the physical world available from contemporary physics which "alters the manner in which

---

[114] Brown, Robert McAfee, *Spirituality and Liberation: Overcoming the Great Fallacy*, London: Hodder & Stoughton Ltd., 1988: 70.
[115] Birch, Bruce C. and Rassmussen, Larry L., *The Predicament of the Prosperous*, Philadelphia: The Westminster Press, 1978: 121 (see Hall, *Imaging God*: 168-171 for a discussion of Birch and Rassmussen's biblical scholarship).
[116] Birch and Rassmussen, *The Predicament of the Prosperous*: 122.
[117] Hall, *Imaging God*: 165, my italics
[118] *Ibid*: 179.
[119] *Ibid*: 179.

humans relate to the world."[120] This alteration may be expressed in terms of a shared suffering, a Tillichian 'participation' that controverts the dominating motif of human superiority over nature. It is the fellowship of suffering that human beings share with all of creation, epitomised in Moltmann's 'creation-community'. Suffering redemption lies at the heart of all creation:

> The whole of the earthen metabolism needs to be understood as having this character. The God met in physics as the divine wellspring from which matter-energy bubbles up, as the upslope epistemic force, is in biology the suffering and resurrecting power that redeems life out of chaos.[121]

The significance of this statement will be discussed more fully in the next section, which explores the extension of the *imago Dei* motif to physical creation itself. More generally, however, it is clear that the motif powerfully integrates key themes explored throughout this book. As those who have been created in God's image, human beings are free to participate in God's ongoing creativity in the world, finding *shalom* fulfilment within God's 'creation-community'.

As we noted in Chapter 2, the pastoral theologian Frank Wright invites us to participate intimately and adventurously in God's good and holy creation precisely because we are thereby enabled to discover the richness of life in all its intensity and depth. But pride – the arrogant Babel-like lust for power and quest for 'pseudotranscendence'[122] – has turned us away from our God-ordained 'ontology of communion' with nature. Indeed, as Moltmann points out, to speak of nature in terms of *our* environment is already to diminish nature's integrity by making it part of the human world. Nature will not – cannot – be saved that way.[123] Nor can human redemption be achieved by returning to nature, as some contemporary spiritual gurus maintain. What is needed is the recognition that "transcendence is immanent in every natural being": when we name the reality in which we live 'creation', we are expressing in the strongest possible way "resistance to the transformation of nature into *human environment*."[124]

Nature as *Imago Dei*?

In his assessment of nature as sacred reality, Langdon Gilkey extends the *imago Dei* motif to creation itself. Tracing the desacralisation of nature to the post-

---

[120] Liderbach, Daniel, *The Numinous Universe*, New York: Paulist Press, 1989:4, cited earlier in Chapter 5.
[121] Rolston, "Does Nature Need to be Redeemed?": 219.
[122] A term used by Hall, *Imaging God*: 179-180; 'pseudo' because this desire does not properly belong to our essential, created being.
[123] See Moltmann, *The Source of Life*: 118-121.
[124] *Ibid*: 121, my italics.

Imaging the Perichoretic God

Renaissance development of modern science and technology, he invites us to reflect upon nature as a creature of God that, like human beings, has value, integrity, order and worth. God speaks through his creation, as the biblical witness testifies, revealing himself in his majesty, power and beauty through images drawn from the grandeur of nature. Furthermore,

> ... experience of *life* in nature, of life in ourselves as part of nature – that is, of our existence in nature – puts us in touch with the awesome and infinitely valuable reality of life, the wonder, power, and terror of life: fertility and birth, blood, breath, vitality, ecstasy (cf. Matt. 22:32; Josh. 3:10; 1 Tim. 4:10; Heb. 10:31). These signs of life are vivid in both our outer and our inner experience of nature ... [125]

It is in these ways, argues Gilkey, that nature incarnates powers and values that we associate with God – infinity, power, life, order, uniqueness or individuality, and self-affirmation – obligating us to treat creation as an *end* as well as a means.[126]

Widening the scope of the *imago Dei* symbol to embrace the natural world should not trouble us too much: it is entirely in keeping with the nature of theology as a contextual discipline to appropriate traditional metaphors and symbols and test their applicability to new areas of theological concern. This is what we referred to in Chapter 2 as *theologia viatorum*, or, to use Anderson's phrase, 'theological innovation.'[127] We live in a vastly different world from that inhabited by the early formulators of the *imago Dei* doctrine, when it was shaped, in part, in response to Gnostic assertions of body-soul dualism. Significantly, however, contemporary ecological concerns are not too far removed from these Gnostic claims, for they both have to do with the issue of how we respond to *physicality*.

In its earliest – and most commonly understood – role, the doctrine has to do with our inner structural make-up as human beings, reflecting 'capacities' that distinguish human beings from other creatures[128] – this is its traditional

---

[125] Gilkey, *Nature, Reality, and the Sacred*: 151, author's italics.

[126] Gilkey closes his book by emphasising the sacramental quality of nature: "To know God truly is to know God's presence also in the power, the life, the order, and the redemptive unity of nature. Correspondingly, to know nature truly is to know its mystery, its depth, and its ultimate value – it is to know nature as an image of the sacred, a visible sign of an invisible grace" (*ibid*: 204).

[127] Anderson, Ray S., *The Shape of Practical Theology: Empowering Ministry with Theological Praxis*, Downers Grove: IVP, 2001: 17-24.

[128] For a helpful summary of two historical conceptions of *imago Dei* – the substantialist and relational – see Hall, *Imaging God*: 88-112. For a scholarly critique of the substantive dualistic metaphysics underlying classical theological anthropology, see Shults, F. LeRon, *Reforming Theological Anthropology: After the Philosophical Turn to Relationality*, Grand Rapids: Eerdmans, 2003.

'substantialist', or ontological, interpretation. Within the framework of its relational significance, we extended the doctrine to include how we relate as human beings to that which lies *outside* us. Throughout this study we have sustained the thesis that humanity is critically related to nature, even dependent upon the natural order for its existence. This can be amplified in terms of *imago mundi* to express our continuity with the dust of the earth. A third possible understanding of *imago Dei* takes us into more controversial theological territory as we conceive of nature itself as an image of the divine Creator. Gilkey supports this more inclusive interpretation of *imago Dei* on the grounds that "the desacralization of nature in traditional Christian faith, in order to make room for the growth of the religious vitality and value of the human, has in the end helped to desacralize both human being and nature."[129] In other words, the failure to uphold the fundamental ecological principle of 'earthkeeping' derives, in part, from an over-emphasis on *imago Dei* as a symbol of *human* value and integrity at the expense of nature's integrity and worth. It is time to be more inclusive.

Conventional interpretations of the image of God doctrine imply a correspondence between human beings and God, with the potentiality for relationship at the level of I-Thou, expressed in the human longing for transcendence. In addition, our capacity to "peer into the mind of God"[130] has also been regarded as an important feature of the doctrine. How valid is it, therefore, to extend the *imago Dei* symbol to a physical creation that is unable to experience the sort of personal relationship that marks out human beings from the rest of creation? Nature cannot love as God loves, and as human beings are called to do. Nature cannot rationally apprehend and behold God. However, to respond to the question within the traditional interpretive framework of *imago Dei* may be too limiting a perspective. As Hall reminds us, "theology was made for human beings, not human beings for theology."[131]

In his intriguing analysis of the contemporary postmodern era, Trainor suggests that postmodernism may be interpreted as a form of 'pre-modern medievalism'. He summarises the medieval view as the conviction that "all living things *participate* in their own way in the Divine Life and that in so doing they, in a sense, 'live the Life of God'."[132] This paradigm of reality assumes an inner spiritual connection between human beings and nature within an 'all-encompassing Nature or World Soul', which was reinforced by medieval Christianity. There is, for Trainor, a certain logic in making the link between the pre-modern notion of 'World Soul' and the Christian understanding of the Spirit:

---

[129] Gilkey, *Nature, Reality, and the Sacred*: 181.
[130] McGrath, *The Re-enchantment of Nature*: 22.
[131] Hall, Douglas John, *Thinking the Faith*, Minneapolis: Fortress Press, 1991: 63.
[132] Trainor, Brian, *The Origin and End of Modernity: Reflections on the Meaning of Post-Modernism*, Quebec: World Heritage Press, 1998: 2, author's italics.

> Certainly, it is but a small step from thinking of 'Nature' as the pervasive pattern or order of the world, as its designing Spirit, as the integrative process which assigns to each of 'its' species its proper place in the scheme of things, or as Life itself, as the womb or mother from whom all life flows, to thinking of Nature under the influence of Christianity as the all-pervasive Spirit of Life (the Holy Spirit, as Lord and Giver of Life) sustaining all living things and providing the principle of unity to the wondrous diversity of the world.[133]

Trainor traces modernism's decisive rejection of medievalism through William of Ockham – an 'apprentice sorcerer in philosophy' who "unleashed and encouraged forces which he himself could not possibly control after setting them free"[134] – and the intellectual optimism of Francis Bacon, to the 'towering figure' of Thomas Hobbes. Hobbes' distinctive contribution to the modernist project was to disentangle the human self from its 'home' in the world, with the result that human beings were seen as confronting nature as an alien and brutish world, a world robbed of both cosmic order and the integrating principle of Divine Reason. In the spirit of Hobbes, the late seventeenth-century philosopher John Locke developed his theory of appropriation, arguing that those who pour themselves into the land are entitled to acquire a property interest in the result. This process of appropriation could continue indefinitely so long as there was enough left for others to take advantage of the natural resources available for cultivation. Unfortunately, under the guise of 'progress', this opened wide the door for the abuse of nature for personal gain.

In contrast to Hobbesian and Lockean philosophies of thought that encouraged the rape of nature – further fuelled by the scientific rationalism of the Enlightenment Era – the eighteenth-century French philosopher and author Jean-Jacques Rousseau's 'noble savage', in touch with nature at the most elemental level, exposes and condemns modernism's wanton ravage of the earth.[135] It is precisely this relationship between human beings and nature that "reappears as a central conviction and guiding principle of post-modern consciousness".[136] Contemporary concerns for the environment and the

---

[133] *Ibid*: 2; in a footnote, the author notes that "[i]n holding that there is a transcendental Creator-God, Christianity has nothing in common with the 'natural beliefs' of humanity, but in holding that God is also immanent and indwelling in all living forms in the world, Christianity entirely coincides with these natural beliefs and reinforces them where its influence is felt" (*ibid*: 8).

[134] Gilson, Etienne, *History of Christian Philosophy in the Middle Ages*, London: Sheed and Ward, 1978: 498.

[135] Trainor makes an important point when he notes that "despite the fact that Rousseau portrayed his noble savage as a kind of thoroughly instinctual, amoral creature, he now stands firmly and proudly on the high moral ground, casting his shadow of censure on the Lockean modernists in the valley below" (Trainor, *The Origin and End of Modernity*: 4).

[136] *Ibid*: 3; Brian Trainor presents us with a more positive assessment of postmodernism in *The Origin and End of Modernity*: he invites us to set aside preconceptions of its

preservation of endangered species suggest that we have come full-circle in acknowledging the medieval understanding of the essential interdependence between human existence and the natural world.[137] However, Trainor goes further in presenting his interpretation of what it means to be *authentically true to oneself*:

> ... the own self can only mean the point of convergence or intersection in each person between the Spirit of the Whole and the depths or innermost recesses of the self. On what other understanding of the own self would we trust ourselves to its intimations, and why would we believe that being attuned to this 'inner ear' will bring us into proper alignment with our fellow human beings, our environment, and our world, *unless* we are implicitly acknowledging all along that our own inner font merges into the font of an all-embracing Nature and that our true, inner spiritual self is informed by the Spirit of the Whole?[138]

This is the language of *imago Dei*: 'alignment with our fellow human beings, our environment, and our world' – the totality of which is informed, or shaped, by the Spirit who integrates and sustains all things, the 'Whole' of reality – represents the journey we have been travelling in this chapter. But, significantly, this sense of 'enveloping Nature' reflects, for Trainor, a correspondence between the interconnectedness that exists between the many different facets of the environment – and not just the immediate ecological environment, but, as we noted in Chapter 5, throughout the whole created universe – and the interconnectedness implicit in our own 'inner' human environment. The history of the world is the history of nature being summoned by the Spirit to *be itself* as a gloriously diverse and integrated perichoretic reality – even as human beings are being summoned by the same Spirit to discover *their true selves* in relationship with each other, with the world of nature and with the triune God who has brought all things into being.

In his counter-reading of Revelation 21.1-22.5 from the perspective of the earth, Reid draws from Moltmann's models of transformation and deification, both of which imply that this present world is valued for what it is as God's

---

relativistic and skeptical attitudes towards universal metanarratives, and to consider in particular the 'return to Nature' that lies at the heart of postmodernism as a reincarnation of 'pre-modern medievalism'. McGrath, on the other hand, suggests that postmodernism has failed to prevent exploitative attitudes towards nature, even to the point of sanctioning technological innovations that enable humanity to change itself and the world in the cause of political correctness (see McGrath, *The Re-enchantment of Nature*: 71-76).

[137] However, as Trainor points out throughout his book, whereas the medieval context was one of *feudalism*, the contemporary context within which the medieval 'return to Nature' has taken place is characterised by modern conditions of *freedom*.

[138] *Ibid*: 84, author's italics.

good creation.[139] Furthermore, in the context of the coming of the new creation, it "is not 'raw material' to be annihilated in the process, but is honoured in the new creation that descends from 'heaven' to transform and renew the earth."[140] Planet Earth is not an after-thought or secondary creation, having instrumental value only in subservience to the human race. An ill-considered anthropocentricism that places human beings at the centre of the world "leads certainly to that loss of sanity and sweetness which an openness to the abiding presence of the non-human living world around us infuses into life."[141] This line of thought takes us beyond Macmurray's personalistic philosophy outlined in Chapter 3, in which the Other is always conceived of in *personal* terms. Lowes argues for the unity of human beings and the universe at large on the grounds that "created persons *are* the universe come-to-consciousness, are stardust made luminous by self- and other-awareness":

> It could be said that [human persons] are *personed* insofar as they *in-person* others, that is, take others into their own personal substance, insofar as they dispossess themselves and dispose of themselves for and in others, including the non-personal 'others' of creation.[142]

The degree of intimacy implicit in the correspondence between the human and the natural suggested by both Trainor and Lowes argues strongly for a re-evaluation of the *imago Dei* concept in order to incorporate, in a modified sense, the status and value of the created universe. To move in this direction should not be interpreted as yielding to the seductive sirens of pantheism, although the possibility of such an interpretation should not be underestimated in the contemporary spiritual climate. Nor should we be dissuaded by those whose vision of *imago Dei* is restricted to the province of theological anthropology, on the grounds that the concept can only be of value in the context of human personality and identity. To claim that creation is, in some sense, *imago Dei*, is to recognise the integrity of nature as a *created* reality, distinct from its Creator, yet at the same time informed and enlivened by the breath of the Spirit – a creation marked by the most surprising interconnectedness between its particular elements, and reflecting the very character of its trinitarian Creator.

Throughout Chapter 5 we articulated a trinitarian theology of creation that not only holds transcendence and immanence together, distinguishing between Creator and creation, but also understands the universe as an emergent, self-

---

[139] See Moltmann, Jürgen, *The Coming of God: Christian Eschatology*, Minneapolis: Fortress Press, 1996: 270-275.
[140] Reid, "Setting Aside the Ladder to Heaven": 242.
[141] Trainor cites Bosanquet, Bernard., *The Principle of Individuality and Value* (the Gifford lectures for 1911), London: MacMillan, 1912: 370n. for this quote.
[142] Lowes, Anthony, "Up Close and Personal: In the End, Matter Matters" in Edwards (ed), *Earth Revealing – Earth Healing*: 143, author's italics.

organising and interconnected network of dynamic processes in which the Spirit is active as the preserver of both gloriously inventive difference and transcendent symbiotic harmony. Interconnectedness and particularity were identified in Chapter 3 as distinctive features of *perichoresis* within the life of the Christian God who lives eternally as the Three-in-One God, features which are evident in the creation that has been brought into being in the freedom of divine love. To make such a statement, supported by the scientific discoveries of quantum physics, evolutionary emergence, chaos and complexity, is to posit a natural world that mirrors the life of God in all of its perichoretic richness, wonder and mystery. And if it is claimed that nature does not answer God in the unique way that is privileged to human beings, does that lessen its integrity and value as a self-expression of the Trinity? Nor should we discount the possibility that one of the mysteries of nature may be the hiddenness of its response to the energies of the Spirit, who is ever at work calling forth from the depths of creation, coaxing creation towards its eschatological goal. Perhaps human beings might concede that nature is more constant in its response to the Spirit than they are, and to that extent a more faithful witness of *imago Dei*.

Imaging the Perichoretic God in the Community of Creation

The ideas expressed above may be represented diagrammatically, as portrayed on pages 283-284. In Diagram 1, the *imago Dei* finds its most complete expression in humanity at the centre, according to the classical Christian tradition. However, it is also reflected in the 'creation-community' of all creatures and environments residing *within* the perichoretic life of God. This way of thinking about *perichoresis* correlates with the more static, or passive, Latin term *circuminsessio*.[143] Another way of depicting this reflects the creative unfolding of creation from the trinitarian centre, with *imago Dei* again most fully expressed in the life of human community, but this time pictured on the edge of the diagram as a historically late development in the evolutionary process.

In Diagram 2, the dynamic unfolding of that which is already within is implicit, with different levels of reality articulating perichoretic life and energy under the impulse of the Spirit. The more dynamic Latin term of *circumincessio* for the Greek word *perichoresis* conveys the idea of 'temporal sequence' here (as distinct from the more limited sense of 'spatial juxtaposition' inherent in *circuminsessio* in Diagram 1).

---

[143] We noted in Chapter 3 that *circuminsessio* is derived from the Latin *circum-in-sedere*, meaning to sit around, and was therefore appropriated by those who preferred to adopt a more passive interpretation of trinitarian relatedness, such as Thomas Aquinas.

Imaging the Perichoretic God

Diagram 1

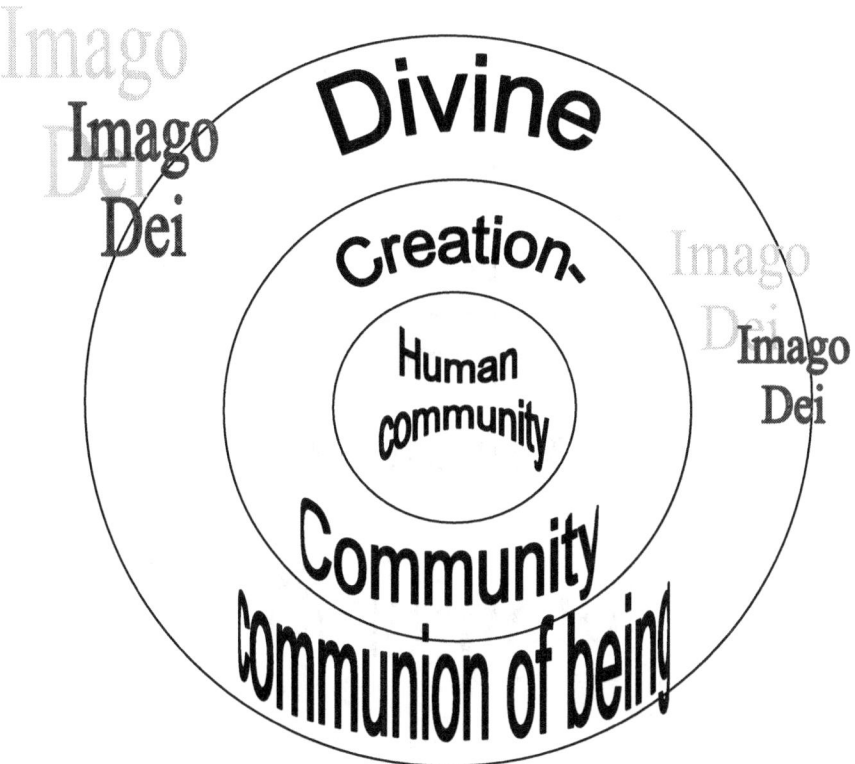

The two diagrams are intentionally simplistic: rather than trying to accommodate the complexities implicit in the three major areas of analysis explored in Chapters 3, 4 and 5 – trinitarian ontology, theological anthropology and scientific cosmology – the focus in this concluding chapter has been on the unfolding of a coherent structure of the *imago Dei* motif consistent with the trinitarian construct of *perichoresis*. A key argument underlying this idea is that the concept of *perichoresis* is a helpful analytical construct at each level of reality – divine, human and natural/physical – as well as *between* those levels. The unique context for this multi-levelled analysis is the pastoral ministry of the Christian community of faith. Specifically, we have maintained that a contextually-aware practical theology cannot ignore explicit engagement with the natural sciences if it is to have contemporary relevance in the practice of ministry. If those who are engaged in pastoral ministry are to examine with more than a passing nod the insights of the scientific community they need a

Diagram 2

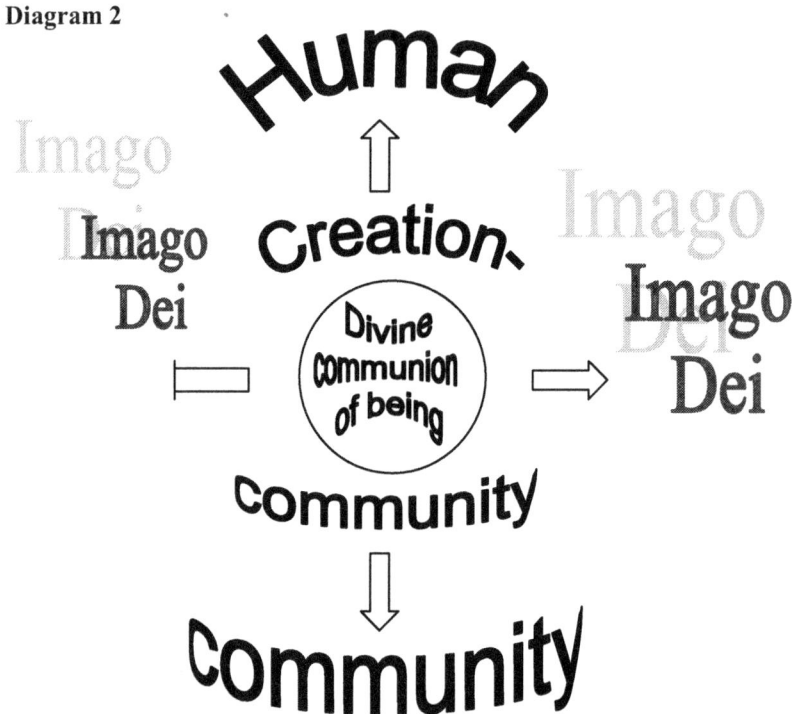

coherent framework within which to recognise the contributions of those who have too often been regarded as 'enemies of the faith'.

Inspired by the patristic scholar G. L. Prestige, Charles Williams refers to the complex interplay among the different elements of creation as 'the Co-inherence', the source of which is found in God, and God alone.[144] In his biblical assessment of creation as a single interdependent system, Houston argues that "self-sufficiency is the outrage of creation. The loss of community wounds creation. Creation 'groans' in the absence of co-inherence."[145] An example of the 'co-inherence' to which these writers refer may be found in the life of the nineteenth-century American 'poet-naturalist' Henry Thoreau, who returned to his native Concord in Massachusetts at the age of 27 in order to study nature, write and simplify his life.[146] At a symposium on 'Science,

---

[144] Cited in Houston, *I Believe in the Creator*: 17, referring to Prestige, G. L., *God in Patristic Thought*, London: SPCK, 1952: 282-302.

[145] Houston, *I Believe in the Creator*: 17.

[146] Some of the insights in this paragraph into Thoreau's life are taken from Furius, Lucius, *Genius Ignored: Rembrandt, Vermeer, Bach, Thoreau, Melville, Van Gogh, Nabokov, and* Casablanca, n.pl., 1977: Chapter 5, cited in http://eserver.org/thoreau/ignored.html, accessed 22.03.04; and Friesen, Carl Victor, "Seeing Beyond the Verge of

Spirituality and the Environment' held in Ontario, Canada, in 1999, Carl Friesen commented that, as a *complete human being*, Thoreau – who was a scientist in the sense that he took voluminous notes and measurements in order to gauge the 'grandeur' of creation – wanted to see more 'life' in scientific descriptions.[147] Shortly before his death in 1862, he described the wilderness as a treasure to be preserved rather than a resource to be plundered. Throughout his life, Thoreau sought to add a spiritual dimension to science, a 'further seeing beyond the verge of sight'. He would wander – he preferred the word 'saunter' – through nature with a sense of wonder, relating to the universe with a mystic-like intensity:

> I had seen into paradisaic regions.... Yet had I hardly a foothold there. I was only sure that I was charmed and no mistake. It is only necessary to behold thus the least fact or phenomenon, however familiar, from a point a hair's breadth aside from the habitual path or routine, to be overcome, enchanted by its beauty and significance.[148]

The suggestion that Thoreau was a pantheist is contradicted by his belief that there is "something superior to any particle of matter, in the idea or mind which uses and arranges the particles".[149] His view of God as immanent in nature was combined with a clear sense of divine transcendence, and so he might more appropriately be thought of as a panentheist. An entry in his journal in 1851 indicates that his profession was to 'find God in nature.'

The life of Henry Thoreau, infused with a rich and profound sense of wonder, reflects a 'complete human being' who had discovered how to live fully *imago Dei* with his fellow beings and with nature, and with a God who was, for him a 'Benefactor and Intelligence that stands over' nature, as he once wrote in *Walden* (which describes the simple life he led at Walden Pond for over two years). "His delicious prose and his descriptions of his interactions with nature testify to his firm belief that there is an unseen power just beyond the veil of the visible ... It is only through developing a proper relationship with

---

Sight: Thoreau's Nature as Incessant Miracle" in http://eserver.org/thoreau/beyond.html, accessed 22.03.04.

[147] For example, he spoke of a botany text having much detail about flowers but little of the flowers' inherent flower-like properties such as smell, taste and feeling (Friesen, "Seeing Beyond the Verge of Sight": [6]). As a youth Thoreau had spent his spare time exploring Concord's woods, fields, rivers, and ponds. He remembered visiting Walden Pond when he was only four years old, where he discovered a species of fish new to science, a striped bream, causing him to write, "I can only think of precious jewels, of music, poetry, beauty, and the mystery of life" (*ibid*: [20]). His later journals were filled with detailed scientific observations as he spent more and more of his time observing and recording.

[148] *Ibid*: [18].

[149] *Ibid*: [24].

nature that individuals and communities can achieve true fulfilment."[150] There is no doubt that, like many today who seek to relate to nature, Thoreau's understanding of God was eclectic, with discernible traces of nature mysticism, but this should not discourage us from seeing in his life an example of a person who was convinced of the interconnectedness between all things in creation. In particular, he insisted that human beings had a responsibility to care for creation in order to allow the natural world to be free to express itself in all its beauty and wonder.

My contention throughout this book is that the trinitarian doctrine of *perichoresis* provides pastoral workers with an effective and theologically robust conceptual instrument with which to engage with scientists "in intimate *dialogue*, rather than a distanced, guilt-ridden (if respectful) *dialectic*."[151] Little progress will be made if pastors fail to acknowledge the reality that binds all things in creation together. The discipline of informed dialogue not only broadens the horizons of those who are seeking to understand the world in which people live and move and have their being, but also generates a richer understanding of what it means to be made in the image of a God who has brought into being a creation that is rich and fecund. With these insights *those in pastoral ministry may be better enabled and willing to re-connect those in their care with the world of nature.* Chapter 2 concluded with the statement that to live more fully *imago Dei* may surely be regarded as the goal of all pastoral ministry. I suggest that this is perhaps the most significant pastoral dividend to be gained from the rich engagement between scientific, trinitarian and pastoral theology proposed throughout this book.

Thoreau's intense and unwavering involvement in God's creation points us towards our role in what Del Re calls the great 'cosmic Dance' of life: "it is the will of God that gives meaning to our life, and God's will is precisely that a person should fully live his or her life as a free, creative, passionate participant

---

[150] McGrath, *The Re-enchantment of Nature*: 136. The following is an example of Thoreau's prose in *Walden: The Pond in Winter* – "Standing on the snow-covered plain, as if in a pasture amid the hills, I cut my way first through a foot of snow, and then a foot of ice, and open a window under my feet, where, kneeling to drink, I look down into the quiet parlor of the fishes, pervaded by a softened light as through a window of ground glass, with its bright sanded floor the same as in summer; there a perennial waveless serenity reigns as in the amber twilight sky, corresponding to the cool and even temperament of the inhabitants. Heaven is under our feet is well as over our heads" (Thoreau, Henry D., *Walden* (edited by Walter Harding), Boston MA: Houghton Mifflin Co., 1995: 275).

[151] Lowes, "Up Close and Personal: In the End, Matter Matters": 142; the context of this statement for Lowes is, at the most general level, the engagement between human persons and the physical creation "through which encounter with the creating and transforming Others of the Trinity is facilitated", but his insight is particularly appropriate for the science-pastoral ministry interface.

in the cosmic Dance."[152] Not only does *imago Dei* encapsulate in all its richness the participation of a human being in the dance of life, a dance that has its genesis in the perichoretic dance of the triune God of love; it also explains why people have throughout the ages sought to understand the physical universe in which they are privileged to participate. To be made in God's image expresses both the *desire* and the *capacity* to investigate God's world, as well as the act of *living* human life within the created order, with all of its joys and sorrows, its ecstasy and its suffering.

Inherent in the human thirst for knowledge, understanding, wisdom and encounter with the natural order is "the drive to find a place for ourselves in a universe into which we never asked to be born."[153] The scientific endeavour is one expression of this ancient quest to locate human meaning and purpose within the perichoretic community of creation. For those who are critically involved in the pastoral ministry of the Christian faith-community, it is a quest that is enticingly situated at the nexus of science and faith. And, as demonstrated throughout this book, one of the pivotal theological concepts that nourishes the dialogue between science and faith is the trinitarian idea of *perichoresis*.

---

[152] Del Re, Guiseppe, *The Cosmic Dance: Science Discovers the Mysterious Harmony of the Universe*, Radnor PA: Templeton Foundation Press, 2000: 391.
[153] Johnson, *Fire in the Mind*: 8.

Bibliography

PASTORAL AND PRACTICAL THEOLOGY

Aden, Leroy and Ellens, J. Harold (eds.), *The Church and Pastoral Care*, Grand Rapids: Baker, 1988

Allmen, J.-J. von, *Worship: Its Theology and Practice*, London: Lutterworth Press, 1965

Anderson, Ray S. (ed.), *Theological Foundations for Ministry: Selected Readings for a Theology of the Church in Ministry*, Edinburgh: T. & T. Clark Ltd, 1979

—, *On Being Human: Essays in Theological Anthropology*, Eerdmans: Grand Rapids, 1982

—, *Ministry on the Fireline: A Practical Theology for an Empowered Church*, Downers Grove: IVP, 1993

—, *The Soul of Ministry: Forming Leaders for God's People*, Louisville: John Knox Press, 1997

—, *The Shape of Practical Theology: Empowering Ministry with Theological Praxis*, Wheaton: IVP, 2001

Arbuckle, Gerald, *Earthing the Gospel*, Homebush NSW: St Paul Publications, 1990

Augsburger, David, *Pastoral Counseling Across Cultures*, Philadelphia: Westminster, 1986

Ballard, Paul and Pritchard, John, *Practical Theology in Action: Christian Thinking in the Service of Christ and Society*, London: SPCK, 1996

Barth, Karl, *Church Dogmatics*, Edinburgh: T. & T. Clark, 1936-1969 (esp. Vols 3.4 and 4.1)

Benner, David G., *Care of Souls: Revisioning Christian Nurture and Counsel*, Grand Rapids: Baker Books, 1998

—, *Sacred Companions: The Gift of Spiritual Friendship and Direction*, Downers Grove: IVP, 2002

Boersma, Hans, "Liturgical Hospitality: Theological Reflections on Sharing in Grace" in *Journal for Christian Theological Research* 8 (2003)

Bosch, David J., *Transforming Mission: Paradigm Shifts in Theology of Mission*, Maryknoll: Orbis Books, 1991

Brister, C.W., *Pastoral Care in the Church*, (3rd edition, revised and expanded) San Francisco: HarperCollins*Publishers*: 1992

Brown, Robert McAfee, *Spirituality and Liberation: Overcoming the Great Fallacy*, London: Spire, 1988

Browning, Don S., (ed.) *Practical Theology,* San Francisco: Harper & Row, 1983

Browning, Don S., *A Fundamental Practical Theology: Descriptive and Strategic Proposals,* Minneapolis: Fortress Press, 1991

Buber, Martin, *I and Thou,* New York: Charles Scribner's Sons, 1958

Buckley, James J. and Yeago, David S (eds.), *Knowing the Triune God: The Work of the Spirit in the Practices of the Church,* Grand Rapids: Eerdmans, 2001

Buxton, Graham, *Dancing in the Dark: The Privilege of Participating in the Ministry of Christ,* Carlisle: Paternoster, 2001

Carr, Wesley, *The Pastor as Theologian,* London: SPCK, 1989

Clebsch, W. and Jaekle, C., *Pastoral Care in Historical Perspective* (2nd edition), New York: Aronson: 1983

Davies, Oliver and Bowie, Fiona, *Celtic Christian Spirituality,* London: SPCK, 1995

Deeks, David, *Pastoral Theology: An Inquiry,* London: Epworth Press, 1987

Donovan, Vincent J., *Christianity Rediscovered,* London: SCM Press, 1978

Engen, Charles van and Tiersma, Jude (eds.), *God So Loves the City: Seeking a Theology for Urban Mission,* Monrovia CA: MARC, 1994

Farley, Edward, *Theologia: Fragmentation and Unity in Theological Education,* Philadelphia: Fortress Press, 1983

Fiddes, Paul S., *Participating in God: A Pastoral Doctrine of the Trinity,* London: Darton, Longman & Todd, 2000

Fiorenza, Elisabeth Schussler, *In Memory of Her: A Feminist Reconstruction of Christian Origins,* London, SCM Press, 1983

Firet, Jacob, *Het agogisch moment in het pastoral optreden,* Kampen: 1968 (translated by Vriend, J. as *Dynamics in Pastoring,* Grand Rapids: Eerdmans, 1986)

Forrester, Duncan B., *Truthful Action: Explorations in Practical Theology,* Edinburgh: T. & T. Clark, 2000

Fowler, James, *Faith Development and Pastoral Care,* Philadelphia: Fortress Press, 1986

Fox, Matthew, *A Spirituality Named Compassion,* San Francisco: Harper, 1979

Frye, Marilyn, *The Politics of Reality: Essays in Feminist Theory,* Freedom CA: Crossing Press: 1983

Giles, Kevin, *The Trinity and Subordinationism: The Doctrine of God and the Contemporary Gender Debate,* Downers Grove: IVP, 2002

Graham, Elaine, *Transforming Practice: Pastoral Theology in an Age of Uncertainty,* London: Mowbray, 1996

Grierson, Denham, *Transforming a People of God,* Melbourne: JBCE, 1984

Hall, Douglas John, *Imaging God: Dominion as Stewardship,* Grand Rapids: Eerdmans, 1986

—, *Thinking the Faith,* Minneapolis: Fortress Press, 1991

Heitink, Gerban, *Practical Theology: History, Theory, Action Domains: Manual for Practical Theology,* Grand Rapids: Eerdmans, 1999

Hiltner, Seward, *Ferment in the Ministry,* Nashville: Abingdon Press, 1969

Hofmann, Hans (ed.), *Making the Ministry Relevant*, New York: Charles Scribner's Sons, 1960

Holmes, Urban T. III, *The Future Shape of Ministry: A Theological Projection*, New York: Seabury, 1971

Hurding, Roger, *The Bible and Counselling*, London: Hodder & Stoughton, 1992

Kallistos of Diokleia, "The human person as an icon of the Trinity" in *Sobornost*, Vol.8 No.2, 1986

Kettler, Christian D. and Speidell, Todd H. (eds.), *Incarnational Ministry: The Presence of Christ in Church, Society and Family*, Colorado Springs: Helmers & Howard, 1990

Kraft, Charles H., *Christianity in Culture*, Maryknoll NY: Orbis, 1979

Kushner, Lawrence, *Honey from the Rock: Visions of Jewish Mystical Renewal*, New York: Harper and Row, 1977

Lewis, C.S., *The Four Loves*, London: Collins Fontana Books, 1960

Lyall, David, "Pastoral Action and Theological Reflection" in *Contact*, Vol 100 (1989)

Macmurray, John, *Persons in Relation*, London: Faber, 1970

Manson, T. W., *The Church's Ministry*, London: Hodder & Stoughton, 1956

McBrien, Richard P., *Ministry: A Theological, Pastoral Handbook*, San Francisco: Harper & Row, 1987

McFadyen, Alistair I., *The Call to Personhood: A Christian Theory of the Individual in Social Relationships*, New York: Cambridge University Press, 1990

Moltmann, Jürgen, *The Church in the Power of the Spirit*, London, SCM Press, 1977

—, "Perichoresis: An Old Magic Word for a New Trinitarian Theology" in Meeks, M. Douglas (ed.), *Trinity, Community, and Power: Mapping Trajectories in Wesleyan Theology*, Nashville: Kingswood Books, an imprint of Abingdon Press, 2000

Mudge, Lewis S. and Poling, James N. (eds.), *Formation and Reflection: The Promise of Practical Theology*, Minneapolis: Fortress Press, 1987

Neuhaus, Richard J., *Freedom for Ministry*, San Francisco: Harper & Row, 1979

Newbigin, Lesslie, *The Good Shepherd: Meditations on Christian Ministry in Today's World*, Grand Rapids: Eerdmans, 1977

Niebuhr, Richard H. (in collaboration with Williams, D. D. and Gustafson, James M.), *The Purpose of the Church and Its Ministry: Reflections on the Aims of Theological Education*, New York: Harper & Bros., 1956

Oden, Amy G. (ed.), *And You Welcomed Me: A Sourcebook on Hospitality in Early Christianity*, Nashville: Abingdon Press, 2001

Oden, Thomas, C., *Contemporary Theology and Psychotherapy*, Philadelphia: Westminster Press, 1967

—, *Pastoral Theology: Essentials of Ministry*, San Francisco, Harper & Row, 1983

Oglesby, William B. (ed.), *The New Shape of Pastoral Theology: Essays in Honour of Seward Hiltner*, Nashville: Abingdon, 1969

Ogletree, Thomas W., *Hospitality to the Stranger: Dimensions of Moral Understanding*, Philadelphia: Fortress Press, 1985

Olthuis, James H., "Dancing Together in the Wild Spaces of Love: Postmodernism, Psychotherapy, and the Spirit of God" in *Journal of Psychology and Christianity* 1999, Vol 18, No 2

O'Meara, Thomas F., *Theology of Ministry* (rev ed), New York: Paulist Press, 1999

Parry, Robin, *Worshipping Trinity: Coming Back to the Heart of Worship*, Milton Keynes: Paternoster, 2005

Pattison, Stephen, "Some Straw for the Bricks: A Basic Introduction to Theological Reflection" in *Contact*, Vol 99 (1989)

Patton, John, *From Ministry to Theology: Pastoral Action and Reflection*, Nashville: Abingdon Press, 1990

—, *Pastoral Care in Context: An Introduction to Pastoral Care*, Louisville: Westminster/John Knox Press, 1993

Pembroke, Neil, *The Art of Listening: Dialogue, Shame, and Pastoral Care*, Grand Rapids: Eerdmans, 2002

Peterson, Eugene H., *Five Smooth Stones for Pastoral Work*, Grand Rapids: Eerdmans, 1980

Pohl, Christine D., *Making Room: Recovering Hospitality as a Christian Tradition*, Grand Rapids: Eerdmans, 1999

Polanyi, Michael, *Personal Knowledge*, Chicago: University of Chicago Press, 1958

Poling, James N. and Miller, Donald E., *Foundations for a Practical Theology of Ministry*, Nashville: Abingdon, 1985

Ratzinger, Joseph, *Church, Ecumenism and Politics: New Essays in Ecclesiology*, Slough: St Paul Publications, 1988

Rogers, Carl, *Client-Centred Therapy: Its Current Practice, Implications, and Theory*, London: Constable, 1951

Ruether, Rosemary Radford, *Sexism and God-Talk: Toward a Feminist Theology*: London, SCM Press, 1983

Schleiermacher, Freidrich, *A Brief Outline of the Study of Theology* (translated by Terrence N. Tice), Richmond VA: John Knox, 1966

Sherlock, Charles, *God on the Inside: Trinitarian Spirituality*, Wanniassa, ACT: Acorn Press, 1991

Spiedell, Todd H., "A Trinitarian Ontology of Persons in Society," in *The Scottish Journal of Theology* 43 (1994)

Spiedell, Todd H. (ed.), *On Being Christian ... and Human: Essays in Celebration of Ray S. Anderson*, Eugene OR: Wipf and Stock Publishers, 2002

St. Athanasius on the Incarnation, translated and edited by a religious of C.S.M.V. (Crestwood: St Vladimir's Orthodox Seminary, 1993)

Stone, Bryan P., *Compassionate Ministry: Theological Foundations*, New York: Orbis, 1996

Storkey, Elaine, *What's Right with Feminism*, Grand Rapids: Eerdmans, 1985
Switzer, David, K., *Pastor, Preacher, Person: Developing a Pastoral Ministry in Depth*, Nashville: Abingdon, 1979
Tacey, David, *ReEnchantment: The New Australian Spirituality*, Sydney: HarperCollins*Publishers*, 2000
Taylor, John V., *The Go-Between God: The Holy Spirit and the Christian Mission*, London: SCM Press, 1972
Teilhard de Chardin, Pierre, *The Phenomenon of Man*, London: Collins, 1959
Thornton, Martin, *Pastoral Theology: A Reorientation*, London: SPCK, 1961
Thurneysen, Eduard, *A Theology of Pastoral Care*, Atlanta: John Knox Press, 1962
Tillich, Paul, *The Courage to Be*, London: Collins Fontana, 1952
Torrance, James B., *Worship, Community and the Triune God of Grace*, Downers Grove: IVP, 1996
Tournier, Paul, *The Adventure of Living*, Crowborough: Highland Books, 1983
Vanier, Jean, *Community and Growth*, Homebush NSW: Society of St Paul, 1979
Vanstone, W.H., *Love's Endeavour, Love's Expense: The Response of Being to the Love of God*, London: Darton, Longman & Todd, 1977
Volf, Miroslav, *After Our Likeness: The Church as the Image of the Trinity*, Grand Rapids: Eerdmans, 1998
Weil, Simone, *Waiting on God*, London: Collins, 1963
Woodward, James and Pattison, Stephen (eds.), *The Blackwell Reader in Pastoral and Practical Theology*, Oxford: Blackwell, 2000
Wright, Frank, *The Pastoral Nature of the Ministry*, London: SCM Press, 1980
Zizioulas, John D., *Being as Communion: Studies in Personhood and the Church*, London: Darton, Longman & Todd, 1985

TRINITARIAN THEOLOGY

Barth, Karl, *Church Dogmatics*, Edinburgh: T. & T. Clark, 1936-1969 (esp. Vols 1.1, 1.2 and 2.1)
Boff, Leonardo, *Trinity and Society*, Maryknoll NY: Orbis, 1988
—, *Holy Trinity, Perfect Community*, Maryknoll NY: Orbis Books, 2000
Colyer, Elmer M. (ed.), *The Promise of Trinitarian Theology: Theologians in Dialogue with T. F. Torrance*, Lanham: Rowman & Littlefield Publishers, 2001
Cunningham, David S., *These Three Are One: The Practice of Trinitarian Theology*, Oxford: Blackwell, 1998
Grenz, Stanley, J., *The Social God and the Relational Self: A Trinitarian Theology of the Imago Dei*, Louisville: Westminster John Knox Press, 2001
Gunton, Colin E., "Augustine, the Trinity and the Theological Crisis of the West" in *The Scottish Journal of Theology* 43 (1990)
—, *The Promise of Trinitarian Theology*, Edinburgh, T. & T. Clark, 1991

—, *The One, the Three and the Many: God, Creation and the Culture of Modernity*, Cambridge: Cambridge UP, 1993
—, *The Triune Creator: A Historical and Systematic Study,* Grand Rapids: Eerdmans, 1998
Harrison, Verna, "Perichoresis in the Greek Fathers" in *St Vladimir's Theological Quarterly*, Vol. 35, No. 1, 1991
Jenson, Robert W., *The Triune Identity: God According to the Gospel*, Philadelphia: Fortress Press, 1982
—, *Systematic Theology,* Vol I - *The Triune God*, New York: Oxford University Press, 1997
Jungel, Eberhard, *God's Being is in Becoming: the Trinitarian Being of God in the Theology of Karl Barth*, Grand Rapids: Eerdmans, 2001
Kelly, J. N. D., *Early Christian Doctrines*, London: Adam & Charles Black, 1965
Kruger, C. Baxter, *Recovering the Trinity and Perichoresis and Their Significance for the 3rd Christian Millennium*, Adelaide; unpublished Perichoresis Lectures 2002
LaCugna, Catherine Mowry, *God For Us: The Trinity and Christian Life*, San Francisco: HarperCollins, 1991
Lossky, Vladimir, *The Mystical Theology of the Eastern Church*, London: James Clarke: 1957
Miller, David L., *Three Faces of God: Traces of the Trinity in Literature and Life*, Philadelphia: Fortress Press, 1986
Moltmann, Jürgen, *The Crucified God: The Cross of Christ as the Foundation and Criticism of Christian Theology*, London: SCM Press, 1974
—, *The Trinity and the Kingdom of God: The Doctrine of God*, London: SCM Press, 1981
—, *History and the Triune God: Contributions to Trinitarian Theology*, London: SCM Press, 1991
—, *The Spirit of Life: A Universal Affirmation*, Minneapolis: Fortress Press, 1992
—, *Theology of Hope: On the Ground and the Implications of a Christian Eschatology*, Minneapolis: Fortress Press, 1993
—, *The Source of Life: The Holy Spirit and the Theology of Life*, London: SCM Press, 1997
—, "'From the Closed World to the Infinite Universe': The Case of Giordano Bruno" in *Science and Wisdom*, Minneapolis: Fortress Press, 2003
Pannenberg, Wolfhart, *Jesus – God and Man*, London: SCM Press, 1968
—, *Theology and the Kingdom of God*, Philadelphia: The Westminster Press, 1969
—, "Problems of a Trinitarian Doctrine of God" in *Dialog*, Vol. 26 No. 4, 1987
—, *Systematic Theology*, Vols. I and II, Grand Rapids: Eerdmans, 1991
—, "Eternity, Time and the Trinitarian God", accessed on 12.03.03 on http://www.ctinquiry.org/publications/pannenberg.htm
—, "A Trinitarian Synthesis" in *First Things* 103 (May 2000)

Peters, Ted, *God as Trinity: Relationality and Temporality in Divine Life*, Louisville: Westminster/John Knox Press, 1993
Pinnock, Clark H. et al, *The Openness of God: A Biblical Challenge to the Traditional Understanding of God*, Downers Grove: IVP, 1994
Pinnock, Clark H., *Flame of Love: A Theology of the Holy Spirit*, Downers Grove: IVP, 1996
—, *Most Moved Mover: A Theology of God's Openness*, Carlisle: Paternoster Press, 2001
Prestige, G.L., *God in Patristic Thought*, London: SPCK 1959
Rahner, Karl, *Theological Investigations, Vol IV*, translated by Kevin Smyth, London: Darton, Longman & Todd, 1966
—, *Hearers of the Word*, translated by Michael Richards, New York: Herder & Herder, 1969
—, *The Trinity*, translated by J. Donceel, London: Burns & Oates, 1970
—, *Foundations of Christian Faith: An Introduction to the Idea of Christianity*, translated by William V. Dych, London: Darton, Longman & Todd, 1978
Richard of St. Victor, *De Trinitate III* in Zinn, Grover A. (trans), *Richard of St. Victor*, New York: Paulist Press: 1979
Schleiermacher, Friedrich, *The Christian Faith*, Edinburgh: T. & T. Clark, 1928
Schwobel, Christoph (ed.), *Trinitarian Theology Today: Essays on Divine Being and Act*, Edinburgh: T. & T. Clark, 1995
Smail, Thomas A., *The Giving Gift: The Holy Spirit in Person*, London: Darton, Longman & Todd, 1988
St. Gregory of Nazianzus, *On God and Christ*, Crestwood NY: St. Vladimir's Seminary Press, 2002
Torrance, Alan J., *Persons in Communion: An Essay on Trinitarian Description and Human Participation*, Edinburgh: T. & T. Clark, 1996
Torrance, Thomas F. *Trinitarian Perspectives: Toward Doctrinal Agreement*, Edinburgh: T. & T. Clark, 1994
—, *The Christian Doctrine of God: One Being Three Persons*, Edinburgh: T. & T. Clark, 1996
Weinandy, Thomas G., *The Father's Spirit of Sonship: Reconceiving the Trinity*, Edinburgh: T. & T. Clark, 1995
Worthing, Mark W., *Foundations and Functions of Theology as Universal Science: Theological Method and Apologetic Praxis in Wolfhart Pannenberg and Karl Rahner*, Frankfurt am Main: Peter Lang, 1996

SCIENCE-THEOLOGY INTERFACE

Abramson, Nils, *The Making and Evaluation of Holograms*, London: Academic Press, 1981
Alexander, Denis, *Rebuilding the Matrix: Science and Faith in the 21st Century*, Oxford: Lion Publishing, 2001

Anderson, Ray S., "Isomorphic Indicators in Theological and Psychological Science" in *Journal of Psychology and Theology*, Vol. 17 No.4 (1989)
Astley, Jeff, Brown, David and Loades, Ann, (eds.), *Creation: A Reader*, London and New York: T. & T. Clark, a Continuum imprint, 2003
Barbour, Ian G., *Issues in Science and Religion*, New York: Harper & Row, 1966
—, *Myths, Models and Paradigms*, New York: Harper & Row, 1974
—, *Religion in an Age of Science*, San Francisco: HarperSanFrancisco, 1990
—, *Religion and Science: Historical and Contemporary Issues*, London: SCM, 1998
—, *When Science Meets Religion: Enemies, Strangers or Partners?*, San Francisco: HarperCollins, 2000
Barth, Karl and Brunner, Emil, *Natural Theology*, London: SCM Press, 1947
Baskhar, Roy, *The Possibility of Naturalism: A Philosophical Critique of the Contemporary Human Sciences*, 3rd edition, London: Routledge, 1998
Benthall, Jonathan, *Science and Technology in Art Today*, Praeger World of Art Series, 1972
Bohm, David, *Wholeness and the Implicate Order*, New York: Routledge and Kegan Paul, 1980
Bohm, David and Peat, F. David, *Science, Order and Creativity*, New York: Bantam Books, 1988
Bohr, Neils, *Atomic Theory and the Description of Nature*, Cambridge: Cambridge University Press, 1934
Brooke, John Hedley, *Science and Religion: Some Historical Perspectives*, Cambridge: Cambridge University Press, 1991
Brooke, John and Cantor, Geoffrey, *Reconstructing Nature: The Engagement of Science and Religion* (1995-6 Gifford lectures), Edinburgh: T. & T. Clark, 1998
Capra, Fritjof, *The Tao of Physics*, London: Collins Fontana, 1976
Clayton, Philip D., *God and Contemporary Science*, Grand Rapids: Eerdmans, 1997
—, "The Emergence of Spirit" in *CTNS Bulletin* 20.4 (Fall 2000)
Clayton, Philip D. and Peacocke, Arthur R. (eds.), *In Whom We Live and Move and Have Our Being: Panentheistic Reflections on God's Presence in a Scientific World*, Grand Rapids: Eerdmans, 2004
Cole-Turner, R. *The New Genesis: Theology and the Genetic Revolution*, Louisville: Westminster/John Knox Press, 1993
Crick, Francis H., *The Astonishing Hypothesis: The Scientific Search for the Soul*, London: Simon and Schuster, 1994
Darwin, Charles [1859], *The Origin of Species*, Baltimore: Penguin Books, 1968
Davies, Paul, *God and the New Physics*, New York: Simon & Schuster, 1983
—, *The Cosmic Blueprint*, London: Unwin, 1989
—, *The Mind of God: Science and the Search for Ultimate Meaning*, London: Penguin, 1993

—, "Physics and the Mind of God" in *First Things* 55 (August-September 1995)
Davis, John Jefferson, *The Frontiers of Science and Faith: Examining Questions from the Big Bang to the End of the Universe*, Downers Grove: IVP, 2002
Dawkins, Richard, *The Blind Watchmaker: Why the Evidence of Evolution Reveals a Universe without a Design,* New York: W.W. Norton & Co., 1986
Deane-Drummond, Celia, "God and Gaia: Myth or Reality?" in *Theology* 95, 766 (1992)
—, *Gaia and Green Ethics: Implications of Ecological Theology*, Grove Ethical Studies No. 88, Bramcote: Grove, 1993
—, "*Gaia* as Science made Myth: Implications for Environmental Ethics" in *Studies in Christian Ethics*, Vol. 9 No. 2
Del Re, Guiseppe, *The Cosmic Dance: Science Discovers the Mysterious Harmony of the Universe*, Radnor PA: Templeton Foundation Press, 2000
Dembski, William A. and Behe, Michael J., *Intelligent Design: The Bridge between Science and Theology*, Downers Grove: IVP, 1999
Dixon, P. *The Genetic Revolution*, Eastbourne: Kingsway, 1993
Draper, John W., *History of the Conflict Between Science and Religion*, New York: Appleton, 1875
Dyson, Freeman J., *Infinite in All Directions*, New York: Harper & Row, 1988
Edwards, Denis, *Jesus the Wisdom of God: An Ecological Theology*, Homebush NSW: St Pauls, 1995
—, *The God of Evolution: A Trinitarian Theology*, Mahwah, NJ: Paulist, 1999
—, *Breath of Life: A Theology of the Creator Spirit*, Maryknoll: Orbis Books, 2004
Edwards, Denis (ed.), *Earth Revealing – Earth Healing: Ecology and Christian Theology*, Collegeville: The Liturgical Press, 2001
Emmeche, C., Køppe, S. and Stjernfelt, F., "Explaining Emergence: Towards an Ontology of Levels" in *Journal for General Philosophy of Science* 28 (1997)
Fuller, Michael, *Atoms and Icons: A Discussion of the Relationships Between Science and Theology*, London: Mowbray, 1995
Gilkey, Langdon, *Nature, Reality, and the Sacred: The Nexus of Science and Religion*, Minneapolis: Fortress Press, 1993
Gleick, James, *Chaos: Making a New Science*, New York: Penguin Books, 1987
Gould, Stephen Jay, *Rock of Ages: Science and Religion and the Fullness of Life*, New York: Ballantine, 1999
Gregersen, Niels Henrik, "The Idea of Creation and the Theory of Autopoietic Processes" in *Zygon: Journal of Religion and Science* Vol. 33, No. 3 (September, 1998)
—, "The Creation of Creativity and the Flourishing of Creation" in *Currents in Theology and Mission* 28:3-4 (June/August 2001)

Gregersen, Niels Henrik (ed.), *From Complexity to Life: On the Emergence of Life and Meaning*, New York: Oxford University Press, 2002

Gregersen, Niels H. and Huyssten, J. Wentzel van (eds.), *Rethinking Theology and Science: Six Models for the Current Dialogue*, Grand Rapids: Eerdmans, 1998

Habel, Norman C. (ed.), *Readings from the Perspective of Earth*, Sheffield: Academic Press, 2000

Habel, Norman C. and Wurst, Shirley (eds.), *The Earth Story in Genesis*, Sheffield: Academic Press, 2000

Haught, John F., *Science and Religion: From Conflict to Conversation*, New York: Paulist, 1995

—, *God After Darwin: A Theology of Evolution*, Boulder, Colo.: Westview Press, 2000

Houston, James M., *I Believe in the Creator*, London: Hodder & Stoughton, 1979

Huyssteen, J. Wentzel van, *Duet or Duel?: Theology and Science in a Postmodern World*, Harrisburg PA: Trinity Press International, 1998

Jammer, Max, *The Philosophy of Quantum Mechanics: The Interpretations of Quantum Mechanics in Historical Perspective*, Chichester NY: Wiley, 1974

Jeeves, Malcolm A., *Human Nature at the Millennium: Reflections on the Integration of Psychology and Christianity*, Grand Rapids: Baker Books, 1997

Johnson, Elizabeth, *Women, Earth, and Creator Spirit*, New York: Paulist Press, 1993

Johnson, George, *Fire in the Mind: Science, Faith and the Search for Order*, London: Viking, 1996

Johnson, Steven, *Emergence: The Connected Lives of Ants, Brains, Cities, and Software*, New York: Scribner, 2001

Joseph, Lawrence E., *Gaia: The Growth of an Idea*, New York: St. Martin's Press, 1990

Kauffman, Stuart, *At Home in the Universe*, Harmondsorth: Penguin, 1995

King, Carolyn M., *Habitat of Grace: Biology, Christianity and the Global Environmental Crisis*, Hindmarsh SA: Australian Theological Forum, 2002

Kuhn, Thomas, *The Structure of Scientific Revolutions*, Chicago: Chicago University Press, 1962

Leopold, Aldo, *A Sand County Almanac: With Essays on Conservation from Round River*, New York: Ballantine Books, 1949

Liderbach, Daniel, *The Numinous Universe*, New York: Paulist Press, 1989

Lovelock, James E., *The Ages of Gaia: A Biography of Our Living Earth*, New York: Bantam Books, 1990

—, "Hands Up for the Gaia Hypothesis" in *Nature* 344 (1990)

Lubac, Henri, S.J. de, *The Faith of Teilhard de Chardin*, London: Burns & Oates Ltd., 1965

Mandelbrot, Benoit, *The Fractal Geometry of Nature*, San Francisco: W. H. Freeman & Co., 1977
McFague, Sallie, *The Body of God: An Ecological Theology*, London: SCM Press, 1993
—, *Super, Natural Christians: How We Should Love Nature*, Minneapolis: Fortress Press, 1997
McGrath, Alister E., *Science and Religion: An Introduction*, Oxford: Blackwell, 1999
—, *A Scientific Theology*, Vol I - *Nature*, Edinburgh: T. & T. Clark, 2001
—, *A Scientific Theology*, Vol II - *Reality*, Edinburgh: T. & T. Clark, 2002
—, *The Re-enchantment of Nature: Science, Religion and the Human Sense of Wonder*, London: Hodder & Stoughton, 2002
Moltmann, Jürgen, *God in Creation: A New Theology of Creation and the Spirit of God*, San Francisco: Harper & Row, 1985
—, *Science and Wisdom*, Minneapolis: Fortress Press, 2003
Monod, Jacques, *Chance and Necessity*, London: Collins, 1972
Monroe, C., "A 'Schrödinger cat' superposition state of an atom" in *Science* 272 (24 May 1996)
Morgan, Conwy Lloyd, *Emergent Evolution*, London: Williams and Norgate, 1923
Morris, Henry (ed.), *Scientific Creationism*, El Cajun CA: Master Books, 1985
Morris, Simon Conway, *Life's Solution: Inevitable Humans in a Lonely Universe*, Cambridge: Cambridge University Press, 2003
Numbers, Ronald L., *The Creationists: The Evolution of Scientific Creationism*, Berkeley: University of California Press, 1992
Ó Murchú, Diarmuid, *Quantum Theology: Spiritual Implications of the New Physics*: New York: Crossroad, 1997
Paley, William, *Natural Theology*, Boston: Gould, Kelly & Lincoln, 1850
Pannenberg, Wolfhart, *Theology and the Philosophy of Science*, London: Darton, Longman & Todd, 1986
— [Ted Peters (ed.)], *Towards a Theology of Nature: Essays on Science and Faith*, Louisville: Westminster/John Knox, 1993
Peacocke, Arthur R., *Creation and the World of Science*, Oxford: Clarendon Press, 1979
—, *Theology for a Scientific Age: Being and Becoming – Natural, Divine and Human*, Minneapolis: Fortress Press, 1993
—, *God and Science: A Quest for Christian Credibility*, London: SCM Press, 1996
—, *Paths from Science Towards God: The End of all our Exploring*, Oxford: Oneworld Publications, 2001
Penrose, Roger, *The Emperor's New Mind: Concerning Computers, Minds and the Laws of Physics*, Oxford: Oxford University Press, 1989
Peters, T. (ed.) *Genetics: Issues of Social Justice*, New York: Pilgrim, 1988
Peters, T. *Playing God?: Genetic Determinism and Human Freedom*, New York: Routledge, 1996

Plantinga, Alvin C., *God, Freedom and Evil*, London: George Allen & Unwin, 1975
Polkinghorne, John, *One World: The Interaction of Science and Theology*, London: SPCK, 1986
—, *Science and Providence: God's Interaction with the World*, London: SPCK, 1986
—, *Science and Christian Belief: Theological Reflections of a Bottom-Up Thinker*, London: SPCK, 1994
—, *Serious Talk: Science and Religion in Dialogue*, Harrisburg PA: Trinity Press International, 1995
—, *Belief in God in an Age of Science*, New Haven CT: Yale University Press, 1998
Polkinghorne, John (ed.), *The Work of Love: Creation as Kenosis*, Grand Rapids: Eerdmans, 2001
Popper, Karl R., *The Logic of Scientific Discovery*, London: Hutchinson, 1959
—, *Realism and the Aim of Science* Totowa NJ: Rowman and Littlefield, 1983
—, *A World of Propensities*, Bristol: Thoemmes, 1990
Powell, Samuel M., *Participating in God: Creation and Trinity*, Minneapolis: Fortress Press, 2003
Pratt, David, "David Bohm and the Implicate Order" in *Sunrise*, Feb./March 1993
Pribram, Karl, *Languages of the Brain: Experimental Paradoxes and Principles in Neuropsychology*, Englewood Cliffs NJ: Prentice-Hall, 1971
Prigogine, Ilya and Stengers, Isabelle, *Order Out of Chaos: Man's New Dialogue with Nature*, New York: Bantam Books, 1984
Prigogine, Ilya and Nicolis, G., *Exploring Complexity*, New York: W.H. Freeman, 1989
Rae, M., Regan, H. and Stenhouse, J. (eds.), *Science and Theology: Questions at the Interface*, Edinburgh: T. & T. Clark, 1994
Regan, Hilary D. and Worthing, Mark William (eds.), *Interdisciplinary Perspectives on Cosmology and Biological Evolution*, Hindmarsh SA: Adelaide Theological Forum, 2002
Richardson, W.M. and Wildman W.J. (eds.), *Religion and Science: History, Method, Dialogue*, New York: Routledge, 1996
Richardson, W. Mark, Russell, Robert John, Clayton, Philip and Wegter-McNelly, Kirk (eds.), *Science and the Spiritual Quest: New Essays by Leading Scientists*, London and New York: Routledge, 2002
Rolston, Holmes, III, "Does Nature Need to be Redeemed?" in *Zygon: Journal of Religion and Science*. Vol. 29, No. 2 (June, 1994)
—, *Genes, Genesis, and God: Values and Their Origins in Natural and Human History*, Cambridge: Cambridge University Press, 1999
Russell, Robert John, "Does the 'God Who Acts' Really Act in Nature?: New Approaches to Divine Action in Light of Science" in *Theology Today* (April 1997)

Russell, Robert J., Stoeger, William R. and Coyne, George V. (eds.), *Physics, Philosophy and Theology: A Common Quest for Understanding*, Vatican City State: Vatican Observatory Publications, 1988

Russell, Robert John, Murphy, Nancey and Isham C.J. (eds.), *Quantum Cosmology and the Laws of Nature: Scientific Perspectives on Divine Action*, Vatican City State: Vatican Observatory; Notre Dame: University of Notre Dame Press, 1993

Russell, Robert John, Stoeger, William R. and Ayala, Francisco J. (eds.), *Evolutionary and Molecular Biology: Scientific Perspectives on Divine Action*, Vatican City State: Vatican Observatory, 1998

Russell, Robert John, Murphy, Nancey, Meyering, Theo C. and Arbib, Michael A. (eds.), *Neuroscience and the Person: Scientific Perspectives on Divine Action*, Vatican City State: Vatican Observatory Publications, California: CTNS, 1999

Russell, Robert J., Murphy, Nancey and Peacocke, Arthur R. (eds.), *Chaos and Complexity: Scientific Perspectives on Divine Action*, Vatican City State: Vatican Observatory Publications, 1995

Sanders, John, *The God Who Risks: A Theology of Providence*, Downers Grove: IVP, 1998

Santmire, H. Paul, *The Travail of Nature: The Ambiguous Ecological Promise of Christian Theology*, Minneapolis: Fortress Press, 1985

Sharpe, Kevin, "David Bohm's Physics and Religion", accessed on 21.11.03 on http://www.ksharpe.com/word/BM03.htm

Sherry, Patrick, *Spirit and Beauty: An Introduction to Theological Aesthetics*, Oxford: Clarendon Press, 1992

Snyder, Howard A., *EarthCurrents: The Struggle for the World's Soul*, Nashville: Abingdon Press, 1995

Southgate, Christopher et al., *God, Humanity and the Cosmos: A Textbook in Science and Religion*, Edinburgh: T & T Clark, 1999

Talbot, Michael, *The Holographic Universe: A Remarkable New Theory of Reality*, New York: Perennial/HarperCollins Publishers, 1991

Teilhard de Chardin, Pierre, *The Divine Milieu: An Essay on the Interior Life*, New York: Harper & Row, 1965

Thomas, J. Mark (ed.), *The Spiritual Situation in Our Technical Society: Paul Tillich*, Macon: Mercer University Press, 1988

Tiessen, Terrance, *Providence and Prayer: How Does God Work in the World?*, Downers Grove: IVP, 2000

Torrance, Thomas F., *Divine and Contingent Order*, Oxford: Oxford University Press, 1981

—, "The Problem of Natural Theology in the Thought of Karl Barth" in *Religious Studies* 6 (1970)

—, *Theological Science*, London: Oxford University Press, 1969

Ward, Keith, *Divine Action*, London: Collins, 1990

—, *God, Chance and Necessity*, Oxford: One World, 1996

—, *God, Faith and the New Millennium: Christian Belief in an Age of Science*, Oxford: One World, 1998

Wegter-McNelly, Kirk, *The World, Entanglement, and God: Quantum Theory and the Christian Doctrine of Creation*, unpublished doctoral dissertation, Berkeley CA: Graduate Theological Union, April 2003

Weinberg, Steven, *The First Three Minutes: A Modern View of the Origin of the Universe*, New York: Basic Books, 1977

Wertheim, Margaret, "The Odd Couple" in *The Sciences*, March/April 1999

Wheatley, Margaret J., *Leadership and the New Science: Learning about Organization from an Orderly Universe*, San Francisco: Berrett-Koehler Publishers, 1999

White, Andrew Dickson, *A History of the Warfare of Science with Theology in Christendom*, New York: Appleton, 1895

Wiles, Maurice, *God's Action in the World: The Bampton Lectures for 1986*, London: SCM Press, 1986

Wilkinson, David, *God, the Big Bang and Stephen Hawking*, Tunbridge Wells: Monarch, 1993

Wilson, Edward O., *Sociobiology: The New Synthesis*, Cambridge MA: Harvard University Press, 1976

Wiseman, James A., *Theology and Modern Science: Quest for Coherence*, New York: Continuum, 2002

Worthing, Mark W., *God, Creation and Contemporary Physics*, Minneapolis: Fortress, 1998

Young, Richard A., *Healing the Earth: A Theocentric Perspective on Environmental Problems and their Solutions*, Nashville: Broadman & Holman, 1994

OTHER TEXTS

Allen, Diogenes, *The Traces of God in a Frequently Hostile World*, Cambridge MA: Cowley, 1981

Anderson, Ray S., *Historical Transcendence and the Reality of God*, London: Geoffrey Chapman, 1975

Balthasar, Hans Urs von, *The Theology of Karl Barth* (translated by John Drury), New York: Holt, Rinehart & Winston, 1971

Barth, Karl, *The Epistle to the Romans* (translated by Edward C. Hoskyns from the Sixth Edition), London: Oxford University Press, 1933

—, *Dogmatics in Outline*, London: SCM Press Ltd., 1949

—, *Evangelical Theology: An Introduction*, London: Collins Fontana, 1965

Berger, Peter L. and Luckmann, Thomas, *The Social Construction of Reality: A Treatise in the Sociology of Knowledge*, Harmondsworth: Penguin, 1971

Bono, Edward de, *Parallel Thinking: From Socratic Thinking to de Bono Thinking*, London: Penguin Books, 1995

Brown, Robert McAfee, *Spirituality and Liberation: Overcoming the Great Fallacy*, London: Hodder & Stoughton Ltd., 1988

Cobb, John B., *A Christian Natural Theology: Based on the Thought of Alfred North Whitehead*, London: Lutterworth, 1966
Cobb, John B. and Griffin, David Ray, *Process Theology: An Introduction*, Philadelphia: Westminster Press, 1976
Darragh, Neil, "Theology from Elsewhere" in *South Pacific Journal of Mission Studies* 2, 1/1991
—, *Doing Theology Ourselves*, Auckland: Accent, 1995
Erickson, Millard J., *Postmodernizing the Faith: Evangelical Responses to the Challenge of Postmodernism*, Grand Rapids: Baker Books, 1998
—, *The Postmodern World: Discerning the Times and the Spirit of Our Age*, Wheaton: Crossway Books, 2002
Forde, Gerhard O., *Where God Meets Man: Luther's Down-to-Earth Approach to the Gospel*, Minneapolis: Augsburg, 1972
Grenz, Stanley J., *A Primer on Postmodernism*, Grand Rapids: Eerdmans, 1996
—, *Renewing the Center: Evangelical Theology in a Post-Evangelical Era*, Grand Rapids: Baker Academic, 2000
Grenz, Stanley J. and Olson, Roger. E, *20th-Century Theology: God and the World in a Transitional Age*, Downers Grove: IVP, 1992
Hare, R. M., *Plato*, Oxford: Oxford University Press, 1983
Hartshorne, Charles, *Creative Synthesis and Scientific Method*, London: SCM Press, 1970
Harvey, David, *The Condition of Postmodernity: An Enquiry into the Origins of Cultural Change*, Oxford: Blackwell, 1990
Inbody, Tyron, "Postmodernism: Intellectual Velcro Dragged Across Culture?" in *Theology Today*, Vol 51 No 4, January 1995
Lundin, Roger, *The Culture of Interpretation: Christian Faith and the Postmodern World*, Grand Rapids: Eerdmans, 1993
Lyotard, Jean-Francois, *The Postmodern Condition: A Report on Knowledge*, Minneapolis, University of Minneapolis Press, 1984
Macquarrie, John, *Principles of Christian Theology*, London: SCM Press, 1966
Middleton, Richard J. and Walsh, Brian J., *Truth Is Stranger Than It Used To Be: Biblical Faith in a Postmodern Age*, Downers Grove: IVP, 1995
Migliore, Daniel, *Faith Seeking Understanding: An Introduction to Christian Theology*, Grand Rapids: Eerdmans, 1991
Moltmann, Jürgen, *The Coming of God: Christian Eschatology*, Minneapolis: Fortress Press, 1996
Mueller, David L., *Karl Barth*, Waco: Word Books, 1972
Pickard, Stephen and Preece, Gordon, *Starting with the Spirit*, Hindmarsh SA: Australian Theological Forum, 2001
Plato, *The Republic*, translated by H. D. P. Lee, London: Penguin Books, 1955
Popper, Karl, *Conjectures and Refutations*, London: Routledge and Kegan Paul, 1963
Ratzinger, Joseph, *Introduction to Christianity*, London: Burns & Oates, 1969
Reid, Duncan and Worthing, Mark (eds.) *Sin and Salvation*, Hindmarsh SA: Adelaide Theological Forum, 2003

Thoreau, Henry D., *Walden* (edited by Walter Harding), Boston MA: Houghton Mifflin Co., 1995
Tillich, Paul, *Dynamics of* Faith, New York: Harper & Row Publishers, 1957
Trainor, Brian, *The Origin and End of Modernity: Reflections on the Meaning of Post-Modernism*, Quebec: World Heritage Press, 1998
Walsh, B. J. and Middleton, J. R., *The Transforming Vision: Shaping a Christian World View*, Downers Grove: IVP, 1984
Webster, John, *Barth*, London: Continuum, 2000
Whitehead, Alfred North, *Process and Reality: An Essay in Cosmology*, New York: Macmillan, 1929

Author Index

Abramson, N. 214.
Aden, L. 73, 188.
Alexander, D. 2, 12, 14, 19-20, 37-38, 43, 45, 47-48.
Allen, D. 85.
Allen, R.J. 144.
Allmen, J.-J. von 177.
Anderson, R.S. 4, 55, 58, 60, 69-70, 79-81, 86, 92, 95, 160, 167-169, 181, 272, 277.
Aquinas 2, 31,33, 40, 73, 101, 131, 183, 282.
Arbuckle, G. 82.
Aristotle 2, 9, 33, 60, 73.
Astley, J. 241.
Athanasius 2, 82, 116, 127, 129, 134.
Augsburger, D. 58, 81.
Augustine 2, 33, 37, 72, 99-101, 107, 133, 135, 179, 253.
Ayala, F.J. 227, 235.
Bacon, F. 20-21, 33, 279.
Ballard, P. 69.
Balsinger, T. 79.
Balthasar, H.U. von 59, 166, 180, 192, 236.
Barbour, I.G. 2, 5, 9, 13-14, 16-17, 20-23, 26, 30-31, 35, 39-41, 48, 50, 197, 199-200, 202, 228-229, 233-234.
Barth, K. 2, 21, 27, 31, 32, 34, 44, 55, 58-59, 64-67, 70-71, 7775-79, 83, 88-89, 96-107, 112, 114-115, 123, 128, 146, 148, 163-164, 169, 180, 182, 211, 255, 247-249, 251.
Basil of Caesarea 108, 110.
Bass, D.C. 170.
Behe, M.J. 35.
Beker, J.C. 256.
Bell, J. 203.
Benner, D.G. 87-88, 175, 188-190.
Benthall, J. 216.
Berger, P.L. 45.
Bergson, H. 269-270.

Bhaskar, R. 26-27, 50.
Birch, B.C. 275.
Blaisdell, B.S. 144.
Boersma, H. 170.
Boff, L. 123, 146, 156-157, 186, 188, 191, 196.
Bohm, D. 35, 200, 202-204, 206, 208-209, 211, 213-221, 228, 234, 252, 267.
Bohr, N. 51, 199-200.
Boisen, A. 75-76.
Bonhoeffer, D. 34, 44, 64, 66, 166, 169.
Bono, E. de 62.
Bosanquet, B. 281.
Bosch, D.J. 184-185.
Boslough, J. 220.
Bowie, F. 175.
Brister, C.W. 53, 57, 68, 91.
Bromiley, G.W. 55.
Brooke, J.H. 3, 6-8, 17-18, 20-21, 31-32, 43, 197.
Brown, D. 241.
Brown, F. 274.
Brown, J.R. 196.
Brown, R.M. 48, 274-275.
Browning, D.S. 56, 58, 61, 66-69, 75, 77-80, 87.
Browning, E.B. 256, 258.
Brunner, E. 32, 34.
Buber, M. 13, 120-121, 243.
Bucer, M. 73.
Buckles, S. 269.
Buckley, J.J. 144-145, 147, 150, 178-179.
Buddaeus 73.
Burkhart, J.E. 74-75.
Burnell, J.B. 51-52.
Butt, J. 70.
Buxton, G. 47, 53, 70, 121, 153, 176, 185, 250.
Byrne, B. 264.
Calvin, J. 43, 77, 88, 126, 266.
Campbell, A. 74, 147.
Cantor, G. 197.

Capra, C. 137, 196-197.
Carr, W. 88.
Clayton, P.D. 51, 227, 231-232, 234.
Clebsch, W. 72.
Clendenin, D.B. 169.
Clinebell, H.J. 72.
Cobb, J.B. 10, 40, 85.
Cole-Turner, R. 4-5, 229.
Colyer, E.M. 92.
Coyne, G.V. 23, 206, 233.
Crick, F.H. 218.
Cross, F.L. 36.
Cunningham, D.S. 124, 144-151, 163-164, 166-167, 171-172, 174, 177-178, 180.
Cyril of Alexandria 109.
Dabney, D.L. 263.
Dalferth, I.U. 111, 116, 118, 232.
Daly, M. 159.
Darragh, N. 61.
Darwin, C. 18, 34, 251.
Davies, O. 175.
Davies, P. 11-13, 22, 24, 30-31, 34, 42, 196, 198, 200-203, 205-206, 212-213, 224, 226.
Davis, J.J. 13.
Dawkins, R. 5, 34-35, 38, 228, 230.
D'Costa, D.G. 10.
Deane-Drummond, C. 224-225, 243.
Deeks, D. 89.
Del Re, G. 140, 195, 197, 209-210, 213, 222, 224, 286-287.
Dembski, W. 35.
Dixon, P. 5.
Donovan, V. 64.
Dostoevsky, F. 89.
Douglas, J.D. 84.
Dowey, E.A. 89.
Draper, J.W. 6, 19.
Duchrow, U. 274.
Duck, R.C. 162.
Dutney, A. 5.
Dyson, F.J. 42.
Edwards, D. 39, 43-44, 51, 221, 239, 235-240, 244, 248, 252, 256, 265, 268, 271, 274, 281.
Eigen, M. 229.
Einstein, A. 9, 12, 33, 197-198, 202-203, 209-210, 212, 267.

Eliot, T.S. 52, 141, 216.
Ellens, J.H. 73, 188.
Emmeche, C. 228-229.
Engen, C. van 183.
Engstrom, T. 255.
Erickson, M.J. 44, 46-47, 49.
Farley, E. 56, 60-61, 63, 68, 75, 80, 183.
Fiddes, P.S. 91, 93-94, 130-132, 139-141, 146, 147, 150-151, 153, 155, 174, 180, 182-183, 191-192, 208, 217, 236, 241.
Finn, T.M. 179.
Finocchiaro, M.P. 17.
Fiorenza, E.S. 158.
Firet, J. 53-54, 72.
Flood, R. 199.
Fontaine, P.M. 48.
Forde, G.O. 250.
Forrester, D.B. 56-57, 60-61, 72-73, 77.
Fowler, J. 61, 80.
Fox, M. 36, 250-251.
Fox, P. 244.
Frei, H. 36, 45.
Friesen, C.V. 284-285.
Frye, M. 258.
Fuller, M. 11, 222.
Furius, L. 284.
Gabor, D. 214, 218.
Gardner, A. 264.
Geertz, C.C. 139.
Gerontius 187.
Giberson, K. 49.
Giles, K. 164.
Gilkey, L. 21-22, 107-108, 124, 262, 276-278.
Gilson, E. 279.
Gingerich, O. 29, 35.
Gleick, J. 14, 212-213.
Gollings, R. 183.
Gould, S.J. 22, 32, 35, 38, 228, 230.
Graham, E. 56, 60, 74, 76, 78.
Greenwood, R. 157.
Gregersen, N.H. 28, 49-50, 225-228, 231, 233, 248.
Gregory of Nazianzus 72, 110, 129-130.
Grenz, S.J. 44, 46, 112, 116-117, 119, 123, 159, 169, 171-173.
Grierson, D. 82-83, 260-261.
Griffin, D.R. 40.

Griffin, G. 67.
Gunton, C.E. 85, 92-93, 108, 110, 112, 124-128, 130-132, 137-140, 148, 150, 164-165, 195, 225, 232, 240, 259, 266.
Gustafson, J.M. 56.
Habel, N.C. 250, 263-265.
Hadewijch 174.
Haisch, B. 23.
Hall, D.J. 54, 61, 64, 68, 88-89, 92, 94, 96, 160, 254, 272, 274-278.
Hare, R.M. 48, 93, 216.
Häring, H. 137.
Harmless, W. 179.
Harrison, V. 129-130.
Hartshorne, C. 40, 85.
Harvey, D. 44.
Haught, J. 4-5, 8, 12, 14-17, 19-20, 22-24, 31, 33, 41-42, 50, 52, 220, 229-230, 232, 235, 239.
Heitink, G. 54, 72-73, 75, 77, 79-80, 87.
Hilary of Poitiers 154.
Hiltner, S. 57, 66-67, 69-70, 75-76, 78-79, 87, 95.
Hobbes, T. 279.
Hodgson, P. 68, 108.
Hoebel, E.A. 9.
Hofmann, H. 87.
Holmes, U.T. III 57, 75-76.
Hopkins, G.M. 89, 195, 216, 251.
Houston, J.M. 259, 284.
Hurding, R. 189.
Hütter, R. 170.
Huyssteen, J.W. van 4, 50.
Inbody, T. 45.
Isham, C.J. 233.
Itano, W.M. 208.
Jaekle, C. 72.
Jammer, M. 198, 210.
Jeeves, M.A. 218.
Jenson, R. 98, 104, 108-112, 119, 126, 163, 166, 182, 196, 240.
Johnson, E. 267.
Johnson, G. 268269, 287.
Johnson, S. 222, 226.
Johnston, S.B. 144.
Jones, L.G. 179.
Joseph, L.E. 223.
Jungel, E. 103-104.

Kaiser, C. 107.
Kauffman, S. 38.
Kellerman, H. 221.
Kelly, J.N.D. 108.
Kettler, C.D. 55, 160, 185-186.
Kielpinski, D. 208.
Kierkegaard, S. 59.
Kimel, A.F. 163.
King, B.E. 208.
King, C.M. 264-265.
King, R.H. 108.
Køppe, S. 228-229.
Kraft, C.H. 83.
Krause, K. 36.
Kruger, C.B. 130, 143.
Kuhn, T. 30, 83.
Kuschel, K.J. 137.
Kushner, L. 167.
LaCugna, C.M. 107-108, 119-124, 126, 131-133, 139, 143, 146, 153-154, 158, 162, 165, 170, 173-174, 180, 272.
Latour, B. 46.
Leopold, A. 264.
Lewis, A.E. 160-162.
Lewis, C.S. 172-174.
Liderbach, D. 209-211, 276.
Liedke, G. 274.
Lindbeck, G. 146.
Livingstone, E.A. 36.
Loades, A. 241.
Locke, J. 279.
Lockwood, M. 199.
Lossky, V. 125-126.
Lovelock, J. 223-224, 243, 252.
Lowes, A. 281, 286.
Lubac, H. de 249.
Luckmann, T. 45.
Lundin, R. 44.
Luther, M. 54, 153, 273.
Lyall, D. 63.
Lyotard, J.-F. 44-45.
MacDonald, C.B. 87.
Macmurray, J. 68, 120-121, 141, 149, 281.
Macquarrie, J. 88, 182.
Mandelbrot, B. 211-213.
Manson, T. 57.
Marcel, G. 152, 172.
Mark, T.J. 270.

Martin, R.P. 84.
Maximus Confessor 130.
Maxwell, J.C. 210, 267.
McBrien, R.P. 65.
McFadyen, A. 149, 152.
McFague, S. 25, 91, 93, 252-254, 258, 260, 263, 265-266, 268.
McGrath, A.E. 1-3, 7-10, 17, 20, 23, 26-27, 29-32, 45-47, 50, 262, 265, 278, 280, 286.
Meeks, M.D. 171, 196.
Middleton, R.J. 44, 48.
Migliore, D. 156.
Miller, D.E. 57, 65, 150.
Miller, D.L. 135.
Mishlove, J. 221.
Moltmann, J. 36-37, 42, 94, 100, 108, 112-116, 119, 123, 126, 130, 133, 135-137, 144-146, 155, 162, 165, 171, 173-175, 179-180, 184, 186-187, 191-192, 195-196, 205, 239-244, 253-254, 256-257, 259-262, 266-268, 270-271, 276, 280-281.
Monod, J. 38, 229.
Monroe, C. 208.
Moore, T. 268.
Morgan, C.L. 228.
Morris, H.M. 22.
Morris, S.C. 230-231.
Mudge, L.S. 58, 81, 90.
Mueller, D.L. 59.
Murphy, N. 29, 221, 233-234, 240.
Myatt, C.J. 208.
Neill, S. 184.
Neuhaus, R.J. 58, 66.
Newbigin, L. 66, 80.
Nicolis, G. 38.
Niebuhr, H.R. 56.
Nouwen, H. 189.
Numbers, R.L. 22.
Oden, A.G. 170-171, 187.
Oden, T.C. 55, 76, 159, 163, 188.
Oglesby, W.B. 67, 87.
Ogletree, T,W, 87, 187.
Olson, R.E. 119, 159.
Olthuis, J.H. 189-190, 193.
O'Meara, T. 58.
Ó Murchú, D. 201, 203-204, 213-217.

Paley, W. 32, 39.
Pannell, W.J. 186.
Pannenberg, W. 42, 78, 80, 92, 100, 108, 111-112, 115-119, 126, 130, 132, 135, 155, 205, 210, 217, 232, 237-238, 240, 266-267.
Parker, S.P. 202.
Parry, R. 178.
Pattison, S. 63, 67, 73-74, 79, 86, 147.
Patton, J. 66, 68-70.
Pauling, L. 96.
Peacocke, A.R. 2-3, 25, 28-29, 35-39, 41, 50, 204, 221, 227-231, 233-234, 240, 251.
Peat, F.D. 206.
Pembroke, N. 152, 172, 191.
Penrose, R. 199, 212-213, 218.
Peters, T. 5, 16-17, 97, 103-104, 106-107, 112, 115-118, 232.
Peterson, E.H. 189.
Pickard, S. 51, 240, 262.
Pinnock, C.H. 115, 119, 136, 140-141, 162, 239, 266-267.
Pirsig, R.M. 268.
Plantinga, A.C. 235-236.
Plato 2, 48, 93, 211, 216, 267.
Plotinus 140-141.
Podolsky, B. 202-203.
Pohl, C.D. 170, 188.
Polanyi, M. 178, 226.
Poling, J.N. 57-58, 65, 81, 90, 150.
Polkinghorne, J. 2, 4, 11-16, 33, 42, 85, 206, 229, 233-236, 240-241, 263.
Pope, A. 70.
Popper, K. 19-20, 30, 86, 227.
Powell, S. 227, 239.
Pratt, D. 203.
Preece, G. 51, 240, 262.
Prestige, G.L. 99-100, 129-130, 284.
Pribram, K. 218-221.
Prigogine, I. 38, 195-196, 223, 229.
Pritchard, J. 69.
Rae, M. 29.
Rahner, K. 51, 101, 105-107, 110, 112, 115, 119-120, 240.
Rakestraw, R.V. 169.
Ramsey, I. 88.
Rassmussen, L.L. 275.

Author Index

Ratzinger, J. 154.
Raven, C.E. 31.
Ray, J. 31.
Reese, W.L. 36.
Regan, H. 29, 169.
Reid, D. 239, 264, 280-281.
Richard of St. Victor 135.
Richardson, W.M. 50-52.
Ridderbos, H.N. 162.
Roethke, T. 89.
Rogers, C. 76.
Rogers, E.F. 150, 183, 186, 191.
Rolston, H. III 8, 50, 238, 271, 276.
Rosen, N. 202-203.
Rousseau, J.-J. 279.
Ruether, R. 158-160.
Runyon, T. 157.
Russell, R.J. 23, 36, 51, 206, 221, 227, 233-235, 237, 240.
Ruthild, W. 229.
Sackett, C.A. 208.
Sanders, E.P. 30.
Sanders, J. 236.
Saniotis, A. 274.
Santmire, P. 247-249, 251, 253-254, 256.
Sayles, L.R. 158.
Schleiermacher, F. 57, 65, 74-75, 77-78, 95, 97-98.
Schweitzer, A. 9.
Schwobel, C. 98, 109, 11, 118, 125, 150, 195, 232.
Scott, N.A. 89.
Shaffer, P. 94.
Sharpe, K. 213-216, 220-221.
Sherlock, C. 172.
Sherry, P. 34.
Shults, F.L. 114, 277.
Simmons, E.L. 207.
Sittler, J. 92.
Smail, T.A. 104.
Smith, E. 157.
Smith, N.K. 21.
Snyder, H.A. 223-224.
Sobosan, J.G. 34.
Soskice, J.M. 25, 162.
Southgate, C. 16, 20, 30, 41, 44, 196-197, 201.
Speidell, T.H. 55, 114, 172, 186, 269.

Stengers, I. 38, 223.
Stenhouse, J. 29.
Stjernfelt, F. 228-229.
Stoeger, W.R. 23, 206, 227, 223-235, 239.
Stone, B.P. 58.
Storkey, E. 158.
Strauss, G. 158.
Switzer, D. 90.
Tacey, D. 90, 175, 266.
Talbot, M. 219.
Taylor, J.G. 196.
Taylor, J.V. 69, 184-185.
Teilhard de Chardin, P. 88, 247-249.
Thimell, D. 69.
Thoreau, H.D. 284-286.
Thornton, M. 89-91.
Thunberg, L. 130.
Thurneysen, E. 67, 75-79, 95.
Tiersma, J. 183.
Tiessen, T. 236.
Tillich, P. 64, 70-71, 76, 88, 173, 247, 270, 272-273.
Torrance, A.J. 100-102, 106-107, 146.
Torrance, J. B. 81-82, 125, 177-178, 181.
Torrance, T.F. 2, 4, 27, 32, 85, 92, 100, 104, 108, 125, 127-128, 130, 132-134, 140, 185-186, 210, 240, 259, 266-267, 269.
Tournier, P. 254.
Tracy, D. 244.
Trainor, B. 278-281.
Turchette, Q.A. 208.
Underhill, E. 255.
Vanhoozer, K.J. 164.
Vanier, J. 168.
Vanstone, W.H. 84, 161-162.
Volf, M. 56, 129, 132, 138-139, 143, 149, 151-152, 154-155, 167, 170, 191, 205.
Wainwright, E. 249-250.
Walsh, B.J. 44, 48.
Ward, K. 4, 39, 236-238, 240-241.
Ware, K. 132, 135-136, 161.
Weber, R. 206, 220.
Webster, J. 59, 104.
Wegter-McNelly, K. 51, 207.
Weil, S. 258.
Weinandy, T.G. 123-124, 134.
Weinberg, S. 23.

Wertheim, M. 4.
West, M. 137.
Westfall, R.S. 21.
Wheatley, M.J. 223.
Whitcomb, J.C. 22.
White, A.D. 6, 19.
White, S. 178.
Whitehead, A.N. 85.
Wildman, W.J. 50.
Wiles, M. 236.
Wilkinson, D. 14, 200.
William of Ockham 73, 279.
Williams, C. 284.
Williams, D.D. 56.
Williams, R. 153.

Wilson, E.O. 8.
Wilson-Kastner, P. 132-133, 139.
Wineland, D.J. 208.
Wiseman, J.A. 36, 42, 233-234.
Wood, S.K. 178.
Woodward, J. 73-74, 86, 147.
Worthing, M.W. 6, 13, 42, 105, 199-200, 203, 205-206, 210, 238-239, 274.
Wright, F. 88-89, 91-95, 276.
Wright, N.T. 25.
Wurst, S. 264.
Yeago, D.S. 144-145, 147, 150, 178-179.
Young, R.A. 243, 248.
Zizioulas, J.D. 56, 108-109, 120-121, 145, 155, 165.

Paternoster Biblical Monographs

(All titles uniform with this volume)
Dates in bold are of projected publication

Joseph Abraham
Eve: Accused or Acquitted?
A Reconsideration of Feminist Readings of the Creation Narrative Texts in Genesis 1–3

Two contrary views dominate contemporary feminist biblical scholarship. One finds in the Bible an unequivocal equality between the sexes from the very creation of humanity, whilst the other sees the biblical text as irredeemably patriarchal and androcentric. Dr Abraham enters into dialogue with both camps as well as introducing his own method of approach. An invaluable tool for any one who is interested in this contemporary debate.

2002 / 0-85364-971-5 / xxiv + 272pp

Octavian D. Baban
Mimesis and Luke's on the Road Encounters in Luke-Acts
Luke's Theology of the Way and its Literary Representation

The book argues on theological and literary (mimetic) grounds that Luke's on-the-road encounters, especially those belonging to the post-Easter period, are part of his complex theology of the Way. Jesus' teaching and that of the apostles is presented by Luke as a challenging answer to the Hellenistic reader's thirst for adventure, good literature, and existential paradigms.

***2005** / 1-84227-253-5 / approx. 374pp*

Paul Barker
The Triumph of Grace in Deuteronomy

This book is a textual and theological analysis of the interaction between the sin and faithlessness of Israel and the grace of Yahweh in response, looking especially at Deuteronomy chapters 1–3, 8–10 and 29–30. The author argues that the grace of Yahweh is determinative for the ongoing relationship between Yahweh and Israel and that Deuteronomy anticipates and fully expects Israel to be faithless.

2004 / 1-84227-226-8 / xxii + 270pp

Jonathan F. Bayes
The Weakness of the Law
God's Law and the Christian in New Testament Perspective

A study of the four New Testament books which refer to the law as weak (Acts, Romans, Galatians, Hebrews) leads to a defence of the third use in the Reformed debate about the law in the life of the believer.

2000 / 0-85364-957-X / xii + 244pp

Mark Bonnington
The Antioch Episode of Galatians 2:11-14 in Historical and Cultural Context

The Galatians 2 'incident' in Antioch over table-fellowship suggests significant disagreement between the leading apostles. This book analyses the background to the disagreement by locating the incident within the dynamics of social interaction between Jews and Gentiles. It proposes a new way of understanding the relationship between the individuals and issues involved.

2005 / 1-84227-050-8 / approx. 350pp

David Bostock
A Portrayal of Trust
The Theme of Faith in the Hezekiah Narratives

This study provides detailed and sensitive readings of the Hezekiah narratives (2 Kings 18–20 and Isaiah 36–39) from a theological perspective. It concentrates on the theme of faith, using narrative criticism as its methodology. Attention is paid especially to setting, plot, point of view and characterization within the narratives. A largely positive portrayal of Hezekiah emerges that underlines the importance and relevance of scripture.

2005 / 1-84227-314-0 / approx. 300pp

Mark Bredin
Jesus, Revolutionary of Peace
A Non-violent Christology in the Book of Revelation

This book aims to demonstrate that the figure of Jesus in the Book of Revelation can best be understood as an active non-violent revolutionary.

2003 / 1-84227-153-9 / xviii + 262pp

Robinson Butarbutar
Paul and Conflict Resolution
An Exegetical Study of Paul's Apostolic Paradigm in 1 Corinthians 9

The author sees the apostolic paradigm in 1 Corinthians 9 as part of Paul's unified arguments in 1 Corinthians 8–10 in which he seeks to mediate in the dispute over the issue of food offered to idols. The book also sees its relevance for dispute-resolution today, taking the conflict within the author's church as an example.

2006 / 1-84227-315-9 / approx. 280pp

Daniel J-S Chae
Paul as Apostle to the Gentiles
His Apostolic Self-awareness and its Influence on the Soteriological Argument in Romans
Opposing 'the post-Holocaust interpretation of Romans', Daniel Chae competently demonstrates that Paul argues for the equality of Jew and Gentile in Romans. Chae's fresh exegetical interpretation is academically outstanding and spiritually encouraging.
1997 / 0-85364-829-8 / xiv + 378pp

Luke L. Cheung
The Genre, Composition and Hermeneutics of the Epistle of James
The present work examines the employment of the wisdom genre with a certain compositional structure and the interpretation of the law through the Jesus tradition of the double love command by the author of the Epistle of James to serve his purpose in promoting perfection and warning against doubleness among the eschatologically renewed people of God in the Diaspora.
2003 / 1-84227-062-1 / xvi + 372pp

Youngmo Cho
Spirit and Kingdom in the Writings of Luke and Paul
The relationship between Spirit and Kingdom is a relatively unexplored area in Lukan and Pauline studies. This book offers a fresh perspective of two biblical writers on the subject. It explores the difference between Luke's and Paul's understanding of the Spirit by examining the specific question of the relationship of the concept of the Spirit to the concept of the Kingdom of God in each writer.
2005 / 1-84227-316-7 / approx. 270pp

Andrew C. Clark
Parallel Lives
The Relation of Paul to the Apostles in the Lucan Perspective
This study of the Peter-Paul parallels in Acts argues that their purpose was to emphasize the themes of continuity in salvation history and the unity of the Jewish and Gentile missions. New light is shed on Luke's literary techniques, partly through a comparison with Plutarch.
2001 / 1-84227-035-4 / xviii + 386pp

Andrew D. Clarke
Secular and Christian Leadership in Corinth
A Socio-Historical and Exegetical Study of 1 Corinthians 1–6

This volume is an investigation into the leadership structures and dynamics of first-century Roman Corinth. These are compared with the practice of leadership in the Corinthian Christian community which are reflected in 1 Corinthians 1–6, and contrasted with Paul's own principles of Christian leadership.

2005 / 1-84227-229-2 / 200pp

Stephen Finamore
God, Order and Chaos
René Girard and the Apocalypse

Readers are often disturbed by the images of destruction in the book of Revelation and unsure why they are unleashed after the exaltation of Jesus. This book examines past approaches to these texts and uses René Girard's theories to revive some old ideas and propose some new ones.

2005 / 1-84227-197-0 / approx. 344pp

David G. Firth
Surrendering Retribution in the Psalms
Responses to Violence in the Individual Complaints

In *Surrendering Retribution in the Psalms*, David Firth examines the ways in which the book of Psalms inculcates a model response to violence through the repetition of standard patterns of prayer. Rather than seeking justification for retributive violence, Psalms encourages not only a surrender of the right of retribution to Yahweh, but also sets limits on the retribution that can be sought in imprecations. Arising initially from the author's experience in South Africa, the possibilities of this model to a particular context of violence is then briefly explored.

2005 / 1-84227-337-X / xviii + 154pp

Scott J. Hafemann
Suffering and Ministry in the Spirit
Paul's Defence of His Ministry in II Corinthians 2:14–3:3

Shedding new light on the way Paul defended his apostleship, the author offers a careful, detailed study of 2 Corinthians 2:14–3:3 linked with other key passages throughout 1 and 2 Corinthians. Demonstrating the unity and coherence of Paul's argument in this passage, the author shows that Paul's suffering served as the vehicle for revealing God's power and glory through the Spirit.

2000 / 0-85364-967-7 / xiv + 262pp

Scott J. Hafemann
Paul, Moses and the History of Israel
The Letter/Spirit Contrast and the Argument from Scripture in 2 Corinthians 3
An exegetical study of the call of Moses, the second giving of the Law (Exodus 32–34), the new covenant, and the prophetic understanding of the history of Israel in 2 Corinthians 3. Hafemann's work demonstrates Paul's contextual use of the Old Testament and the essential unity between the Law and the Gospel within the context of the distinctive ministries of Moses and Paul.
2005 / 1-84227-317-5 / xii + 498pp

Douglas S. McComiskey
Lukan Theology in the Light of the Gospel's Literary Structure
Luke's Gospel was purposefully written with theology embedded in its patterned literary structure. A critical analysis of this cyclical structure provides new windows into Luke's interpretation of the individual pericopes comprising the Gospel and illuminates several of his theological interests.
2004 / 1-84227-148-2 / xviii + 388pp

Stephen Motyer
Your Father the Devil?
A New Approach to John and 'The Jews'
Who are 'the Jews' in John's Gospel? Defending John against the charge of antisemitism, Motyer argues that, far from demonising the Jews, the Gospel seeks to present Jesus as 'Good News for Jews' in a late first century setting.
1997 / 0-85364-832-8 / xiv + 260pp

Esther Ng
Reconstructing Christian Origins?
The Feminist Theology of Elizabeth Schüssler Fiorenza: An Evaluation
In a detailed evaluation, the author challenges Elizabeth Schüssler Fiorenza's reconstruction of early Christian origins and her underlying presuppositions. The author also presents her own views on women's roles both then and now.
2002 / 1-84227-055-9 / xxiv + 468pp

Robin Parry
Old Testament Story and Christian Ethics
The Rape of Dinah as a Case Study

What is the role of story in ethics and, more particularly, what is the role of Old Testament story in Christian ethics? This book, drawing on the work of contemporary philosophers, argues that narrative is crucial in the ethical shaping of people and, drawing on the work of contemporary Old Testament scholars, that story plays a key role in Old Testament ethics. Parry then argues that when situated in canonical context Old Testament stories can be reappropriated by Christian readers in their own ethical formation. The shocking story of the rape of Dinah and the massacre of the Shechemites provides a fascinating case study for exploring the parameters within which Christian ethical appropriations of Old Testament stories can live.

2004 / 1-84227-210-1 / xx + 350pp

Ian Paul
Power to See the World Anew
The Value of Paul Ricoeur's Hermeneutic of Metaphor in Interpreting the Symbolism of Revelation 12 and 13

This book is a study of the hermeneutics of metaphor of Paul Ricoeur, one of the most important writers on hermeneutics and metaphor of the last century. It sets out the key points of his theory, important criticisms of his work, and how his approach, modified in the light of these criticisms, offers a methodological framework for reading apocalyptic texts.

***2006** / 1-84227-056-7 / approx. 350pp*

Robert L. Plummer
Paul's Understanding of the Church's Mission
Did the Apostle Paul Expect the Early Christian Communities to Evangelize?

This book engages in a careful study of Paul's letters to determine if the apostle expected the communities to which he wrote to engage in missionary activity. It helpfully summarizes the discussion on this debated issue, judiciously handling contested texts, and provides a way forward in addressing this critical question. While admitting that Paul rarely explicitly commands the communities he founded to evangelize, Plummer amasses significant incidental data to provide a convincing case that Paul did indeed expect his churches to engage in mission activity. Throughout the study, Plummer progressively builds a theological basis for the church's mission that is both distinctively Pauline and compelling.

***2006** / 1-84227-333-7 / approx. 324pp*

David Powys
'Hell': A Hard Look at a Hard Question
The Fate of the Unrighteous in New Testament Thought
This comprehensive treatment seeks to unlock the original meaning of terms and phrases long thought to support the traditional doctrine of hell. It concludes that there is an alternative—one which is more biblical, and which can positively revive the rationale for Christian mission.

1997 / 0-85364-831-X / xxii + 478pp

Sorin Sabou
Between Horror and Hope
Paul's Metaphorical Language of Death in Romans 6.1-11
This book argues that Paul's metaphorical language of death in Romans 6.1-11 conveys two aspects: horror and hope. The 'horror' aspect is conveyed by the 'crucifixion' language, and the 'hope' aspect by 'burial' language. The life of the Christian believer is understood, as relationship with sin is concerned ('death to sin'), between these two realities: horror and hope.

2005 / 1-84227-322-1 / approx. 224pp

Rosalind Selby
The Comical Doctrine
The Epistemology of New Testament Hermeneutics
This book argues that the gospel breaks through postmodernity's critique of truth and the referential possibilities of textuality with its gift of grace. With a rigorous, philosophical challenge to modernist and postmodernist assumptions, Selby offers an alternative epistemology to all who would still read with faith *and* with academic credibility.

2005 / 1-84227-212-8 / approx. 350pp

Kiwoong Son
Zion Symbolism in Hebrews
Hebrews 12.18-24 as a Hermeneutical Key to the Epistle
This book challenges the general tendency of understanding the Epistle to the Hebrews against a Hellenistic background and suggests that the Epistle should be understood in the light of the Jewish apocalyptic tradition. The author especially argues for the importance of the theological symbolism of Sinai and Zion (Heb. 12:18-24) as it provides the Epistle's theological background as well as the rhetorical basis of the superiority motif of Jesus throughout the Epistle.

2005 / 1-84227-368-X / approx. 280pp

Kevin Walton
Thou Traveller Unknown
The Presence and Absence of God in the Jacob Narrative
The author offers a fresh reading of the story of Jacob in the book of Genesis through the paradox of divine presence and absence. The work also seeks to make a contribution to Pentateuchal studies by bringing together a close reading of the final text with historical critical insights, doing justice to the text's historical depth, final form and canonical status.
2003 / 1-84227-059-1 / xvi + 238pp

George M. Wieland
The Significance of Salvation
A Study of Salvation Language in the Pastoral Epistles
The language and ideas of salvation pervade the three Pastoral Epistles. This study offers a close examination of their soteriological statements. In all three letters the idea of salvation is found to play a vital paraenetic role, but each also exhibits distinctive soteriological emphases. The results challenge common assumptions about the Pastoral Epistles as a corpus.
***2005** / 1-84227-257-8 / approx. 324pp*

Alistair Wilson
When Will These Things Happen?
A Study of Jesus as Judge in Matthew 21–25
This study seeks to allow Matthew's carefully constructed presentation of Jesus to be given full weight in the modern evaluation of Jesus' eschatology. Careful analysis of the text of Matthew 21–25 reveals Jesus to be standing firmly in the Jewish prophetic and wisdom traditions as he proclaims and enacts imminent judgement on the Jewish authorities then boldly claims the central role in the final and universal judgement.
2004 / 1-84227-146-6 / xxii + 272pp

Lindsay Wilson
Joseph Wise and Otherwise
The Intersection of Covenant and Wisdom in Genesis 37–50
This book offers a careful literary reading of Genesis 37–50 that argues that the Joseph story contains both strong covenant themes and many wisdom-like elements. The connections between the two helps to explore how covenant and wisdom might intersect in an integrated biblical theology.
2004 / 1-84227-140-7 / xvi + 340pp

Stephen I. Wright
The Voice of Jesus
Studies in the Interpretation of Six Gospel Parables
This literary study considers how the 'voice' of Jesus has been heard in different periods of parable interpretation, and how the categories of figure and trope may help us towards a sensitive reading of the parables today.
2000 / 0-85364-975-8 / xiv + 280pp

Paternoster
9 Holdom Avenue,
Bletchley,
Milton Keynes MK1 1QR,
United Kingdom
Web: www.authenticmedia.co.uk/paternoster

Paternoster Theological Monographs
(All titles uniform with this volume)
Dates in bold are of projected publication

Emil Bartos
Deification in Eastern Orthodox Theology
An Evaluation and Critique of the Theology of Dumitru Staniloae

Bartos studies a fundamental yet neglected aspect of Orthodox theology: deification. By examining the doctrines of anthropology, christology, soteriology and ecclesiology as they relate to deification, he provides an important contribution to contemporary dialogue between Eastern and Western theologians.

1999 / 0-85364-956-1 / xii + 370pp

Graham Buxton
The Trinity, Creation and Pastoral Ministry
Imaging the Perichoretic God

In this book the author proposes a three-way conversation between theology, science and pastoral ministry. His approach draws on a Trinitarian understanding of God as a relational being of love, whose life 'spills over' into all created reality, human and non-human. By locating human meaning and purpose within God's 'creation-community' this book offers the possibility of a transforming engagement between those in pastoral ministry and the scientific community.

***2005** / 1-84227-369-8 / approx. 380 pp*

Iain D. Campbell
Fixing the Indemnity
The Life and Work of George Adam Smith

When Old Testament scholar George Adam Smith (1856–1942) delivered the Lyman Beecher lectures at Yale University in 1899, he confidently declared that 'modern criticism has won its war against traditional theories. It only remains to fix the amount of the indemnity.' In this biography, Iain D. Campbell assesses Smith's critical approach to the Old Testament and evaluates its consequences, showing that Smith's life and work still raises questions about the relationship between biblical scholarship and evangelical faith.

2004 / 1-84227-228-4 / xx + 256pp

Tim Chester
Mission and the Coming of God
Eschatology, the Trinity and Mission in the Theology of Jürgen Moltmann
This book explores the theology and missiology of the influential contemporary theologian, Jürgen Moltmann. It highlights the important contribution Moltmann has made while offering a critique of his thought from an evangelical perspective. In so doing, it touches on pertinent issues for evangelical missiology. The conclusion takes Calvin as a starting point, proposing 'an eschatology of the cross' which offers a critique of the over-realised eschatologies in liberation theology and certain forms of evangelicalism.
2006 / 1-84227-320-5 / approx. 224pp

Sylvia Wilkey Collinson
Making Disciples
The Significance of Jesus' Educational Strategy for Today's Church
This study examines the biblical practice of discipling, formulates a definition, and makes comparisons with modern models of education. A recommendation is made for greater attention to its practice today.
2004 / 1-84227-116-4 / xiv + 278pp

Darrell Cosden
A Theology of Work
Work and the New Creation
Through dialogue with Moltmann, Pope John Paul II and others, this book develops a genitive 'theology of work', presenting a theological definition of work and a model for a theological ethics of work that shows work's nature, value and meaning now and eschatologically. Work is shown to be a transformative activity consisting of three dynamically inter-related dimensions: the instrumental, relational and ontological.
2005 / 1-84227-332-9 / xvi + 208pp

Stephen M. Dunning
The Crisis and the Quest
A Kierkegaardian Reading of Charles Williams
Employing Kierkegaardian categories and analysis, this study investigates both the central crisis in Charles Williams's authorship between hermetism and Christianity (Kierkegaard's Religions A and B), and the quest to resolve this crisis, a quest that ultimately presses the bounds of orthodoxy.
2000 / 0-85364-985-5 / xxiv + 254pp

Keith Ferdinando
The Triumph of Christ in African Perspective
A Study of Demonology and Redemption in the African Context
The book explores the implications of the gospel for traditional African fears of occult aggression. It analyses such traditional approaches to suffering and biblical responses to fears of demonic evil, concluding with an evaluation of African beliefs from the perspective of the gospel.
1999 / 0-85364-830-1 / xviii + 450pp

Andrew Goddard
Living the Word, Resisting the World
The Life and Thought of Jacques Ellul
This work offers a definitive study of both the life and thought of the French Reformed thinker Jacques Ellul (1912-1994). It will prove an indispensable resource for those interested in this influential theologian and sociologist and for Christian ethics and political thought generally.
2002 / 1-84227-053-2 / xxiv + 378pp

David Hilborn
The Words of our Lips
Language-Use in Free Church Worship
Studies of liturgical language have tended to focus on the written canons of Roman Catholic and Anglican communities. By contrast, David Hilborn analyses the more extemporary approach of English Nonconformity. Drawing on recent developments in linguistic pragmatics, he explores similarities and differences between 'fixed' and 'free' worship, and argues for the interdependence of each.
***2006** / 0-85364-977-4 / approx. 350pp*

Roger Hitching
The Church and Deaf People
A Study of Identity, Communication and Relationships with Special Reference to the Ecclesiology of Jürgen Moltmann
In *The Church and Deaf People* Roger Hitching sensitively examines the history and present experience of deaf people and finds similarities between aspects of sign language and Moltmann's theological method that 'open up' new ways of understanding theological concepts.
2003 / 1-84227-222-5 / xxii + 236pp

John G. Kelly
One God, One People
*The Differentiated Unity of the People of God in the Theology of
Jürgen Moltmann*
The author expounds and critiques Moltmann's doctrine of God and highlights the systematic connections between it and Moltmann's influential discussion of Israel. He then proposes a fresh approach to Jewish–Christian relations building on Moltmann's work using insights from Habermas and Rawls.
2005 / 0-85346-969-3 / approx. 350pp

Mark F.W. Lovatt
Confronting the Will-to-Power
A Reconsideration of the Theology of Reinhold Niebuhr
Confronting the Will-to-Power is an analysis of the theology of Reinhold Niebuhr, arguing that his work is an attempt to identify, and provide a practical theological answer to, the existence and nature of human evil.
2001 / 1-84227-054-0 / xviii + 216pp

Neil B. MacDonald
Karl Barth and the Strange New World within the Bible
Barth, Wittgenstein, and the Metadilemmas of the Enlightenment
Barth's discovery of the strange new world within the Bible is examined in the context of Kant, Hume, Overbeck, and, most importantly, Wittgenstein. MacDonald covers some fundamental issues in theology today: epistemology, the final form of the text and biblical truth-claims.
2000 / 0-85364-970-7 / xxvi + 374pp

Keith A. Mascord
Alvin Plantinga and Christian Apologetics
This book draws together the contributions of the philosopher Alvin Plantinga to the major contemporary challenges to Christian belief, highlighting in particular his ground-breaking work in epistemology and the problem of evil. Plantinga's theory that both theistic and Christian belief is warrantedly basic is explored and critiqued, and an assessment offered as to the significance of his work for apologetic theory and practice.
2005 / 1-84227-256-X / approx. 304pp

Gillian McCulloch
The Deconstruction of Dualism in Theology
With Reference to Ecofeminist Theology and New Age Spirituality
This book challenges eco-theological anti-dualism in Christian theology, arguing that dualism has a twofold function in Christian religious discourse. Firstly, it enables us to express the discontinuities and divisions that are part of the process of reality. Secondly, dualistic language allows us to express the mysteries of divine transcendence/immanence and the survival of the soul without collapsing into monism and materialism, both of which are problematic for Christian epistemology.
2002 / 1-84227-044-3 / xii + 282pp

Leslie McCurdy
Attributes and Atonement
The Holy Love of God in the Theology of P.T. Forsyth
Attributes and Atonement is an intriguing full-length study of P.T. Forsyth's doctrine of the cross as it relates particularly to God's holy love. It includes an unparalleled bibliography of both primary and secondary material relating to Forsyth.
1999 / 0-85364-833-6 / xiv + 328pp

Nozomu Miyahira
Towards a Theology of the Concord of God
A Japanese Perspective on the Trinity
This book introduces a new Japanese theology and a unique Trinitarian formula based on the Japanese intellectual climate: three betweennesses and one concord. It also presents a new interpretation of the Trinity, a co-subordinationism, which is in line with orthodox Trinitarianism; each single person of the Trinity is eternally and equally subordinate (or serviceable) to the other persons, so that they retain the mutual dynamic equality.
2000 / 0-85364-863-8 / xiv + 256pp

Eddy José Muskus
The Origins and Early Development of Liberation Theology in Latin America
With Particular Reference to Gustavo Gutiérrez
This work challenges the fundamental premise of Liberation Theology, 'opting for the poor', and its claim that Christ is found in them. It also argues that Liberation Theology emerged as a direct result of the failure of the Roman Catholic Church in Latin America.
2002 / 0-85364-974-X / xiv + 296pp

Jim Purves
The Triune God and the Charismatic Movement
A Critical Appraisal from a Scottish Perspective

All emotion and no theology? Or a fundamental challenge to reappraise and realign our trinitarian theology in the light of Christian experience? This study of charismatic renewal as it found expression within Scotland at the end of the twentieth century evaluates the use of Patristic, Reformed and contemporary models of the Trinity in explaining the workings of the Holy Spirit.

2004 / 1-84227-321-3 / xxiv + 246pp

Anna Robbins
Methods in the Madness
Diversity in Twentieth-Century Christian Social Ethics

The author compares the ethical methods of Walter Rauschenbusch, Reinhold Niebuhr and others. She argues that unless Christians are clear about the ways that theology and philosophy are expressed practically they may lose the ability to discuss social ethics across contexts, let alone reach effective agreements.

2004 / 1-84227-211-X / xx + 294pp

Ed Rybarczyk
Beyond Salvation
Eastern Orthodoxy and Classical Pentecostalism on Becoming Like Christ

At first glance eastern Orthodoxy and classical Pentecostalism seem quite distinct. This ground-breaking study shows they share much in common, especially as it concerns the experiential elements of following Christ. Both traditions assert that authentic Christianity transcends the wooden categories of modernism.

2004 / 1-84227-144-X / xii + 356pp

Signe Sandsmark
Is World View Neutral Education Possible and Desirable?
A Christian Response to Liberal Arguments
(Published jointly with The Stapleford Centre)

This book discusses reasons for belief in world view neutrality, and argues that 'neutral' education will have a hidden, but strong world view influence. It discusses the place for Christian education in the common school.

2000 / 0-85364-973-1 / xiv + 182pp

Hazel Sherman
Reading Zechariah
The Allegorical Tradition of Biblical Interpretation through the Commentary of Didymus the Blind and Theodore of Mopsuestia
A close reading of the commentary on Zechariah by Didymus the Blind alongside that of Theodore of Mopsuestia suggests that popular categorising of Antiochene and Alexandrian biblical exegesis as 'historical' or 'allegorical' is inadequate and misleading.
2005 / 1-84227-213-6 / approx. 280pp

Andrew Sloane
On Being a Christian in the Academy
Nicholas Wolterstorff and the Practice of Christian Scholarship
An exposition and critical appraisal of Nicholas Wolterstorff's epistemology in the light of the philosophy of science, and an application of his thought to the practice of Christian scholarship.
2003 / 1-84227-058-3 / xvi + 274pp

Damon W.K. So
Jesus' Revelation of His Father
A Narrative-Conceptual Study of the Trinity with Special Reference to Karl Barth
This book explores the trinitarian dynamics in the context of Jesus' revelation of his Father in his earthly ministry with references to key passages in Matthew's Gospel. It develops from the exegeses of these passages a non-linear concept of revelation which links Jesus' communion with his Father to his revelatory words and actions through a nuanced understanding of the Holy Spirit, with references to K. Barth, G.W.H. Lampe, J.D.G. Dunn and E. Irving.
2005 / 1-84227-323-X / approx. 380pp

Daniel Strange
The Possibility of Salvation Among the Unevangelised
An Analysis of Inclusivism in Recent Evangelical Theology
For evangelical theologians the 'fate of the unevangelised' impinges upon fundamental tenets of evangelical identity. The position known as 'inclusivism', defined by the belief that the unevangelised can be ontologically saved by Christ whilst being epistemologically unaware of him, has been defended most vigorously by the Canadian evangelical Clark H. Pinnock. Through a detailed analysis and critique of Pinnock's work, this book examines a cluster of issues surrounding the unevangelised and its implications for christology, soteriology and the doctrine of revelation.
2002 / 1-84227-047-8 / xviii + 362pp

Scott Swain
God According to the Gospel
Biblical Narrative and the Identity of God in the Theology of Robert W. Jenson
Robert W. Jenson is one of the leading voices in contemporary Trinitarian theology. His boldest contribution in this area concerns his use of biblical narrative both to ground and explicate the Christian doctrine of God. *God According to the Gospel* critically examines Jenson's proposal and suggests an alternative way of reading the biblical portrayal of the triune God.
2006 / 1-84227-258-6 / approx. 180pp

Justyn Terry
The Justifying Judgement of God
A Reassessment of the Place of Judgement in the Saving Work of Christ
The argument of this book is that judgement, understood as the whole process of bringing justice, is the primary metaphor of atonement, with others, such as victory, redemption and sacrifice, subordinate to it. Judgement also provides the proper context for understanding penal substitution and the call to repentance, baptism, eucharist and holiness.
2005 / 1-84227-370-1 / approx. 274 pp

Graham Tomlin
The Power of the Cross
Theology and the Death of Christ in Paul, Luther and Pascal
This book explores the theology of the cross in St Paul, Luther and Pascal. It offers new perspectives on the theology of each, and some implications for the nature of power, apologetics, theology and church life in a postmodern context.
1999 / 0-85364-984-7 / xiv + 344pp

Adonis Vidu
Postliberal Theological Method
A Critical Study
The postliberal theology of Hans Frei, George Lindbeck, Ronald Thiemann, John Milbank and others is one of the more influential contemporary options. This book focuses on several aspects pertaining to its theological method, specifically its understanding of background, hermeneutics, epistemic justification, ontology, the nature of doctrine and, finally, Christological method.
2005 / 1-84227-395-7 / approx. 324pp

Graham J. Watts
Revelation and the Spirit
A Comparative Study of the Relationship between the Doctrine of Revelation and Pneumatology in the Theology of Eberhard Jüngel and of Wolfhart Pannenberg

The relationship between revelation and pneumatology is relatively unexplored. This approach offers a fresh angle on two important twentieth century theologians and raises pneumatological questions which are theologically crucial and relevant to mission in a postmodern culture.

2005 / 1-84227-104-0 / xxii + 232pp

Nigel G. Wright
Disavowing Constantine
Mission, Church and the Social Order in the Theologies of John Howard Yoder and Jürgen Moltmann

This book is a timely restatement of a radical theology of church and state in the Anabaptist and Baptist tradition. Dr Wright constructs his argument in dialogue and debate with Yoder and Moltmann, major contributors to a free church perspective.

2000 / 0-85364-978-2 / xvi + 252pp

Paternoster
9 Holdom Avenue,
Bletchley,
Milton Keynes MK1 1QR,
United Kingdom
Web: www.authenticmedia.co.uk/paternoster